Social Policy and Practice in Canada

A HISTORY

D0827385

Social Policy and Practice in Canada

A HISTORY

ALVIN FINKEL

Wilfrid Laurier University Press
www.wlupress.wlu.ca

This book has been published with the help of a grant from the Canadian Federation for the Humanities and Social Sciences, through the Awards to Scholarly Publications Program, using funds provided by the Social Sciences and Humanities Research Council of Canada. Wilfrid Laurier University Press acknowledges the financial support of the Government of Canada through the Canada Book Fund for our publishing activities.

Library and Archives Canada Cataloguing in Publication

Finkel, Alvin, 1949–
    Social policy and practice in Canada : a history / Alvin Finkel.

Includes bibliographical references and index.

ISBN 13: 978-0-88920-475-1

1. Canada – Social policy. 2. Public welfare – Canada – History. 3. Welfare state – Canada – History. I. Title

HV108.F56 2006   361.6′10971   C2006-901185-0

Cover and text design by Sandra Friesen. The cover photograph of an unemployment demonstration in Edmonton, Alberta, was taken in October 1933 by McDermid Studio. The photograph is used with permission from the Glenbow Museum Archives.

Printed in Canada

For Ann, Antony, Kieran

CONTENTS

Acknowledgements

This book tries both to narrate and analyze the history of social policy in Canada from pre-contact times to the present, integrating the extensive existing literature on the period before the 1930s with mostly primary research on the period since 1930. It has been the product of over a decade's work. Along the way, I have been helped by the insights and willingness to read my writing of a variety of people, including Harold Chorney, Philip Hansen, Shirley Tillotson, Georgina Taylor, Bryan Palmer, Mark Goldblatt, and Ann Goldblatt. The three anonymous reviewers for the publisher also made a valuable contribution to the final product. Steve Boddington provided research assistance. The archivists at Library and Archives Canada (LAC), the Archives of Ontario, the Provincial Archives of Alberta, the British Columbia Archives, and the library staff at the LAC, the University of Alberta, and the Alberta Legislature Library have all been very helpful in finding materials that I might otherwise have missed. Of course, I take sole responsibility for any deficiencies in the final product, but would like to share credit for anything that might be worthwhile in these pages.

Among those who also deserve credit are the anonymous reviewers of articles and book chapters on social welfare that I have published over the years. Two of the chapters in this book are largely based on earlier journal articles of mine. I thank the editors of *Journal of the Canadian Historical Association/ Revue de la Société historique du Canada* for their permission to make use of my article "Paradise Postponed: A Re-examination of the Green Book Proposals of 1945," which appeared in *New Series*, 4 (1993): 120–42; and the editors of *Labour/Le Travail* for their permission to copy large parts of my article "Even the Little Children Cooperated: Family Strategies, Child care Discourse, and Social Welfare Debates 1945–1975," which appeared in 36 (Fall 1995): 91–118. The former forms the basis of chapter 7 of this book, the latter of chapter 10. Though the rest of this work represents original writing, readers may catch a glimpse of materials and ideas from the following articles, among others: "The State of Writing on the Canadian Welfare State: What's Class Got to Do with It?" *Labour/Le Travail* 54 (Fall 2004): 151–74; "Welfare for Whom? Class, Gender, and Race in Social Policy," *Labour/Le Travail* 49 (Spring 2002): 247–61; "Changing the Story: Gender Enters the History of the Welfare State," *Tijdschrift voor sociale geschiedenis* 22, 1 (1996): 67–81; "Trade Unions and the Welfare State in Canada, 1945–1990," chapter 3 in Cy Gonick, Paul Phillips, and Jesse Viorst, eds., *Labour Gains, Labour Pains: Fifty Years of PC 1003* (Halifax: Fernwood, 1995): 59–77; "Social Programs, the West and the Constitution," in James McCrorie and Martha L. Macdonald, eds., *The Constitutional Future of the Prairie and Atlantic Regions of Canada* (Regina: Canadian Plains Research Centre, 1992): 167–80; and "Origins of the Welfare State in Canada," in Leo Panitch, ed., *The Canadian State* (Toronto: University of Toronto Press, 1977): 344–70.

Funds from the Social Sciences and Humanities Research Council for a Standard Research Grant from 1991 to 1994, along with research grants from the Academic Research Fund at Athabasca University, made it possible to travel to archives outside of my home base in Edmonton and to employ a research assistant. Athabasca University also provided one sabbatical for the research and another for the writing of this work. Several secretaries at the university during this period, particularly Myrna Nolan and Sandra Davidson, have assisted me in various ways with keeping track of materials.

The editors at Wilfrid Laurier University Press have contributed a great deal to this book. I wish to thank Brian Henderson, Jacqueline Larson, Beth McAuley, and Carroll Klein for their input. Thanks also to Cheryl Lemmens, who prepared the index.

Studying Social Policy

APPROACH AND STRUCTURE OF THIS BOOK

This book surveys the evolution of social policies in Canada from the period of Aboriginal occupation to the present. It focuses on how the residents of what is today Canada have, at various periods, attempted to care for the unfortunate in their midst. While other social policies are referred to from time to time, the main focus is on care of the destitute, the ill, the elderly, and the young.

Such policies cannot be studied without an appreciation of the larger social context in which they have evolved. The book's focus is on the social values that have predominated in various periods and the struggles over social values that have led to change. This leads to an emphasis on social class, gender, and race/ethnicity as factors in social development in Canada. The book interrogates reforms closely to determine who benefited from the particular design of social policies or from the ways in which the program was implemented. A key concern throughout is the role of social struggles in shaping outcomes.

Part 1, "Non-State Provision" (chapters 1 to 3), assesses various periods before Confederation, each different but characterized by a reliance primarily upon the charitable or private provision of social assistance. Part 2, "Beyond the

Poor Law" (chapters 4 to 6), covers the period from 1867 to 1950 and studies the factors that influenced broad social acceptance of a "welfare state." Parts 1 and 2 are largely chronological, demonstrating emerging social trends in various periods. Chapters 1 to 4 are based primarily on secondary sources, reflecting an extensive Canadian literature. Chapters 5 and 6, by contrast, rely more on primary research, as do the chapters in Part 3.

Part 3, "The Welfare State" (chapters 7 to 11), discusses the years between 1945 and 1980, the period that witnessed the greatest progressive social experimentation in Canada. This is the era that we associate with the establishment of the Keynesian "welfare state," a period in which social programs came to dominate state activities. Part 3 attempts to evaluate critically the evolution of a large number of these programs, with a focus on how they affected the distribution of wealth and power in Canada. A chronological approach here might emphasize how much more dynamic this period was for social program development than the period covered in Part 2, but it might easily degenerate into a positivist catalogue of state achievements. Instead, I have chosen to assess policy areas in separate chapters, and to demonstrate in this manner the limits as much as the achievements of social policy-making in the period often viewed as the "welfare state" period.

Part 4, "Neo-Liberalism" (chapters 12 and 13), analyzes the decline of the postwar Keynesian welfare state and the rise of neo-liberal notions of the relationship of states and individuals. It also documents the continued struggles of workers, women, Aboriginal peoples, and others to win back the programs achieved by earlier generations, and, indeed, to deepen, rather than gut, the social infrastructure of Canada.

Though this is a history book, it is far more than a collection of facts and dates. Like all scholarly works, it embodies a set of social values. The author is a socialist whose writings focus on how wealth and power are concentrated and what the results of this concentration are for the poor and powerless. While my intellectual influences are eclectic, they begin with Marxism and its emphasis on the struggles among social classes for power. The political economy tradition, which incorporates Marxist concepts into empirical analyses of the operations of the state and their interactions with the market economy, informs much of this book. The book is also influenced by the extensive feminist literature on the welfare state and the related literature that stresses the state's role in moral regulation of society. As a result, it discusses the different discourses that competed with one another at various periods and their influence on social policy development. It takes very seriously the proposition that how people talk about a subject influences the way in which government policies are established and implemented.

Ultimately, however, this is a materialist reading of the development of social policy. While I reject any simple relationship between particular constellations of social forces and the actions of the state, I also reject the view that state policies can be assessed purely in terms of competing and free-floating discourses. Material social forces, including the capitalist system and patriarchy, while subject to change, are constants throughout post-contact Canadian history. It is important to always keep sight of the power structure at given moments of social change and to be clear whether real changes in the distribution of wealth and power were occurring, as opposed to the changes simply being in the ways the social system was talked about.[1]

DEFINING SOCIAL POLICY

In this book, I define social policy as the set of non-market decisions, public and private, that determine the distribution of wealth to individuals and families and the degree of availability of human services to all members of society. The focus on the results of social policy in terms of distribution of income provides a critical framework for evaluating social policies and for interrogating the intentions of those who created these policies. It inevitably leads to a discussion of the kinds of inequalities that market-based economic decisions produce and to an analysis of who exercises power within both the economy and the state. Otherwise, it is all too easy to take at face value the rhetoric of "reformers" who claimed that such-and-such policy benefited all of society or even that it mainly benefited the underprivileged.

Elite politicians have often viewed social policy as a means to avoid redistribution of wealth in favour of the disadvantaged. A.J. Balfour, a future British Conservative prime minister, running for office in 1895, told his electors: "Social legislation, as I conceive it, is not merely to be distinguished from Socialist legislation but it is its most direct opposite and its most effective antidote. Socialism will never get possession of the great body of public opinion…among the working class or any other class if those who wield the collective forces of the community show themselves desirous to ameliorate every legitimate grievance and to put Society upon a proper and more solid basis."[2] In office, Balfour and his successors fashioned social programs that largely involved forced savings. These assured some benefits for the needy but largely through a redistribution of wealth within the working class rather than through any shift of income from the rich to the poor.

Along with compulsory schooling, supervision of recipients of social assistance, and state interventions in families on behalf of children, forced-savings programs reveal the power of the state to shape notions of proper social behaviour. Notions of what constitutes a "family" and what practices are sufficiently desirable or undesirable to be either enforced or banned by the state also form part of social policy. While many such decisions are beyond the scope of this book—for example, legislation regarding pornography or prostitution—others such as how the state or private charities have regarded unmarried mothers and their children at different periods are central to the discussion. For example, social legislation in the area of unmarried mothers has sometimes supported their right to an income as they raise children, but at other times it has actively encouraged the giving up of their children for adoption. In short, social policy can either foster a range of choices for individuals and households in society or it can impose a restricted set of options for citizens.

There is a type of revolutionary defeatism that dismisses all state actions as detrimental to the working class, the poor, women, or ethnic and racial minorities. But pressures from below have been important in influencing the design and the implementation of social policy. Grassroots agitation rarely produces legislation that fully meets the demands of oppressed groups, but it often leads to compromises in social policy between elite perspectives and popular perspectives.[3]

APPROACHES TO SOCIAL POLICY HISTORY

Scholars portray the evolution of social policy and particularly the emergence of the welfare state in myriad ways. Writing in 1984, Derek Fraser suggested at least seven paradigms for the history of social policy, ranging from functionalism that regards state policy as a rational state reaction to problems created in the wake of industrialization, to Marxism that (in his view) suggests welfare measures are designed to serve the interests of large businesses and the wealthy.[4] Functionalism, among other theoretical approaches, emphasizes structure over human agency. This book largely rejects approaches that privilege structure over agency. If structure alone created policy frameworks, then all countries at similar stages of economic development would have broadly similar social policies. They do not, and that is because different constellations of social forces in each country result in different policy choices.

Fraser's typology of seven perspectives interestingly omits feminism, reflecting the relatively recent appearance of gender-centred writing on the welfare state. He also slights one popular set of theories of welfare-state development with the label "conspiratorial." Its advocates, however, prefer the term "moral regulationist" and build upon the work of the late French philosopher Michel Foucault. Foucault argues that the state reinforces not only the power of big business but also of an entire moral universe in which many of the repressive social values are of a non-economic nature. For Foucault, moral regulation does not begin with the state but rather with deeper social forces ("governmentality") that lead to pressures upon all individuals to conform to oppressive rules.

Governmentality, which studies the complex ways in which individuals and institutions come to share ways of seeing and behaving, has become a popular academic approach to social phenomena.[5] Sociologists Philip Corrigan and Derek Sayer note the clear relationship of moral regulation with state-level policy-making. "State agencies," they note, "attempt to give unitary and unifying expression to what are in reality multifaceted and different experiences of groups within society, denying them their particularity. The reality is that bourgeois society is systematically unequal, it is structured along lines of class, gender, ethnicity, age, religion, occupation, locality. States act to erase the recognition and expression of these differences."[6] But, while moral regulation theorists are critical theorists at odds with functionalists who largely support the status quo, they often share with them the view that much of what the state does is impervious to rebellion from below.

Marxists are at times also accused of simply dismissing everything the state does in non-socialist societies as in the interests of capital. However, because Marxism focuses on class struggles, many Marxists do regard the welfare state as, at least in part, the product of workers' efforts to win concessions from employers and the state. Marxists suggest that the state legislates social policies for two associated reasons: to promote the accumulation of capital and to promote the legitimation of the social system. So, for example, unemployment insurance might be legislated to allow capitalists to introduce new technologies and fire redundant employees at will. The existence of unemployment insurance promotes accumulation because it ensures that unemployed workers have some purchasing power despite losing their jobs and can buy some of the products industry produces. Yet it also promotes legitimation of an economic system in which employers can dismiss willing workers by promoting some continuity of income after losing a job.

Disagreements arise among Marxists on the question of whether workers played a large, direct role in convincing governments to implement unemployment insurance, in establishing the rules for who gets access to this program, and the level of payouts. Most Marxists and most historians of social policy generally agree that pressures from workers below need to be assessed as closely as pressures from economic elites above when we explain how social programs evolve. But they often differ in their perspectives on the relative importance of accumulation (which stresses the agency of the elites) and legitimation (which pays attention to both elites and the people). These two goals of social welfare often come into conflict, since business groups often argue that the cost of programs that legitimize the system is reflected in higher taxes that allegedly restrict capital accumulation.[7]

It is important, then, in attempting to untangle the threads that weave together social policies in various places and periods, to be cognizant not simply of the overall cultural inheritance of a society but also of the specific social forces at play. These include the conscious organization of citizens on the basis of social class, gender, and race/ethnicity, and the impact of various social groups on politicians and state bureaucracies. Certain typologies of the welfare state help us to distinguish the degree to which various social forces have been influential in shaping the overall model of social programming in a particular state in various periods.

Swedish welfare-state scholar Gøsta Esping-Anderson notes three ideal types that approximate the approaches of various countries to social welfare. The social-democratic welfare state stresses state-run universal programs and social equality, with state programs compensating heavily for the inequitable distribution of wealth in the marketplace. Access to health care, daycare, pensions, and a decent income for the unemployed are regarded as rights of citizenship. By contrast, in conservative or corporatist welfare states, programs are class-based, with administration of programs delegated by the state to institutions representing different class and group interests. Such states use social policy as much to reinforce market and non-market inequalities as to ameliorate them. Finally, in residual welfare states, there are few universal programs; social policy aims only to prevent the destitute from starving or going without any form of medical care. Social assistance is begrudging, closely monitored, and results in little redistribution of social wealth. Esping-Anderson suggests that the Scandinavian countries are the representatives par excellence of the social-democratic model; Germany, Austria, and Holland of the conservative model; and the United States of the residual model.[8]

As for Canada, Esping-Anderson relegates it to the residual model, though without any close analysis of the country's social programs. Indeed, Canada has had periods when the residual model seemed to best describe the thrust of policy-making. But at other times elements of the social-democratic model have been at play and have distinguished the Canadian welfare state from its American counterpart.

WOMEN AND THE WELFARE STATE

A feminist typology of welfare states developed by British welfare-state scholar Jane Lewis stresses the ways in which different countries use social policy to influence gender roles, a phenomenon that the Esping-Anderson typology ignores. Like Esping-Anderson, Lewis notes three broad types of welfare states. First are strong male-breadwinner states such as Ireland and Britain whose policies strongly reinforce patriarchy. Then there are modified male-breadwinner states such as France where patriarchal control is exercised within the family but state policies have favoured women's work and resulted in greater redistribution in favour of families headed by single mothers than in strong male-breadwinner countries. Finally, Sweden represents a weak male-breadwinner society since state policy consciously promotes a dual-breadwinner model.[9] Canada, throughout most of its history, has been a strong male-breadwinner state, though in recent years it has straddled the boundaries between strong and modified male-breadwinner states, shaping at least some of its social policies to recognize women's right to work.

Debates about the impact of the welfare state on women are of recent duration and highlight the ways in which writings about the history of the welfare state have often been blinkered.[10] Introducing her feminist text on social policy, Gillian Pascall observes that bringing women on stage "suggests questions about the structures which have left women out; about the way academic disciplines work; about language, concepts, methods, approaches and subject areas."[11]

Before the 1980s, most writing on social policy was gender-blind. Whether historians emphasized functionalism, class conflict, or bureaucratic struggles within the state, they tended to ignore issues of gender in discussions of policy-making and of the recipients and providers of social services. The comprehensive texts on national social welfare history for Canada, the United States, and Britain all gave only the most incidental attention to gender issues.[12] Feminist historians, whose work began to appear in the late 1970s, rejected the assumption of earlier historians that male and female social roles are grounded in biology and provide a natural framework for social policy. Differences in the social roles of the sexes, the feminists argued, were socially constructed rather than biologically constructed. They dissected the development and implementation of a variety of state policies to demonstrate that key social programs had as their deliberate aim the subordination of women both in the home and the workplace.[13]

The new feminist syntheses suggested that the "welfare state" subordinated women to men and imposed a single model of the "family"—male breadwinner with dependent wife and mother. This model disadvantaged women in the home where they were subordinated to the economic and physical power of husbands and in the workplace where they were paid less and given limited economic opportunities because allegedly their "real place" was in the home. From this vantage point, once uncritically celebrated national proposals for cradle-to-grave "welfare," such as Britain's Beveridge Report and Canada's Marsh Report, were re-examined. Jane Lewis noted, for example: "Beveridge's conviction that adult women were normally dependent became embodied in legislation which then had a prescriptive effect, leaving little room for change in gender roles."[14]

The "gender control" literature revealed that entitlement programs, much like the various social insurance programs, have tended to benefit males disproportionately. Unemployment insurance in the United States, Canada, and Britain was implemented in ways that made collection of benefits difficult for most women workers, particularly married women workers.[15] Means-tested and punitive programs—for example, social assistance with its armies of snoops assessing recipients' behaviour—have by contrast, a largely female clientele. The feminist historical scholarship on the welfare state, focusing on state attempts to impose a particular role—mother and housekeeper—and a particular morality—monogamous wife—on women, has also helped to clarify why certain social programs with primarily female recipients have proved more acceptable to male legislators than others. Widows' pensions, for example, have been generally acceptable because a widow is seen as someone who lost the male breadwinner upon whom she was dependent through no fault of her own. In Quebec, where the state and the Roman Catholic Church formed a tight antifeminist bond, it was symbolic that, in 1937, the same year that the provincial government cut single mothers off public assistance, it also began to provide widows' and (married) mothers' pensions.[16]

8

By contrast, family allowances paid to mothers have been controversial because they implicitly challenge the rights of fathers to supply or withhold the income needed by a nuclear family and because they also give benefits to mothers with no male breadwinner in their household but who are not widowed. Trade unions in both Britain and Canada initially attacked them as threats to male attempts to win a "family wage." Though pronatalist and Keynesian consumption arguments won the day, there was sufficient antipathy to family allowances from proponents of the "traditional family" and the "family wage," representing respectively right-wing and left-wing male-stream thinking, to prevent family allowances from growing after the Second World War to match inflation. In Canada, the allowances were abolished in 1992. Public provision of child care has also been implemented in only a token way in many countries because of a continued perception that it is a mother's responsibility to provide child care. If she must work, the onus is therefore largely on her and not on society to ensure that adequate provision for the care of her children is provided.[17]

In 1992, sociologist Jane Ursel, building on the work of feminist scholars in the United States and Britain, attempted to explain Canadian social-welfare policy developments in terms of changing state goals with regards to gender roles in the family. But this effort to reduce state policy-making to one objective largely failed to explain empirical developments. So, for example, the period from 1914 to 1939 is summarized in gender terms as one of "more systematic structures for the support of the family (welfare law) while extending the limitations on female and child labour (labour law) and elaborating on legislation to ensure familial support of its members (family law)."[18] In fact, as chapter 5 demonstrates, the desire not to tax and spend proved far more influential in the overall scheme of policy development for this period than Ursel's schema would predict.

Much of the feminist work in the 1990s and early 2000s has, however, nuanced the earlier arguments that suggested the state and patriarchy were inseparable. Linda Gordon, for example, has argued that some of the pioneer work provided too instrumentalist a view of the state and understated the role of women's agency both in the establishment of social programs and in their implementation. Policy-makers, she notes, have "fragmented and inconsistent goals" and "most welfare policies represent the jerry-built compromises which are the artifacts of political and social conflict—a dynamic that functionalism cannot encompass."[19]

The formulation "patriarchal state," like any other formulation that isolates one factor, can be a barrier in interpreting fully the evolution of various developments in social policy. It overstates the bonds of gender to the detriment of class and race. Jill Quadagno has demonstrated the extent to which American social security policies since the 1930s have favoured white males over black males. Others have documented the conscious design of certain social programs to have differential impacts on white women and women of colour. Organizations of white women are sometimes complicit in maintaining such discrimination. In Australia, for example, notes Marilyn Lake, white working-class women won a maternity allowance for white women after a campaign that stressed the concept of the "mother of the race." This "idea of a maternal citizenship" defined black women as ineligible for motherhood and citizenship both. Unsurprisingly, non-white women were often less sanguine than white women that the state was a potential friend since they were victims not only of state practices of sexism but also of state-supported racism.[20]

Comparative work on the social programs of various countries has also tended to highlight important differences in national experiences that social-control models, including feminist social-control models, cannot explain.[21] While single mothers and their children are everywhere poorer than nuclear families, their levels of poverty in France and in Sweden are a small fraction of the American rate, with Canada falling in between.[22] In short, some of the early feminist work on the welfare state under-theorizes the state and is too defeatist about women's ability in the past to shape programs both before and after they were implemented. So, for example, Gillian Creese, examining women's activism in British Columbia in the 1930s, notes that women wrested from the state authorities social assistance for single unemployed women, milk for women with babies, the extension of social assistance to needy Japanese and Chinese families, and clothing allowances for impoverished married women and their children.[23]

There is now a large literature that paints the welfare state as a paradox in gender terms. Though in most countries the preservation or recreation of patriarchal families was a fundamental goal of early reformers, programs that put cash in the hands of working-class women and created occupations for middle-class women weakened women's dependence on male wages. The breadwinner/ mother-housewife ideology survived everywhere sufficiently to keep women's wages below men's, but in some countries, particularly in Scandinavia and in France, the gender gap in wages narrowed significantly even though occupations remained largely gender-stratified.[24] The small army of women suppliers of social services are today among the better-paid women workers, and they and their clients "mediate constantly between the domestic and state spheres."[25]

Some feminist commentators simply view the female employees of state welfare bureaucracies as incorporated within a patriarchal regime rather than transforming that regime.[26] But this one-sided view of social workers and their clients is challenged as ahistorical by Linda Gordon and other feminist historians. In one book, focusing on casework within private agencies in the pre-welfare period in the United States, she demonstrates the ways in which clients utilized agencies to suit their own ends. Staff, responding to clients as individuals rather than the stereotypes built into written agency policy, also often bent the rules. In a later book, Gordon documents how during the welfare-state period as well, women have managed to make use of programs meant to compel their dependence on men to achieve a degree of independence.[27]

Jane Lewis's typology of welfare states is an effort to demonstrate the continuum that exists among welfare states with respect to how the state influences and shapes women's lives. Lewis cautions that the advantages for women in the French and Swedish models are fragile because they were made possible by a male-controlled state in response to pressures largely unrelated to the demands of organized feminists. France was attempting to increase its birth rate and Sweden faced a persistent labour shortage. Barbara Einhorn's survey of post-Communist states in eastern Europe confirms the danger that Lewis identifies. In the "state socialist" regimes women were expected to participate in the paid labour force and social policies virtually compelled that participation, even though women faced the double burden of waged work and housework/child care. With little help in the home from either male partners or state programs, many women in the Communist states regarded their paid jobs as a form of compulsion rather than a token of economic independence. So, as the post-Communist regimes moved quickly to establish capitalist social relations, only muted protests from organized women's groups initially met the closings of daycares and the discrimination against women that occurred in hirings and firings.[28]

In Western countries, as well, women have disagreed about the extent to which state-organized programs can be potentially beneficial to women. Jill Vickers has pointed out that Canadian feminists' greater willingness than their American counterparts to consider the state a potential ally has resulted in more women-friendly policies in this country than in the United States.[29]

This brief overview of the international literature on welfare states should alert the reader to the need to approach critically any presentation of the "facts" about why a particular program was initiated at a particular time, and how it was implemented. In this survey text, social policy is presented as a response to popular pressures, but in the context of class-divided societies with particular stratifications of class and gender and sometimes ethnicity. The strength of social elites is such that they have often managed to ensure that social programs, which the working class, women's organizations, and other popular groups have demanded, are either not implemented at all or are implemented in ways that result in little or no redistribution of wealth. Sometimes they have been able to win cancellation of or huge cutbacks in long-established programs, at times using their control over the media to win public support for meaner and leaner social policies. Throughout, however, if we always ask who benefited and who lost from particular courses of action in social policy, we can maintain a critical perspective when evaluating the rhetoric of the various players in the field of social policy.

Notes

1 A fascinating and award-winning study of Canadian social welfare history that focuses purely on discourse is Nancy Christie, *Engendering the State: Family, Work, and Welfare in Canada* (Toronto, ON: University of Toronto Press, 2000). Christie closely examines the gendered debates from 1914 to 1945 about what sorts of families the Canadian state should attempt to promote. Ultimately, however, as I have argued elsewhere, Christie fails to demonstrate a convincing link between particular discourses at various junctures and the actual making of policy. See Alvin Finkel, "Welfare for Whom? Class, Gender, and Race in Social Policy," *Labour/Le Travail* 49 (2002): 247–61.

2 Derek Fraser, *The Evolution of the British Welfare State: A History of Social Policy since the Industrial Revolution*, 2nd ed. (Houndmills, Basingstoke, Hampshire, UK: Macmillan, 1984), 139.

3 The contradictory character of the welfare state is discussed in Ian Gough, *The Political Economy of the Welfare State* (London, UK: Macmillan, 1979), 13–14.

4 Fraser, *The Evolution of the British Welfare State*, xxii–xxix.

5 For one of the works by Michel Foucault that stress moral regulation, see *The Birth of the Clinic: An Archaeology of Medical Perception* (New York, NY: Vintage, 1973). Governmentality is central to his narrative in *Discipline and Punish: The Birth of the Prison* (London, UK: Pantheon, 1977).

6 Philip Corrigan and Derek Sayer, *The Great Arch: English State Formation as Cultural Revolution* (Oxford, UK: Basil Blackwell, 1985), 4. See also Carolyn Strange and Tina Loo, *Law and Moral Regulation in Canada, 1867–1939* (Toronto, ON: University of Toronto Press, 1997).

7 For key works on the accumulation-legitimation debate, see James O'Connor, *The Fiscal Crisis of the State* (New York, NY: St. Martin's, 1973); Rick Deaton, "The Fiscal Crisis of the State in Canada," in *The Political Economy of the State; Québec, Canada, U.S.A.*, ed. Dimitrios Roussopoulos (Montreal, QC: Black Rose, 1973), 18–56; Claus Offe, *Disorganized Capitalism: Contemporary Transformations of Work and Politics* (Cambridge, MA: MIT Press, 1985); Goran Therborn, "Classes and States: Welfare State Developments 1881–1984," *Studies in Political Economy* 13 (1984): 7–41; and Michael Kalecki, *Essays on the Dynamics of the Capitalist Economies* (Cambridge, UK: Cambridge University Press, 1971).

8 Gøsta Esping-Anderson, *The Three Worlds of Welfare Capitalism* (Cambridge, UK: Polity, 1990).

9 Jane Lewis, "Gender and the Development of Welfare Regimes," *Journal of European Social Policy* 2 (1992): 159–73.

10 Alvin Finkel, "Changing the Story: Gender Enters the History of the Welfare State," *Tijdschrift voor Sociale Geschiedenis* 22, 1 (1996): 67–81.

11 Gillian Pascall, *Social Policy: A Feminist Analysis* (London: Tavistock, 1986), 1.

12 Dennis Guest, *The Emergence of Social Security in Canada*, 3rd ed. (Vancouver, BC: University of British Columbia Press, 1997); Walter I. Trattner, *From Poor Law to Welfare State: A History of Social Welfare in America*, 3rd ed. (New York, NY: Free Press, 1984); Fraser, *The Evolution of the British Welfare State*.

13 Among pioneering works were Elizabeth Wilson, *Women and the Welfare State* (London, UK: Tavistock, 1977); Jane Lewis, "Dealing with Dependency: State Practices and Social Realities, 1870–1945," in *Women's Welfare: Women's Rights*, ed. Jane Lewis (London, UK: Croom Helm, 1983), 17–37; Jane Lewis, *The Politics of Motherhood: Child and Maternal Welfare in England, 1900–1939* (Montreal, QC: McGill-Queen's University Press, 1980); Hilary Land, "The Introduction of Family Allowances: An Act of Historic Justice?" in *Change, Choice and Conflict in Social Policy*, ed. Phoebe Hall, Hilary Land, Roy Parker, and Adrian Webb (London, UK: Heinemann, 1975), 159–230; Jill Roe, "The End Is Where We Start From: Women and Welfare since 1901," in *Women, Social Welfare and the State in Australia*, ed. Bettina Cass and Cora V. Baldock (London, UK: Allen and Unwin, 1983), 1–19; Mimi Abramovitz, *Regulating the Lives of Women: Social Welfare Policy from Colonial Times to the Present* (Boston, MA: South End Press, 1989); Jane Ursel, *Private Lives, Public Policy: 100 Years of State Intervention in the Family* (Toronto, ON: Women's Press, 1992); Harriet Holter, ed., *Patriarchy in a Welfare Society* (Oslo, Norway: Universitetsforlaget, 1984).

14 Lewis, "Dealing with Dependencies," 19.

15 Jen Dale, "Feminists and the Development of the Welfare State—Some Lessons from Our History," *Critical Social Policy* 6 (1986): 58; Nancy E. Rose, "Gender, Race, and the Welfare State: Government Work Programs from the 1930s to the Present," *Feminist Studies* 19 (1993): 326; Diana M. Pearce, "Toil and Trouble: Women Workers and Unemployment Compensation," *Signs* 10 (1985): 435–59; Ruth Roach Pierson, "Gender and the Unemployment Insurance Debates in Canada, 1934–40," *Labour/Le Travail* 25 (1990): 77–103; and Ann Porter, *Gendered States: Women, Unemployment Insurance, and the Political Economy of the Welfare State in Canada, 1945–1997* (Toronto, ON: University of Toronto Press, 2003).

16 Andrée Lévesque, *La norme et les déviantes: des femmes au Québec pendant l'entre-deux-guerres* (Montreal, QC: Éditions du rémue-ménage, 1989), 48–49, 136.

17 The impact of the propaganda against working mothers on child care policy is explored, inter alia, in Denise Riley, "'The Free Mothers': Pronatalism and Working Women in Industry at the End of the Last War in Britain," *History Workshop* 11 (1981): 59–118; Sonya Michel, *Children's Interests/Mothers' Rights: The Shaping of America's Child Care Policy* (New Haven, CT: Yale University Press, 1999); and Susan Prentice, ed. *Changing Child Care: Five Decades of Child Care Advocacy and Policy in Canada*, (Halifax, NS: Fernwood, 2001).

18 Ursel, *Private Lives*, 154.

19 Linda Gordon, "The Welfare State: Towards a Socialist-Feminist Perspective," in *Socialist Register, 1990*, ed. Ralph Miliband and Leo Panitch (London, UK: Merlin, 1990), 186.

20 Jill Quadagno, *The Color of Welfare: How Racism Undermined the War on Poverty* (New York, NY: Oxford University Press, 1994); Rose, "Gender, Race, and the Welfare State," 319–42; Marilyn Lake, "A Revolution in the Family: The Challenge and Contradictions of Maternal Citizenship in Australia," in *Mothers of a New World: Maternalist Politics and the Origins of*

Welfare States, ed. Seth Koven and Sonya Michel (New York, NY: Routledge, 1993), 378–95; Teresa L. Arnott, " Black Women and AFDC: Making Entitlement out of Necessity," in *Women, the State, and Welfare*, ed. Linda Gordon (Madison, WI: University of Wisconsin Press, 1990); Jacqueline Jones, *Labor of Love, Labor of Sorrow: Black Women, Work, and the Family from Slavery to the Present* (New York, NY: Vintage, 1985), 201, 224–25, 263; Eileen Boris, "The Power of Motherhood: Black and White Women Redefine the Political," in *Mothers of a New World*, ed. Koven and Michel, 213–45; Marilyn Lake, "The Independence of Women and the Brotherhood of Man: Debates in the Labour Movement over Equal Pay and Motherhood Endowments in the 1920s," *Labour History* 63 (1992): 6.

21 Lewis, "Gender and the Development of Welfare Regimes"; Alisa Klaus, *Every Child a Lion: The Origins of Maternal and Infant Health Policy in the United States and France, 1890–1920* (Ithaca, NY: Cornell University Press, 1993); Gertrude Schaffner Goldberg and Eleanor Kremen eds., *The Feminization of Poverty: Only in America?* (New York, NY: Greenwood, 1990); Jane Jenson, "Both Friend and Foe: Women and State Welfare," in *Becoming Visible: Women in European History*, 2nd ed., ed. Renate Bridenthal, Claudia Koonz, and Susan Stuard (Boston, MA: Houghton Mifflin, 1987), 535–56.

22 Jane Jenson and Ruth Kantrow, "Labor Market and Family Policy in France: An Intersecting Complex for Dealing with Poverty," in *The Feminization of Poverty*, ed. Goldberg and Kremen, 107–28; Marguerite G. Rosenthal, "Sweden: Promise and Paradox," in *The Feminization of Poverty*, ed. Goldberg and Kremen, 129–55.

23 Gillian Creese, "The Politics of Dependence: Women, Work and Unemployment in the Vancouver Labour Movement before World War II," in *British Columbia Reconsidered: Essays on Women*, ed. Veronica Strong-Boag and Gillian Creese (Vancouver, BC: Press Gang, 1992), 364–90.

24 Frances Fox Piven and Richard A. Cloward, "Welfare Doesn't Shore Up Traditional Family Roles: A Reply to Linda Gordon," *Social Research* 55 (1988): 631–47.

25 Anne Showstack Sassoon, "Women's New Social Role: Contradictions of the Welfare State," in *Women and the State: The Shifting Boundaries of Public and Private*, ed. Anne Showstack Sassoon (London, UK: Hutchinson, 1987), 173.

26 Wendy Brown, "Finding the Man in the State," *Feminist Studies* 18 (1992): 11; Gisela Bock, "Challenging Dichotomies: Perspectives in Women's History," in *Writing Women's History: International Perspectives*, ed. Karen Offen, Ruth Roach Pierson, and Jane Rendall (Bloomington, IN: Indiana University Press, 1991), 5.

27 Linda Gordon, *Heroes of Their Own Lives: The Politics and History of Family Violence: Boston, 1880–1960* (New York, NY: Viking, 1988); Linda Gordon, *Pitied but Not Entitled: Single Mothers and the History of Welfare, 1890–1935* (Boston: Free Press, 1994).

28 Barbara Einhorn, *Cinderella Goes to Market: Citizenship, Gender and Women's Movements in East Central Europe* (London, UK: Verso, 1993).

29 Jill Vickers, "The Intellectual Origins of the Women's Movement in Canada," in *Challenging Times: The Women's Movement in Canada and the United States*, ed. Constance Backhouse and David H. Flaherty (Montreal, QC: McGill-Queen's University Press, 1992), 39–60.

Non-State Provision
(The Pre-Confederation Period)

Part 1 deals with the period before Canadian Confederation and traces how societies in the area that became Canada in 1867 dealt with those in need. While Part 1 deals with several rather distinct eras, the societies discussed are united by the perspective that individuals who required help from others generally had to get it from sources other than governments. The discussion begins with the people who lived in Canada for millennia without, for the most part, producing formal state structures. As chapter 1 demonstrates, Canada's Aboriginal societies had all evolved ways of insuring that the sick, the disabled, and the old were cared for by the community and for limiting inequalities of goods among their members. Chapter 2 deals with New France, whose feudal structures at once guaranteed both inequality among its residents and a land base for the majority. In New France, the Church, and especially its female religious orders, played the major role in providing services for the destitute and the ill. But the state was gradually forced to become involved as well.

Chapter 3 looks at the ways in which social provision evolved in British North America, a set of colonies with capitalist economic structures but dominated by small landowners and small businesses. Those without land or businesses lived precarious lives, with widows, "illegitimate" children, single women, and the old and infirm at particular risk. Voluntary organizations, usually led by women, arose to serve the needs of the helpless. But, over time, as the numbers of people dependent upon wage labour to survive increased, voluntary organizations became overwhelmed with the demands being made upon them. The state, while largely leaving social provision to the voluntary sector, gradually began making subventions to the volunteer groups and also opened poorhouses for those whose income problems were longer term. On the whole, both the state and the volunteers looked down on their charges, and argued that individual weaknesses, rather than the structure of the economy, caused destitution.

CHAPTER 1

First Peoples and Social Needs

North American Native peoples were dumbfounded by the extent of social inequalities in Europe. In 1611, Sauvignon, an eighteen-year-old Huron, visited France with Samuel de Champlain, the founder of Quebec. On his return home, Sauvignon proclaimed that he never wished to return to France, which he considered inferior to his homeland. He was appalled by the "great number of needy and beggars" in France, "saying that if [they] had some intelligence [they] would set some order in the matter, the remedies being simple."[1]

The European newcomers assumed their superiority over the millennial residents of the Americas, and many Natives were prepared to tell them that the reverse was true. The *Jesuit Relations,* a detailed chronicle of that religious order's efforts to convert Native Canadians in the eastern half of Canada during the seventeenth century, observed that the Mi'kmaq of the Atlantic region "consider themselves better than the French. 'For,' they say, 'you are always fighting and quarreling among yourselves; we live peaceably. You are envious and are all the time slandering each other; you are thieves and deceivers; you are covetous and are neither generous nor kind; as for us, if we have a morsel of bread we share it with our neighbor.'"[2]

The Aboriginal reaction to European social structures in the sixteenth and seventeenth centuries highlights the fact that Aboriginal societies had very different underlying values than European societies at the time of contact and their own economic structures as hunter-gatherers, agriculturists, and fishers. Different political systems had emerged as well. Across the country, the hunter-gatherers lived in stateless, largely egalitarian societies and agriculturists were governed by loose confederations, while the fishers on the West Coast lived in ranked societies under the control of relatively powerful chiefs. On the West Coast slavery was relatively common, and slaves were usually treated as chattels. But all of the Aboriginal peoples of Canada had certain features in common that affected what we might term their "social policies." In all of these societies, spiritual life was the organizing principle and all else flowed from people's relationship with the Creator. This included people's treatment of one another.

HUNTER-GATHERER SOCIETIES

Among hunter-gatherers, egalitarian principles were the norm. People lived in relatively small bands, with size determined by the abundance of game and plants in a given area. So, for example, Ojibwa bands in northern Ontario might be as large as two hundred, while bands in the Northwest Territories might be as small as twenty. Among Plains Natives, power was exercised collectively by all men who had proven their abilities in war and demonstrated their generosity. European observers sometimes confirmed the Aboriginal perspective that Plains peoples were far more generous overall than Europeans. Explorer David Thompson, writing about First Nations of the Plains, commented: "These acts that pass between man and man for generous charity and kind compassion in civilized society are no more than what is every day practiced by these Savages [the Cree]; as acts of common duty; is any one unsuccessful in the chase, has he lost his little all by some accident, he is sure to be relieved by the others to the utmost of their power." And Captain W.F. Butler, reporting to Parliament on conditions in the vast Western territories purchased by the Parliament of Canada from the Hudson's Bay Company in 1869, observed: "This wild man who first welcomed the newcomer is the only perfect socialist or communist in the world....He holds all things in common with his tribe—the land, the bison, the river, and the moose."[3]

The Blackfoot, recounting their own history, stress that spiritual laws guided their people's behaviour. The people were organized in clans, each composed of many families. Groups termed "inaki" had the responsibility to ensure law and order. Societies, such as the horn society, took the responsibility of helping people in their daily lives. For the Cree, as well, the need to follow the laws of the Creator governed relations among the people. Their educational, medical, and social institutions obeyed the same fundamental spiritual laws. Ceremonies provided a means for affirming the relations between the nation's social institutions and their debt to the Creator.[4]

Each Native nation had an extensive cornucopia of medical treatments and practices that had evolved over the centuries. Medicine men, individuals trained in the traditional healing knowledge of their people, prepared and administered the natural potions that were meant to cure various diseases. Some of the Native medical knowledge would be picked up by the Europeans—for example, the Natives of eastern Canada taught early explorers, whose men died in huge numbers from scurvy, that a broth made from the bark and needles of white cedar trees could provide the vitamin C needed to prevent the disease. For the most part, however, Europeans' sense of superiority would result not only in a failure to adopt Native cures but also in extensive and often successful efforts to prevent Native peoples from following their traditional healing practices.

Sex roles among hunter-gatherers were distinct, but, for the most part, appear to have been complementary, rather than marked by domination and subservience. One study of the Dene suggests the need to counter mythologies of women's exploitation and subordination found in explorers' and missionaries' accounts but without going "so far as to suggest that precontact life was a sort of egalitarian 'golden age' in which men and women were equally valued."[5] The greater incidence of female over male infanticide during famines, men's sharing and exchanging of wives without the latter's consent, and the disparaging of childless women but not of men, all point to a greater valuing of men than women.

Just as female babies might be seen as dispensable in times of famine, the elderly—in normal times respected as advisers to all those younger than they and as educators of the youth—might be abandoned when times were tough. The need for mobility meant that the mentally and physically infirm, of whatever age, might have to be left behind as a band moved with the seasons to a new camp in search of seasonal food. While early European commentators often disparaged Native practices and were quick to suggest that both the Dene and Inuit simply did not value the lives of the old and the infirm, there is much evidence, and not only in oral tradition, that this was not true. For example, "When the explorer Ross met the Netsilik people a century and a half ago, he saw Iliktat, an old man who was being pulled on a sleigh by his family across a difficult land. Early in this century Chief Robuscan of Abitibi carried his very heavy crippled wife on his back in their travels for almost twenty years."[6]

The fate of the infirm and baby girls in hard times aside, egalitarian practices characterized Western subarctic societies. For the Slavey of the Mackenzie District, mutual sharing of resources within a band was the norm. The principle of usufruct across territories as opposed to private ownership of property meant that the sharing of resources went beyond the immediate band. For example, for each territory a particular band had customary rights to hunt and gather at various times of the year, but a band short of food could hunt in another band's territory without payment after asking permission.[7]

Hunter-gatherer societies outside the North had a richer resource base and were rarely forced to abandon the infirm. Aboriginal peoples in the South attempted to fend off scarcity by exploiting diverse ranges—parkland and grassland, parkland and boreal forest, shield upland and Hudson Bay lowland (even in the North, most tribal groups exploited both northern transitional forest and tundra). As in the North, hoarding of wealth by individuals was actively discouraged. Prestige came not from having wealth but from giving it away. Even wealth earned from trade was distributed by chiefs or "trading captains" among their followers, thus increasing their prestige.[8] Sharing occurred not only within tribes but within the larger "national" groupings of Aboriginal peoples, as well as among people from different linguistic/national groupings. Plains Cree elder Danny Musqua makes it clear that usufruct prevailed in the woodland and plain regions occupied by the Cree: "We had agreements between one another, hunting territories that we shared, trapping lands that we shared, gathering lands that we shared, medicinal lands that we shared [sacred lands], peace territorial lands that we designated for the shelter and safety of all people."[9]

Nations with Embryonic State Formations

Decision-making within and among Native nations followed well-entrenched rituals but, for the most part, lacked a formal code along European lines. Alliances among Native groups also relied on traditional understandings rather than on formal bureaucratic governmental arrangements. A significant, if partial, exception had begun to develop among the Mi'kmaq and many of the Iroquoian nations in the century or two preceding contact with the Europeans.

The Mi'kmaq, who moved seasonally from the Atlantic coast to inland areas, were fishers as well as hunters and gatherers. The favourable climate and abundant fishery in their region allowed them to live in much larger villages than the hunter-gatherer groups we have discussed. By the time of European contact, the Mi'kmaq had formed district organizations, each of which had a grand chief and a grand captain as well as elected advisers and a leader of the warriors. The Grand Council, composed of the seven grand chiefs and the seven grand captains, met only once annually. But it served an important function from the perspective of social policy. The Council's task was to ensure that each family had adequate fishing stations for spring and autumn, hunting ranges for winter, and gathering grounds for summer. Where there were disputes among families that went beyond a given community, the Grand Council would serve as an arbitrator. With an expanding population, the Council ensured that families' traditional rights to certain hunting grounds and fishing waters were balanced against the needs of the Mi'kmaq people as a whole.[10]

The Iroquoian nations, living in the fertile areas of the Great Lakes–St. Lawrence lowlands region, had become primarily agricultural peoples in the millennium preceding contact with the Europeans. They were sedentary, living in large extended-family longhouses within palisaded villages of up to two thousand people. The women were the farmers and therefore controlled most of the food supply. While the men hunted large game and the women small game close to home, trade with hunter-gatherer nations such as the Ojibway and Cree was an important source of game and other products for Iroquoians. The charitable notions that governed relations inside tribes also governed relations in trade. Despite the greater wealth of the Iroquoian groups relative to most other Native groups, their society was held together by shared ideals and mutual consent. Prestige was earned through public service rather than the acquisition of property. In a stateless society, such property could not, in any event, be protected.[11]

However the outlines of an emerging state were evident in Huron society—an Iroquoian nation—by the time of contact. Each clan segment usually had a civil chief and a military chief chosen from particular family lines. Two councils ran village affairs: the warriors' council composed of men of the village over a certain age, likely about thirty, and the civil chiefs' council. The councils met almost daily. Each tribe was a collection of villages made up of clan segments and sporadic tribal councils occurred at the behest of any chief of a segment. The five Huron tribes had formed a loose confederacy, and a confederacy council was held at least once a year to renew the ties between the tribes. Agreement of all tribes was needed for a decision to be made and the Huron Confederacy appears in the early 1600s to have still been more relevant in a symbolic than a legislative sense.

The social communities of the Huron were built around the role of the long-house. Although the Jesuits believed living in longhouses meant living in filth and without privacy,

> in actual fact, communal life with one's nearest kin in a longhouse offered social and economic benefits that an outsider could only be dimly aware of. These benefits derived mainly from the fact that members of the longhouse were completely inter-dependent. Furthermore, the system of marriage outside the kin group spread this interdependency to other kin groups, tying longhouses and ultimately villages to-gether. The longhouse was therefore the physical symbol of social and psychological security, not only at the family level, but ultimately at the village and tribal level. No one needed to feel that he was alone in his house, village or tribe, as long as he met his obligations and responsibilities to his relations and his neighbours.[12]

In Iroquoian society, the aged and ill were cared for, as were those whose crops had failed. Yet despite these egalitarian practices, Iroquoian nations were, by no means, without internal and external conflict. Warfare was common, and the Five Nations then living in what is today northern New York state had formed the first Iroquois Confederacy in the late fourteenth or early fifteenth century in an effort to end the internecine warfare that had come to plague their na-tions. Dekanawidah, a Huron who lived among the Seneca, and Hiawatha, an Onondaga who lived with the Mohawk, were, according to legend, the leaders responsible for gathering the Five Nations together to create the "Constitution of the Iroquois Nations, the Great Binding Law." Because the Iroquois had no written language, the constitution was passed on to the members of the Five Nations orally and transmitted from generation to generation. It was quite elaborate in its efforts to ensure that, despite the growing population of the Five Nations, its society would be organized along as democratic and egalitar-ian lines as possible. This included an important role for both sexes in insur-ing that chiefs, who were always male, represented the interests of society as a whole.

The women of certain prestigious families, called the Royaneh, would choose the chiefs and, if a chief failed to perform his duties, the women would "select another of their sons as a candidate." Both men and women would de-termine whether a chief was doing his job. Either "the men or women of the Confederacy, or both jointly" could complain to the Confederacy Council if a chief "has not in mind the welfare of the people or disobeys the rules of this Great Law." Three such reports and the chief was out. Women's economic status was assured by clause 44 of the Great Law, which stated simply: "The lineal descent of the people of the Five Nations shall run in the female line. Women shall be considered the progenitors of the Nation. They shall own the land and the soil. Men and women shall follow the status of the mother."[13]

PACIFIC COASTAL CHIEFDOMS

The position of women was likely not as equal to men's among the Pacific coastal peoples, whose societies were patrilineal and authoritarian rather than matrilineal and democratic like the Iroquoian societies. Each individual's position within society was closely ranked. Positions of authority and prestige were inherited, rather than earned, and elaborate ceremonies marked an individual's receipt of honours set aside for him or her. Nonetheless, "the principle of sharing prevailed as far as the basic necessities of life were concerned: a village's hunting, fishing, and gathering territories were divided among its kinship groups and exploited accordingly."[14] However, such equality must be seen in perspective. Slaves could comprise as much as a third of the population of a particular village and had no rights. They were the property of their owners who could dispose of them at will, though there is some debate as to how roughly their owners treated them.[15]

Nor were slaves entitled to the benefits of the potlatch, the chief ceremony for "redistributing" the goods of a nation. While the purpose of a potlatch from the outside might have seemed to be simply for a chief or other leading person to give away most of his worldly goods, in practice there were strict conventions that governed the operation of the potlatches and determined who gave and who received what. Over a series of potlatches, the status of each free individual would be reaffirmed rather than changed. The potlatch ensured that all members of the nation, that is all non-slaves, received a minimum of the collective goods of the nation but also reaffirmed the legitimacy of the caste-like structures that made certain families more important and richer than others. Despite inequalities in the distribution of wealth, the land, houses, and important tokens of wealth belonged to the community with individuals only having the right to look after such community property. The distinction was important because it meant that property could not be sold or traded by individuals without the express approval of the community.

During the twenty to thirty millennia before Europeans arrived in the Americas, complex social structures evolved. All of the societies that emerged appear to have maintained some degree of egalitarianism in the pre-contact years. Medicine men administered to the medical needs of all people without distinction (except perhaps slaves in the Pacific coastal societies). Clans ensured that the infirm and elderly were looked after to the best of a First Nation's ability. Co-operation across clans and across national groupings, via both trade and usufruct, made it possible for each group to have a fighting chance of survival when game or plants were scarce or when crops had failed. But new societies were about to take root in the Americas, and would introduce entirely different social structures and principles of social organization. These would have an impact not only on the Europeans who moved to the "New World" but on the descendants of the original inhabitants as well.

Notes

1 James Axtell, "Through Another Glass Darkly: Early Indian Views of Europeans," in *Out of the Background: Readings on Canadian Native History*, 2nd ed., ed. Ken Coates and Robin Fisher (Toronto, ON: Copp Clark, 1996), 26.

2 A.G. Bailey, *The Conflict of European and Eastern Algonkian Cultures 1504–1700: A Study in Canadian Civilization*, 2nd ed. (Toronto, ON: University of Toronto Press, 1969), 14. For Aboriginal peoples' views more generally, see Cornelius J. Jaenen, "Amerindian Views of French Culture in the Seventeenth Century," in *Out of the Background: Readings on Canadian Native History*, ed. Robin Fisher and Kenneth Coates (Toronto, ON: Copp Clark Pitman, 1988), 121.

3 David Thompson, *Explorations in Western America, 1784–1812*, ed. J.B. Tyrell (Toronto, ON: Champlain Society, 1916), 81; Paul F. Sharp, *Whoop-Up Country: The Canadian-American West, 1865–1885* (Norman, OK: University of Oklahoma Press, 1973), 25.

4 Treaty 7 Elders and Tribal Council with Walter Hildebrandt, Sarah Carter, and Dorothy First Rider, *The True Spirit and Original Intent of Treaty 7* (Montreal, QC: McGill-Queen's University Press, 1996), 83; Harold Cardinal and Walter Hildebrandt, *Treaty Elders of Saskatchewan: Our Dream Is That Our Peoples Will One Day Be Clearly Recognized as Nations* (Calgary, AB: University of Calgary Press, 2000), 14–15.

5 Kerry Abel, *Drum Songs: Glimpses of Dene History* (Montreal, QC: McGill-Queen's University Press, 1993), 23.

6 Keith J. Crowe, *A History of the Original Peoples of Northern Canada*, rev. ed. (Montreal, QC: McGill-Queen's University Press, 1991), 24.

7 Indian Brotherhood of the Northwest Territories and Métis Association of the Northwest Territories, "Past and Present Land-Use by Slavey Indians of the Mackenzie District": Summary of Evidence of Michael Asch, Department of Anthropology, University of Alberta, before the Mackenzie Valley Pipeline Inquiry, Yellowknife, NWT, April 1976; Arthur Ray and Donald Freeman, *Give Us Good Measure: An Economic Analysis of Relations between the Indians and the Hudson's Bay Company before 1763* (Toronto, ON: University of Toronto Press, 1978), 17.

8 Arthur J. Ray, "Periodic Shortages, Native Welfare, and the Hudson's Bay Company, 1670–1930," in *The Subarctic Fur Trade: Native Social and Economic Adaptations*, ed. Shepard Krech III (Vancouver, BC: University of British Columbia Press, 1984), 1–20; G. Copway or Kah-

Ge-Ga-Gah-Bowh, Chief of the Ojibway Nations, *The Traditional History and Characteristic Sketches of the Ojibway Nation* (1850; reprint, Toronto, ON: Coles, 1972).

9   Cardinal and Hildebrandt, *Treaty Elders of Saskatchewan*, 39.

10 Canada, Royal Commission on Aboriginal Peoples, *Final Report*, vol. 1, *Looking Forward Looking Back* (Ottawa, ON: Minister of Supply and Services, 1996), available online from www.ainc-inac.gc.ca/ch/rcap/sg/sgmm_e.html.

11 Father Gabriel Sagard, *The Long Journey to the Country of the Huron*, ed. George M. Wrong (Toronto, ON: Champlain Society, 1939), 139–40; Bruce Trigger, *The Huron: Farmers of the North*, rev. ed. (New York, NY: Holt, Rinehart and Winston, 1990).

12 Conrad Heidenreich, *Huronia: A History and Geography of the Huron Indians 1600–1650* (Toronto, ON: McClelland and Stewart, 1971), 171.

13 "Dekanawidah." *Humanistic Texts*. Retrieved from www.humanistictexts.org/dekanawidah.htm

14 Olive Patricia Dickason, *Canada's First Nations: A History of Founding Peoples from Earliest Times*, 2nd ed. (Toronto, ON: Oxford University Press, 1997), 47.

15 Eugene Ruyle, "Slavery, Surplus and Stratification on the Northwest Coast: The Ethnogenetics of an Incipient Stratification System," *Current Anthropology* 14, 5 (1973): 603–17.

CHAPTER 2

New France: The Church, the State, and Feudal Obligations

In 1721, Michel Begon, the intendant of Canada, decreed that a son-in-law must "receive in his house Antoine Dionne...aged 90, father of his wife, to lodge him, to feed him and to care for him throughout his life. Bartholemi Gobille, the other son-in-law must contribute half his expenses."[1]

This involvement by the state to ensure care for an infirm and elderly individual demonstrates some of the principles of the society that had been established in Canada in the early post-contact period. If Aboriginal societies could rely on custom to ensure that no one starved, New France sometimes had to resort to formal laws to achieve the same end. As the intendant's decree suggested, wherever possible, the state expected families to care for the infirm and the destitute among their relatives. As this chapter demonstrates, there was sufficient poverty and misery in New France to make the family an inadequate resource for many *Canadiens* (residents of the St. Lawrence colony of Canada) and *Acadiens* (French-speaking residents of Atlantic Canada) in their struggle for survival. Both the Church and the seigneurial system played important roles alongside the family to deal with destitution and illness, but their combined efforts still left many people without necessary supports.

SOCIAL STRUCTURE AND ECONOMY

The starting point for understanding social policy in New France is to explore the social structure of the colonies: Canada (today's Quebec), Acadia (today's Maritime provinces), Newfoundland, and Louisiana. France bequeathed to New France a modified version of its own late feudal structures. In France, feudal structures had changed since the Middle Ages, and the emerging commercial capitalism was hampered by a myriad of feudal rules. The French authorities, crafting plans for the royal government for Canada in 1663, attempted to remove some of the deadweight of imperial institutions from the colony. But the seigneurial system of landholding, the fundamental institution of feudalism, was confirmed.

In theory, feudalism meant that the king alone owned the land. Seigneurs exercised control over seigneuries in return for their loyalty to the Crown, particularly military service in wartime. The habitants or serfs lived on land within the seigneury and had customary rights to work that land in return for several days of work each week on the seigneur's land. Over time, such labour duties were commuted to rents in kind. The seigneur owed the habitants certain obligations, such as provision of a grist mill and a court. While the system emphasized the two-way obligations, it guaranteed great wealth for the seigneur and poverty for the habitants. Apart from paying up to half their crop to a landlord, French habitants paid a tithe of one-tenth of their crop for support of the Roman Catholic Church.

The rules were more lenient in Canada where the French government was unwilling to spend the monies required to maintain a comparable level of repression. Tithes were lower than in France. While French habitants could be put to death for hunting and fishing on a seigneur's land, both rural and urban settlers of New France had abundant territories open to them for hunting and fishing. They also had far more land available per family. But the land was only available after they had hacked down forests, a process that was slow and cumbersome. Although there was greater opportunity for families in New France than in France, large disparities of wealth and social status marked the overseas colonies. Ancestry and occupation established social boundaries that only small numbers of individuals were able to cross. In towns, such as Montreal, Quebec, and Louisbourg, a small number of civil servants and merchants accounted for most of the wealth, with tradespeople, labourers, and domestics living modest lives. In church, in courts, and in the streets, all individuals knew their rank in a rigid social system.

The Atlantic fishery and the fur trade sparked a deeper expansion of French ventures into Canada, and the establishment of more colonial settlements. Agriculture was encouraged so that fur traders would have local food sources. By 1760, three-quarters of the population of Canada lived in the rural areas and had largely become self-sufficient, but the ups and downs of the fur trade had an impact on the availability of jobs in the towns. The urban job market was important both to permanent residents of the towns and to habitants who fell on hard times and needed to temporarily supplement their farming.

THE ROLE OF THE CHURCH

From the beginnings of colonial settlement in Canada and Acadia, members of Roman Catholic orders, both cloistered and non-cloistered, were the providers of social services. Both women and men were involved in educating colonists and Aboriginals alike in Christian and French ways, while women were leaders in providing health care services to colonists. Eventually both female and male religious orders also provided shelters for the poor, while the women's orders looked after foundlings, prostitutes, the insane, and the aged.

The Récollets and the Jesuits, both communities of men, were the first religious orders in New France. They devoted their early efforts to the conversion of the "heathen" Natives to Christianity. The process of conversion moved quite slowly and the religious brethren felt the need to recruit more devout Catholics from France both to help in the laborious work of conversion among the Natives and to minister to the slowly increasing flock of French-origin settlers. They turned to women's religious orders to meet these objectives, and the call was answered by individuals and groups of religious women who believed that God wanted them to spread the faith in a new land.

First came Marie Guyart, or Mère Marie de l'Incarnation, a widow who had managed a family transport company for ten years. Supported by a wealthy female sponsor, Madame de la Peltrie, she established a convent of the Ursulines in Quebec. The Ursulines opened their first boarding school in 1639, where the pious Marie de l'Incarnation attempted to educate young Aboriginal girls in the faith. Most of the students ran away from their austere teachers who preached a strange religion, and eventually the Ursuline schools that came to be established in the colony serviced young French girls from wealthy families.[2]

Also in 1639, religious women established the first hospital in New France, the Hôtel-Dieu de Québec. The Soeurs Hospitalières de Dieppe, under the supervision of Marie Guenet and Marie Forestier, were responsible for this institution. The second hospital was also founded by women. Jeanne Mance, a founding member of the colony of Ville Marie (later renamed Montreal) in 1642, established the Hôtel-Dieu de Ville Marie the following year, aided by other members of the Soeurs Hospitalières de la Flèche. Mance travelled to France frequently to ensure continuing financial support for the hospital. Her efforts underscored both the role of private benefactors and the important role of independent women, motivated by religious zeal, in establishing hospitals and other institutions serving public needs. Eventually the Hôtel-Dieus in Montreal and Quebec (and in Trois-Rivières, where the third Hôtel-Dieu opened in 1702) ran short of funds and the governors and intendants implored the king to provide them with long-term funding.[3]

By 1658, Montreal's Hôtel-Dieu occupied a building that normally held ten beds but could hold twenty during an epidemic. In Quebec, seventeen cloistered nuns in the Hôtel-Dieu served a population of 1,976 in 1663. When French government policies resulted in population expansion, the hospital had expanded as well and by 1672 could boast a men's and a women's wing, along with a small chamber for wealthier patients. From 1689 to 1698, the Hôtel-Dieu of Quebec admitted 3,297 men and 1,765 women, the equivalent of one admission for every resident of the area at the time. Twice each year Montreal's Hôtel-Dieu employed master surgeons, always male, on three-month contracts to visit the wards and handle charity cases, but most medical care was provided by the nursing sisters.[4]

The scope of the church's charitable and educational institutions expanded throughout the French period in tandem with increases in the population and increases in social problems. In New France's early years, almost the whole population was young and able-bodied. By the end of the seventeenth century, many of the earlier colonists had become aged or infirm, and, if they had no family to support them, survival required moving to one of the three towns in the colony and becoming beggars.

Bishop Saint-Vallier recognized the problem by founding several institutions to house the destitute. First, he established an almshouse in Quebec in 1692 for older women beggars. Inmates worked in the institution's workshop or on its farmland, with able-bodied beggars expected to help care for the ill. The following year, the bishop established the Hôpital-Général de Québec to house chronically indigent males, particularly the impoverished aged and ill. It was placed under the supervision of the Frères Charon, a group of lay brothers who were soon entrusted with a similar institution in Montreal. Only in 1747, when Marguerite d'Youville and the Soeurs Grises (Grey Nuns) took over the Hôpital, were women, including prostitutes seeking rehabilitation, allowed entry as well. In Quebec, by contrast, by 1725, the Hôpital-Général had become home to destitute women as well as men. A separate wing for the insane had been added in 1721.[5]

There was, interestingly, a difference in class origins among the nuns in the charitable organizations in Quebec. While the nuns of the Hôtel-Dieu as well as the Ursulines came from families that could provide good dowries, the nuns of the Hôpital-Général had their beginnings in the minor nobility in France. On the initiative of the higher-born women, the Hôpital-Général added a boarding school for girls in 1725.[6]

Class differences were not only evident in the origins of the nuns or monks who were in charge but also in terms of what the facilities offered. For example, the Ursulines' boarding schools were reserved for girls from wealthy families whose parents could afford to pay the fees required by the sisters to maintain their institutions. Like all schools for girls in the colony, the Ursuline schools gave no consideration to teaching a trade. Instead they taught music, art, singing, and a foreign language to girls who were being groomed as the wives of wealthy men. Day students of the Ursulines came next in the educational hierarchy, and below them were the boarders who attended the schools founded by Marguerite Bourgeoys.

Bourgeoys had arrived in Ville Marie in 1653 and opened a school in a building near the Hôtel-Dieu. Her order, the Congrégation des Filles seculières de Ville Marie, later called the Sisters of the Congregation of Notre Dame, rejected Bishop François Laval's demand that they merge with the cloistered Ursulines. Providing free education, instruction for girls, reading in French rather than Latin, and limited use of corporal punishment, her schools had little cachet relative to the fee-paying Ursuline schools. Since they were educating girls who would be the wives of habitants or artisans, these schools also gave instruction in housekeeping duties. Peter Moogk suggests that the efforts of the Sisters of the Congregation of Notre-Dame meant that "many country girls were better educated than their brothers."[7]

Schools for boys also had class overtones, with Jesuit schools designated mainly for the upper classes and a vocational school for boys from the popular classes. The Jesuit schools did, however, offer some assistance for talented children of poor families, insuring that education was not exclusively available to the wealthy. Nonetheless, the number of girls and boys in New France who received any sort of formal education before 1760 always remained small. Most settlers could not sign their names, and only about 10 per cent of the habitants were literate.[8]

The Soeurs Grises were founded in 1737 by Marguerite Dufrost de Lajemmerais, a widow who was more commonly known as Madame d'Youville, along with three friends. She and her friends rented a house and devoted themselves to caring for the sick, the poor, and the old. Their main focus was on abandoned children, whose numbers increased sharply between 1750 and 1770 as first the French and then the British army took up residence in the colony. The soldier/lovers who died or who returned to their homes or barracks left many an unmarried mother with no means of raising her love child. While Madame d'Youville and her associates rejected being cloistered, they were motivated by religious fervour and had little alternative, under colonial rules, but to form a secular association that conformed to the Church's laws. Their official name was "desmoiselles de la Charité chargées par Sa Majesté de la direction de l'Hôpital-Général de Montréal." [9]

What sort of service did this diverse set of Church-run institutions provide for the small colony? Both contemporaries and modern scholars have praised the unstinting efforts of the religious communities, dominated by the women's communities, to look out for the health and well-being of the colonists. In 1733 Intendant Hocquart praised "the zeal with which the nuns hospitallers in the three towns in this colony have gone to the relief of the sick; their charity and their cares have known no limits." The nuns themselves noted the special challenges faced by the Hôtel-Dieus when epidemics struck, though fortunately epidemic outbreaks were infrequent. In Quebec, in 1685, the nuns of the Hôtel-Dieu cared for members of a crew ridden with typhus and one recorded the scene as follows: "There were so many sick in this ship that soon the wards, the chapel, the barns, the chicken coop and all the hospital grounds, wherever a place could be found for them—even tents were put up in the yard—were filled. We redoubled our efforts to serve them and they had great need of our help—fevers, terrible and burning, delirium and much scurvy. There came into our hospital more than three hundred sick."[10]

But historian Allan Greer cautions that the work of the religious communities must be seen on its own terms. The members of these communities were not promoting a political agenda such as the elimination of poverty or the universal availability of medical services. He writes: "The aim was not to solve 'social problems.' The accent was on the act of alms-giving and on its spiritual significance to the giver, rather than the needs of the recipient. The religious were not necessarily expected to adjust their handouts when times were hard, and they certainly did not aim to eliminate poverty. Accordingly, we find indigent people begging in the streets while widows of military officers occupy comfortable lodgings at the hospital."[11]

Similarly, it may be imposing a present-day secular viewpoint on the past, to conclude, as did the Clio Collective in their comprehensive history of Quebec women, that the nuns and lay women who provided health and educational services found in New France "a privileged place where they could express their independence and initiative."[12] For those firmly committed to a life spent demonstrating their submission to the Roman Catholic version of God, there could be no bourgeois individualistic "independence and initiative." Instead, there could be only submission to God's will and rejection of all material happiness.

The Church's role in providing social services was most noticeable in the towns. In Acadia, where French rule was intermittent and more short-lived than in New France—after 1713, only Cape Breton remained in French hands—a smaller population and the lack of urban development did not permit the same level of institutional development. But in Louisbourg, the fortress developed by France on Cape Breton Island (Île Royale) in 1720, the church played an important role in providing social services. Récollet priests distributed alms to the poor. The Brothers of Charity and the Sisters of the Congregation of Notre Dame played parallel roles to the Charon Brothers and the various female orders in Canada. The Sisters of the Congregation cared for orphaned girls while the Brothers of Charity operated a home for indigent men.[13]

Funds for the charitable work of the Louisbourg religious communities came mostly from the French-appointed state apparatus. Emphasis on the role of the churches in providing social services in New France should not obscure the important role that the state played in funding charitable endeavours in the French colonies and in determining a variety of social policies.

THE ROLE OF THE STATE

Before 1663, the fur-trade monopoly in Canada exercised the powers of government. Beginning in 1663, however, the fur trade and government were separated, and royal officials were appointed to positions of governor, intendant, and bishop with specific jurisdictions of governance. While the bishop, as the head of the Church, had at least nominal authority over the various religious communities involved in the social welfare area, the intendant, as the leading civic official, played an important role in determining the thrust of social policy. He was assisted by the appointed Sovereign Council, a body that registered royal edicts and acted as a court of appeal.

The Sovereign Council's involvement in social policy began with a decree in August 1677 that banned begging in Quebec and ordered the beggars to leave town and return to their farms. There were an estimated three hundred beggars in the town, whose total population was less than two thousand. Trying to choke off the supply of alms to beggars, the Council imposed stiff fines on colonists who helped them out. The 1677 law may have been effective at the time, but six years later the Council felt compelled to issue a similar decree—this time with the threat that beggars who failed to leave town would be placed in the stocks for a first offence and flogged for a second offence. Only beggars incapable of working would be allowed to beg, and their right to this privilege would be determined by the state authorities who would issue a license to beg if they accepted a beggar's application as valid.

The Council's early edicts established a philosophy of social policy that had already taken root in Europe. The poor were to be categorized as "deserving" or "undeserving" of charity. The able-bodied, particularly if they were men, were assumed to be capable of working and therefore were deemed ineligible for state help. Little thought was given to whether there was a job available to an unemployed, able-bodied person. The individual, rather than the state, was presumed to have the responsibility of finding a job. Thus began in Canada the never-ending debates about who should be considered able-bodied, who should be considered "deserving" of state income rather than being forced to seek employment, and what level of support the "deserving" poor should receive from the state.

Historian W.J. Eccles provides a classic conservative explanation for the growth of begging by the 1670s. "It was inevitable, however, given the hasty manner in which many of the emigrants had been recruited in France, that some of them would find conditions in Canada too arduous and would abandon the attempt to wrest a living from the wilderness. Thus, within a few years after the establishment of royal government, Quebec was beset by beggars."[14] The evidence of other historians of New France suggests that Eccles's claims are purely ideological. While many colonists were unprepared for wilderness conditions, it makes little sense to suggest that the habitants were free farmers who could enjoy the fruits of their own efforts provided they were willing to do the work. Tithes collected by the Church along with dues paid to the seigneur could eat up half the crop grown by a habitant. This left little possibility of storing up surpluses or of selling them off.[15] A poor crop year, illness or death that prevented a farm family from getting in a crop, or the ill luck of having poor land could result in destitution. The willingness of colonists to help alms-seekers suggested that many ordinary folk were sympathetic to the view that temporary hardship, rather than calculated idleness, brought strangers a-begging to their door.

Before 1688, the only help a poor person deemed "deserving" of charity received from the state was a license to beg. That year, more comprehensive legislation to deal with poverty was drawn up by the Sovereign Council on order from Intendant Jean Bochart de Champigny. The Council drafted a lengthy document with three aims: to prevent starvation; to find work for all those capable of working; and to end public begging. Determined to draw a clear line between the deserving and undeserving poor, the Council gave the seigneurs the power to decide who in the rural areas deserved charitable help and how much. In the three towns, however, *bureaux des pauvres* (offices of the poor) would be established. The local curé, along with three directors, would have the authority to collect money for alms and then dispense the charity. The destitute were required to register with one of the bureaus. Bureau officials would seek work for the employables and provide alms to the unemployables. Individuals who refused a job offered to them at wages deemed acceptable by the bureau were declared to be idlers and deprived of eligibility for alms. As the fur trade gradually revived after 1689, and almshouses for the chronically indigent were established by the religious communities, the need for the bureaus subsided, and they were discontinued, only to be re-established in 1698, when the fur trade entered a slump again. Women figured prominently among the "deserving" poor who were aided. In Montreal, at the end of the seventeenth century, two-thirds of alms recipients were women, mostly widows and abandoned wives.[16]

One area in which the state gradually assumed financial responsibility was the care of foundlings. Contemporary attitudes regarded unwed mothers as sinners and rejected providing them with financial aid that would allow them to keep their children. Instead, they were forced to give up their children, usually at the door of a church, for others to raise. In 1726, Intendant Bégon had ordered seigneuries to care for foundlings, but seigneurs resisted having to pay for the upkeep of "illegitimate" babies and, a decade later, the state assumed these costs. By 1736, there were 390 abandoned children being raised with state funds, and in 1748, an *ordonnance* decried the high death rate among foundlings and set out regulations to protect them better. A generous rate of pay was set for the wet nurses required by these babies so as to ensure that women with enough breast milk to nurse could be found for the work. The Crown would seek foster parents for the children when they reached eighteen months, and would pay the parents an honorarium.[17]

The state also began to pay urban midwives, and at mid-century, four midwives were on the state payroll. Midwives, whose expertise was passed on from mother to daughter, both helped the mother and administered baptism to newborns on the verge of dying. It became customary for the women of the parish to choose from among their number for the task. A rural midwife received no remuneration from the state, though she could expect that the family of a delivering mother would reward her with a gift in kind for her practical and psychological help with a birth. The beginnings of state involvement in childbirth in New France reflected the need to reduce the number of deaths of mothers giving birth wherever possible. Pregnancies were hazardous in the seventeenth and eighteenth centuries and it is estimated that 1.5 per cent of pregnancies in New France resulted in the mother's death. Since the average woman would give birth to eight or nine children, perhaps 10 per cent of all women before 1760 died either in childbirth or in the months immediately following giving birth.[18]

The democratic hiring and informal pay of rural midwives indicated the presence of an informal, voluntary sector alongside the formal Church and state sectors in the social welfare field in New France. Another example of cooperative efforts to ensure the availability of a social service occurred in the late 1600s in Montreal, where forty-two citizens contracted a master surgeon for five livres a year per family to ensure treatment for whatever diseases or injuries might befall them, excepting plague, smallpox, leprosy, and lithotomy.[19]

Both the state and the Church became involved in providing necessities to families only when families proved unable to rely on their own resources to survive. But every effort was made by families to prevent this. Most widows and widowers remarried quickly.[20] Widows and deserted wives who failed to remarry might give their children under five to a church-run orphanage. They had little option but to place older children with an employer willing to indenture the child till adulthood. So, for example, an abandoned wife in Quebec in 1736, unable to feed her eight-year-old son, indentured him to a merchant as a "domestic servant...until the full age of twenty years." Pauper children were also indentured by their families or by the church if they were orphaned, with the result that two-thirds of the household servants in New France in the closing days of the French regime were indentured children.[21]

By custom, children cared for their aged parents. A father who could no longer work turned his property over to his children in return for an amnesty in cash or in kind. If the amnesty was large, a couple or an individual surviving parent might live separately from their kids. The elderly who lived in the "hôpitals" were usually indigents whose children were simply too poor to care for them, or, in a few cases, fee-paying elderly people who had chosen to live apart from their children.[22]

Apart from the direct involvement of the state authorities in Canada in the provision of social services, the indirect involvement of the French state must be emphasized. The French state provided subventions to the Church in the colony to compensate for the smaller tithe paid by the settlers relative to the French. This aided the Church in running the institutions that provided social services to colonists. In Louisbourg, the government largely funded all charitable activities, including church-operated institutions.[23]

The colonies of New France were socially stratified along lines similar to France, though greater prosperity overall meant that habitants and town dwellers alike were better off on the whole than their French counterparts. The basic economic unit was the nuclear family and families strove to provide for themselves rather than relying on the state or the Church for any portion of their economic needs. But economic inequalities and economic misfortunes left many people in poverty. Church institutions and later state institutions developed to care for the poor, though in a manner that did not call into question the colonies' social structure and distribution of wealth. The Church's involvement in health services and in housing indigents, including the aged, the insane, and destitute widows, and state provisions for foundlings and for the aid of midwives for pregnant women meant that Canada, with fewer than 65,000 people at the time of the British conquest in 1760, had a rich social service institutional life by the end of the French regime. Through the Church, women played at least an equal role to men in the provision of health and social services.

NOTES

1 Translated by the author from André Lachance, *Vivre, aimer et mourir en Nouvelle-France: la vie quotidienne aux xvii è et xviii è siècles* (Montreal, QC: Libre Expression, 2000), 176.
2 Clio Collective, *Quebec Women: A History* (Toronto, ON: Women's Press, 1987), 32.
3 André Vachon, *Dreams of Empire: Canada before 1700* (Ottawa, ON: Public Archives of Canada, 1982), 332.

4 Alison Prentice et al., *Canadian Women: A History* (Toronto, ON: Harcourt Brace Jovanovich, 1988), 42; W.J. Eccles, "Social Welfare Measures and Policies in New France," in *Essays on New France*, W.J. Eccles (Toronto, ON: Oxford University Press, 1987), 45; Vachon, *Dreams of Empire*, 333.

5 Vachon, *Dreams of Empire*, 333; André Vachon, *Taking Root: Canada from 1700 to 1760: Records of Our History* (Ottawa, ON: Public Archives of Canada, 1985), 255.

6 Vachon, *Taking Root*, 255.

7 Peter N. Moogk, "'Les Petits Sauvages': The Children of Eighteenth-Century New France," in *Childhood and Family in Canadian History*, ed. Joy Parr (Toronto, ON : McClelland and Stewart, 1982), 39. See also Clio Collective, *Quebec Women*, 36–9, 63; and Nadia Fahmy-Eid, "L'éducation des filles chez les Ursulines de Québec sous le Régime français," in *Maîtresses de maison, maîtresses d'école : femmes, famille et éducation dans l'histoire du Québec*, ed. Nadia Fahmy-Eid and Micheline Dumont (Montreal, QC: Boréal Express, 1983), 49–76.

8 Louise Dechêne, *Habitants and Merchants in Seventeenth-Century Montreal* (Montreal, QC: McGill-Queen's University Press, 1992), 271; Allan Greer, *The People of New France* (Toronto, ON: University of Toronto Press, 1997), 46.

9 Clio Collective, *Quebec Women*, 95.

10 Vachon, *Taking Root*, 256; Greer, *The People of New France*, 25–26.

11 Greer, *The People of New France*, 25–26.

12 Clio Collective, *Quebec Women*, 40.

13 Kenneth Donovan, "Tattered Clothes and Powdered Wigs: Case Studies of the Poor and Well-to-Do in Eighteenth-Century Louisbourg," in *Cape Breton at 200: Historical Essays in Honour of the Island's Bicentennial 1785–1985*, ed. Kenneth Donovan (Sydney, NS: University College of Cape Breton Press, 1985), 6–7.

14 Eccles, "Social Welfare Measures and Policies in New France," 41.

15 Roberta Hamilton, *Feudal Society and Colonization: The Historiography of New France* (Gananoque, QC: Langdale Press, 1988).

16 Vachon, *Dreams of Empire*, 334; Eccles, "Social Welfare Measures and Policies in New France," 43; Lachance, *Vivre, aimer et mourir en Nouvelle France*, 146.

17 Vachon, *Taking Root*, 259.

18 Prentice et al. *Canadian Women*, 54; Lachance, *Vivre, aimer et mourir en Nouvelle France*, 31, 39.

19 Eccles, "Social Welfare Measures, and Policies in New France" 45.

20 Dechêne, *Habitants and Merchants in Seventeenth-Century Montreal*, 242, 254.

21 Moogk, "Les Petits Sauvages," 26.

22 Dechêne, *Habitants and Merchants in Seventeenth-Century Montreal*, 256.

23 Donovan, "Tattered Clothes and Powdered Wigs," 6–7.

CHAPTER 3

British North America
and the Poor Law

The British conquest of New France, which began with the cession of Acadia in 1713 and was completed with the conquest of Canada in 1760, was followed by the immigration of English-speaking peoples from the Anglo-American colonies and Britain. While Roman Catholic institutions continued to direct educational and social service programs in the St. Lawrence colony, British models and social values guided social policy in the new colonies of Nova Scotia, New Brunswick, and Upper Canada (today's Ontario) that were established in the eighteenth century.

In 1834, the British Parliament passed the Poor Law Amendment Act, which forced the destitute requiring state assistance to move into spartan state-run workhouses. The intention was to force working people to take whatever jobs employers placed on offer regardless of wages or working conditions. Britain's North American colonies quickly passed parallel legislation, reflecting the power in North America of the budding class of business people who wanted to guarantee themselves a cheap source of labour. Alongside this rather crass public policy towards the poor, charitable agencies had been established, composed mainly of wealthy and middle-class women, who espoused more humane solutions to destitution, though rarely challenging the social construct of the poor as the authors of their own sufferings. The gradual growth of urban centres and a social class dependent upon a precarious employment market soon overwhelmed the volunteer organizations. By 1867, state action of various kinds began to supplement volunteer activities. This chapter traces the development of both voluntarism and state action, exploring why neither prevented the development of dramatic inequalities of wealth and power in pre-Confederation British North America.

THE PIONEER YEARS

For most of the pre-Confederation period, British North America's economy could be characterized as pre-industrial. Over 80 per cent of British North Americans farmed or fished, leaving only a minority to live in towns where they depended on earning wages. For individuals and families in distress the towns provided cash relief. As late as the 1810s in Upper Canada (Ontario), authorities in charge of dispensing municipal aid made little discrimination between able-bodied persons in distress and the disabled. The notion of relief for the former was that it was temporary, and the individuals in question would soon be back on their feet.[1]

In rural areas, such views prevailed throughout the pre-Confederation period, and often resulted in a blurring of state aid and private charity. Petitions to the Quarter Sessions of the Peace before 1850, and various municipal and county councils after 1850, demonstrate "an overwhelming sense of community responsibility towards the dependent aged."[2] The courts of the General Quarter Sessions, responding to public opinion, granted public funds for relief of the poor, and neighbours frequently argued for individuals mistreated by their kin. One example was Elizabeth Bowens whose case was heard by the Northumberland District Quarter Sessions in 1833. Blinded by smallpox in her youth and later abandoned by her husband, she lived with her father till he died. She then handed over all her property to her brother in return for a promise of care. Instead, she was mistreated and locked in an unheated room. When she escaped, her neighbours supported her request for independence, convincing the Sessions that she should receive state aid and that they themselves would supplement that aid with a great deal of community service.

British policy, by contrast, promoted inequality within the colonies. Britain tried to recreate its own highly stratified class structure in a North American environment, though it had to balance this aim with the colonists' demands for American-style democratic institutions. The result was hybrid political structures that included appointed executive councils along with appointed legislative councils that could overrule the resolutions of elected assemblies. Political appointees—individuals who received huge tracts of land, large government contracts, and plum government appointments, and who isolated themselves socially and residentially from other citizens—became the core of the social elites in all colonies. By the 1850s, political pressure in the colonies and rebellions in both Upper and Lower Canada forced the granting of responsible government. Nonetheless, a system of social classes had been implanted, although the elites were now forced to make more subtle alliances with some leaders of the popular forces in order to preserve their considerable economic advantages.

In Britain, a few thousand landlords owned most of the agricultural land of the kingdom, with tenants managing the land and an army of landless labourers making up most of the agricultural population. In the colonies, too, the British authorities hoped to ensure a cheap labour force for both farmers and urban business operators. Colonial Secretary Lord Goderich argued "the necessity that there should be in every society a class of Labourers as well as a class of capitalists or landowners. The high rate of wages and the scarcity of labour, is the complaint of every growing Society. To force that condition artificially, by tempting into the class of Landowners those who would naturally remain labourers, appears to me a course opposed to the dearest interests of the Colony."[3]

Such pro-capitalist sentiments were embodied in huge land grants given to a small number of companies and individuals. But large landowners, unable to find desperate farmworkers in the scarcely populated colonies, found it lucrative to resell the land to immigrants who were able to buy it. Immigrants who could not afford to buy land became dependent upon wage labour and bore the brunt of hardship during periods of economic crisis and, indeed, were susceptible to a seasonal economy that offered few job prospects in winter.

POVERTY IN BRITISH NORTH AMERICA

John McTaggart, former clerk of the Rideau Canal construction works, wrote in 1829 that the Irish in Bytown (Ottawa) "burrow into the sand-hills; smoke is seen to issue out of holes which are opened to answer the purpose of chimneys." He opined "that one-tenth of all the poor Irish emigrants who come to Canada perish during the first two years they are in the country." Diseases and accidents killed them. Lacking blankets and stockings, they were weakened by frostbite. Away from spring or river water, they drank swamp water. And who was to blame for this sorry state of affairs? In McTaggart's opinion, it was the Irish themselves. Many were killed in the works because they were untrained for their jobs. The view that the poor were the authors of their own doom was widespread among the elites, but historians largely dispute that view. The landless were forced to move to towns, where they were again confronted by public policy-making that favoured a small elite. The poor pay received by the Rideau Canal workers prevented the majority from ever escaping wage labour and the British military crushed their efforts to use strikes to improve their wages.[4]

Landlessness became a problem by the 1810s in Lower Canada (now the province of Quebec) as the new British authorities rejected both the extension of the seigneurial system to new areas and the granting of free land to habitants; instead the British insisted on freehold tenure as new lands were opened up. Even within the seigneurial belt, a version of freehold prevailed. The state allowed seigneurs to charge habitants whatever dues they wished, transforming former feudal arrangements with customary dues into capitalist arrangements in which landlords charged whatever rent the market would bear. Forced to pay high rents for their lands, habitants could not save money to buy or rent additional properties for their children. Even such defenders as rebel leader Louis Joseph Papineau of the paternalism of the pre-conquest seigneurial system could not resist the temptation to become heartless landlords. Since the land could only be subdivided so far, many younger sons became dependent on town and city employers to provide them with employment. By 1828, 50 per cent of the landholders in the Montreal district owned fifty arpents or less. In 1844, 38 per cent of householders in the rural Montreal district were landless, an increase of 10 per cent over 1831.[5]

In the cities, the workers faced class discrimination. In Quebec City, the British merchant class that controlled civic administration, as well as the military elite, lived in the Upper Town. Half the area's roads had been paved by 1831, and the area enjoyed adequate drainage. By contrast, in working-class Saint-Roch, the streets were little more than mud paths, most drains were wooden and broke frequently, and the city ignored problems of disease, crime, and fire. Bitterness against the city's rich rulers also had ethnic overtones since most of the workers were francophones while the important naval construction yards, ship-building firms, and timber companies, were overwhelmingly in the hands of anglophones.[6]

Similar conditions were evident in every British North American town, where winter posed special challenges to the working class. In the period before industrial factories provided year-round employment, town economies were largely seasonal. The shipbuilders in Saint John and Quebec City could look forward to year-round industrial work; but construction jobs, public works, dock work, shipboard work, along with farm labour and fishing largely ended with the onset of winter, and illness and death awaited many of the unemployed destitute. Inquests revealed that their deaths were hastened by living in hovels with improper heating, and little in the way of either blankets or winter clothes.

Wages when work was available allowed most families to pay for their most immediate needs, but left little for saving against the inevitable decline in household income that the cold weather would bring. Private charities begged for funds to help those whom winter made destitute, ironically making benefactors of some of the same employers whose policies of low wages and winter job cuts created most of the need for relief in the first place. Winter activities in British North America underlined the social-class divide:

> Winter, then, provided the common bond which united the well-to-do in charitable undertakings, a collective pastime to supplement sleighing, theatricals, assemblies, and parties. Winter afforded colonial employers with the convenient *raison d'être* to lay off operatives, cut wages, and acclimatize the poor to regular hardship. Winter transformed the labouring poor into a seasonally exploited class, dependent on relief and demoralized by the insecurity, distress, and drinking habits of the pre-industrial economy. Winter reduced the helpless poor to unbearable, heart-rending privations. In winter British North America most emphatically was not a "poor man's country" and, furthermore, if the cold climate produced the nineteenth-century myth of ruggedness, independence, and self-reliance, it was a myth in which the urban poor played no part and from which they drew no inspiration.[7]

PRIVATE CHARITIES

"Charitable undertakings," including the collection of money, clothing, and food to aid the poor, were undertaken by both bourgeois men and women. For women, in particular, charity offered an opportunity to participate in public life, since tradition kept "ladies" out of paid employment. Church teachings, class obligations, and personal convictions combined to influence women's social-welfare activism.[8] In the early nineteenth century, throughout the various colonies, women helped to found and administer asylums, orphanages, and refuges for the destitute. Sometimes, as in the case of the Protestant Orphan

Asylum in Montreal, they ran the institutions alone. In other cases, they ran everything but had an advisory committee of men to assist fundraising efforts. Often both men and women served together on the administration committees. In all cases, the women were involved in hiring personnel, raising funds, and making day-to-day decisions. Many of the organizations they established were shelters for children without parents or for destitute women. Examples in the Canadas before Confederation included the Protestant Orphan Asylum in Montreal, in 1822; the Female Orphan Asylum in Quebec City about 1830; the Catholic Orphanage in Montreal, in 1832; the Orphans' Home in Kingston, in 1857; the Protestant Home for Women in Quebec, in 1859; the Home of the Friendless in Hamilton, in 1859; the Girls' Home in Hamilton, in 1862; the Orphans' Home of the City of Ottawa, in 1865; and the Working Boys' Home in Toronto, in 1867. While white middle-class women formed the backbone of the volunteer effort in anglophone British North America, there were important exceptions. Ellen Abbot, a former domestic servant who had married a free black in the U.S. and migrated with him to Upper Canada in 1835, founded Toronto's Queen Victoria Benevolent Society to aid indigent black women in the city.[9]

Much of this women's activism reflected an understanding of the precarious position of women in British North American society. With limited economic opportunities, single and widowed women were usually among the working poor. Most of the work available to them was domestic labour in other women's homes, though some took in boarders while others ran schools from their homes or established millinery, dress, and hat shops.[10]

Some organizations ran several institutions. The Female Benevolent Society, organized in Montreal in 1817, established the Montreal General Hospital four years later, which provided free services from physicians and employed a small paid staff. The Society established the Protestant Orphan Asylum in 1822 and during the 1832 cholera crisis, it established a soup kitchen, a house to receive widows and children, and an employment office for domestics.

There were also some institutions whose purpose was to provide work rather than medical services or handouts. In St. John's, Newfoundland, women founded the St. John's Factory during the winter of 1832–33 to supply indoor winter work making and mending fishing nets. Their objective was "to find employment for the destitute, and to stimulate the poorer classes to independence, by shewing them the means of earning their own livelihood."[11] In 1837, the Factory provided employment year-round. By the 1850s, the Saint Vincent de Paul Society, a Catholic male charity, had moved into the second floor of the Factory and provided jobs in net-making and mending as well as in textile handicrafts. In Halifax, the Poor Man's Friend Society secured firewood for distribution to the poor in the winter of 1824–25 and soup kitchens opened in many other cities.

Most Protestant charitable organizations were groups of inter-denominational lay people. The Catholic Church, by contrast, discouraged independent lay activity. The female religious communities in Quebec continued their health and social work activities after the conquest, though the British government forced the male religious communities to return to France. The British authorities provided the nuns with state subsidies so they could continue their work in Montreal, Quebec, and Trois Rivières. From 1800 to 1823, they received a grant of 17,103 pounds to care for the sick and homeless. The Hôtel-Dieu of Montreal had thirty beds, and the town's Hôpital-Général an additional eighty beds. The latter treated 485 Protestant and 367 Catholic patients in 1823, of whom only forty-one died. The Hôpital was administered by talented nuns such as Thérèse-Geneviève Coutlée, who served as director from 1792 to 1821. She restored its finances by renting out part of its land and developing workshops where nuns made candles and vestments, embroidered cloth, and bound books.[12]

After the rebellions of 1837 and 1838, Britain, anxious to bolster conservative forces in Quebec, allowed the bishops to bring back the male religious communities and to recruit additional members for female religious communities, of which there were twenty-one new ones established between 1840 and 1902. This expansion of religious institutions encouraged new church-based social welfare initiatives. Though the male religious communities were mainly oriented towards teaching, the Saint Vincent de Paul Society, a transplant to British North America of a charitable organization founded in France in 1837, provided relief to destitute males.

The women's orders tended to focus on social services and health. The sisters who later took the name Soeurs de la Miséricorde opened a hospice for single pregnant women in Montreal in 1848. Rosalie Jette, a widow, had been asked to care for single pregnant women in her own home by Bishop Bourget early in his tenure. Later, at his suggestion, she left her own children to rent a house to serve as the home for unwed pregnant women. Eventually, she and seven other women formed the Congrégation des Soeurs de la Miséricorde and opened the Hôpital de la Miséricorde. The Church's condemnation of unwed mothers forced most of them to give their babies to the nuns to raise. Rates of illegitimacy in French Canada from 1770 to 1810 have been estimated at 2 to 3 per cent in urban areas, and at 1.5 to 2 per cent in the countryside. Rates in predominantly Protestant Ontario were similar. Adoptions were still rare, and the nuns continued, as they had in the pre-conquest period, to farm out found-lings. In the 1850s, about 80 per cent of them died.[13]

In 1858, the Soeurs Grises opened the first daycares in British North America, the so-called *salles d'asile* where preschool children could be left dur-ing the day while mothers worked or recovered from illnesses. They were set up in the working-class districts of Montreal and Quebec and in the towns of Longueuil, Saint-Jean, Saint-Jérôme, and Saint-Hyacinthe. Tens of thousands of children were looked after by the Soeurs Grises by the end of the century.[14]

We have only anecdotal evidence, for the most part, of how the recipients of charitable activities in the pre-Confederation period viewed their benefac-tors. Few agencies kept detailed records. The keeping of case histories and case records only began in earnest when urban charities "were confronted with the numbers and anonymities of the late nineteenth-century city, when the particularized knowledge of people and their histories characterizing smaller communities no longer existed."[15] Even from extensive records that have been kept, we get little sense of what the recipients of charity thought. For example, the Sisters of Providence and the Grey Nuns wrote daily reports on the elderly residents of their shelters, but the reports centred on the eternal souls of their clients. While the homes provided decent food and a bed for the elderly, their main objective was to prepare for the spiritual needs of a clientele approaching death and to administer the rites of the dying to them.

The nuns' records do suggest that they attempted to care for all the needs of the elderly in their charge, and demonstrate that the perceptions of old age were changing. Once viewed as a gift from God for leading a good life, old age was now seen as a period of physical frailty. There were more old people than ever before, and the young increasingly believed that the elderly had to be insti-tutionalized at a certain point and cared for much like children. Some scholars believe that such prejudices resulted in most old people being treated as if they were infirm, sometimes unfairly. By the 1860s, the asylums for the elderly oper-ated by the Sisters of Providence and the Grey Nuns were home to over three hundred Montrealers, a large proportion of the city's aged.[16]

The position of women as providers of social services was subtly changing as well by mid-century. They were increasingly removed from positions of man-agement in the social welfare institutions that they had founded. In Montreal, wealthy merchants "turned the women's wooden hospices and rented houses into the great pillared and iron-railed institutions of Victorian Canada," while

Bishop Ignace Bourget gave men the lead in "a new network of Catholic welfare institutions" where "women continued to supply much of the labour."[17]

The community-minded efforts of private individuals and churches to care for the aged, the ill, working mothers, and the unemployed increasingly fell far short of meeting the needs of the casualties of a market economy. In 1852, according to Dr. Wolfred Nelson, 47 per cent of Montreal's prison population was women. The sheriff of Montreal observed that the old, sick, infirm, and mad were often sent to prison on vague charges of disturbing the peace. Dr. Nelson said of the prison: "One could almost call it a maternity hospital, because so many of the women who go there are pregnant and give birth there...One could call it a children's home since very large numbers of very young children are taken in there." The children were the progeny of prisoners, some of whom simply had nowhere else to go.[18] With the limited success of private efforts to deal with problems of poverty and illness, there was increasing pressure on the state to become active in dealing with social problems.

The Poor Law Legacy

State involvement in British North American relief of the poor owed its origins to traditions in the "mother country," much as state involvement in New France copied practices at home. When Henry VIII ended the Catholic Church's status as Britain's state church in the 1530s, he chose to make the state, rather than the new Anglican Church, the main dispenser of aid to the poor. With the feudal system in England in rapid decline, the medieval notion that landlords must ensure the survival of their serfs had disappeared. Tenants were unceremoniously tossed off their tiny plots of land to create huge enclosures for the grazing of sheep, whose wool was much in demand by the expanding textile industry. Cities and towns became gathering places for a swelling crowd of landless and unemployed people, placing enormous pressures on charitable agencies.

State policies for dealing with the destitute evolved into what were called the Poor Laws. Under Elizabeth I, the Poor Law of 1601, for example, decreed that towns and counties must appoint overseers of the poor to provide "indoor relief," relief in specially designed institutional settings. But "outdoor relief"—aid that allowed families to stay in their own homes—could also be provided. Two types of institutions provided indoor relief. The poorhouse served as the shelter for destitute unemployables, including mothers of young children, the sick, and the aged. By contrast, the workhouse would house those deemed employable and was meant to operate without state subsidy. Inmates were to produce goods for sale on the market and to be available as farm and town labour in order to repay their room and board.

Overseers decided who deserved aid, and whether individuals were assigned to the workhouse or the poorhouse. By the late eighteenth century, London alone had at least 100 institutions that housed the poor. From 1795 to 1834, however, under the so-called Speenhamland system, outdoor relief became more common in Britain. But capitalists in both cities and the countryside claimed it converted taxes on the rich into incomes for the poor, tempted the poor not to seek work, and forced employers to pay higher wages to potential workers. Changes in the Poor Law in 1834, therefore, severely restricted outdoor relief. The poor would be housed in workhouses and hired out for casual work until they could find longer-term work and leave the workhouse.[19]

The "mixed workhouse," which placed the families of luckless employables in the same building as the elderly infirm, the insane, and alcoholics was instantly unpopular in the cities. Charles Dickens's trenchant criticisms of institutions that placed children in unsavoury settings were widely shared. However, the fundamental principles of the Poor Law Amendment Act of 1834—local rather than national responsibility for poor relief, with no outdoor relief—were responsible for the deaths of millions in Ireland in the 1840s. When the Irish potato crop failed three years out of four between 1845 and 1848, the Whig government of the United Kingdom chose to do nothing, clinging to the principles of the New Poor Law. As many as a million Irish died during the famines, and several million more fled the country to resettle in English slums or to emigrate abroad. Whig legislator Thomas Babington Macaulay argued: "Our rulers will best promote the improvement of the nation by strictly confining themselves to their own legitimate duties, by leaving capital to find its own most lucrative course, commodities their fair price, industry and intelligence their natural reward, idleness and folly their natural punishment, by maintaining peace, by defending property, and by observing strict economy in every department of the state. Let the government do this: the people will assuredly do the rest."[20]

The New Poor Law had an almost instant effect on social policy in British North America. Beginning in the late 1830s, so-called Houses of Industry opened in major towns, and in common parlance were referred to as poorhouses and workhouses. Municipalities were largely responsible for funding these workhouses and attempted to minimize costs by requiring inmates to maintain the home and to do work that the Houses of Industry contracted from private employers. The elderly, who formed the largest element within the poorhouses, often became cheap labour for employers along with young children living with a parent or parents in the workhouse. The children were often separated from their parents and apprenticed to respectable people in the country, the boys as farm labourers, the girls as housemaids. Operators of the poorhouses regarded child labour as a boon to a family since it might provide them the income needed to live outside the poorhouse. The poorhouse became an enduring institution, particularly in Nova Scotia and New Brunswick, where poorhouses remained the major, indeed almost the only, form of state relief until the 1950s.

A female House of Industry opened in Saint John in 1835 and concentrated on training domestic servants. In the winter of 1836–37, Houses of Industry opened in Montreal and Quebec, with Toronto opening a winter-only home the following year aided by a grant from the colonial government. One in twelve residents of Toronto lived in the House of Industry at some point during its first half-year of operation. They lived a grim existence, with their diet consisting only of milk and bread. In Kingston, where the House of Industry opened its doors in December 1837, 183 people sought shelter the very first month of its operation. Of these, 175 were Irish immigrants. In the total group, 47 were widows and 63 were children under ten. Landless immigrants, unsurprisingly, loomed large in the population of the workhouses. Women looked to escape the House of Industry by seeking work as dressmakers' assistants, charwomen, or washerwomen. Their children broke stones for roads, worked as servants or agricultural labourers, ran errands, or worked with their mothers as pedlars, washers, or beggars.[21]

The House of Industry Act was passed by the Assembly in Upper Canada in 1837. It authorized construction under public auspices of institutions to accommodate "all poor and indigent persons who are incapable of supporting themselves; all persons, able of body to work and without any means of maintaining themselves, who refuse or neglect to do so; all persons living a lewd, dissolute vagrant life or exercising no ordinary calling or lawful business sufficient to procure an honest living." The placing of the "dissolute" within the same subgroup as the merely unemployed speaks volumes to the mindset of the elites who framed social policy. Upper Canada's governor, Sir Francis Bond Head, commented that "workhouses should be made repulsive" so that anyone capable of eking out a living any other way would avoid them.[22]

In the pre-Confederation period, no rural councils established a House of Industry. For some historians, this is evidence of rural taxpayers refusing to allow their property taxes to pay the costs of public relief of the poor. Others suggest that a strong sense of the need to help their neighbours led them instead to continue to support both voluntary and municipal help to individuals and families who had been luckless and needed help to remain in their own homes.[23] Interestingly, in Lower Canada, the reform-minded *patriotes* opposed outdoor relief. They preferred that public funds be spent on Houses of Industry for the moral uplift of the poor, and on jails.[24]

Apart from establishing workhouses and granting occasional direct relief to individuals deemed "deserving," governments also used public works as a means of creating work to aid the unemployed. "Less eligibility," the principle that state-aided workers should earn less than privately employed workers, was generally applied to such projects so as to avoid any upward pressures on wages in the private sector. So, for example, in 1832, Halifax had poor people break stones for road improvement projects but paid them only token wages. Common jobs for which the poor man might earn some money from the state included stone breaking, canal building, snow removal, digging wells, and laying water pipes. Women and girls were given knitting and spinning work. Quebec used shipbuilding for winter relief.[25]

In Upper and Lower Canada, the state also provided subsidies to private charities. In Upper Canada, as early as 1828, the government gave grants to the Emigrant Temporary Asylum as well as subsidies to road contractors who hired the needy. By Confederation, direct spending by the United Province of Canada also included spending on primary schools, prisons, old-age homes, and insane asylums. The governments in the Atlantic colonies were less willing to develop separate institutions for various groups of poor people, and forced most of the destitute into workhouses. Gradually in the Canadas, state aid to charities allowed the insane and the aged to leave the workhouses for other institutions, turning workhouses increasingly into homes for destitute single men. Charities and poorhouses tried to keep families in their homes. So, for example, the Annual Report of Toronto's House of Industry in 1857 claimed to have helped three thousand individuals. Most had lived in the House at some point during the year, but the House had also distributed 200 cords of wood and 3,176 loaves of bread to the homes of indigent families. [26]

The increasing use of institutions to warehouse the poor marked a distinct contrast with the early nineteenth-century practices in British North America of providing cash relief for those in distress. Writes Rainer Bahre: "The Emigrant Asylum and the House of Industry were a notable departure in poor relief practices. They were formal institutions, nineteenth century-asylums like the penitentiary and the lunatic asylum, establishing rules and regulations governing internal discipline, demanding labour, and watched over by an appointed board or committee." Nor did residence in a workhouse guarantee protection from the winter cold. Efforts to cut expenditure by limiting the provision of warm clothing and the amount of wood cut to heat the institution resulted in deaths. In the "Camps," the poorhouses of St. John's, there were frequent reports of deaths from freezing, and many inmates in the Kingston House of Industry froze from lack of proper clothing in 1855.[27]

HEALTH CARE

State involvement in the area of health care had also begun by the time of Confederation. Insufficient private funds to provide health care for the destitute and to deal with epidemics such as cholera pushed governments to take an active but limited role in aspects of health care.

In the early post-conquest period, the women's Catholic religious orders continued to operate their hospitals with the help of state subsidies. Steady immigration of Protestants from the United States and Great Britain, however, spurred the new Protestant elite to raise funds to open hospitals for their co-religionists. In Lower Canada, once Protestant hospitals such as the Montreal General Hospital (MGH) began operation, they too received some state aid but were, like the francophone hospitals, largely dependent on other sources for their funds. The MGH's management committee reported that in the quarter ending 1 November 1824, 336 indigent sick received services at the hospital, a 10 per cent increase over the corresponding period the previous year. Only twelve of these patients paid for their treatment; over half were outpatients; and 159 were hospitalized at some point during the quarter. The management committee, hoping to reduce costs, advertised in the newspapers that paupers from outside the parish of Montreal would not be served by the MGH unless their parishes had contributed financially to the operations of the hospital.[28]

While the MGH leadership was ecumenical, the initial management of the York Hospital, predecessor of the Toronto General Hospital, which opened its doors in 1829, was exclusively Anglican. As a consequence of its ties to the Anglican Church, the state, and the Upper Canadian elite in the period before the Rebellion of 1837, the York Hospital received free land from the government of Upper Canada.[29]

Serving mainly the indigent population, hospitals often owed their popularity among the well-to-do to their usefulness as places to isolate the infectious from the general population. Even relatively modest-sized towns such as Owen

Sound could raise money from a local elite for a hospital so that they could isolate individuals suffering from typhoid and smallpox until they either recovered or died.[30] In the period before antiseptic practices became common, the wealthy viewed hospitals as places where diseases and death were rampant. Few with the means to avoid the risks of a hospital stay chose this route over hiring a physician to minister to their health. As late as the 1850s, British North Americans were as likely to choose a homeopathic physician or use a home cure or Native remedy as to visit an allopathic physician.

In 1850, none of the Maritime colonies had a medical school or a legal system of professional self-regulation. By contrast, an anglophone medical school had opened in Lower Canada in 1823, followed by a francophone school in 1845. John Rolph, a Reformer forced into exile during the Upper Canadian rebellion, provided today's Ontario with its first medical school in 1843 in Toronto. With their claims to have science on their side for their chemical and surgical responses to illnesses, the allopathic physicians organized to lobby governments to give biomedical practitioners the exclusive right to call themselves doctors. The Halifax Medical Society, formed in 1853, also set as its objectives enhancing professional standards, promoting a positive image of the allopathic profession, and lobbying the legislature for state payments of charity cases. The following year, spearheaded by the Halifax medical elite, Nova Scotia doctors formed a provincial medical society. Prince Edward Island physicians formed a parallel society in 1855, and New Brunswick followed in 1861. Doctors' efforts, aided by charitable groups, resulted in the establishment of the Nova Scotia Hospital for the Insane in 1859 and the City and Provincial Hospital in 1867, both in Halifax, as well as a hospital in Saint John in 1860.[31]

The physicians had gained much credibility because of their role in dealing with epidemics, particularly the dreaded cholera. The need for a co-ordinated strategy to deal with cholera outbreaks also increased state involvement in setting health policy. Cholera had made its way from India throughout British Empire in the early 1830s, and several deadly epidemics struck British North America before Confederation. Immigrants, arriving on ships from Britain, often carried the deadly disease into the colony. In 1832, the first cholera outbreak resulted in 5,820 deaths in Lower Canada and 504 in Upper Canada, according to the government's Board of Health reports. In anticipation of the spread of a cholera epidemic from Britain, the Lower Canadian government had established two quarantine hospitals, one at Pointe Levy, across the river from Quebec in 1830, the second at Grosse Île, down the river from Quebec, the following year. The arrival of the disease in 1832 led to an expansion of the facilities at Grosse Île and its designation as a permanent site for inspecting immigrants and detaining the already ill and infectious.

Dr. E.B. O'Callaghan, later one of the leaders of the armed insurrection in 1837, played an important role during the cholera outbreak of 1832. He took charge of a cholera "hospital" in Quebec, which consisted simply of hastily rented buildings. Both in Quebec and Montreal, the facilities used to quarantine the victims of cholera were cold warehouses where bodies were piled one on top of the other. The physicians and the civic authorities joined in urging citizens who had been spared cholera to keep clean and to avoid contact with people who had contracted the disease.

Once the 1832 outbreak was over, the inspection of immigrants and the quarantine hospital at Grosse Île remained as a legacy. However, Lower Canada imposed a head tax on immigrants that year as a way to maintain the quarantine hospitals. In 1842, New Brunswick introduced a similar head tax for the support of indigents among the immigrants. When one hundred thousand Irish immigrants entered British North America in 1847, the United Province of Canada and New Brunswick increased their head taxes, and Nova Scotia introduced one.[32]

New outbreaks of diseases forced the colonial governments to implement further public health measures. A typhus epidemic in 1847 killed thousands of immigrants and resulted in the British imposing controls on the accommodations and food served to passengers on ships. These were, however, often poorly enforced. That year, another outbreak of cholera proved particularly devastating in Kingston, where it killed twelve hundred of the town's ten thousand residents.[33] In 1854, another major cholera outbreak left a wave of deaths in British North America. In 1866, though the cholera outbreak proved relatively benign, the government of the United Province of Canada required municipal governments to establish local boards of health. It then held a conference on cholera for medical doctors, and named doctors to the Central Board of Health, where they determined the detailed regulations for local boards to follow. As sociologist Bruce Curtis observes, "The scare's durable relevance to the formation of the Canadian state lies in the practical attempts it spawned to extend projects for the organization of surveillance, the centralization of knowledge, the consolidation of expertise, and the government of conduct."[34]

The extent of the problem of infectious diseases in British North America is evident in the mortality figures for immigrants. From a quarter to a third of immigrants to British North America and then Canada before 1891 died of infectious diseases, many en route to their prospective new home. One-seventh of all travellers died before reaching British North American shores. This rate of infectious diseases, along with high child-mortality rates, contributed to a death rate in British North America of thirty seven per one thousand persons in 1870, compared to six or seven per thousand in the last years of the twentieth century.[35]

We have already observed the primary role that women played in administering hospitals for the poor. This extended beyond medical care for the physically ill to care for those deemed to be mentally ill. The Grey Nuns began to house supposedly insane patients in Montreal in the 1820s. They kept them in six-by-eight-foot cells, but fed them well, and claimed that about half the patients were cured at the time of their release. However, they could only care for about eight mentally disturbed people at a time, leaving the city jail to handle an equal number. In 1845, the government of the United Province of Canada decided to establish an asylum at Beauport where inmates could be classified, treated, and receive exercise. Their model was an asylum in Glasgow.

As in the case of infectious diseases, state officials increasingly believed that governments could play an important role in co-ordinating treatment of the insane, by collecting statistics, categorizing individuals, and determining success rates for various treatments. But "no all-encompassing 'psychiatric state' was established." Instead, medical experts, the state, and families, all somewhat in conflict, produced a system of "lunatic asylums" in which reformers and asylum promoters played key roles but over which they could not exercise full control either over budgets or admissions.[36]

Beauport, though receiving state funds and holding a monopoly for many years in Lower Canada over mental-health treatment, was privately operated by physicians. They claimed that "moral therapy" could cure the mentally disturbed and allow them to be reintegrated into their families and communities. Moral therapy linked work, religion, and recreation, and the administrators of Beauport created a rigid routine for inmates to ensure that they received all three elements in just the right doses. Overcrowding in the facility, however—there were 428 patients in 1861, for example—often meant that Beauport seemed simply to be warehousing patients. Toronto's lunatic asylum, which was state operated, also failed to live up to the modern medical principles that it espoused. Underfunded, it suffered from constant overcrowding despite an expansion of its facilities between 1856 and 1861.

Admission to "lunatic asylums" sometimes pitted families against medical "experts." Families often wished to commit a family member whose behaviours seemed to be getting in the way of their making a living. But asylum managers had their own notions of who needed help. To the chagrin of many desperate families, the asylum physicians rejected so-called incurables, and used this designation with great frequency to limit admissions. Lunatic asylums were part of the bureaucratic network over which the Inspectorate of Prisons, Asylums, and Public Charities took charge for Upper Canada in 1859. By contrast, there was no such network in the pioneering colony of British Columbia in the years before it entered Confederation. The colonial government preferred to spend whatever monies it received from Britain or through taxes on infrastructure, particularly roads. Until asylums were built in the late 1870s the "insane" were thrown into jails or forced to leave British Columbia altogether.[37]

While women had played the major role in establishing hospitals first in New France and then in British North America, the fledgling medical establishment strictly forbade women to train as doctors. Emily Howard Stowe faced a wall of rejection from medical schools when she attempted to enrol in the 1860s. Instead, she earned her medical degree from the New York Medical College in 1867 and then had to operate without a license for thirteen years before the College of Physicians and Surgeons of Ontario agreed to accredit her and she could practise in the province. [38]

CHILDREN

The growing trend towards institutionalization that was evident in the social and medical services was even more evident in the area of education. In 1800, parents decided whether to send their children to privately run schools, educate them at home, or not educate them at all. Although a program of compulsory schooling was not implemented in any of the colonies before Confederation, from the 1820s onwards there was a growing movement towards state-supported education for children. By 1867, it was increasingly common for Protestant children to attend "public schools" and for Catholic children to attend schools operated by the clergy. Both sets of schools were then receiving public funding from the colonial governments in the United Province of Canada and in Nova Scotia and there is some dispute among educational historians about the governments' goals in extending public money to the schools. Some historians believe that the economic elites who came to dominate public life were mainly interested in the social control of the population. They wanted to train workers and farmers to be docile in the presence of their social betters, and to have enough knowledge of reading, writing, and mathematics to be efficient employees. Others argue that the goals of the educational reformers such as Egerton Ryerson, whose career as the superintendent of education for Upper Canada and then Ontario stretched from the 1840s to 1880s, was to mould a citizenry with common understandings of the social order. Even in the latter historiography, however, the suggestion is that the education system was preparing students to accept the society that they were part of, with all its social inequalities, rather than to become social critics. Education was also seen by some as a means for the more ambitious, at least among males, to escape humble origins and establish themselves as members of the emerging middle class in an increasingly industrial society.

Staffing a growing public school system posed problems of cost. The local boards of education that emerged to collect property taxes for the operation of the schools and to disburse funds were usually short of cash. Charging parents high fees for the education of their children would defeat efforts to make the schools accessible to all social classes. The solution that most boards accepted was to hire young women as the teaching force and pay them miserable salaries on the grounds that they would supposedly soon marry and leave teaching to be supported financially by their husbands. By contrast, men were employed at relatively decent wages for the positions of superintendents, inspectors, principals, and headmasters. As in the health field, there was a gender hierarchy for the workforce that left women in a subordinate position to men.[39]

While education might be a means for a minority of individuals to escape their class origins, this was not the case for the poor. Children who were placed in the Protestant Orphans' Homes—many of whom were not orphans but simply sons and daughters of widowed, deserted, or single mothers who had to seek paid work—would always remain on the bottom rungs of society. While some children lived in the orphanages, many were boarded out. "Uniformly, the work that they were trained into and encouraged to do was to serve their betters on farm or in household. Boys invariably became agricultural labourers and girls domestic servants."[40] The children who remained tended livestock and gardens and did household chores.

Native Peoples

Though the fur trade resulted in disruption of Native peoples' lives, it did not result in their impoverishment unless local resources were denuded. The Hudson's Bay Company recognized that its fur-trading operations depended upon good relations with the Native hunters and intermediaries who were crucial to the fur trade. Though treatment of Natives by Company personnel was inconsistent, Company policy mandated that the Natives be treated with respect and be guaranteed a degree of economic security. The fear was that otherwise they might abandon the trade and return to traditional subsistence activities, leaving the Company without a realistic opportunity to trap and prepare furs cheaply.[41]

But as the fur trade was superseded by colonization in various areas, the mutual economic interests that had forced the Company to respect Native needs disappeared. As European settlers poured into British North America, the authorities coerced Native populations off their land and onto "reserves," leaving the unpopulated land to the disposal of the immigrants. Native communities attempted to survive as best they could, following traditional subsistence practices where possible and supplementing them by selling various products to Europeans or working as cheap labour for the new settlers. But disease and poverty stalked them everywhere, and the Native population declined throughout the nineteenth century. Though Indian Affairs offices existed in the colonies, they were poorly staffed and seemed more concerned with keeping Native peoples out of the way of the advancing settlements than with their welfare. This lack of concern for their welfare was evident, for example, in Nova Scotia's passage of a law in 1842 to provide for "Instruction and Permanent Settlement" of Natives. Supervision of land distribution was placed under the authority of an Indian Commissioner, for whom no pay was provided. The colony set aside 20,500 acres (8,114 hectares) for the province's Natives, but reserved none of it for specific bands and most of the land was of poor agricultural quality.[42]

On the whole, Native peoples were shut out of the expanding institutional structure that assured at least some help for European-origin indigents, whether they were the elderly, single mothers, abandoned children, the ill, or the unemployed. They were also excluded from the public-school systems that were developing at mid-century, as were the small black and Chinese populations of the colonies. Race played an important role in determining who received services from both private and state sources.

By 1867 the conditions for the transformation from pre-industrial to industrial society were evident in British North America. Extensive immigration, the growth of towns, and the commercial success of first the lumber and then grain industries provided the capital and the labour for a variety of commercial and, eventually, industrial initiatives. State policies and the workings of the marketplace ensured that an ever-increasing group of British North Americans, at any given time, were destitute. The Roman Catholic Church's religious communities, particularly the female ones, continued to aid as many of the destitute as they could, and their efforts were extended by a variety of equally female-dominated Protestant charitable groupings. Eventually, however, the casualties of unplanned town economies overwhelmed the charitable sectors and the state began tentative efforts to deal with destitution amid prosperity. Such efforts initially were largely punitive, as is evidenced by the focus on Houses of Industry that removed the poor from their communities and homes and made them, to an extent, social lepers. The political elites, who were nearly coterminous with the economic elites, believed that state aid must respect the principle of "less eligibility." If citizenship alone allowed families or individuals to claim a decent living from society, then how would employers assure themselves of a supply of relatively cheap and compliant workers?

Economic concerns, more than compassionate concerns, guided state policies with regards to the poor. Distinctions were made between the "deserving poor," that is, individuals whom social custom argued could not be expected to be in the labour force, and the "undeserving poor," that is, the able-bodied unemployed. The latter were treated in the Canadas as slackers and denied outdoor relief, while, in Nova Scotia and New Brunswick, practically all impoverished people, whether regarded as unfortunates or idlers, ended up in the workhouse. The state proved most progressive in extending benefits to all citizens when the rich had a stake along with the poor. So, for example, in the case of infectious diseases, policy-makers recognized that diseases had no respect for class distinctions.

Perhaps a telling sign about the relative importance that governments placed upon social programs at the time of Confederation is that the British North America Act, the constitution cobbled together by the founding colonies, gave control over all of them to the provincial governments. Quebec was particularly insistent that federalism must mean that matters involving civil rights and property, which included both education and social welfare, must be under provincial jurisdiction. Quebec supporters of Confederation wanted to protect the francophone and Catholic heritage of the province, and a strong provincial government was key to this objective. But Quebec politicians did not want the province to make direct use of its powers in the social welfare area; instead, they wanted to preserve clerical control. Even resolute proponents of a strong central government such as John A. Macdonald saw no problem with placing education, hospitals, and charities under the jurisdiction of the provinces. Trade, defence, and railways were all seen as far more important goals for the national government than health, social services, and education. Tellingly, the

average expenditure of the British North American colonies on charities, welfare, and education combined in 1866 was only 9 per cent of their fairly modest
budgets.[43] Looking after society's unfortunates was simply not the priority of
governments in British North America.

NOTES

1 Rainer Bahre, "Paupers and Poor Relief in Upper Canada," *Historical Papers* 60 (1981): 57.

2 Edgar-André Montigny, *Foisted Upon the Government? State Responsibilities, Family
   Obligations, and the Care of the Dependent Aged in Late-Nineteenth-Century Ontario* (Montreal,
   QC: McGill-Queen's University Press, 1997), 65.

3 Leo Johnson, "Land Policy, Population Growth and Social Structure in the Home District,
   1793–1851," *Ontario History* 63,1 (March 1971): 57–58.

4 Virginia R. Robeson, ed., *Upper Canada in the 1830s* (Toronto, ON: Ontario Institute for
   Studies in Education, 1977), 14; William T.N. Wylie, "Labour and the Construction of the
   Rideau Canal, 1826–32," *Labour/Le Travailleur* 11 (1983): 29; H. Clare Pentland, *Labour and
   Capital in Canada, 1650–1860* (Toronto, ON: James Lorimer, 1981), 52.

5 Claude Baribeau, *La Seigneurie de la Petite-Nation 1811–1854 : le rôle économique et social
   du seigneur* (Hull, QC: Éditions Asticou, 1983); Fernand Ouellet, *Lower Canada, 1791–1840:
   Social Change and Nationalism* (Toronto, ON: McClelland and Stewart, 1980), 330.

6 David-Thiery Ruddel and Marc La France, "Québec: 1785–1840 : problèmes de croissance
   d'une ville coloniale," *Histoire Sociale/Social History* 18, 36 (1985): 315–33.

7 Judith Fingard, "The Winter's Tale: The Seasonal Contours of Pre-Industrial Poverty in British
   North America," *Historical Papers* 53 (1974): 86.

8 Elizabeth Jane Errington, *Wives, Mothers, School Mistresses and Scullery Maids: Working
   Women in Upper Canada* (Montreal, QC: McGill-Queen's University Press, 1995), 180–81.

9 Wendy Mitchinson, "Early Women's Organizations and Social Reform: Prelude to the Welfare
   State, " in *The Benevolent State: The Growth of Welfare in Canada*, ed. Alan Moscovitch and
   Jim Albert (Toronto, ON: Garamond, 1987), 77, 90; Alison Prentice et al., *Canadian Women:
   A History* (Toronto, ON: Harcourt Brace Jovanovich, 1988), 104; Judith Fingard, "The Relief of
   the Unemployed: The Poor in Saint John, Halifax and St. John's, 1815–1860," in *The Canadian
   City: Essays in Urban and Social History*, ed. Alan J. Artibise and Gilbert Stelter (Montreal,
   QC: McGill-Queen's University Press, 1984), 341–67. Among recent works on the "separate
   spheres" of women and men in nineteenth-century British North America and the place of
   charitable activities within this nexus, see Cecilia Morgan, *Public Men and Virtuous Women:
   The Gendered Language of Religion and Politics in Upper Canada, 1791–1850* (Toronto, ON:
   University of Toronto Press, 1996), and Janet Guildford and Suzanne Morton eds., *Separate
   Spheres: Women's Worlds in the Nineteenth-Century Maritimes* (Fredericton, NB: Acadiensis
   Press, 1994).

10 Errington, *Wives, Mothers*, 19, 190–212.

11 Fingard, "The Winter's Tale," 83.

12 Jan Noel, "'Femmes Fortes' and the Montreal Poor in the Early Nineteenth Century," in
   Canadian Women: A Reader, ed. Wendy Mitchinson et al. (Toronto, ON: Harcourt Brace,
   1996), 72–73.

13 Andrée Lévesque, "Deviants Anonymous: Single Mothers at the Hôpital de la Miséricorde
   in Montreal 1929–1939," *Historical Papers* 63 (1984):168–84; W. Peter Ward, "Unwed
   Motherhood in Nineteenth-Century English Canada," *Historical Papers* 60 (1981): 34–56.

14 Clio Collective, *Quebec Women: A History* (Toronto, ON: Women's Press, 1987), 141.

15 Dorothy E. Smith, "Cases and Case Histories," in *The Conceptual Practice of Power: A Feminist Sociology of Knowledge,* Dorothy Smith, ed. (Toronto, ON: University of Toronto Press, 1990), 89.

16 Bettina Bradbury, "Elderly Inmates and Caregiving Sisters: Catholic Institutions for the Elderly in Nineteenth-Century Canada," in *On the Case: Explorations in Social History,* ed. Franca Iacovetta and Wendy Mitchinson (Toronto, ON: University of Toronto Press, 1998), 129–55.

17 Noel, "Femmes Fortes," 82.

18 Clio Collective, *Quebec Women,* 172.

19 Anthony Brundage, *English Poor Laws 1700–1930* (Houndmills, Basingstoke, Hampshire, UK: Palgrave Macmillan, 2002); Eric Midwinter, *The Development of Social Welfare in Britain* (Buckingham, UK: Open University Press, 1994), 33–34, 52; Derek Fraser, "Introduction," in *The New Poor Law in the Nineteenth Century,* ed. Derek Fraser (New York: St. Martin's Press, 1976), 1–24; Raymond G. Cowherd, *Political Economists and the English Poor Laws: A Historical Study of the Influence of Classical Economics on the Formation of Social Welfare Policy* (Athens, OH: Ohio University Press, 1977), 245–46.

20 Martin O'Brien and Sue Penna, *Theorising Welfare: Enlightenment and Modern Society* (London, UK: Sage, 1998), 24; the quotation is from Anthony Arblaster, *The Rise and Decline of Western Liberalism* (Oxford, UK: Basil Blackwell, 1984), 252.

21 Fingard, "The Winter's Tale," 82–83; Bahre, "Paupers and Poor Relief"; Patricia Malcolmson, "The Poor in Kingston, 1815–1850," in *To Preserve and Defend: Essays on Kingston in the Nineteenth Century,* ed. Gerald Tulchinsky (Montreal, QC: McGill-Queen's University Press, 1976), 281–97; Patricia T. Rooke and R.L. Schnell, *Discarding the Asylum: From Child Rescue to the Welfare State in English Canada (1800–1950)* (Landham, MD: University Press of America, 1983).

22 Stormie Stewart, "The Elderly Poor in Rural Ontario: Inmates of the Wellington County House of Industry, 1877–1907," *Journal of the Canadian Historical Association,* New Series, 3 (1992): 220; J.K. Johnson, "'Claims of Equity and Justice': Petitions and Politicians in Upper Canada 1815–1840," *Histoire sociale/Social History* 28, 55 (1995): 239; Allan Irving, "'The Master Principle of Administering Relief': Jeremy Bentham, Sir Francis Bond Head and the Principle of Less Eligibility in Upper Canada," *Canadian Review of Social Policy* 23 (1989): 17.

23 Stewart, "The Elderly Poor in Rural Ontario," 221; Montigny, *Foisted Upon the Government?*

24 Allan Greer, *The Patriots and the People: The Rebellion of 1837 in Rural Lower Canada* (Toronto, ON: University of Toronto Press, 1993), 131.

25 Fingard, "The Winter's Tale," 81.

26 Mariana Valverde, "The Mixed Social Economy as a Canadian Tradition," *Studies in Political Economy* 47 (Summer 1995): 42; Michael S. Cross, ed., *The Workingman in the Nineteenth Century* (Toronto, ON: Oxford University Press, 1974), 201.

27 Bahre, "Paupers and Poor Relief," 67; Fingard, "The Winter's Tale," 71.

28 Cross, *The Workingman in the Nineteenth Century,* 187.

29 J.T.H. Connor, *Doing Good: The Life of Toronto's General Hospital* (Toronto, ON: University of Toronto Press, 2000), 27–31.

30 David Gagan, *"A Necessity Among Us": The Owen Sound General and Marine Hospital, 1891–1915* (Toronto, ON: University of Toronto Press, 1990).

31 Paul Rutherford, ed., *Saving the Canadian City: The First Phase, 1880–1920* (Toronto, ON: University of Toronto Press, 1974); Geoffrey Bilson, *A Darkened House: Cholera in Nineteenth-Century Canada* (Toronto, ON: University of Toronto Press, 1980), 147; Colin D. Howell, "Medical Science and Social Criticism: Alexander Peter Reid and the Ideological Origins of

the Welfare State in Canada," in *Canadian Health Care and the State*, ed. C. David Naylor (Montreal, QC: McGill-Queen's University Press, 1992), 20.

32 Bilson, *A Darkened House*, 27; Ninette Kelley and Michael Trebilcock, *The Making of the Mosaic: A History of Canadian Immigration Policy* (Toronto, ON: University of Toronto Press, 1998), 49–50.

33 Malcolmson, "The Poor in Kingston, 1815–1860."

34 Bruce Curtis, "Social Investment in Medical Forms: The 1866 Cholera Scare and Beyond," *Canadian Historical Review* 81, 3 (2000): 357. See also Bruce Curtis, *State Formation, Statistics, and the Census of Canada, 1840–1875* (Toronto, ON: University of Toronto Press, 2001).

35 Herbert C. Northcott and Donna M. Wilson, *Death and Dying in Canada* (Toronto, ON: Garamond, 2001), 21, 26.

36 Noel, "Femmes Fortes," 75; James E. Moran, *Committed to the State Asylum: Insanity and Society in Nineteenth-Century Quebec and Ontario* (Montreal, QC: McGill-Queen's University Press, 2000), 172.

37 Gerry Ferguson, "Control of the Insane in British Columbia, 1849–78: Care, Cure, or Confinement," in *Regulating Lives: Historical Essays on the State, Society, The Individual and the Law*, ed. John McLaren, Robert Menzies, and Dorothy E. Chunn (Vancouver, BC: University of British Columbia Press, 2002), 63–96.

38 Prentice et al., *Canadian Women*, 160.

39 Susan Houston and Alison Prentice, *Schooling and Scholars in Nineteenth-Century Ontario* (Toronto, ON: University of Toronto Press, 1988); Bruce Curtis, *Building the Educational State: Canada West, 1836–1871* (London, ON: Althouse Press, 1988); R.D. Gidney and W.P.J. Millar, "From Voluntarism to State Schooling: The Creation of the Public School System in Ontario," *Ontario History* 66, 4 (1985): 443–73; Alison Prentice, "The Feminization of Teaching," in *The Neglected Majority: Essays in Canadian Women's History*, ed. Susan Mann Trofimenkoff and Alison Prentice (Toronto, ON: McClelland and Stewart, 1977), 49–65.

40 Rooke and Schnell, *Discarding the Asylum*, 165.

41 Arthur Ray and Donald Freeman, *Give Us Good Measure: An Economic Analysis of Relations Between the Indians and the Hudson's Bay Company before 1763* (Toronto, ON: University of Toronto Press, 1978), 8; Arthur J. Ray, Jim Miller, and Frank Tough, *Bounty and Benevolence: A History of Saskatchewan Treaties* (Montreal, QC: McGill-Queen's University Press, 2000), chap. 1 and 2.

42 Olive Patricia Dickason, *Canada's First Nations: A History of Founding Peoples from Earliest Times*, 2nd ed. (Toronto, ON: Oxford University Press, 1997), 203–204.

43 Elisabeth Wallace, "The Origin of the Social Welfare State in Canada, 1867–1900," *Canadian Journal of Economics and Political Science* 16, 3 (1950): 385.

Beyond the Poor Law:
Canada, 1867–1950

Part 2 traces the social and legislative changes that gradually discredited the Poor Law approach to helping the destitute. The focus is on popular pressures for greater state responsibility for social services and the distribution of wealth, on the one hand, and the elites' efforts to maintain both a class society and patriarchy, on the other. Chapter 5 discusses the effects of rapid industrialization before the First World War on popular and state attitudes to the question of individual versus collective responsibility for public health, and the welfare of children and families; the rise of the social gospel and the social work profession; and the introduction of workers' compensation. Chapter 6 studies the First World War and the interwar period and assesses the impact of both the war and the Depression on struggles for greater social justice. Chapter 7 focuses on the Second World War and its aftermath, a period when the Poor Law approach became discredited and universal programs such as unemployment insurance and family allowances were legislated. It also demonstrates how the power of the elites restricted "welfare state" developments that responded to popular pressures for greater equality.

CHAPTER 4

Early Canada: Continuity
and Change, 1867–1914

This chapter examines the evolution of both state and charitable institutions in Canada from Confederation to the First World War. It was a period in which much of Canada witnessed a transformation from pre-industrial, largely rural societies to industrial, urban agglomerations. This was an uneven transformation. The chapter explores the growing divergences among provinces (and between Canadian provinces and Newfoundland, which did not join Canada until 1949) and the impact on the design and delivery of social welfare programs. The origin of workers' compensation is discussed in the light of the relative importance of employer and worker pressures for such a program, as is the social provision for Native peoples in a period when both industrial and agricultural expansion encroached upon Native territories. During this period social work gradually emerged as a distinct profession, and it is important to look at why social welfare, once the province of unpaid volunteers, increasingly relied on trained "experts." Finally, the evolution of notions of social right in Canada is compared with other industrial nations during this period. Throughout, the extent to which state intervention adequately met the needs of Canadians in an emerging industrial society is questioned, and I argue that despite the rhetoric of reform, the owners of private businesses emerged as the chief beneficiaries of social policies that aimed at reforming individuals, largely leaving existing political and economic structures intact.

Prosperity and Poverty in Pre-War Canada

Economic growth before the First World War was spectacular. The expansion of manufacturing industries, supported by protective tariffs, and an orgy of publicly subsidized railway building were the major success stories. Resource industries, including agriculture, forestry, and mining, also had large increases in output, thanks especially to the development of the four western provinces. Immigration contributed to more than a doubling of the population. But economic growth occurred unevenly throughout this period, and its benefits were unequally distributed. An international depression in the 1870s stalled the economic development that the proponents of Confederation had expected. When manufacturing took off in the 1880s, it was mainly concentrated in the Toronto–Montreal corridor, while the Maritime economies floundered. Within Quebec, the new prosperity seemed largely confined to Montreal and new resource towns. Out-migration from the Atlantic region and Quebec was extensive. Even in areas where manufacturing advanced, early manufacturers were mainly quite small, and bankruptcies were frequent. When the "second industrial revolution" of the early twentieth century produced mergers and the modern corporation, job losses often accompanied both consolidation and technological changes.

Market forces and state policies worked hand in hand to maintain class disparities in all regions. The benefits of the tariff flowed directly to factory owners. Neither federal nor provincial governments passed legislation to protect workers' rights to either organize or strike. On the eve of the First World War, only about one non-agricultural employee in fifteen belonged to a trade union, with most of the membership consisting of white males in skilled occupations. The rest of the working class was treated as semi-skilled or unskilled and therefore interchangeable. Their incomes during good times were modest and, in the case of most immigrants and women, often below subsistence levels, leaving most workers susceptible to destitution when jobs were unavailable.

The growth of industry and urbanization, and the concomitant growth in the absolute and relative numbers of poor and propertyless people requiring outside aid, taxed the institutions established in the pre-industrial era. Between 1867 and 1914, existing social welfare institutions were reshaped and new ones were created to deal with the large number of women, seniors, Natives, immigrants, and labourers who faced being washed away by the industrial tide. By the early 1900s, however, this had produced a diffuse reform movement that advocated state intervention to aid the casualties of capitalism. Within the trade union movement, this included both moderates who wanted the state to compensate for the worst excesses of capitalism and socialists who wanted to eradicate the market-based economic system altogether. Responding to the horrors of early industrialism and to the "godless socialists" who regarded the economic and religious elites together as oppressors of working people, a "social gospel" movement arose in the Protestant churches that played a strong role in motivating governments to intervene on behalf of the most indisputable victims of a capitalist economic system.

The Spread of Workhouses

As the pace of industrialization quickened, the number of workhouses that segregated the unemployed from the rest of the community grew. The earlier resistance to workhouses in rural areas broke down as large towns, either industrial or commercial, began to dot the rural landscape. The mutual reciprocity that characterized agricultural communities gave way to capitalist social relations in which employers determined the numbers and wages of workers in accordance with potential profits.

The elites blamed the poor, particularly the able-bodied poor, for their own poverty, using their media to propagate this perspective. Toronto's *Daily Globe* argued typically in an editorial in 1877 that "to talk about hard-heartedness is a very cheap and easy proceeding. A very large proportion of both men and women who are the recipients of public bounty are notoriously dissipated. Though they are so, we do not advocate a system which would leave them to starve, but we do say that if they are ever to be taught economical and saving habits they must understand that the public have no idea of making them entirely comfortable in the midst of their improvidence and dissipation."[1]

Such thinking led the workhouses to institute "labour tests" for able-bodied destitute males seeking refuge. In Toronto, the House of Industry made stone-breaking the labour test in 1881, adding cutting wood as an alternative in the winter of 1883–84. In 1888, this workhouse began to refuse food and shelter to individuals who declined the work test, though some of the homeless were too weak to comply; but it continued its extensive outdoor relief program for families. The Toronto House of Providence, by contrast, provided only indoor relief but received twice as large a provincial subsidy thanks to a provincial bias against social assistance for indigents who did not move to workhouses.[2]

Despite this bias, many municipalities in Ontario established outdoor relief programs. By 1888, 130 of the province's cities, towns, and villages offered one, and five thousand individuals received state-funded social assistance in their homes. The funds paid out were always modest, consistently less than the potential wages for an employed unskilled labourer, in keeping with the requirements of "less eligibility." "Moral" considerations determined who received money. Campbellford, for example, provided monthly grants to widows and deserted wives, but refused aid to a woman whose husband deserted her because she was rumoured to have had an affair with a "coloured man." Women often served as snoops for the local government, informing them when recipients' conduct defied the norms of conventional morality. Belleville put women in charge of relief distribution because they were seen as more tight-fisted than men.[3]

The Quebec government also limited its funds for the poor by only giving grants to houses of industry, but these were operated by the churches that tried to keep families out of the poorhouses. In February 1872, the Protestant House of Industry's outdoor relief section in Montreal provided firewood, clothes, blankets, and food to 279 families while the major Catholic charities, the Grey Nuns and the Sisters of Providence, likely aided three times as many families. Such aid was minimal, and both families of the working poor and the unemployed doubled and tripled up to save on rent, share resources, and avoid ending up in the poorhouse.[4]

The Maritime provinces were tougher still on the poor. Prince Edward Island had no real system for state aid, relying on occasional small grants to municipalities or individuals as conditions warranted, with political patronage often determining recipients. New Brunswick and Nova Scotia built more workhouses in the post-Confederation period, and rejected at-home relief by the state for any category of citizens. In New Brunswick, even in the late 1940s, the municipal poorhouse served as home to orphans and mentally challenged children along with a population of the aged, the poor, alcoholics, unwed mothers, and paraplegics. While the churches in the two larger Atlantic provinces provided some outdoor relief, they received no state aid and could therefore help only a limited number of families.

The availability of employment shifted with both the business cycle and the seasons. As much as 18 per cent of the labour force in Toronto was unemployed in 1892, at the nadir of a business recession. Workhouse residents included railway construction workers, farm labourers, and sailors who had been laid off for the winter, along with general labourers, grocers, clerks, painters, carpenters, printers, and servants. Yet governments and businesses explained demands on the poorhouses in terms of the moral failings of the workforce rather than the operation of the economy. Their solution was to make life difficult for the unemployed. The Casual Poor Committee of the House of Industry wanted to send beggars to prison and to force the long-term unemployed into labour colonies where they would be trained for industry. "Hitherto we have brought the tramp up to a certain stage in recovering industrious inclinations, but we have allowed him to slip from our hands before these inclinations have been formed into habits of industry."[5]

Overcrowding in the workhouse was endemic, and in 1884, about 130 to 150 men lived in a room in Toronto's House of Industry that would only comfortably house about a third of them. The inmates resisted patronizing treatment and demanded an improvement in conditions. When they were given a stack of religious periodicals to read on Sunday, they burned them.[6]

Young women without work also sometimes ended up in the poorhouses, though many resorted to prostitution to avoid this fate. Well-off women in the Toronto Relief Society tried to provide an alternative for poverty-stricken women by opening the Industrial Room in 1883. The Room provided jobs for women to make night shirts and children's clothing for a wage sufficient to pay for modest room and board. In the winter of 1889, this relief agency employed 154 young women.[7]

In rural areas, children, mothers without husbands, and the elderly were the major economic casualties who ended up in Houses of Industry. In 1895, the Children's Protection Act of Ontario, originally passed in 1893, was amended to keep children out of institutions that accepted dependent adults. By 1900, the legislation was sufficiently enforced that a poorhouse could serve neither as an orphanage nor as a shelter for a dependent family with children.[8]

The relatively large percentage of the workhouse population who were elderly caused some politicians to complain that children were no longer caring for their aging parents. However, studies, such as the one of Brockville, Ontario, suggest that a larger percentage of aged citizens lived under the same roof as their adult children in 1901 than ever before. Only 2 per cent of Ontarians over the age of sixty in 1891 lived in institutions. The next decade saw little change in percentage terms, but with an aging population, that translated into a large absolute increase in the number of institutionalized seniors. This caused concern among politicians, many of whom believed that a crisis in care for the elderly was developing.[9]

Most men as well as single women in the waged labour force worked until their deaths unless illness made this impossible. Studies of the inmates of town workhouses suggest that they were dominantly elderly people without work, relatives, or friends to support them. In Wellington County, from 1877 to 1907, men accounted for 69 per cent of inmates and 82 per cent of aged inmates. In general, men ended up in the poorhouse when there was no work for them, and women when there were no relatives to support them.[10] In 1903, Ontario made construction of houses of refuge mandatory in each county because of increases in people requiring care, especially the elderly. However, the government continued to make the family and not the state primarily responsible for their care.

SAVING CHILDREN

In contrast to the treatment of the elderly, the state did express greater interest in involving itself directly in children's welfare. The income of children remained necessary in the "family economy" of many working-class households because low pay and seasonal incomes for male "heads of household" and proscriptions against married women's work outside the home limited family options. However, in the early 1880s factory legislation in Ontario and Quebec, followed by similar legislation in other provinces, outlawed the labour of children under the age of twelve. While such legislation was often laxly enforced, the percentage of young people in the workforce began a steady decline. Another reason for the decline in child labour was that in the 1870s, provinces—except for Quebec, which only made education compulsory in 1943—had begun to make it mandatory for children under twelve (and later fourteen) to attend school.

In general, as Canada became more industrialized, the view that children were solely the responsibilities of their parents was challenged by the state. Its newly formed bureaucratic apparatus proclaimed that the creation of good citizens required the state's intervention in the parent–child relationship. J.J. Kelso, one of the most celebrated of the "child savers" and the key proponent of the children's aid societies movement in Ontario, expressed the growing view of "experts" that early childhood experiences shaped the character of an adult. In 1893, Kelso began a forty-one-year stint as Ontario's superintendent of neglected and dependent children. Writing in *The Canadian Magazine* the following year, he linked criminality with early childhood influences and defended the state's consequent right to dictate to parents, even to remove their children if they disobeyed state-dictated prescriptions on child raising. "For the protection of the child the removal is made; for the protection of the community, the unworthy parent should be compelled to pay to the last farthing."[11]

Such views led to the legislation that closed the workhouses to children in Ontario and kept orphanages separate from poorhouses. Child savers had secured a provincial law in 1888 entitled Act for the Protection and Reformation of Neglected Children. It allowed courts to make children wards of the state, compelling local governments to pay for their care either in institutions or in foster homes. Three years later Kelso formed the Children's Aid Society of Toronto, convinced reformers in other areas to establish parallel organizations, and campaigned for amendments to the child protection law to give children's aid societies the power to determine whether children should be removed from their homes. In 1895, the province allowed these volunteer-created societies to become legal guardians of homeless children and children deemed at either physical or "moral" risk if they remained in their home. Children's aid societies would operate municipal shelters for such children and charge municipalities for costs incurred. By 1912, sixty Children's Aid Society (CAS) offices in Ontario were carrying out this mandate.

The CAS preferred to board children out rather than institutionalize them. Kelso believed that children needed a family environment and orphanages were notorious for their high incidence of diseases. In Newfoundland, the St. John's Methodist Orphanage faced a quarantine of several months in 1912 when twenty-one of thirty-three girls contracted diphtheria. Neither the Orphanage nor the home run by the Church of England in the city had sufficient funds to maintain adequate kitchen and food standards, provide proper sewage, ventilation, and toilets, or to prevent overcrowding. In 1915, the Church of England home could spend on average only 18 cents per child.[12]

Nor was mistreatment of rural children uncommon. Between 1880 and 1925, about eighty thousand British boys and girls, mostly under the age of fourteen, were indentured to Canadians as agricultural labourers and domestic servants. In one sample of children from the Barnardo Homes in Britain, 15 per cent of the girls and 9 per cent of the boys had suffered excessive abuse in Canada. Only when there was a death was prosecution likely, and, unfortunately, children did die because of ill treatment. An example was of a fourteen-year-old boy who was sent to Grenfell in the Northwest Territories (now within

Saskatchewan). He was punished for his incontinence by being forced to sleep outside in the stable. One night, as temperatures dropped to minus 45 degrees Farenheit, his feet became frost-bitten and then gangrenous.[13]

While state involvement likely saved some children from intolerable homes, some loving parents lost their children simply because they lacked the financial resources to care for them. The most glaring example of "child saving" abuse involved Aboriginal children. The federal government coerced Native parents, particularly in western Canada, to put their children in "residential schools" or "industrial schools" where they were forced to learn European ways. The church-run schools, subsidized by the federal government, were generally punitive in their approach. While some teachers treated the children kindly, many others used repeated beatings and insults to prevent them from using their own languages, following their own customs, or running away. Poor nutrition, overwork, and the stress of being away from their families and in an unwelcoming environment contributed to many deaths. Sexual predators among the teaching staff caused irreparable psychological harm to many of the young students. The residential schools were gradually closed in the 1960s and 1970s. Native peoples attribute alcoholism, failure to learn parenting skills, and lack of knowledge of their ancestors' culture to the effects of being forced to attend schools devoted to the annihilation of their traditions.[14]

The "child savers," though focused on imposing middle-class values on all families, were also concerned about the health of babies and children. The death rate of babies in Toronto was 160 out of every 1,000 in 1901; by 1907, the figure had climbed to 196. Montreal had the highest rate of infant deaths in North American cities; one baby in three born at the turn of the twentieth century failed to reach the age of one.[15] In 1910, the Ontario government appointed Dr. Helen MacMurchy to investigate the causes of infant mortality and make recommendations to reduce its incidence. MacMurchy was a graduate of the University of Toronto Faculty of Medicine and a former medical inspector for the schools. She issued three reports between 1910 and 1912 that would strongly influence the course of provincial social policy in protecting the health of infants. From the outset she argued for government intervention, noting, "We are only now discovering that Empires and States are built of babies. Cities are dependent for their continuance on babies. Armies are recruited only if and when we have cared for our babies."[16]

Her recommendations included legislating inspection of commercially sold milk to ensure that it was clean; registering births and deaths of infants to aid in public health supervision of children; awarding allowances to mothers who breast-fed their babies; establishing a government bureau of infant welfare along with a network of infant-welfare clinics staffed by doctors and nurses; requiring medical visits by experts to new moms to instruct them on the healthy care of their infants; distributing free diphtheria antitoxin to the poor; and providing free ice to poor mothers in the summertime. It was an ambitious set of recommendations, and its emphasis on public health measures was progressive. But there was an undertone to the report which suggested that part of the problem of infant mortality was due to the mother's lack of knowledge about hygiene and nutrition. This attitude reflected MacMurchy's estrangement from working-class families. For far too many families, overcrowding, poor municipal sanitation, and budgets too small to afford fresh vegetables and fruits were the problems, not lack of knowledge. MacMurchy also opposed child care centres and other measures that might encourage mothers to seek employment and bolster family incomes, arguing forcefully, though without evidence, that maternal employment contributed to infant deaths. She did, however, support some special programs for the poor, including more parks in poor neighbourhoods and more chances for open-air holidays.

Even before MacMurchy's report, middle-class and farm feminists had taken action to save babies' lives. The National Council of Women of Canada (NCWC), founded in 1893 as an umbrella organization for women's volunteer organizations, established the Victorian Order of Nurses (VON) in 1897. One of its key objectives was to make regular visits to mothers and their children, and by 1900, VON employed thirty-two nurses across Canada. In addition, the Women's Institutes in rural areas of English Canada and Les Cercles des Fermières in Quebec made layettes for newborns and school lunches that they distributed to families, as well as providing health information. In 1901, the Montreal Local Council of Women, the Foundling Hospital, and a group of doctors established a pure milk depot on the model of the Gouttes de lait de Paris. Toronto volunteers followed suit.

Governments proved reluctant to pass much of the legislation called for by the child reformers, if only because they did not wish to impose the taxes that they might necessitate. Until 1917, there was no federal income tax in Canada either on individual or corporate wealth. The federal government relied largely on the tariff for its revenues, while the provinces depended on sales and leasing of Crown lands along with federal grants and municipalities relied on property taxes. Government spending on child welfare was less than 10 per cent of the gross national product on the eve of the First World War. But some concessions were made to the child savers' ideas. Most importantly, water supplies were gradually purified and legislation regarding milk supplies, while not forbidding the sale of unpasteurized milk until the 1920s, ensured that fewer children were exposed to tainted products. These measures contributed to dramatic declines in infant mortality in the years leading up to the war. In Winnipeg, the infant mortality rate fell from 207 per 1,000 live births in 1912 to 106 in 1915, with London, Brantford, and Vancouver posting similar dramatic reductions. The Gouttes de lait in Montreal also contributed to a falling infant mortality rate in that city.[17]

Another concession to the reformers was the gradual introduction of systematic medical inspections in the schools. Montreal's Board of Health led the nation in 1906, and by 1910, it had been followed by Sydney, Hamilton, Halifax, London, Toronto, Brantford, Winnipeg, Edmonton, and Nelson. That year British Columbia passed the Schools Health Inspection Act that provided for a co-ordinated approach to school inspections across the province. By 1922, Saskatchewan had fourteen school nurses travelling the province acting as inspectors. School inspectors both educated children and their parents regarding sanitary habits and identified problems with the schools that contributed to ill health for children. Often, however, funding limitations made it difficult to implement the findings of the inspectors. So, for example, a rural medical officer in Nova Scotia complained in 1920 that only one of thirty schoolhouses that he inspected had satisfactory toilets.

Historians, as were contemporaries of the time, are divided regarding the motives for the campaigns to educate and direct mothers in their child-raising practices. Neil Sutherland pays tribute to the child savers for increasing consciousness of the physical needs of children. He writes: "There were undoubtedly thousands of mothers who had not studied domestic science at school, who had never visited a pure-milk depot or baby welfare station, who had never received a visit by a public health nurse, who had not read a copy of the Canadian Mother's Book or a Metropolitan Life pamphlet, but whose infant and child care practices were nonetheless very much influenced by the climate of opinion generated to improve the life chances of the newly born."[18]

Feminist scholars have analyzed the child savers more critically. Katherine Arnup, in a study of advice literature to mothers in twentieth-century Canada, suggests that gender and class biases caused many reformers to underestimate the knowledge of mothers, especially working-class mothers. Like temperance advocates, who focused on drink rather than low wages as the cause of working-class poverty, the child savers often ignored the impact of poverty on the mothers' behaviour. Women were criticized for raising babies in overcrowded, filthy homes with little regard for what options their meagre family incomes afforded them. Veronica Strong-Boag, focusing on the interwar period, notes that few women could afford the luxury of following advice to stay in bed for two weeks after giving birth, to provide a baby with a room of her own, or even to have an indoor bathroom with modern plumbing.[19]

For Arnup and Strong-Boag, increasing prosperity rather than expert advice produced gradual improvements in children's health. Sutherland concedes that poverty, rather than ignorance, was sometimes the cause of families failing to act in the interests of children. He notes, for example, that efforts in the 1890s to encourage mothers to have their babies vaccinated with a new anti-diphtheria antitoxin had desultory results. But when governments, such as Ontario in 1907 and Saskatchewan in 1917, made the antitoxin available for free, mothers lined up to have their babies vaccinated.[20]

Wives without employed husbands, deserted wives, and widows could not heed the advice of the reformers that mothers should leave the labour force. Newfoundland was well in advance of the Canadian provinces in singling out deserted wives for financial support from the state, providing modest help beginning in 1872. Ontario followed in 1888 with the assistance of $5 per week to deserted wives. Between 1900 and 1911, Manitoba, British Columbia, and Saskatchewan accepted the same principle in legislation. In all of these jurisdictions, never-married women and women who left their husbands, regardless of the cause, were deemed ineligible for state assistance. New Brunswick and Nova Scotia denied funding to all mothers outside the workhouse.[21]

British Columbia was the only province where the government provided state aid to at least a section of working mothers. In 1910, the Infants' Hospital, which enjoyed municipal and provincial subsidies, opened a centre for preschool children of working mothers. Six years later, the city's health department accepted responsibility for operation of a crèche organized by a charitable group. In other provinces, charitable groups ran some day homes for the children of working mothers. In Montreal, the crèches run by Roman Catholic women's orders since the 1850s continued to operate. Protestant English-speaking Montreal working women finally had a daycare where they could take their children in 1887. In 1891 and 1906, respectively, the first crèches were opened in Toronto and Winnipeg. Missions and settlement houses sponsored by churches were responsible for daycares established in Ottawa in 1911 and Halifax during the First World War. The centres tended to be overcrowded and spartan, providing children with lessons about manners, obedience, and religion, but giving them little affection. The philanthropic women who ran the centres also tried to impose their notions of thrift and morality on the moms of children who attended the centres. Still, the centres were a welcome alternative to the orphanages, which most breadwinner mothers had to resort to in order to earn wages.[22]

HEALTH AND STATE POLICIES

Public health measures between Confederation and the First World War involved more than the protection of babies and children. As public authorities accepted the germ theory of disease, the need for public health measures to prevent the spread of disease became clear. Pre-Confederation campaigns to deal with outbreaks of infectious diseases had created only temporary organizations that disbanded when the crisis had passed. Now permanent boards of health were created to halt the spread of disease.

Britain's Public Health Act of 1875 became the model for Canadian provinces. It required local authorities to establish boards to carry out preventive measures. In 1882, Ontario introduced similar legislation and, by 1909, all provinces had implemented a parallel act. Public health physicians and sanitary inspectors became the core staff of the new public health organizations, with public health nurses later added in significant numbers. Ontario organized a successful propaganda campaign for vaccination against smallpox in 1885 as an epidemic struck the country. Only eighty-four Ontarians died from the disease, while in Quebec, where little was done to counter popular paranoia about vaccination, there were over five thousand deaths, with 3,175 in Montreal alone.[23]

The public health movement's greatest success was its campaign for clean water supplies and sanitary systems for disposing of wastes. In the nineteenth century, waterworks and sewers were the privileges of wealthy people usually living in residential enclaves. The *Patriot* in Charlottetown noted in 1874 that while the rich could live in unpolluted suburbs or buy spring water if they lived in the cities, the poor man "must bring up his family in the neighborhood of reeking cesspools and filthy pig-sties. He can not well afford to buy pure water at a very expensive rate; and he has to think twice before he calls in a doctor."[24]

A waterworks was established in Charlottetown in 1888 and sanitation was improved towards the end of the century. Other cities witnessed slower progress. In Winnipeg in 1890, about 10 per cent of residents had access to sewers and waterworks. There was no comprehensive health bylaw until 1899, though it was generally accepted that impure water carried the bacteria that caused typhoid fever, scarlet fever, diphtheria, and other infectious diseases.

In the immigrant and working-class North End, water mains were not built until the twentieth century. Montreal's class structure similarly marked health divisions, as pointed out in Herbert Brown Ames's classic survey of Montreal's living conditions published as *The City below the Hill*, in 1897. Ames found that in the area of west-end Montreal—bounded by Westmount, the city limits, and the St. Lawrence River—one home in five had proper sanitary equipment and overcrowding was rampant. One quarter of Griffintown residents had modern plumbing. In the upper city, by contrast, population densities were small and all the homes were clean and enjoyed modern plumbing.[25]

As it became clear that neighbourhoods with impure water supplies and un-sanitary disposal of wastes could spread diseases to better-off areas, the public health movement convinced cities to provide purified water supplies and a safe system of sewerage for all citizens. In the 1890s and early twentieth century, this often meant municipal ownership of waterworks and sewers. "Faith in professional management, confidence in the results of scientific study, and, for some, the evangelical conviction that the causes of contagious disease, like the temptation to sin, had to be rooted out by the force of individual will" all con-tributed to the expansion of the infrastructure.[26] Pressure from business people also played a role. In their competition to entice firms to locate within their boundaries, municipalities provided high levels of direct and indirect subsidies to businesses. The presence of a public waterworks was attractive to industries because a waterworks was necessary for fire protection and for convincing in-surance companies to charge a lower premium for fire protection.[27]

Municipalities also became increasingly involved in the establishment and maintenance of hospitals. Efforts to have provincial governments pay more of the costs largely failed. As late as 1917, Ontario paid only 60 cents a day per pa-tient to hospitals for care of indigents while municipalities contributed on aver-age $1.75. Other provinces were even less generous.[28] State subsidies provided only a small part of the operating costs of hospitals, and their clientele before the late nineteenth century were largely the destitute. This began to change as the new knowledge of germs led to campaigns to make hospitals antiseptic, though many surgeons continued to perform surgery with their bare hands up until the First World War. Nonetheless, hospitals advertised themselves as safe places for surgeries and, as medical technology developed, as the centres for new equipment that physicians could not transport to homes for paying patients. Paying patients became important to the plans of hospital administra-tors for financing their institutions and ultimately for defining the purposes of their institutions. Administrators and boards appealed to the middle class by carefully distinguishing services available to paying patients from services available to indigents. In the 1890s, the Victoria General Hospital in Halifax and the Hamilton City Hospital built private wards that were separate from the areas where poor patients were served. In 1893, paying patients provided 20 per cent of the revenues of Kingston General Hospital, and 29 per cent at Montreal General Hospital in 1907. Owen Sound's General and Marine Hospital was receiving a majority of its income from fees paid by better-off patients by 1905.

Hospitals in the Maritimes received only tiny state subsidies, making income from paying patients a necessity. The Moncton Hospital, an independent community venture with neither large endowments nor ties to medical schools, opened in 1898 in the local almshouse with fewer than twenty beds. Income from paying patients rose from 27 per cent in 1898–99 to 58 per cent in 1908–09 and 84 per cent in 1929–30. In 1918, it cost $2 a day for a semi-private room and $3.71 for a private room. Anaesthetics, drugs, operating room use, surgery fees, X-ray charges, and laboratory expenses were extra costs.[29]

Hospitals proudly advertised the spacious, comfortable rooms, fine furniture and appointments, and sumptuous meals available in the wing occupied by paying patients, which was physically separated from the charity wing so that paying patients never need see charity patients. By contrast, in 1907, charity patients at the Hamilton Sanatorium stayed in tents and wooden shacks, and those who were not absolutely bedridden were sent to work on the hospital's farm that produced their food. The Inspector of Prisons and Charities reported in 1913 that Hamilton City Hospital's public wards were overcrowded and poorly ventilated; the conditions of these wards were "almost up to the shade of being criminal."[30]

How did such glaring differences arise? Some historians suggest that hospital administrators, conscious of the need to raise more money to serve charity patients, inadvertently recreated the class divide of the larger society within the hospital itself.[31] Others, focusing on the rhetoric of the "expert" male hospital administrators who were replacing the largely female hospital "matrons" of an earlier period, suggest that the class structure of hospital services was deliberate. The administrators often regarded the hospital as a quasi-business venture providing desirable services to those who could afford them. They came to see the paying patients as the desirable and deserving clients of the hospital, and viewed the non-paying patients as a burden on their business for whom costs should be minimized.[32]

Within the hospitals, as in private practice, almost all of the physicians before the Second World War were men. So were the administrators, who were increasingly trained physicians. Catholic institutions in Quebec were an exception, still administered by the nuns, though physician control over hospital decisions deemed to be medical was becoming common. The absolute ban on women training to become doctors gradually lifted after Confederation, but because of the hostility that greeted them in the existing medical schools, small medical colleges for women were set up in Kingston and Toronto in 1883.[33]

Most women in the health sector were low-wage nurses and hospital cleaners. With most health services still provided in the home, most nurses were privately employed. Even in the hospitals, patients, rather than the hospital itself, employed nurses. Before the twentieth century, most nurses were charwomen or domestics and supplemented their main incomes with part-time hospital work. Though the first training program for nurses had been established in 1874 at Mack's General and Marine Hospital in St. Catharines, there were fewer than three hundred trained nurses in Canada in 1900. In the next two decades, along with the growth in private and public hospitals, two to three year hospital training programs for nurses were established across the country. Yet they remained poorly-paid assistants to doctors, their extensive medical training giving them no right to formal decision-making power. By 1918, there were over twenty thousand trained nurses in the country. Quebec's francophone hospitals followed their Ontario counterparts in providing formal training of nurses in order to win recognition of their hospitals by hospital accreditation bodies. Along with standard medical courses, they provided courses in Catholic teachings and only reluctantly admitted lay students.[34]

The medical profession's authority within the health field increased steadily. In 1869, the Ontario Medical Association won legislative approval for professional self-regulation by physicians. The Ontario Medical Act established the College of Physicians and Surgeons of Ontario, an examining and licensing board for physicians. The College would also control the curriculum of medical schools. This legislation effectively shut out non-allopathic healers from using the designation of "doctor" or "physician." Nova Scotia followed Ontario's example in 1872, New Brunswick in 1881, and Prince Edward Island in 1884. Quebec followed suit with a series of laws between 1876 and 1898 that limited the right to practise medicine to university-trained physicians.

By the end of the century, doctors not only presented themselves as healers whose practices were based on hard scientific evidence but also as social scientists able to diagnose underlying social problems. Much of their critique focused on heredity rather than environment, and on reactionary solutions such as eugenics, which called for only those deemed physically and mentally healthy by the medical profession to be allowed to breed. The overwhelming dominance of males in the profession also led to a discourse about women's bodies and mental health that made it appear that women were both more physically frail than men and mentally unstable. The medical profession, dressing up long-standing social prejudices in the garb of scientific language, reinforced gender stereotypes that limited women's advancement in Canada.

Nonetheless, women played key roles both in nursing and in the volunteer sector. In Montreal, the YWCA began home visits in 1879 for the distribution of healthy food to those who were poor and sick. In 1901, they distributed aid to almost seventeen thousand people and the YMCA in other cities had by then copied the same program. The women's section of the Fédération Nationale Saint-Jean-Baptiste opened l'Hôpital Sainte-Justine in 1907 as a hospital for sick children, focusing on the indigent, though accepting paying patients as well. In Quebec, women's voluntary organizations increasingly hired trained nurses for a variety of functions once performed by volunteers, such as home visits to new mothers.[35]

Hospitals for the mentally ill, like those for the physically ill, claimed to apply the most recent "scientific" treatments. Studies of inmates of the asylums suggest that many were quite capable of looking after themselves and were eccentric rather than delusional or suicidal. Often they were simply an inconvenience to their families—young women who transgressed conventional sexual morality, middle-aged women no longer desired by their husbands in a society where few divorces were granted, alcoholics, and drug addicts. The prevalence of women in the asylums suggested the greater power of males within the family and society. At the Homewood Retreat, established in Guelph, Ontario in 1883, fashions alternated between the view that heredity caused psychiatric problems and the perspective that blamed neurological and physical problems. Historian Cheryl Krasnick Warsh, analyzing Homewood's treatment of over one thousand patients, observes that patriarchal practices prevailed, but met with acts of rebellion from patients attempting to exercise some control over their lives in institutions that sought to regiment their lives. She notes that "variable levels of equivocal authority, reward and punishment, rebellion and secrecy, negligence and caring interventions, mirrored the dynamics of the household."[36]

CRIME AND PUNISHMENT

The new interest in psychiatry gradually led to some rethinking of traditional views of the causes of criminality and the possibilities of rehabilitating criminals.

The British North America Act gave the federal government control over institutions housing prisoners who had committed major crimes. The Penitentiary Act of 1868 underlined the federal government's intention to maintain the punitive approach to convicted criminals, and several new penitentiaries were built in the 1870s and 1880s.

Gradually, the federal penitentiaries began to use the carrot of reduced sentences to encourage prisoners to do the work that they were assigned in prison. In part, this was because the prisons became dependent on labour contracts to defray their expenses, but there were also glimmers of rehabilitative philosophy here since it was argued that prisoners who learned good work habits would have a better chance to reintegrate into society. In the early 1900s, the silence and darkness that once shrouded prisoners' evenings gave way to an environment in which reading and conversation were viewed as steps towards preparing the prisoner to re-enter society with a better moral understanding of society's rules for behaviour.

Provincial prisons, which housed prisoners with sentences of less than two years, took longer to develop humane attitudes. Central Prison, Ontario's first prison, opened in Toronto in 1874, and, from the outset, the government stressed that harsh conditions and hard labour were the keys to preventing recidivism. A royal commission investigating charges of cruelty laid by the prisoners defended the authorities' use of beatings and even called for their intensification. The case of William O'Neill is a good example. O'Neill was kept in solitary confinement for three months and given only bread and water, before being declared insane; the commissioners suggested that even greater punishment might have been justified. Such views reflected the desire of the middle classes for social control over citizens. Social control did not, however, always mean providing a punitive environment. The Mercer Reformatory for Women, also in Ontario, minimized corporal punishments in favour of a program that socialized inmates to accept middle-class maternal values, values often at odds with the realistic expectations for many of these lawbreakers.[37]

The "child saver" movement gradually extricated younger offenders from adult prisons. In the late nineteenth century, younger offenders were placed in "reformatories," industrial schools that, like adult prisons, emphasized inmate labour. Child savers suggested that unsavoury home environments, rather than heredity, created young criminals. J.J. Kelso estimated in 1889 that about seven to eight hundred Toronto children were sent to the streets "by drunken and avaricious parents to earn money by the precarious selling of newspapers, pencils, etc." but were often engaged in petty theft and begging. Such children, in his view, were prime candidates for the children's aid societies to seize as wards of the state and place in a new home environment. Like other moral regulationists, Kelso condemned beggars and did not question whether they had realistic options.[38]

In 1908, the federal government legislated the Juvenile Delinquents Act, which created separate courts and different punishments for young offenders than adults. Vancouver Judge Helen Gregory MacGill, among other reformers, argued that treatment, not punishment, must be the goal of the juvenile court. "Treatment" practices of the time included having Winnipeg truancy officers stalk the city's streets and department stores and Vancouver's probation officers removing juveniles from pool halls and theatres late at night. By the First World War, juvenile courts had been established in Winnipeg, Halifax, Charlottetown, Montreal, Ottawa, Toronto, Vancouver, and Victoria.[39]

WORKMEN'S COMPENSATION

Juvenile courts stressed that young people should aim their sights at honest work, yet many jobs were dangerous. The labour faction of the Royal Commission on Relations of Labour and Capital, which reported in 1889, charged that railways failed to take safety precautions such as installing guardrails on roofs of freight cars. By 1914, it was clear that Factory Acts were indifferently enforced, and the state legislated no responsibilities upon employers to either keep workers in work or to pay them a decent wage. Unions were legal, but employers had a legal right to fire workers who joined unions. A worker maimed on the job or the family of a worker killed in an industrial accident could sue the employer if they could afford legal counsel and court fees. But court decisions largely went against the workers. The Trades and Labour Congress—organized in 1883 as a national union central largely composed of Canadian branches of American "international" craft unions—along with its provincial affiliates lobbied governments for "workmen's" (now workers') compensation. The eventual concession of such a program by provincial governments was, in part, a tribute to rising militancy on the part of unions by the early twentieth century. The rise of radical workers' organizations such as the Industrial Workers of the World, the formation of socialist parties, and the increasing frequency and militancy of strikes in the early 1900s played a role in state calculations.[41]

There were also employers who wanted workmen's compensation. Several Canadian provinces, beginning with Ontario in 1886, had passed employer liability laws. Such laws removed some common-law defences that employers had earlier used to avoid responsibility for an accident at their workplace. While employers still managed to win most cases, jury trials often resulted in sympathy for the employee or the employee's family and, after 1900, increasingly large awards were levied against employers. Employers grew tired of legal fees and the risk of being forced to pay restitution to injured workers or their families. The notion of a no-fault workmen's compensation fund into which all employers would make contributions and from which injured workers or the families of workers who died on the job could draw, appeared a better solution to many employers in industries where accidents were common.[42]

The first province to legislate workmen's compensation was Quebec in 1909. The province's charities proved unable to keep up with the additional demand upon them created by the victims of industrial carnage. The provincial factory inspector, Louis Guyon, became an untiring campaigner for workmen's compensation so that a fixed schedule of payments for industrial victims, including death benefits for families, would replace charity and the courts in attempting to deal with the human consequences of work-related accidents. Guyon's task was aided by the support offered both by organized labour and organized business for workmen's compensation.[43]

In Ontario, it was organized labour that led the campaign, and its cause was helped when a provincially appointed commission of inquiry to investigate the desirability of such a program reported in favour of a bill for workmen's compensation. The Canadian Manufacturers Association (CMA), usually an opponent of governments doing much other than providing shamelessly high levels of tariff protection for industry, had indicated its support for the principle of compensation to the commission of inquiry. Many firms carried liability insurance but complained about its costs; surely a state-run no-fault program would remove the plague of lawyers and adjusters who forced up the costs of insuring industries against lawsuits arising out of job accidents. In 1914, the province finally passed a bill to establish workmen's compensation with industries charged payroll fees based on past experience of industrial accidents in their sector. These payroll deductions provided the funds that a provincial commission would use to distribute payments to injured workers or their families based on a fixed schedule. Farm workers and domestics were, however, excluded from coverage.

The CMA, interestingly, while pleased that the bill followed their suggestion for a system of collective insurance under state control, regarded the level of compensation payments set by the province as too high. By contrast, the provincial labour movement called for higher rates of compensation, including payment of injured workers' medical bills. The stage was set for the continuous class struggle regarding workers' compensation, not over the principle as such, but over eligibility and levels of compensation. In general, organized business argued compensation levels should provide only a sufficient subsistence for workers' families that they had no claims on organized charity and no need to enter the poorhouse; organized labour, by contrast, believed that the family of a worker either killed or left unable to work because of an accident should enjoy the standard of living they would have enjoyed had there been no accident.[44]

British Columbia and Nova Scotia established workmen's compensation in 1915 and New Brunswick in 1918. In the latter province, the New Brunswick Federation of Labour supported the Liberals in a provincial election that year when the Conservative provincial government proved dilatory in delivering upon a promise to introduce workmen's compensation. The successful Liberals established a program similar to Ontario's.[45]

INTERNATIONAL BORROWINGS

Workmen's compensation was an innovation borrowed from other countries. Germany had decreed in 1885 that all companies had to provide accident insurance for their employees. Between 1889 and 1906, Finland, New Zealand, and the United Kingdom adopted no-fault systems that included both benefits for injured workers and death benefits. Similarly, the public health and child-saving measures, as well as the establishment of mental asylums, all borrowed European and American precedents. But Canada proved conservative in its efforts to mimic other countries' social programs, and by 1914, it was clearly a laggard in the provision of social benefits to its citizens. Germany, in contrast, had introduced sickness and accident insurance in 1884 and old age pensions in 1889 in an effort to stave off the growth of a powerful socialist movement.

By the First World War, Austria, France, Italy, Holland, the United Kingdom, Scandinavia, and even Czarist Russia, among other countries, had all instituted some or all of the German social insurance programs. France had established a public network of medical clinics and crèches, the latter allowing mothers of young children to be in the workforce. Several countries had implemented unemployment insurance, beginning with France in 1905, usually providing the trade union movement the task of administering insurance funds.[46] Indeed, in every country, the extent of reforms, while dependent on several factors, seemed most to be influenced by the relative political and economic strength of the trade union movement. In all countries, however, the benefits paid to individuals tended to be paltry. Canada's labour movement was strong enough to influence the development of workmen's compensation, but was too weak to wring many other concessions before the First World War. Middle-class reform movements in the country associated with the mainstream Protestant churches had, however, aligned themselves with trade unions in calling for state programs.

THE SOCIAL GOSPEL

Charles Darwin's evolutionary theories had caused splits among Protestants regarding the literal truth of the Bible that led to soul-searching regarding the churches' role in society. Some continued to view the churches' mission as one of individual moral reform, and limited their political horizon to measures such as prohibition which had overtones of moral regulation. But a new group of social reformers in the Protestant churches, while rarely opposing prohibition, argued that the way to combat poverty and ignorance was to have the state pursue policies that guaranteed individuals and families a minimum income and ensured that all citizens enjoyed access to health services and to clean air, water, and milk.

The Moral and Social Reform Council of Canada, formed in 1907, attempted to blend both the concerns of individualists and collectivists within the Protestant churches, though its renaming as the Social Service Council of Canada in 1913 suggested the greater influence among reformers in the church of the socially minded. Proponents of what came to be called the "social gospel," unlike fundamentalists, believed that it was possible to work for the Kingdom of Heaven on earth, and recognized that it was necessary to engage in the political process to achieve their aims. Many of the "child savers" and health reformers discussed above subscribed to "social gospel" teachings. However, social gospel advocates often mixed their reformist views with reactionary ideas, such as xenophobia and eugenics. The former led them to want to shape Canadian citizenship by closing the immigration gate to all non-whites and anyone else they regarded as a "misfit," and to force all immigrants to adopt Anglo-Protestant values. The latter led them to propose that the state prevent "misfits" from breeding.[47]

Religiously inspired reformers established settlement houses in poor areas at once to bring the church's message to the labouring classes and to ensure that the worldly concerns of the latter became the concerns of all churches. Winnipeg's All People's Mission—whose superintendent from 1907 to 1913 was J.S.

Woodsworth, later the first national leader of the Co-Operative Commonwealth Federation (CCF)—Toronto's Fred Victor Mission, and Halifax's Jost Mission focused respectively on immigrants, the destitute, and working mothers. Jost Mission was one of several missions and settlement houses that sponsored day homes for the children of working mothers.[48]

EMERGENCE OF SOCIAL WORK PROFESSION

Settlement houses were not the exclusive agencies of the religiously minded. The settlement house movement had begun in Britain as a campaign of socially minded, university-trained philosophers. Toynbee Hall, opened in 1884, sought to blend British idealism and empiricism to deal with the problems of the poor. Its founders looked to wealthy college-trained men to give of their time and funds to help the poor individually to overcome their problems and become independent members of the community.

Within a few years, settlement houses had also been established in the United States. The two major houses, Hull House in Chicago and Henry House in New York City, were founded by women reformers, with Jane Addams in the former and Lillian Wald in the latter becoming the public figures most associated with these social welfare institutions. The American settlement houses were distinguished from their British counterpart not only by feminization but also by the Americans' greater emphasis on social, as opposed to individual, problems. Living in settlement houses, among the people they sought to help, Addams, Wald, and other "social workers" became aware of the social structures that created poverty. While they followed Toynbee Hall workers in trying to "reform the poor," to a large extent they also worked to have conditions that led to poverty obviated.

The American social workers pioneered notions of "casework," in which individuals and families were interviewed closely when they first came into contact with an agency and then monitored throughout their dealings with the agency. While some charitable organizations had kept records of their clients in the past, "casework" advocates presented detailed protocols that should be followed and made claims to "scientific" accuracy for their methods of tracking clients and judging their progress towards economic independence. For many women in the United States and then Canada as well, "casework" provided the possibility of arguing for social work to become a recognized profession, with women in the lead. Women, they argued, could combine the scientific approaches that were being developed to individuals' problems in adjusting to society with their allegedly superior intuition to men regarding people's mental states.

As children's aid societies, orphanages, municipal relief departments, and mental health institutions expanded, opportunities for paid social worker positions for women increased. However, the men who operated these agencies paid them poorly and belittled notions that training was required for this work. The social workers responded by attempting to create university training programs that would elevate the social work profession much as university programs for physicians and lawyers had elevated these professions in the nineteenth century. Their first success came at the University of Toronto in 1914, but it involved quite a struggle.[49]

In 1910, W.J. Ashley, founder of the University of Toronto's Department of Political Economy, established the University of Toronto Settlement House along the lines of Toynbee Hall. Ashley fought hard to keep the new settlement house and social work as a male and voluntarist endeavour. Ultimately, however, the combination of the campaign of women social workers and the needs of the expanding network of social agencies undid Ashley's efforts. In 1914, the Department of Social Service opened at the university with a program that combined training in casework with a broad humanist education for social workers, with its first director, E.J. Urwick, emphasizing sociology and social philosophy over psychology. Urwick's position fed into the tension that had become apparent in the field of social work— that is, the tension between approaches that emphasized the individual's need to adapt to social institutions and approaches that emphasized the need of social institutions to adapt to individuals' needs. Urwick leaned to the latter approach.[50] Both radicals and conservatives framed their arguments in secular terms. As one commentator says of the profession as it was emerging in 1914: "Professional social workers and the agencies for which they worked consciously moved away from church affiliation, proclaiming themselves as secular and professing a new faith in science and its application."[51]

NATIVE PEOPLES AND WELFARE

Both religious-minded and science-minded whites wanted to force Native peoples to abandon their traditional cultures. Government policy was summed up by Clifford Sifton, Minister of the Interior, in 1902: "We have them with us, and we have to deal with them as wards of the country. There is no question that the method we have adopted [will bring] these people to an improved state…There is a difference between the savage and a person who has become civilized, though perhaps not of a high type."[52]

Native peoples viewed their poverty as the result of European usurpation of their lands. Though the signing of treaties led them to believe that they were merely agreeing to share their lands with the Europeans, the Canadian government regarded the treaties as land surrenders. The government deprived Natives of their land base and restricted their traditional economic pursuits, the "gifts" that they promised in return constituting rather thin gruel. For example, the promised farm tools and seed to Prairie Natives often did not materialize, thanks to government budget restraints. Many starved and their general health suffered because of the government's determination to provide rations for only three years during the transition from a hunting economy to a farm economy. When chiefs from across the Prairies met with Governor-General the Marquis of Lorne, in 1881, one chief told him, "The horses that have had the scab have been given to the children to eat. That is why there is sickness and they are weak and die." The Marquis, echoing the philosophy the British government applied when confronted with the Irish potato famine, replied: "I am sure that the red men to the East when they work do well and do not starve and I have noticed that the men who talk most and ask most do not work."[53]

An interesting "welfare" clause did appear in Treaty 6, which was signed in 1876 and covered the Cree of today's central Saskatchewan and central Alberta. It read: "That a Medicine Chest shall be kept at the house of the Indian Agent for the use and benefit of the Indians, at the discretion of each agent." The Cree, having suffered several epidemics of smallpox and other diseases, interpreted the "medicine chest" clause as a commitment by the government to provide all the health services required by all Aboriginal peoples. The federal government always argued that this clause only provided limited health care for a defined group of Natives, and did not create a federal responsibility for Aboriginal peoples' health.[54]

In 1904, the Department of Indian Affairs appointed its first general medical superintendent, Dr. Peter Bryce. His dedicated efforts to improve Native health were hampered by "lack of interest and sometimes outright racist attitudes of his colleagues toward his work."[55] Bryce noted in his annual report in 1906 that the death rate for Natives in Canada was twice the rate for non-Natives and in some provinces three times as high. Tuberculosis was the culprit, and he argued for a series of hospitals and sanatoria to be established on or near reserves. Aboriginal peoples avoided the mission hospitals, which focused as much on proselytization as on medicine. The government was loath to spend the money necessary to implement Bryce's vision. It preferred to fund "tent houses" to isolate tubercular children in the residential schools rather than to build and staff hospitals. Similarly, it rejected any suggestion that poorly ventilated and overcrowded housing, contaminated water supplies, and inadequate clothing and diet contributed to increasing rates of TB, though rates were falling for non-Natives. Instead, it blamed the "immorality" of Natives for their illnesses.[56]

In the early post-Confederation years, social assistance was meted out when there were special requests from a Native band, or a priest or Indian agent working with Aboriginal peoples, for government aid to avoid a bout of starvation. Such unsystematic aid gradually gave way, just before the First World War, to casework ideas that emphasized individual Natives or Native families rather than bands. Relief was minimal and short term since the philosophy of relief policy was "to control Indian behaviour and coerce the able bodied into the marketplace."[57]

In the half century following Confederation, Canada was gradually transformed from an agricultural country to an urban-based industrial country. While 80 per cent of the population lived in rural areas at the time of Confederation and a majority farmed, by 1914 half the population lived in towns and cities, and the relative number of agriculturalists in the nation was declining. Most of the new town and city dwellers were dependent upon wage labour and, as a result, there was an increasing number of Canadians who were vulnerable to both seasonal labour conditions and to the booms and busts of the international capitalist marketplace.

With increased urbanization, there was a steep decline in informal neighbourly means of caring for the temporarily or permanently down-and-out. Both organized charities and the state stepped in to fill the breach, though the approach of the social elites and government was quite cautious relative to their European counterparts, who had greater reason to fear social unrest. The numbers of workhouses and hospitals expanded and new specialized institutions, such as asylums for the mentally ill and children's aid societies, opened their doors. State funds and private charitable administration often went hand in hand in both the old and new institutions for dealing with social problems. Much was done to make water supplies and waste disposal more sanitary with excellent consequences for reducing infant mortality.

Overall, however, there was no "welfare state" in Canada at the end of the period under study, despite pressures for reform from both advocates of the social gospel and from workers' movements. Apart from workmen's compensation, no major social program was implemented in Canada before 1914. Pressures from below over the next twenty-five years would gradually cause Canadian federal and provincial governments to implement reforms that had been instituted in Europe before the outbreak of the war.

NOTES

1 Edgar-André Montigny, *Foisted Upon the Government? State Responsibilities, Family Obligations, and the Care of the Dependent Aged in Late-Nineteenth-Century Ontario* (Montreal, QC: McGill-Queen's University Press, 1997), 91.
2 Michael S. Cross, ed., *The Workingman in the Nineteenth Century* (Toronto, ON: Oxford University Press, 1974), 195.
3 Lynne Marks, "Indigent Committees and Ladies Benevolent Societies: Intersections of Public and Private Poor Relief in Late-Nineteenth-Century Small Town Ontario," *Studies in Political Economy* 47 (Summer 1995): 61–87. The standard account of the development of social welfare provision in Ontario in the nineteenth century is R.B. Splane, *Social Welfare in Ontario, 1791–1893: A Study of Public Welfare Administration* (Toronto, ON: University of Toronto Press, 1965).
4 Mariana Valverde, "The Mixed Social Economy as a Canadian Tradition," *Studies in Political Economy* 47 (Summer 1995): 43; Bettina Bradbury, "The Family Economy and Work in an Industrializing City: Montreal in the 1870s," *Historical Papers* 58 (1979): 142, 145; Patricia T. Rooke and R.L. Schnell, *Discarding the Asylum: From Child Rescue to the Welfare State in English Canada (1800–1950)* (Landham, MD: University Press of America, 1983), 341–42.
5 James M. Pitsula, "The Treatment of Tramps in Late-Nineteenth-Century Toronto," *Historical Papers* 59 (1980): 130.
6 Ibid., 123.
7 Cross, ed., *The Workingman in the Nineteenth Century*, 209.
8 Stormie Stewart, "The Elderly Poor in Rural Ontario: Inmates of the Wellington County House of Industry, 1877–1907," *Journal of the Canadian Historical Association*, New Series 3 (1992): 222.
9 Montigny, *Foisted Upon the Government?*, 48, 99, 100.
10 Stewart, "The Elderly Poor in Rural Ontario," 224.
11 Cross, ed., *The Workingman in the Nineteenth Century*, 213. On the treatment of children in the late nineteenth century, the most detailed account is found in John Bullen, "Children of the Industrial Age: Children, Work and Welfare in Late-Nineteenth-Century Ontario" (PhD diss., University of Ottawa, 1989). Also see Bullen, "Hidden Workers: Child Labour and the Family Economy in Late-Nineteenth-Century Urban Ontario," *Labour/Le Travail* 18 (1986): 163–87, and "J.J. Kelso and the 'New' Child-Savers: The Genesis of the Children's Aid Movement in Ontario," *Ontario History* 82 (1990): 107–28. For a critical appraisal of the child savers, see also Terrence R. Morrison, "The Child and Urban Social Reform in Late-Nineteenth-Century Ontario" (PhD diss., University of Toronto, 1971), and his articles, "'Their Proper Sphere': Feminism, the Family, and Child-Centred Social Reform in Ontario, 1875–1900," Part 1, *Ontario History* 68, 1 (1976): 45–64, and Part 2, *Ontario History* 68, 2 (1976): 65–74. A sympathetic portrait of J.J. Kelso is found in Andrew Jones and Leonard Rutman, *In the Children's Aid: J.J. Kelso and Child Welfare in Ontario* (Toronto, ON: University of Toronto Press, 1989).

12 Rooke and Schnell, *Discarding the Asylum*, 312.

13 Joy Parr, *Labouring Children: British Immigrant Apprentices to Canada, 1869–1924* (Montreal, QC: McGill-Queen's University Press, 1980).

14 Among useful sources on residential schools in Canada are J.R. Miller, *Shingwauk's Vision: A History of Native Residential Schools* (Toronto, ON: University of Toronto Press, 1996); and Celia Haig-Brown, *Resistance and Renewal: Surviving the Indian Residential School* (Vancouver, BC: Tillacum Library, Arsenal Press, 1988).

15 Katherine Arnup, *Education for Motherhood: Advice for Mothers in Twentieth-Century Canada* (Toronto, ON: University of Toronto Press, 1994), 14–15.

16 Ibid., 21.

17 Neil Sutherland, *Children in English-Canadian Society: Framing the Twentieth-Century Consensus* (Toronto, ON: University of Toronto Press, 1976), 68; Denyse Baillargeon, "Gouttes de lait et soif de pouvoir : les dessous de la lutte contre la mortalité infantile à Montréal, 1910–1953," *Canadian Bulletin of Medical History* 15 (1998): 27–57.

18 Sutherland, *Children in English-Canadian Society*, 68.

19 Arnup, *Education for Motherhood*, 80; Veronica Strong-Boag, *The New Day Recalled: Lives of Girls and Women in English Canada, 1919–1939* (Toronto, ON: Copp Clark Pitman, 1988), 146.

20 Sutherland, *Children in English-Canadian Society*, 43.

21 Alison Prentice et al., *Canadian Women: A History* (Toronto, ON: Harcourt Brace Jovanovich, 1988), 187–88.

22 Patricia Vandebelt Schulz, "Day Care in Canada: 1850–1962," in *Good Day Care: Fighting For It, Getting It, Keeping It*, ed. Kathleen Gallagher Ross (Toronto, ON: Women's Press, 1978), 137–58.

23 Eric Midwinter, *The Development of Social Welfare in Britain* (Buckingham, UK: Open University Press, 1994), 78; Sutherland, *Children in English-Canadian Society*, 40; Michael Bliss, *Plague: A Story of Smallpox in Montreal* (Toronto, ON: Harper Collins, 1991).

24 Doug Baldwin, "'But Not a Drop to Drink': The Struggle for Pure Water," in *Gaslights, Epidemics, and Vagabond Cows: Charlottetown in the Victorian Era*, ed. Doug Baldwin and Thomas Spira (Charlottetown, PE: Ragweed Press, 1988), 110.

25 Alan Artibise, *Winnipeg: An Illustrated History* (Toronto, ON: James Lorimer, 1977); Herbert Brown Ames, *The City Below the Hill* (1897; reprint, Toronto, ON: University of Toronto Press, 1972).

26 Colleen MacNaughton, "Promoting Clean Water in Nineteenth-Century Public Policy: Professors, Preachers, and Polliwogs in Kingston, Ontario," *Social History* 32, 63 (1999): 51.

27 John Hagopian, "Debunking the Public Health Myth: Municipal Politics and Class Conflict During the Galt, Ontario Waterworks Campaigns, 1888–1890," *Labour/Le Travail* 39 (1997): 39–68.

28 Valverde, "The Mixed Social Economy," 44–45.

29 A comprehensive account of the changing character of Canadian hospitals in the early twentieth century is found in David Gagan and Rosemary Gagan, *For Patients of Moderate Means: A Social History of the Voluntary Public General Hospital in Canada, 1890–1950* (Montreal, QC: McGill-Queen's University Press, 2002). See also David Gagan, "For Patients of Moderate Means: The Transformation of Ontario's Public General Hospitals, 1880–1950," *Canadian Historical Review* 70 (1989): 152; Herbert C. Northcott and Donna M. Wilson, *Dying and Death in Canada* (Toronto, ON: Garamond, 2001), 21; W.G. Godfrey, "Private and Government Funding: The Case of the Moncton Hospital, 1898–1953," *Acadiensis* 31, 1 (Autumn 2001): 9–10; Paul Rutherford, ed., *Saving the Canadian City: The First Phase, 1880–1920* (Toronto, ON: University of Toronto Press, 1974), 7, 17–18.

30 James M. Wishart, "Class Differences and the Reformation of Ontario Public Hospitals, 1900–1935: 'Make Every Effort to Satisfy the Tastes of the Well-to-Do,'" *Labour/Le Travail* 48 (2001): 47.

31 See, for example, Gagan and Gagan, *For Patients of Moderate Means*; David Gagan, *"A Necessity Among Us": The Owen Sound General and Marine Hospital 1891–1915* (Toronto, ON: University of Toronto Press, 1990); and Mark Cortiula, "Social Class and Health Care in a Community Institution: The Case of Hamilton City Hospital," *Canadian Bulletin of Medical History* 6 (1989): 133–45.

32 Wishart, *Class Differences*, 27–61.

33 Prentice et al., *Canadian Women*, 160.

34 Kathryn McPherson, *Bedside Matters: The Transformation of Canadian Nursing, 1900–1990* (Toronto, ON: Oxford University Press, 1996), 4, 26–28; Yolande Cohen, *Profession infirmière : Une histoire des soins dans les hôpitaux du Québec* (Montreal, QC: Presses de l'Université de Montréal, 2000), 30–31, 84–85, 108.

35 Rutherford, *Saving the Canadian City*; Wendy Mitchinson, *The Nature of Their Bodies: Women and Their Doctors in Victorian Canada* (Toronto, ON: University of Toronto Press, 1991); Yolande Cohen and Esther Lamontagne, "Le bénévolat féminin dans le secteur de la santé : distribution de services et développement d'expertises" (paper presented at the Canadian Historical Association Conference, Toronto, ON, May 2002) ; Aline Charles, *Travail d'ombre et de lumière : le bénévolat féminin à l'Hôpital Ste-Justine, 1907–1960* (Quebec, QC : IQRC, 1990). On women's voluntary medical activities in rural Quebec, see Yolande Cohen, *Paroles de femmes : une histoire des Cercles de fermières* (Montreal, QC : Le Jour, 1990); Cohen, *Profession : Infirmière*, 30, 43, 84–85, 105–107.

36 Cheryl Krasnick Warsh, *Moments of Unreason: The Practice of Canadian Psychiatry and the Homewood Retreat, 1883–1923* (Montreal, QC: McGill-Queen's University Press, 1989), 173.

37 Donald Wetherell, "To Discipline and Train: Adult Rehabilitation Programmes in Ontario Prisons, 1874–1900," *Social History* 12, 23 (1979): 145–65; Peter Oliver, "'A Terror to Evil-Doers': The Central Prison and the 'Criminal Class' in Late-Nineteenth-Century Ontario," in *Patterns of the Past: Interpreting Ontario's History*, ed. Roger Hall, William Westfall, and Laurel Sefton MacDowell (Toronto, ON: Dundurn, 1988), 206–37; Peter Oliver, *"Terror to Evil-Doers:" Prisons and Punishment in Nineteenth-Century Ontario* (Toronto, ON: University of Toronto Press, 1998); Carolyn Strange and Tina Loo, *Making Good: Law and Moral Regulation in Canada, 1867–1939* (Toronto, ON: University of Toronto Press, 1997).

38 Sutherland, *Children in English-Canadian Society*, 103–104.

39 Ibid., 125–26.

40 Eric Tucker, *Administering Danger in the Workplace: The Law and Politics of Occupational Health and Safety Regulation in Ontario, 1850–1914* (Toronto, ON: University of Toronto Press, 1990); Jeremy Webber, "Labour and the Law," in *Labouring Lives: Work and Workers in Nineteenth-Century Ontario*, ed. Paul Craven (Toronto, ON: University of Toronto Press, 1995), 105–203; Robert H. Babcock, "Blood on the Factory Floor: The Workers' Compensation Movement in Canada and the United States," in *Social Welfare Policy in Canada: Historical Readings*, ed. Raymond B. Blake and Jeff Keshen (Toronto, ON: Copp Clark, 1995), 109.

41 Bryan D. Palmer, *Working-Class Experience: Rethinking the History of Canadian Labour, 1800–1991* (Toronto, ON: McClelland and Stewart, 1992), 155–213.

42 The debate on the real reasons for the introduction of workmen's compensation is sharper in the American literature than the Canadian. Contending views are found in Brian Robertson, *Capital, Labor, and State: The Battle for American Labor Markets from the Civil War to the New Deal* (Lanham, MD: Rowman and Littlefield, 2000), 232–37; Robert Asher, "Failure and Fulfillment: Agitation for Employers' Liability Legislation and the Origins of Workmen's

Compensation in New York State, 1876–1910," *Labor History* 24 (Spring 1983): 198–222; and John Fabian Witt, *The Accidental Republic: Crippled Workingmen, Destitute Widows, and the Remaking of American Law* (Cambridge, MA: Harvard University Press, 2004).

43 Babcock, "Blood on the Factory Floor," 115–16.

44 Michael J. Piva, "The Workmen's Compensation Movement in Ontario," *Ontario History* 67 (1975): 39–56; Ontario, Commission on Laws Relating to the Liability of Employers to Make Compensation to Their Employees for Injuries Received in the Course of Their Employment. *Final Report* (Toronto, ON: King's Printer, 1912–13); Michael Bliss, *A Living Profit: Studies in the Social History of Canadian Business 1883–1911* (Toronto, ON: McClelland and Stewart, 1974), 42; J. Castell Hopkins, ed., *Canadian Annual Review of Public Affairs* (Toronto, ON: Annual Review Publishing Company, 1914), 391–95.

45 Babcock, "Blood on the Factory Floor," 110, 116–18.

46 Gøsta Esping-Anderson, *The Three Worlds of Welfare Capitalism* (Cambridge, UK: Polity, 1990), 24, 59; Michael Sullivan, *The Development of the British Welfare State* (London, UK, Prentice Hall/Harvester, Wheatsheaf, 1996), 8; Robertson, *Capital, Labor and State*, 242; John Myles, *Old Age in the Welfare State: The Political Economy of Public Pensions* (Boston, MA: Little, Brown and Company, 1984); Midwinter, *The Development of Social Welfare in Britain*, 77.

47 Gale Wills, *A Marriage of Convenience: Business and Social Work in Toronto 1918–1957* (Toronto, ON: University of Toronto Press, 1995), 19; Ramsay Cook, *The Regenerators: Social Criticism in Late Victorian English Canada* (Toronto, ON: University of Toronto Press, 1985); Richard Allen, *The Social Passion: Religion and Social Reform in Canada, 1914–28* (Toronto, ON: University of Toronto Press, 1971). The xenophobia of many church-based reformers at this time is evident in J.S. Woodsworth, *Strangers within Our Gates* (1909, reprint, Toronto, ON: University of Toronto Press, 1973). On eugenicists in Canada, see Angus McLaren, *Our Own Master Race: Eugenics in Canada, 1885–1945* (Toronto, ON: McClelland and Stewart, 1990).

48 Christina Simmons, "'Helping the Poorer Sisters': The Women of the Jost Mission Halifax, 1905–1945," *Acadiensis* 14 (1984): 3–27.

49 Sara Z. Burke, *Seeking the Highest Good: Social Service and Gender at the University of Toronto, 1888–1937* (Toronto, ON: University of Toronto Press, 1997).

50 Ken Moffatt, *A Poetics of Social Work: Personal Agency and Social Transformation in Canada, 1920–1939* (Toronto, ON: University of Toronto Press, 2001), 23–28.

51 Wills, *A Marriage of Convenience*, 19.

52 James S. Frideres and René Gadacz, *Aboriginal Peoples in Canada: Contemporary Conflicts*, 6th ed. (Toronto, ON: Prentice Hall, 2001), 9.

53 Maureen K. Lux, *Medicine that Walks: Disease, Medicine, and Canadian Plains Native People, 1880–1940* (Toronto, ON: University of Toronto Press, 2001), 140.

54 Peter A. Barkwell, "The Medicine Chest Clause in Treaty No. 6," *Canadian Native Law Reporter* 4 (1981): 1–23; Lux, *Medicine That Walks*, 27

55 Canada, Royal Commission on Aboriginal People, *Final Report*, vol. 3, *Gathering Strength* (Ottawa, ON: Minister of Supply and Services, 1996), chap. 3, "Health and Healing," Available online from, www.ainc-inac.gc.ca/ch/rcap/sg/sgmm_e.html.

56 Lux, *Medicine that Walks* 153–54, 193–97. Another excellent study that contrasts Native and European notions of health and healing in the context of the colonial subjugation of First Nations is Mary-Ellen Kelm, *Colonizing Bodies: Aboriginal Health and Healing in British Columbia, 1900–1950* (Vancouver, BC: University of British Columbia Press, 1998).

57 Hugh Shewell, *"Enough to Keep Them Alive": Indian Welfare in Canada, 1873–1965* (Toronto, ON: University of Toronto Press, 2004), 166.

CHAPTER 5

War, Depression, and Social Policy: 1914–1939

On 18 August 1914, just two weeks after Britain declared war on Germany, the Canadian Patriotic Fund (CPF) was launched with great fanfare in Ottawa, with Canada's political and economic elite in attendance. Herbert Ames, millionaire footwear manufacturer, was at the head of this ambitious national organization whose goal was to care for the dependants of men who volunteered to serve in the Canadian Expeditionary Force. Branches of the CPF would be started throughout the country and the funds that they collected would be pooled to be distributed where needed most. The organization provided allowances to soldiers' wives and sometimes to their mothers, and arranged domestic jobs and housing for wives and medical services for children, as required.

Yet the CPF was reminiscent of other charities in that it advised and inspected recipients. Unwillingness to accept charity and concomitant intrusiveness caused about two-thirds of potential recipients not to apply. The charitable character of the CPF linked it to the traditional methods of dealing with poverty in Canada. However, its national and redistributive character—which was meant to ensure that recruitment in poorer areas would not stumble because of lack of funds to maintain soldiers' families—pointed to a future in which the national government would play a major role in providing economic security to citizens.[1]

Pressure from below for changes that went beyond charity increased as Canadians suffered from the carnage on the battlefields of Europe and from inflation at home that resulted from war profiteering. While the women's suffrage and prohibition movements won important legislative victories, victories on the economic front were harder to come by in the face of employer opposition. The Housewives' Leagues mounted campaigns for price controls on foodstuffs and other necessities, but the government response was timid. When the war ended in 1918, governments confronted a burgeoning and militant trade union movement, but state and employer repression, and a punishing postwar recession that lasted until early 1924, thwarted the union advance. Canada's elites recognized that some reforms were necessary to avert radicalism over the long term. In the private sector, reform took the shape of "corporate welfarism," which featured company-sponsored social insurance among other programs as a way to stave off unionism.

Reforms undertaken at the federal level in the first decade after the war were half-hearted: apart from veterans' benefits, there was a modest program of social housing, a national program of employment exchanges, and the introduction of legislation for a modest, means-tested old age pension, with financing shared by the federal and provincial governments. Most provinces, in turn, legislated mothers' allowances for widows and sometimes for deserted wives. While these programs benefited some poverty-stricken Canadians, they were poorly funded, and none stimulated the economy. Private enterprise, not governments at various levels, accounted for most economic activity. The state provided a negligible economic cushion when private investment decreased in the early 1920s and especially throughout the Great Depression.

Urban jungles, mass squalor, relief camps for single men, lack of provision for single women, and inadequate social assistance for families without a wage-earner prevailed in the 1930s. This provoked discussion about the need for the state both to support the victims of capitalist economic cycles and to invest public money when panic dampened private investment. The revival of radicalism by workers, farmers, and the unemployed forced both the established political parties and capitalists to consider seriously the need for reforms. Yet "reform" meant something different to the socialists and communists who called for massive social and economic restructuring than to conservatives who foresaw an increased state role in the economy that would actually enhance the power of the elites rather than compromise it. The struggle over how to finance an unemployment insurance program and what benefits to pay demonstrated the disagreements between conservative and radical "reformers."

THE WAR AND "REFORM"

The wartime mobilization of the economy had both positive and negative effects on the development of social policy in Canada. For many social gospellers and advocates of a planned social order, the extent to which the federal government could plan the economy in wartime was encouraging. Unemployment disappeared in the face of demand for both soldiers and munitions workers. Labour shortages led to government campaigns that recruited single women (though not married women) into manufacturing and skilled-trades jobs once reserved for men.

However, the conservative character of wartime economic planning provoked public ire. Conservative Prime Minister Robert Borden relied largely on wealthy business owners to staff the dollar-a-year jobs that headed the agencies established to mobilize the Canadian economy for war. However, as these wealthy corporate owners profited and inflation reduced the real wages of workers, there was a popular outcry for a greater equality of sacrifice among Canadians. The government responded only slowly and with little conviction, creating agencies in the later war years to control prices that seemed largely ineffectual.

The government also introduced allegedly temporary corporate income taxes in 1916 and personal income taxes in 1917; however, the level of taxes imposed was tiny. Corporations would pay no tax on the first 7 per cent of profits, and 25 per cent on all profits over that amount. Though average incomes were about $1000 per year, only single people making $2,000 a year and families earning over $5,000 a year would pay income tax. A married man earning the fabulous sum of $20,000 per year paid $2,460 in tax in 1917, and $4,085 in 1919.[2] The huge costs associated with fighting the war and the federal government's reluctance to commit to longer-term taxation bode poorly for postwar advocates of state planning as a way to stabilize the economy and help the poor. Though corporate and personal income taxes proved permanent, governments were reluctant to raise them more than fractionally in the early postwar years.

Some government responsibilities were inevitable after the war, particularly the establishment of programs to reintegrate able-bodied veterans into the economy, to care for the injured, and to provide for the families of dead soldiers. Veterans regarded these programs as restrictive and formed organizations such as the Great War Veterans' Association (GWVA) to fight for better provisions for veterans and the families of fallen soldiers.[3]

The two government agencies mainly responsible for veterans' affairs were the Department of Soldiers' Civil Re-establishment (DSCR) and the Military Hospitals Commission. The DSCR administered military pensions, retraining, and employment programs. While the government claimed retraining programs successfully aided four out of five enrollees, 80 per cent of applicants for retraining were rejected on the grounds that they appeared physically able to return to their previous employments. Only 7 per cent of injured soldiers were ruled eligible for pensions and 71 per cent of them received only 20 per cent of the maximum pension.[4] Soldiers whose mental health suffered from their war experiences were rarely accepted as disabled. Only in 1930, after years of lobbying by veterans' organizations, did one group of veterans—destitute men over sixty years of age—receive a fixed pension: $20 a month for singles and $40 a month for married men. Gradually the War Veterans' Allowance Act, which awarded these pensions, was amended to provide fixed pensions for younger veterans whose physical or psychological wounds prevented their gainful re-entry into the labour force.[5]

The government also introduced a Soldier Settlement scheme that provided loans to soldiers who wished to buy land and farm, but the government saved money by only making the loans available for homesteads in remote areas. Poor land and the government's unwillingness to allow for longer repayment periods to reflect the dismal harvests of the early postwar years doomed the efforts of most veterans in the program. Within five years, 80 per cent of the prospective farmers had gone bankrupt.[6]

While veterans were disappointed with the level of support they received from the Canadian state, victims of the economic dislocation occasioned by the closing of wartime factories and the postwar recession received even less support. The federal government's only response was to establish labour exchanges in the major cities which would attempt to match unemployed persons with prospective employers. Even these exchanges were abandoned a few years after the end of the war.[7]

As rural Canadians moved into cities to take factory jobs during the war, urban housing shortages resulted, creating high rents and overcrowding as families doubled and tripled up in their search for affordable shelter. Social housing programs had been undertaken in Britain and other European countries. Responding to provincial pressures, particularly from Ontario, the federal government decided to set aside funds for a modest federal-provincial program meant to make it more affordable for Canadians to build their own homes. It set aside $25 million for loans at a rate of 5 per cent interest to provinces that established programs to encourage private house building. But, ironically for a program meant to quell popular revolt, only the top 20 per cent of income earners could afford to build homes under the terms of the program.

Only in Halifax—where the federal government joined the British government and the government of the state of Massachusetts to help the city rebuild the Richmond Heights area which had been levelled in a horrific explosion on 6 December, 1917—were working-class people the main recipients of state housing aid in this period. The explosion was caused when two ships, one of which was carrying munitions, collided in the harbour. Two thousand people died and the buildings within a two-square kilometre area were destroyed. The Halifax Relief Commission, set up by the city, planned a suburban-style neighbourhood on the model of the garden-city movement in Britain which emphasized green spaces, play areas for kids, and community facilities within a compact neighbourhood. Altogether, 328 homes were built, all of hydrostone cement blocks, which gave the area its common name of Hydrostone.[8]

MOTHERS' ALLOWANCES

While the federal government rejected responsibility for providing income and social services to non-veterans after the war, the provinces faced increasing pressure to provide support for widows and their children and sometimes for deserted wives and wives of incapacitated husbands. A variety of pre-war reform movements joined the movement for mothers' allowances in Canada. Feminists, social gospellers, and the emerging social work profession, used somewhat different logic in their call for state aid to "virtuous" mothers living without a male breadwinner. While workmen's compensation, the major social program available to men, made no judgment of the moral worth of a recipient, mothers' allowances, the major social program serving women, placed moral judgment at its very centre.

The exclusion of single mothers from the purview of the reformers reflected contemporary morality and a rigid view of gender roles. Men were expected to be the income earners in a household, women the child-bearers and caregivers within the household. Women who had children out of wedlock were regarded as transgressors against this vision of the orderly, gendered household. They were expected to give their children to orphanages, which in turn, in the postwar years, increasingly sought to find adoptive homes that conformed to the preferred gender-role model. In Quebec, "the social stigma attached to il-legitimacy would pursue such a child for the rest of her or his life. The label was in the parish registers, and some religious orders did not accept bastards, hence denying them the highest aspirations of a Catholic."[9]

Feminists arguing in favour of state aid to widows and deserted wives stressed that women were capable of looking after their children without husbands, but they required state financial aid when a male breadwinner was unavailable so that they could keep their children. The alternative for mothers left with young children was often the placement of children in orphanages, since the costs of having someone care for the children while the mother worked would be pro-hibitive. Social gospellers, who focused particularly on the needs of children, believed that the state had a moral obligation to ensure that children were not separated from their mothers. Unsurprisingly, in Ontario, J.J. Kelso became an early and persistent advocate, and "child savers" generally viewed state aid to "virtuous" but destitute mothers as essential for preventing family breakups. For social workers, whose lobbying was likely most influential in convincing prov-inces of their efficacy, mothers' allowances were a perfect opportunity to create state jobs for the social work profession. Here was a program for which the casework method seemed a natural fit. The Social Service Council of Canada, where social workers predominated among the social gospellers, passed a reso-lution in favour of mothers' allowances in 1914.[10]

Provincial government reaction to the campaigns for mothers' allowances varied and demonstrated the differing patterns of social welfare that were aris-ing within the country. Perhaps unsurprisingly, the Prairie provinces, where the suffrage forces had won their first victories, were first to implement them. In Manitoba, the campaign began with charitable organizations experimenting with allowances to needy mothers. The Social Workers' Club of Winnipeg then conducted a study of mothers' allowance programs in American states, as well as a survey of widows. This resulted in a report recommending that the prov-ince initiate mothers' allowances, which the Club circulated to all members of the legislature. The report was soon embraced by the Convention of Manitoba Municipalities and taken up by the major women's organizations.

In 1916, the Liberal government of Premier Norris, which had been elected on a reformist platform that included full women's suffrage and prohibition of the sale of alcohol, repaid its feminist constituency with not only the vote but also mothers' allowances. Similar campaigns brought mothers' allowances to Saskatchewan in 1917 and to Alberta in 1919.[11] In 1920, British Columbia and Ontario succumbed to similar reformist campaigns. But the remaining four provinces held out much longer, with Nova Scotia acting in 1930, Quebec in 1937, New Brunswick in 1943, and Prince Edward Island in 1949. That year, Newfoundland joined Confederation and also implemented mothers' allowances.

Some provinces were far more generous than others. In 1942, for example, Alberta paid up to $45 a month for mothers' allowances and British Columbia paid a maximum of $42. By contrast, Nova Scotia's maximum was $15 and Saskatchewan's was $10. These disparities mirrored the contrasts in old age pension rates among provinces and demonstrated the difficulties faced by poorer provinces in attempting to provide for their destitute. While the rest of the country boomed from 1924 to 1929, the Maritime economies went into deep recession as soon as the First World War ended, and never recovered in the interwar period. A Royal Commission on Maritime Claims in 1926, headed by British industrialist Sir Andrew Rae Duncan, proposed federal subsidies to poorer provinces so that they could better discharge their responsibilities to their citizens. Prime Minister William Lyon Mackenzie King rejected this early proposal for equalization payments. With the Maritime provinces having lost many federal seats as population growth occurred everywhere else in the country, the region's political clout was diminished. With both federal Liberal and Conservative governments largely unwilling to increase taxes significantly, equalization would have to await a different political and economic climate. Meanwhile, the larger incidence of destitution in the region meant that Nova Scotia and New Brunswick, despite their harsh reliance on the poorhouse for dealing with indigents, spent more per capita on social assistance and services than the Canadian average. Indeed, in 1945, only British Columbia and Saskatchewan outspent these two provinces on a per capita basis.[12]

Did poor provinces have no options but to remove people from their homes and institutionalize them? Newfoundland, an independent colony, had per capita incomes as low as the Maritime provinces. Yet, early on, because of its dependence on a precarious fishery, it developed the practice of treating poverty as structural rather than the fault of individuals. While public assistance was never generous, it was offered to most destitute people in their homes without efforts to categorize them as deserving or undeserving, and without the erection of poorhouses or the imposition of work requirements. In the winter of 1932–33, perhaps one-fourth of all Newfoundlanders received public relief. Assistance "allowed independent commodity producers to remain in the fisheries rather than to be forced to sell their fishing equipment and rely completely on wage labour."[13] This differed significantly from the practice in

Canada's provinces of only supplying relief after individuals or families had sold all their personal effects, including their homes. Arguably, Newfoundland paid a price for using public relief to redistribute wealth, however mildly. In 1933, the colony was bankrupt and agreed to give up its independence to be governed by a British-appointed commission.

While mothers' allowances were too small in the Maritimes to prevent many widows and deserted wives from placing their children in orphanages and seeking paid labour, they were insufficient even in provinces like Ontario to keep most recipient families out of poverty. Ontario's rates were less generous than British Columbia's or Alberta's. In 1942, British Columbia paid up to $42 for one child with $7.50 for each additional child. Ontario's maximum rate was $35 in cities and $25 in rural areas for mothers of one child with $5 added for additional children. These rates forced most Ontario recipients to seek at least part-time paid work outside or inside the home to get by.[14]

Recipients often found themselves living in a fish bowl, closely monitored by the state to ensure that they were "respectable," that is celibate and obsessively house-proud. Mothers' allowances were administered by a provincial board staffed by civil servants, but the municipalities, which contributed a portion of the allowances, appointed their own officials to determine eligibility on the local level. In big cities, this meant work for professional social workers. Towns and smaller cities relied on volunteers from charitable agencies. An array of snoops, mostly middle-class women, watched over widows to ensure that they were living sufficiently boring, conventional lives to merit the mothers' pensions. Children's Aid Society volunteers, churchgoers, the men of Kiwanis, and others were conscripted into this army of moral regulators of women living without breadwinners in their households. The notion that women who received allowances must be dependents of the state was inscribed even in the more generous programs such as British Columbia's, which did not discriminate against deserted wives. Women with property valued at $500 or more, or who held $500 in cash, were deemed ineligible for allowances until the money was gone or the property was sold.[15]

The 1901 census reported that 13.9 per cent of households in Canada were headed by single parents, usually women, who, in turn, were overwhelmingly widows. Advocates of mothers' allowances largely fought for the widows because it was easiest to present them as morally deserving. Deserted wives were often excluded from mothers' allowances in the early years on the grounds that the state should focus on finding the deserting husband and forcing him to pay for the upkeep of his family. This was easier in theory than in practice. Society's negative attitude to divorce made state aid for divorced mothers a political impossibility. Single mothers were even more of an offence against society's gendered moral code. They were fortunate if municipal relief programs, where they existed, allowed them to qualify for aid. Quebec closed off even that avenue for single mothers and their babies as a way to survive. In 1937, the same year that it introduced La Loi de l'aide aux mères nécessiteuses, its mothers' allowance legislation, the Quebec government ordered an end to municipal relief for single mothers, forcing Montreal to cut these women from the welfare rolls. Racism, which was pervasive in Canadian society in the interwar period, also affected eligibility for mothers' allowances. In British Columbia, Native women and women of Japanese ancestry were specifically disqualified from eligibility.[16]

Ironically, though legislators claimed recipients should supplement mothers' allowances with paid labour, they opposed the provision of affordable daycare for working mothers. There were, however, some academic efforts to establish model daycares in the context of research on ideal ways to raise children. In 1926, the Institute of Child Study was established at the University of Toronto. The Institute and its laboratory school, St. George's Nursery School, trained nursery school personnel. A similar institute, established at McGill University, was short-lived. Nursery schools provided half-day programs to socialize young children. Their emphasis was on emotional development and social skills. While mothers working part-time might make use of the nursery schools, their primary audience was the stay-at-home mother who wanted her preschoolers to get a head start on school and to give herself a brief break from parenting duties.

At the time, the all-too-few daycares in the country were fairly bleak charitable institutions except for a few municipally sponsored centres in British Columbia. Toronto's Victoria Day Care Services, the renamed original Toronto crèche, was described in a 1930 report on Toronto nurseries as "barren and cheerless in appearance and quite inadequate for the 80 children who range in age from two months to 14 years. There were only six iron cots for the runabout children so two children shared a bed. There was practically no recreational equipment except a piano and it appeared to be unused."[17]

As depressing an environment as the existing daycares provided for children, at least these children saw their parent or parents at the end of their workday. A larger group of Canadian children with parents were in orphanages or foster homes. Daycare historian Patricia Vandebelt Schulz recalls that she ate her lunch in an orphanage when her mother worked, because no other facilities were available. Her half-sisters were placed in foster homes when their mother died, partly because no day care was available. And, in 1940, one of her school friends lived with her sister in the Earlscourt Children's Home, Toronto, although her mother was living and visited the children frequently."[18]

Working-class women with children, recognizing the precariousness of their position, campaigned in the interwar period for maternity benefits for all mothers. Instead of helping mothers financially, the federal government and some provincial governments spent modest amounts of money to aid and sometimes take control of the "child-saver" programs that had been established by volunteer groups before the war. The focus was on dispensing information to mothers about how to care for their children. Since co-operation with public health measures, increasingly under state control, became a primary emphasis of such programs, medical doctors were usually put in charge. The overall result was a state public health and child-saving movement whose eye was on improving childrearing techniques within the framework of an industrial capitalist system bent on maintaining the unequal distribution of wealth. Mothers were to inculcate the work ethic in their children rather than demand medical insurance and other social rights.[19]

OLD AGE PENSIONS

Apart from mothers' allowances at the provincial level, the major new state program of income support to emerge in the 1920s was the old age pension that was jointly funded by the federal and provincial governments. Means-tested, though unlike mothers' allowances not morals-tested, it shared several features with mothers' allowances. It designated a specified group of destitute Canadians as more deserving of direct state aid than other destitute Canadians; but it provided them with such limited support that they remained in poverty, though they were less likely than other poor people to end up in the poorhouse.

Provincial and municipal authorities continued to believe that care of indigent seniors was the responsibility of families. Ontario's Parents' Maintenance Act of 1921 allowed magistrates to compel children to make a weekly payment for the upkeep of indigent parents. Yet, despite stringent enforcement of such rules, the authorities were forced to accept that there were many elderly people without living relatives who could be tracked down or whose relatives were too poor themselves to care for a senior. These were the elderly people who, if they were unable to find work, ended their lives in the province's "refuges" or poorfarms. Counties, required by provincial law to maintain poorfarms, received no provincial subsidies to do so and hired untrained couples to manage them, making it clear that cutting costs rather than providing care was the condition for not getting fired. Elderly residents who ended their days on poorfarms found themselves living in overcrowded and unsanitary conditions, eating mediocre food, and enjoying little recreation and no privacy. At the Ontario County Refuge, even in the early 1940s, there were sixty-six inmates sleeping in the attic, nine in hallways, and sixteen in the basement.[20]

The social gospellers and social workers of the early twentieth century proposed that old age pensions, similar to the ones that European governments had passed before the First World War, be introduced in Canada as well. There was a gradual growth throughout Canadian society of the view that people beyond a certain age had earned the right to quit work and receive a state pension to maintain them. This was reflected in the resolutions adopted by the National Liberal Federation at their 1919 convention. With the support of Mackenzie King, who won his leadership at the convention, the Liberals committed themselves to establishing national programs for old age pensions, unemployment insurance, and health insurance.

But the Liberal victory in the 1921 federal election delivered nothing in the way of social reform. The Liberals were as determined as the Conservatives before them to avoid new national taxes and resolved to reduce tariffs, the major source of federal revenue, in order to blunt the regional power of the Progressive Party, which had emerged as the second biggest political bloc in the House of Commons during the 1921 election. The Liberals fell to second place to the resurgent Conservatives in the 1925 federal election. King, desperate to hold on to power, made various promises to the Progressives in return for their support. He also looked for support from the two Independent Labour Party MPs elected from Winnipeg, J.S. Woodsworth and A.A. Heaps. These two members, who viewed both old parties as tools of big business, took advantage of the minority Parliament to demand that King implement his pension promises in order to gain their votes of confidence in the government. King agreed, though he was willing only to support a means-tested pension at age seventy, funded half and half by the federal and provincial governments. In 1930, only 3.5 per cent of Ontarians and 1.5 per cent of residents of the four Western provinces had reached this age. King argued both the necessity of controlling expenditures on pensions and of not invading the provincial jurisdiction over civil rights and property.

Ironically, thanks to a scandal in the customs department, both the Progressives and Labour abandoned their support for the Liberals fairly shortly after making their deals with Mackenzie King. But King won the subsequent election, and with both Labour members returned to Parliament, he agreed to keep his promise to them. Legislation to establish a federal–provincial shared-cost program, the first social insurance program of its kind in the country, passed the House of Commons in 1927. As with mothers' allowances, the four Western provinces proved quickest off the mark in establishing a provincial program. Ontario followed reluctantly in 1929. The Maritime provinces and Quebec waited several years more, their reluctance to participate mollified by the federal decision in 1931 to raise its share of the pensions from 50 per cent to 75 per cent.[21]

The federal legislation establishing old age pensions restricted eligibility to people over seventy whose annual income was no more than $125. The size of the pension was reduced if the potential pensioner had assets that could be sold to provide a subsistence income. In several provinces, programs were in place to force relatives to care for the elderly before consideration had to be given to a pension. Ironically, in order to reduce state expenditures, governments were following procedures that penalized thrift and entrepreneurship, values that were otherwise espoused by elites in Canada. Differences in the generosity of old age pension programs among the provinces mirrored differences in mothers' allowances. Quebec and the Maritime provinces had tougher eligibility requirements than the provinces to their west.

In Newfoundland, old age pensions for needy men over seventy-five had been legislated as early as 1911, but the budget ceiling for the program was tiny and both the numbers of men allowed to receive pensions and the size of the pensions were modest. For needy older women and for men younger than 75, both under self-government and under the British-appointed commission government, institutionalization was the only option. The St. John's Home for the Aged and Infirm was understaffed and its residents were poorly fed and living in filth in 1934 before the government committed to policies of increased staffing and rigorous enforcement of rules of hygiene and cleanliness. However, its efforts to impose work roles on the elderly residents led to a residents' revolt.[22]

The existence of pensions created a popular dynamic of its own. While the state emphasized the means-tested character of the program, it could not hold back the tide of sentiment in favour of making such a program universal. While this did not happen until 1951, eligibility requirements were gradually softened in several provinces in response to a public opinion increasingly against the young being burdened with the care of indigent parents. The Old Age Pensioners' Association of British Columbia, formed in 1932, was particularly influential and spawned other provincial organizations. It proclaimed as its aims the defence of the interests of BC seniors, insuring speedy consideration of their applications, fighting for fair pension legislation, and "to preserve their status as citizens, entitled to pensions, as [a] social and legal right, and not by way of relief or charity."[23]

In Ontario, where the municipalities administered the old age pension and had to pay 20 per cent of the cost of the pension, there was a strong disincentive towards liberalization. Rural municipalities proved quite tight-fisted and the proportion of the elderly in Ontario who received pensions for which they applied was lower than anywhere else in the country, except Prince Edward Island.[24]

PRIVATE INSURANCE

For most working people in the 1920s, the state provided little assurance of income during a working life. There were no state programs of unemployment insurance or medical insurance. Only when all other sources of income had been expended could a working-class family apply for municipal aid, and in Nova Scotia and New Brunswick, such aid was only provided in the poorhouses. Little wonder, then, that when wartime worker shortages made it difficult for state and employer repression to prevent them from unionizing, workers organized in unprecedented numbers. Unions united workers in demands for better wages and working conditions and generally offered their members modest social benefits, including sickness insurance and death benefits. But during the postwar recession, a major employer counter offensive, aided by governments, smashed trade union power, and union membership dropped from about 380,000 in 1919 to 240,000 in 1924, with almost no recovery in union fortunes occurring during the subsequent economic boom between 1924 and 1929.[25]

Workers who had built unions and lost them sometimes received concessions because of their former struggles. So-called welfare capitalism covered only a minority of Canadian workers, usually those in mass-production industries and monopolies. Employers in large manufacturing firms, whether Canadian firms such as Massey-Harris and Stelco, or American branch-plants such as Imperial Oil's refineries, International Harvester, General Motors, and General Electric opposed unions as potential threats to management's rights to exercise whatever authority it wished. These firms also recognized that repression alone would not prevent workers from turning to the unions again nor would it encourage the labour force to be productive. Even before the war, a number of American companies had established "industrial councils" in which elected workers' representatives sat with management to discuss problems. Mackenzie King, having lost his position as Canada's minister of labour in 1911, had become a corporate adviser whose name became synonymous with "industrial councils." Industrialists dealing with militant labour forces hoped that industrial councils could co-opt the workforce and keep the unions at bay. Massey-Harris organized an elected workers' council in 1919 in Toronto while a metal-trades strike raged in the city. Similarly, BESCO's Employee Representation Plan in its Nova Scotia steel plants was introduced after the company had broken a union drive in 1923. In Canada, perhaps as many as two hundred thousand workers in the late 1920s worked for companies that sponsored industrial councils.[26]

Most of these companies introduced company welfare programs during this period. Sickness insurance and pensions were common benefits, and other benefits might include mortgage loans, but recreational programs meant to foster worker loyalty were also important. In return for company pensions and baseball tournaments, workers were expected to accept uncomplainingly speed-ups, close surveillance, compulsory overtime work, unsafe and polluted workplaces.[27] The limited insurance that such programs offered workers in comparison with universal state programs became obvious during the Depression. As workforces were decimated, most workers approaching retirement age were simply laid off without receiving a pension. Sickness insurance programs, established in good times, were curtailed or eliminated in hard times.

Unemployment Insurance

State policies that limited social spending mainly to residual social assistance in the 1920s contributed to the onset of the Great Depression of the 1930s. The move away from independent commodity production towards industrial employment as the major means of earning income increased the vulnerability of a growing proportion of the population to capitalist economic cycles. Influenced by both pre-war and wartime technological discoveries and the discipline of factory production, industrial productivity soared in the 1920s. But the benefits of this increasing productivity flowed quite unequally among sectors of the population. While dividends to shareholders fattened, industrial wages and farm income did not keep pace and workers could not take advantage of the new consumer products in the marketplace. Despite an increasing availability of consumer credit, inventories piled up. Greater bargaining power for workers and independent commodity producers might have helped, but state policies acquiesced to "yellow-dog contracts" (labour contracts in which a worker agreed not to join a union as a condition of employment), the blacklisting of unionists, the use of state power to assure the right of scabs to replace striking workers, and other policies that limited the ability of workers to unionize and demand better wages. Farmers and fishers were at the mercy of the corporations that bought their products. The Canadian Wheat Board, established during the First World War for orderly marketing of grain, was dismantled.

As it became clear by 1929 that industrial production exceeded the capacity of consumers to purchase what was being produced, companies began to curtail production. Stock prices declined and investment quickly disappeared. Factories reduced employment dramatically and consumption tanked, forcing firings in the wholesale and service sectors. Without a countervailing power to the marketplace system to stop such a downward spiral, the Depression proved a devastating decade for Canadians. Only wartime, it seemed, demonstrated that economic planning and government spending could easily end a depression. It required only political will.

There was no such political will in 1930. The political and economic elites defended the primacy of the marketplace, the morality of economic inequalities, and the inevitability of recessions. Governments presumed the Depression would be short-lived and were determined not to increase their debts significantly to help the victims of the vicious economic downturn. As unemployment rose sharply during the winter of 1929–30, the federal and provincial governments left it up to the municipalities to handle the growing number of indigents. Municipalities' only source of income was residential and corporate property taxes, which were quite inflexible. Property owners were quick to object if it appeared that anyone who could survive without it received "relief" and if the relief was greater than bare subsistence.

Nonetheless, the need to maintain social peace and to prevent starvation forced municipalities to stretch their social assistance budgets, once minimal, to unplanned levels. The consequence was often that municipalities went so far into debt that they could not pay back their loans, even when they ran the political risk of raising property taxes. Municipalities were also forced to establish permanent departments for public welfare, with full-time administrators, social workers, and clerical staff to determine eligibility for welfare, issue cheques, and keep tabs on recipients. The extent of destitution had overwhelmed the capacities of charitable organizations and resulted in a permanent shift of social assistance administration towards municipal and provincial government departments.[28]

The municipalities approached provincial governments for aid, but their revenues were also restricted by Depression conditions. So both the municipalities and the provinces approached the federal government for help in dealing with municipal relief. There had been some federal help for public works programs during the recession of the early 1920s, and the lower levels of government urged Ottawa to at least provide that level of support again. King responded sourly that he would not spend "a five-cent piece" to help Tory provincial administrations, a statement that reflected not only partisanship but parsimony since six of the country's nine provinces were governed by the Conservatives at the time. King reinforced traditional views of how the poor were to be helped. Their families were the first line of defence, with the municipalities coming next. If necessary, the provinces might step in, but the federal government simply had no responsibility for the unemployed.

King's penury contributed to his losing the federal election of 1930. The victor, Conservative leader R.B. Bennett, proved more willing to grant federal funds to the provinces so they could help the municipalities support the unemployed without any visible means of helping themselves. Over the next five years Bennett would spend over $200 million on such aid, an unprecedented sum, but it was a drop in the bucket relative to the needs of the unemployed. An estimated 26 per cent of the labour force was unemployed in the winter of 1932, "and this did not include the young, or the wives who had never had a job, or the destitute farmers and fishermen." Only a third of employables without work that year received some form of state relief though that figure doubled by 1936. In the winter of 1933, the 1,427,746 Canadians on relief accounted for about half of the unemployed.

All levels of government spent a total of $173 million on relief in 1935, up from less than $20 million in 1930. Initially, most relief spending was in the form of public-works employment at subsistence wages, with Ottawa and the provinces paying 25 per cent each of the cost of local public works, leaving the municipalities to pay half. Useful civic improvements such as the building of the Winnipeg Auditorium, Regina's dredging and beautification of Wascana Lake, and Saskatoon's repairs to City Hospital resulted from this program. But in 1932, Bennett's government concluded that it could not afford the greater costs associated with a works-projects approach. With federal monies shifted to direct relief, the provinces and municipalities largely followed suit.[29]

The impact of living on social assistance was devastating for families. Relief paid for only a bare subsistence—rent in an overcrowded suite and a minimal amount of food and clothing, with unavoidable health expenses covered in some circumstances. Families that had always managed to survive in the past, if only barely, suddenly required state and charitable support to keep alive. Not only did their economic independence vanish but so did their privacy, as an army of welfare workers employed by the state and by charitable organizations kept close surveillance on their lives and expenditures. In many cities, "relief vouchers" specified the food items that social assistance recipients were eligible to purchase, and stores required "reliefers" to line up separately from paying customers so that their purchases could be scrutinized. Women did most of the shopping in that period, and it was humiliating for them to be treated as if they could not budget the monies they received from the state.[30]

Single people, especially the young, were often ignored by relief authorities. In 1931, in Vancouver, about one thousand homeless men lived in four "jungles" in the city's east end—instant neighbourhoods of makeshift homes. "Near Prior Street, the men used packing boxes, corrugated iron, tar paper, barrels, tea boxes, and even old Ford cars found in the nearby dump to construct huts." They used water from a tap on adjacent city property. In the jungle under the Georgia Viaduct, one privy was shared by about 250 men.[31]

Campaigns by women's organizations, emphasizing that the only alternative for many was prostitution, resulted in some public assistance being provided for single women. But single men were regarded as a particular threat to public order. Public protests against state treatment of the destitute featured single young men prominently in their ranks. Such demonstrations, often led by organizations of the unemployed with Communist leadership, scared the state authorities. The solution of the Bennett government was to create military-run camps in remote areas to keep young males under tight supervision. From Bennett's point of view, he was defending public order, while from the point of view of radicals, he was defending bourgeois order, the system of inequalities that had produced so much immiseration in the first place.

Camp inmates received only 25 cents a day and were expected to work for their keep. While they were generally fed well, their living conditions were overcrowded and grim, since the government's goal was to keep the costs of maintaining the single unemployed as low as possible. Over one hundred thousand single men would pass through the camps from their establishment in 1932 to their abolition in 1936. Little more than inmates, they had no hopes of finding real jobs, of establishing families, or enjoying much in the way of recreational activities. The Communists' Relief Camp Workers Union (RCWU), which the military authorities tried to suppress, found little difficulty in recruiting supporters for its call for "Work and Wages." Essentially, what the Communists proposed was that the government move to shut down the camps and create real jobs for the unemployed, providing work in the camps at union wages in the interim.[32]

In 1935, the RCWU planned the On-to-Ottawa Trek. This involved having men from the camps across the country converge on Ottawa to demand better camp conditions and the union's objective of "Work and Wages" as an alternative to camps. Beginning with the inmates of camps in the interior of British Columbia marching to Vancouver, where local sympathizers housed them, the march picked up steam as it moved eastwards. Bennett, whose purpose in shoving the single unemployed men into camps had been to prevent them from organizing and demonstrating, ordered the RCMP to suppress the march at Regina and force the men back to their camps.

But the confidence of many right-wingers, including Bennett himself, in the efficacy of repression as the answer to protest had already been badly shaken. Early in 1935, in a series of radio speeches, Bennett had announced that the era of the uncontrolled marketplace was over. Government's new role, he said improbably, was to "be a permanent guide and regulator with the right and power of correction, with the duty and responsibility of maintaining hereafter in our whole industrial and capitalist system a better and more equitable distribution of benefits."[33] Much of what the prime minister proposed in the way of "reform" amounted to little more than state acceptance and regulation of price-fixing codes on the part of various industries.

A similar effort to tame the market had been tried by Franklin Delano Roosevelt in the United States but had lost the support of industry itself and ultimately the courts. Nonetheless, what the press termed the "Bennett New Deal" was modelled mainly on this aspect of FDR's New Deal. Bennett seemed less enamoured of the American president's embrace of pump-priming public works expenditures. He did, however, endorse the latest phase in the American New Deal: social insurance. While he spoke of health insurance and of a broader scheme of old-age insurance in his radio speeches, the only insurance program that Bennett introduced in the 1935 legislative session, the last of his term of office, was unemployment insurance.

The exegesis of the first unemployment insurance bill and of Bennett's "reform" philosophy divided contemporaries. Bennett's sympathizers claimed that the prime minister's conversion to a program of social reform was a heartfelt Protestant response to suffering in the country. His opponents suggested that his "death-bed" conversion was a cynical and ultimately unsuccessful ploy to turn his party's political fortunes around before the federal election of 1935. His failure to consult the provinces, whose acquiescence to programs such as unemployment insurance the constitution demanded, was cited as proof of his insincerity. The courts, in the end, struck down the legislation, a completely predictable outcome of unilateral federal action.[34]

It was, in any case, not radical legislation if one looks at the alternative that radicals were proposing. The Communist-controlled Workers' Unity League had gathered almost one hundred thousand signatures nationally in favour of non-contributory unemployment insurance. Put simply, this would mean that general revenues would finance unemployment pay, and the program could begin immediately. Such a program, which its supporters suggested should be financed by higher taxes on high-income earners, would indeed have produced "a better and more equitable distribution of benefits." The three Labour members of Parliament and the United Farmers of Alberta members who had coalesced with Labour in the fledgling socialist Co-operative Commonwealth Federation (CCF), had pressed the government to introduce non-contributory unemployment insurance. But Bennett was aghast at the idea, insisting that insurance meant collecting dues from potential recipients rather than from the rich. His bill provided for only one-fifth of unemployment insurance to be paid by the state, with the other four-fifths being provided by employers and employees equally. Because only those who had contributed to the insurance fund for a considerable period were eligible for a payout when they lost their jobs, the army of existing unemployed people could hope for no relief from the fund. The period for which benefits were available was tied to the number of months the unemployed person had worked before losing a job and limited to a maximum of one year. So the redistributive impact of the bill was minimal.[35]

Indeed, because Bennett and the actuaries his government consulted wanted to keep demands on the fund in check, the workers most vulnerable to unemployment, including most women workers, were excluded from coverage. In fact, less than three in five workers were covered. Farmers, fishers, and nurses were deemed self-employed and thus denied coverage; civil servants, including teachers, were deemed to enjoy sufficient job security and therefore did not require insurance. Farm labourers and loggers, whose work was seasonal, were denied insurance during the periods when no work was available in their field. Domestic workers, still the largest group of female employees, were also uninsured along with the pieceworkers who dominated the clothing industry and most part-time workers. Married women would be left without coverage on the assumption that they were leaving the labour force to have children and had no intention of returning to work. In short, patriarchal and class prejudices were deftly woven into the various clauses of the bill.[36]

When Bennett introduced his contributory, non-redistributive version of unemployment insurance, he was aware of the growing support for this measure among his capitalist friends. Bennett was an almost archetypal capitalist, having become a multi-millionaire through his involvement in the creation of monopolies in the grain elevator and cement industries, through his shareholdings in oil, tobacco, and packinghouse oligopolies along with the Royal Bank, as well as through his ownership of the monopoly E.B. Eddy Match Company. As a lawyer, he defended the Canadian Pacific Railway and Imperial Oil, among other large firms.[37]

Capitalists gave the prime minister various arguments in favour of unemployment insurance. Sir Charles Gordon, president of the Bank of Montreal and Dominion Textiles, argued from the financial sector's point of view. Municipalities, he wrote to Bennett, were yielding to pressures from the streets to be relatively generous in their granting of relief. While the modest rates of relief across the country might seem to contradict his claims, Gordon pointed to the growing number of municipal bankruptcies that were harming bank profits. Though the hotheaded single unemployed men had been relegated to the camps, there were a vast number of strikes by married reliefers, and that made it unlikely that the municipalities would get tougher with the unemployed and save their finances. From Gordon's point of view, unemployment insurance, if largely paid for by the workers' forced savings, would prevent future municipal defaults when unemployment rates rose. Other bankers echoed these views.[38]

The president of the Canadian Chamber of Commerce and the president of Canadian Cottons, A.O. Dawson, had incurred a bitter strike in 1929 when layoffs accompanied the introduction of assembly line techniques of operation at his plant. In his view, unemployment was an inevitable feature of the capitalist system; but, unlike the socialists who saw this as a reason to abandon that system, he argued that social insurance could help stabilize capitalism. Supporting unemployment, old-age, and sickness insurance, Dawson advocated that they be financed through a fund to which employees, employers, and government would make equal contributions. Many manufacturers echoed Dawson's views, adding that such a fund would ensure that unemployed workers continued to spend money while searching for jobs.[39]

Many capitalists, however, opposed unemployment insurance altogether. While bank and manufacturing firms, both of which operated in a national marketplace, supported unemployment insurance, the resource industries opposed it. Even in its largely non-redistributive form, it required contributions from employers, and the resource industries, focused on an international market, were less impressed than manufacturers with the potential stabilization of the national economy that unemployment insurance entailed.[40]

As Bennett's critics predicted in 1935, unemployment insurance did not withstand its referral to the courts by Mackenzie King's government, nor did a variety of other economic reforms Bennett had proposed. These included a national limitation of working hours to forty per week. King, despite his early rhetorical support for social insurance legislation, largely opposed Bennett's vision of the state acting as an umpire among capitalists rather than as a minor player in the economy, but he did not oppose unemployment insurance. Its popularity among capitalists, always assuming that the workers themselves paid a major share of it through monthly deductions from their pay, was confirmed by the recommendations of the National Employment Commission appointed by King in 1936 and headed by Arthur R. Purvis. The president of CIL and Dunlop, Purvis, whose firms' employment of new technologies had recently created job losses, recommended not only unemployment insurance but also a national network of labour exchanges, a national housing policy, and state loans for housing improvements. In short, he preferred a national approach to the problem of unemployment.[41]

Initially Mackenzie King was not convinced, though he shared Bennett's concern about the dangers of radicalism on the part of the unemployed. He had closed down Bennett's relief camps, regarding them as incubators for radicalism, and emphasized programs that sent young unemployed males as cheap labour to farms, where they were likely to be beyond the influence of left-wing organizers. Both fiscally tight and unwilling to do battle with provincial governments jealous of control in their own jurisdictions, particularly Ontario and Quebec, King responded warily to calls to attempt to relegislate unemployment insurance. A bill was prepared in 1938 for discussion with the provinces, but the government gave it little priority.

In the end, it was the Second World War that provided King with both a conservative rationale and a political window for finally implementing unemployment insurance painlessly. The conservative rationale was that the payroll deductions from workers and employers in wartime would provide funds needed for the war effort. Wartime mobilization of troops and industries for the war effort would wipe out unemployment, and so there would be few payouts from the fund during the war. That would allow federal loans from the fund to help finance the war effort. Once the war was over, veterans and wartime workers would have a fund from which they could draw when they found themselves involuntarily unemployed.

At least, male industrial breadwinners outside seasonal industrial employment would have such a fund, if they could land 180 days of employment in the two years before they became unemployed. The restrictions on eligibility for insurance that particularly hit women workers hard were retained, if sometimes in somewhat altered form, in the 1940 legislation. While gender-based contributions and payouts were not spelled out as they had been in the 1935 program, rates of insurance payouts were tied to income, a provision that penalized low-income workers, and therefore most women workers. The specific exclusion of married women was replaced with a transparent requirement that claimants be "capable and available for work," a clause which the Unemployment Insurance Commission would soon interpret to mean that married women were ineligible. Seasonal workers were still excluded along with farm labourers, fishers, and forestry workers. In 1940, only 42 per cent of Canadian workers qualified for insurance. Thus, actuarial ideology trumped notions of serving the interests of the unemployed in the original design of the program; only workers who were unlikely to face unemployment during good economic times were included. This would ensure that the unemployment insurance fund ran surpluses during booms that would pay for the costs of insurance during busts.[42]

The passage of unemployment insurance as a federal initiative would require a constitutional amendment, and this meant at the time that all nine provinces would have to approve the amendment. Most Quebec governments would have balked immediately, but the provincial Liberals, led by Adelard Godbout, had defeated the Union Nationale provincial government in Quebec in October 1939 with federal Liberal help. Beholden to King, Godbout acquiesced to national unemployment insurance.[43] So did Ontario premier Mitch Hepburn and Alberta premier William Aberhart, earlier opponents of a national program who did not want to appear to be squabbling with the federal government in wartime. In July 1940, King announced that the British government had amended the British North America Act to provide the federal government exclusive control over unemployment insurance.

The national character of the program was a contrast with its counterpart in the United States, which had been introduced in 1935 and placed the administration of unemployment insurance in state hands. Southern politicians, determined not to let African Americans draw much benefit from a social insurance program, had insisted on state rights and predictably such programs were marked by intense racism in the South.[44] Canada's program, by contrast, would be in the hands of a federal Unemployment Insurance Commission. This provided no protection against racism or sexism per se but it ensured that battles against prejudice regarding this program had to be fought at only one level of government.

Unemployment insurance, despite its conservative character, was a significant advance for Canadian workers. It provided recognition that unemployment was generally not voluntary and that at least some segments of the unemployed had a social right to state aid. Unlike social assistance, which was charitable and stigmatizing, unemployment insurance implied a social right. It was, however, a right that the King government, like the Bennett government before it, attempted to hem in within a framework that buttressed the status quo. As in Britain, side by side with the creation of unemployment insurance, the government created a network of labour exchanges to match the unemployed with employers. Government regulations were clear that, if necessary, workers must uproot themselves and their families from communities where they had relatives and friends and relocate to places where jobs existed. Rather than have the state plan to ensure jobs where workers already lived, it planned to ensure that workers were available to go wherever capital had decided jobs would be located.[45]

SOCIAL WORK DEBATES

The destitution caused by the Depression intensified debates in the emerging social work profession between conservatives who emphasized techniques for changing individual behaviour and humanists who focused on the need for social change. In the 1920s, advocates of the technical approach seemed to prevail. The constitution of the Canadian Association of Social Workers (CASW), founded in 1926, proclaimed: "The association aims to bring together professional social workers for such cooperative effort as may enable them more efficiently to carry out their ideals of service in the community. To this end the association may seek to promote professional standards; encourage proper and adequate training; cultivate an informed public opinion which will recognize the professional and technical nature of social work."[46]

Apart from CASW, which served as the social workers' professional body, the Canadian Welfare Council (CWC), founded in 1922, became the main voice for social work perspectives. The Council called for professional supervision over child placement and pressed the view that all children ought to be protected and dependent until their late teens. Charlotte Whitton, executive director first of the Canadian Council on Child and Family Welfare and then of the CWC from 1920 to 1941, provided a classic definition of the casework approach that both the CASW and the CWC endorsed:

> Treatment of every individual as a case different from that of every other human being, because each person is different in endowment, character, and circumstances from every other person; and the service which will be given will differ with this different character, his or her different circumstances, and background. Meeting the need of this basis involves the most patient and skilled inquiry of each application for help, with the purpose of finding out the fundamental cause of the person being in the plight in which she, or he, is, and of giving treatment that will provide material aid if that is necessary, but most of all personal understanding, advice, encouragement, character strengthening, and a plan to work the person out of this need as soon as possible if there is any hope of re-establishment.[47]

During the Depression, however, there was a new emphasis on state interventionism to achieve minimum household incomes via universal social programs. While social workers would continue trying to adapt individuals to their environment, the latter would have to change significantly. There was little point in inculcating a work ethic in individuals or building their self-esteem as contributors to society if work was scarce and the work that was available did not provide a decent standard of living. A minority of social workers, including activists in the CCF, embraced state planning and ownership of industry as the solution. They were opposed, however, by Whitton and other social work leaders who embraced individualism. But Whitton, whose individualism extended to opposition to universal social programs, was increasingly becoming a minority voice.[48]

Before the Second World War, the public voice of social work was largely male and was largely cautious. Though women predominated in the rank and file of the profession, the administrators and academics were generally men. Business leaders dominated the boards of social agencies and these agencies in turn were dependent on business co-operation to raise private funds and to influence governments to provide grants. The social work leadership believed that it was imprudent for the profession to publicly associate itself with radical critiques of capitalism. The business hold over social agencies had been increased by the formation of centralized financial federations in various cities, beginning with Toronto and Montreal during the First World War and extending gradually to other major cities in the interwar period. These were the forerunners of today's United Ways and Community Chests, and their goal was to co-ordinate fundraising for charity organizations.[49]

NATIVE PEOPLES

The interwar period witnessed a transition, though rather slight, in government notions about state responsibilities for the Native population. The colonialist notions that had governed Native policies did not change, and in official circles, there were no serious challenges to policies that relegated Native communities to the margins of Canadian society. Government and big business continued to seize lands that Natives had never surrendered or, indeed, had reconfirmed as their own in earlier treaties with the newcomers. Native parents, particularly in Western Canada, were still being coerced to send their children to off-reserve, church-run residential schools where their traditional cultures and languages were scorned. Questionably trained missionaries and RCMP men often improvised as health care providers, while the practices of traditional healers were suppressed.

In 1930, the federal government began to establish on-reserve nursing stations to deal with the horrendous death rates among registered Indians. The first of these was set up in Fisher Branch, Manitoba. By the early 1950s, the Department of National Health and Welfare operated thirty-three nursing stations, sixty-five health centres, and eighteen regional hospitals for Native people across Canada. While humanitarian considerations played a role in the establishment of these institutions, an equal factor was fear that tuberculosis, a scourge on reserves, would spread to the non-Native population.[50]

Corporate interests played no small role in bringing the government into Northern Canada. The Hudson's Bay Company traditionally provided relief to Natives involved in the fur trade when the fur supply or demand for furs was weak. If it allowed them to starve to death or move, the Company would lose its labour force and collapse. By the 1920s, however, with fur prices in decline and destitution among its Native workforce widespread, the HBC pressured the federal government to pick up the tab for the relief of these workers during hard times.[51]

In the short term, the steps taken by the federal government had only a marginal impact on Native health. In the 1940s, Natives had a life expectancy of only about half that of other Canadians. As settlers encroached upon their lands and resources, Natives experienced poor diets, minimal income with which to access a market economy, poor housing, and lives of despair marked by drunkenness, violence, disease, and early death. The modest expenditures of government on health were no substitute for an all-round attack on the causes of ill health, but prevailing opinion blamed Native peoples rather than their dispossessors for their plight.

The federal government proved reluctant to provide either health care or relief to Native peoples whom they regarded as the constitutional responsibility of the provinces. In 1931, for example, they drastically cut medical aid to the Inuit of Ungava, whom they maintained ought to be provided for by the Government of Quebec. Quebec disagreed, and also withheld medical care and social assistance while the issue slowly moved through the courts. In some communities, Inuit starved to death as the constitutional wrangling dragged on. They were unable to feed themselves since their traditional territories had been depleted of caribou, seal, and fox.[52]

As well, medical provisions were not made for non-status Indians and Métis. The situation of the Métis was desperate. An Alberta official inquiry in 1934 determined that up to 90 per cent of that province's Métis suffered from TB while paralysis, blindness, and syphilis were endemic in Métis settlements, which were small, dispersed, and lacking in resources. The province's Social Credit administration established six Métis colonies in 1939 where schools and health care service were provided, though unemployment remained rampant. Saskatchewan's Métis were even worse off, living in shacks without sewage disposal or water.[53]

By 1939, traditional perspectives on the causes of poverty had been radically shaken by the ten-year Depression. There were nine hundred thousand Canadians registered with the public authorities as unemployed in a non-agricultural workforce of about 3.8 million.[54] Remarkably, though, the interwar period brought few changes to Canada's social policies. The workhouses still stood gloomily in every county in Nova Scotia and New Brunswick, with direct state aid limited to small old age pensions in the two provinces and token mothers' allowances in Nova Scotia. Quebec's church-run social services still combined institutional support for various classes of the destitute, providing "legitimate" families with very modest outdoor relief. Wealthy Ontario's limited modifications to pre-war programs included only the poorly funded mothers' allowances and old age pensions, while agriculture-dependent Manitoba and Saskatchewan, despite being early participants in both of these programs, funded them on an even more limited basis. Alberta and British Columbia stood out as more generous funders of the two main interwar social programs and also proved more generous in the provision of social assistance to families in the 1930s than other provinces. But even in these two provinces, the 1930s were dominated by relief camps, soup kitchens, relief strikes, and generalized hopelessness.

While even sections of the corporate elite had begun to question whether the limited character of state policy made sense in an industrial society, divisions among the capitalists—along with federal–provincial squabbles and conservative notions among elites regarding government financing—all conspired to virtually strangle social advances. Though the clamour from below for change was impressive, the fact was that the state's repression and collaboration with industry's anti-democratic policies kept unionization limited and the voices of workers at the margins of state planning. All these obstacles to social advance would be modified during the Second World War, as chapter 6 suggests, with the legislation of unemployment insurance in July 1940 providing a glimmer of what was to come.

Notes

1 Desmond Morton, *Fight or Pay: Soldiers' Families in the Great War* (Vancouver, BC: University of British Columbia Press, 2004), 59, 95; Cynthia R. Comacchio, *The Infinite Bonds of Family: Domesticity in Canada, 1850–1940* (Toronto, ON: University of Toronto Press, 1999), 68.

2 R. Craig Brown and G. Ramsay Cook, *Canada, 1896–1921: A Nation Transformed* (Toronto, ON: McClelland and Stewart, 1974), 232.

3 Morton, *Fight or Pay*, 157; Desmond Morton and Glenn Wright, *Winning the Second Battle: Canadian Veterans and the Return to Civilian Life, 1915–1930* (Toronto, ON: University of Toronto Press, 1987).

4 Morton, *Fight or Pay*, 146–47.

5 Jeff Keshen, "Getting It Right the Second Time Around: The Reintegration of Canadian Veterans of World War 2," in *The Veterans Charter and Post-World War II Canada*, ed. Peter Neary and J.L. Granatstein (Montreal, QC: McGill-Queen's University Press, 1998), 63–4.

6 Ibid.

7 Georges Campeau, *De l'assurance-chômage à l'assurance-emploi : l'histoire du régime canadien et de son détournement* (Montreal, QC : Les Éditions du Boréal, 2001), 74–78.

8 John C. Bacher, *Keeping to the Marketplace: The Evolution of Canadian Housing Policy* (Montreal, QC: McGill-Queen's University Press, 1993), 55–61. On the Hydrostone project, see Suzanne Morton, *Ideal Surroundings: Domestic Life in a Working-Class Suburb in the 1920s* (Toronto, ON: University of Toronto Press, 1995).

9 Andrée Lévesque, "Deviants Anonymous: Single Mothers at the Hôpital de la Miséricorde in Montreal, 1929–1939," in *Rethinking Canada: The Promise of Women's History*, 2nd ed., ed. Veronica Strong-Boag and Anita Clair Fellman (Toronto, ON: Copp Clark Pitman, 1991), 333.

10 James Struthers, *The Limits of Affluence: Welfare in Ontario, 1920–1970* (Toronto, ON: University of Toronto Press, 1994), 21; Veronica Strong-Boag, "'Wages for Housework': Mothers' Allowances and the Beginnings of Social Security in Canada," in *Social Welfare Policy in Canada: Historical Readings*, ed. Raymond B. Blake and Jeff Keshen (Toronto, ON: Copp Clark, 1995), 124.

11 Strong-Boag, "'Wages for Housework,'" 124–25. '

12 Gerard William Boychuk, *Patchworks of Purpose: The Development of Provincial Social Assistance Regimes in Canada* (Montreal, QC: McGill-Queen's University Press, 1998), 28: Appendix, table A1.

13 Ibid., 39.

14 Struthers, *The Limits of Affluence*, 39.

15 Margaret Little, *No Car, No Radio, No Liquor Permit: The Moral Regulation of Single Mothers in Ontario, 1920–1997* (Toronto, ON: Oxford University Press, 1998); Margaret Little, "He Said, She Said: The Role of Gossip in Determining Eligibility for Mothers' Allowance," *Journal of Policy History* 11, 4 (1999): 433–54; Allan Irving, "The Development of a Provincial Welfare State: British Columbia, 1900–1939," in *The "Benevolent" State: The Growth of Welfare in Canada*, ed. Allan Moscovitch and Jim Albert (Toronto, ON: Garamond, 1987), 159; Margaret Little, "The Introduction of Mothers' Pensions in B.C.," in *Family Matters: Papers in Post-Confederation Family History*, ed. Lori Chambers and Edgar-André Montigny (Toronto, ON: Canadian Scholars' Press, 1998), 91–114; and Megan J. Davies, "'Services Rendered, Rearing Children for the State': Mothers' Pensions in British Columbia, 1911–1931," in *Not Just Pin Money: Selected Essays on the History of Women's Work in British Columbia*, ed. Barbara K. Latham and Roberta J. Pazdro (Victoria, BC: Camosun College, 1984), 249–63.

16 James Struthers, *The Limits of Affluence*, 29–30; James G. Snell, *In the Shadow of the Law: Divorce in Canada, 1900–1939* (Toronto, ON: University of Toronto Press, 1991), 262; Andrée Lévesque, *La Norme et les déviantes: des Femmes au Québec pendant l'entre-deux-guerres* (Montreal, QC: Les Éditions du rémue-menage, 1989), 136 ; Irving, "The Development of a Provincial Welfare State," 159.

17 Patricia Vandebelt Schulz, "Day Care in Canada: 1850–1962," in *Good Day Care: Fighting For It, Getting It, Keeping It*, ed. Kathleen Gallagher Ross (Toronto, ON: Women's Press, 1978), 143.

18 Ibid., 219–20.

19 Cynthia R. Comacchio, *"Nations Are Built of Babies": Saving Ontario's Mothers and Children, 1900–1940* (Montreal, QC: McGill-Queen's University Press, 1993), 14, 52, 83.

20 On changing attitudes to old age in Canada, see James G. Snell, *The Citizen's Wage: The State and the Elderly in Canada, 1900–1951* (Toronto, ON: University of Toronto Press, 1996); and Struthers, *The Limits of Affluence*, 55–59.

21 On the early political history of old age pensions, see Ken Bryden, *Old age pensions and Policy-Making in Canada* (Montreal, QC: McGill-Queen's University Press, 1974); and Snell, *The Citizens' Wage*.

22 James G. Snell, "The Newfoundland Old Age Pension Program, 1911–1949," *Acadiensis* 13, 1 (Autumn 1993): 86–109; Snell, *The Citizen's Wage*, 50.

23 Snell, *The Citizens' Wage*, 159.

24 Struthers, *The Limits of Affluence*, 69.

25 Bryan D. Palmer, *Working-Class Experience: Rethinking the History of Canadian Labour, 1800–1991* (Toronto, ON: McClelland and Stewart, 1992), 219–20.

26 H.M. Grant, "Solving the Labour Problem at Imperial Oil: Welfare Capitalism in the Canadian Petroleum Industry, 1919–1929," *Labour/Le Travail* 41 (1998): 69–96; Margaret E. McCallum,

"Corporate Welfarism in Canada, 1919–39," *Canadian Historical Review* 71 (1990): 46–79; Bruce Scott, "A Place in the Sun: The Industrial Council at Massey-Harris, 1919–1929," *Labour/Le Travailleur* 1 (1976): 158–192; and Robert Storey, "Unionization Versus Corporate Welfare: The Dofasco Way," *Labour/Le Travailleur* 12 (1983): 7–42.

27 Craig Heron and Robert Storey, "Work and Struggle in the Canadian Steel Industry," in *On the Job: Confronting the Labour Process in Canada*, ed. Craig Heron and Robert Storey (Montreal, QC: McGill-Queen's University Press, 1986), 226–27, 231; Palmer, *Working-Class Experience*, 278.

28 James Struthers, *No Fault of Their Own: Unemployment and the Canadian Welfare State, 1914– 1941* (Toronto, ON: University of Toronto Press, 1983), 71–103.

29 R.B. Bryce, "The Canadian Economy in the Great Depression," in *Interpreting Canada's Past*, vol. 2: *Post-Confederation*, ed. J.M. Bumsted (Toronto, ON: Oxford University Press, 1993), 470; Struthers, *No Fault of Their Own*, 60; Patrick H. Brennan, "'Thousands of Our Men Are Getting Practically Nothing at All to Do': Public Works Relief Programs in Regina and Saskatoon, 1929–1940," in *Age of Contention: Readings in Canadian Social History, 1900–1945*, ed. Jeffrey Keshen (Toronto, ON: Harcourt Brace, 1997), 316–30; Eric J. Strikwerda, "From Short-Term Emergency to Long-Term Crisis: Public Works Projects in Saskatoon, 1929– 1932," *Prairie Forum* 26, 2 (2001): 169–86.

30 Alvin Finkel, *The Social Credit Phenomenon in Alberta* (Toronto, ON: University of Toronto Press, 1989), 225.

31 Jill Wade, *Houses for All: The Struggle for Social Housing in Vancouver, 1919–1950* (Vancouver, BC: University of British Columbia Press, 1994), 60.

32 Lorne Brown, *When Freedom Was Lost: The Unemployed, the Agitator and the State* (Montreal, QC: Black Rose Books, 1987); Victor Howard, *"We Were the Salt of the Earth!" The On-to-Ottawa Trek and the Regina Riot* (Regina, SK: Canadian Plains Research Centre, 1985); Laurel Sefton MacDowell, "Relief Camp Workers in Ontario During the Great Depression of the 1930s," *Canadian Historical Review* 76, 2 (1995): 205–28.

33 Alvin Finkel, *Business and Social Reform in the Thirties* (Toronto, ON: James Lorimer, 1979), 36.

34 Partisan views of Bennett's intentions regarding the New Deal are found in Ernest Watkins, *R.B. Bennett: A Biography* (London, UK: Secker and Warburg, 1963); R.H. Wilbur, *The Bennett Administration* (Ottawa, ON: Canadian Historical Association, 1969); and Larry A. Glassford, *Reaction and Reform: The Politics of the Conservative Party under R.B. Bennett, 1927–1938* (Toronto, ON: University of Toronto Press, 1938). More dismissive is H. Blair Neatby, *The Politics of Chaos: Canada in the Thirties* (Toronto, ON: Macmillan, 1972). Neatby was the official biographer for Mackenzie King.

35 Finkel, *Business and Social Reform*, 83–85. The role of actuaries in influencing the character of the unemployment insurance program is documented in Leslie Pal, *State, Class and Bureaucracy: Canadian Unemployment Insurance and Public Policy* (Montreal, QC: McGill-Queen's University Press, 1988).

36 Ruth Pierson, "Gender and the Unemployment Insurance Debates in Canada, 1934–1940," *Labour/Le Travail* 25 (Spring 1990): 77–103.

37 Finkel, *Business and Social Reform*, 11.

38 Ibid., 86–87.

39 Ibid., 87–90.

40 Capitalist resistance to unemployment insurance is documented in Carl J. Cuneo, "State, Class and Reserve Labour: The Case of the 1941 Canadian Unemployment Insurance Act," *Canadian Review of Sociology and Anthropology* 16 (May 1979): 147–70.

41 Finkel, *Business and Social Reform*, 94–95.
42 Ruth Pierson, "Gender and the Unemployment Insurance Debates," 93–100; Campeau, *De l'assurance-chômage à l'assurance-emploi*; 116–17.
43 On the change in Quebec's attitude towards unemployment insurance and other issues of federal–provincial co-operation, see Herbert F. Quinn, *The Union Nationale: A Study in Quebec Nationalism* (Toronto, ON: University of Toronto Press, 1963), 105–107, 115.
44 Ann Shona Orloff, "The Political Origins of America's Welfare State," in *The Politics of Social Policy in the United States*, ed. Margaret Weir, Ann Shona Orloff, and Theda Skocpol (Princeton, NJ: Princeton University Press, 1988), 40.
45 Campeau, *De l'assurance-chômage à l'assurance-emploi*, 13.
46 Ken Moffatt, *A Poetics of Social Work: Personal Agency and Social Transformation in Canada, 1920–1939* (Toronto, ON: University of Toronto Press, 2001), 26.
47 Patricia T. Rooke and R.L. Schnell, *Discarding the Asylum: From Child Rescue to the Welfare State in English Canada (1800–1950)* (Landham, MD: University Press of America, 1983), 341–42; Moffat, *A Poetics of Social Work*, 27–28, 80.
48 Patricia T. Rooke and R.L. Schnell, *No Bleeding Heart: Charlotte Whitton, A Feminist on the Right* (Vancouver, BC: University of British Columbia Press, 1987); James Struthers, "A Profession in Crisis: Charlotte Whitton and Canadian Social Work in the 1930s," in *The "Benevolent" State*, ed. Moscovitch and Albert, 116–17; James Struthers, "'Lord Give Us Men': Women and Social Work in English Canada, 1918 to 1953," in *The "Benevolent" State*, Moscovitch and Albert ed. 137.
49 Shirley Tillotson, "Class and Community in Canadian Welfare Work, 1933–1960," *Journal of Canadian Studies* 32, 1 (Spring 1997): 63–92; Gale Wills, *A Marriage of Convenience: Business and Social Work in Toronto 1918–1957* (Toronto, ON: University of Toronto Press, 1995), 29–31, 43–45.
50 Canada, Royal Commission on Aboriginal Peoples, *Final Report*, vol. 3, *Gathering Strength* (Ottawa: Government of Canada, 1996), chap. 3, "Health and Healing."
51 Arthur J. Ray, "Periodic Shortages, Native Welfare, and the Hudson's Bay Company," in *Out of the Background: Readings on Canadian Native History*, ed. Ken S. Coates and Robin Fisher (Toronto, ON: Copp Clark, 1996), 83–101.
52 Walter J. Vanast, "'Hastening the Day of Extinction': Canada, Quebec, and the Medical Care of Ungava's Inuit, 1867–1967," in *Social Welfare Policy in Canada*, ed. Blake and Keshen, 48–52.
53 Murray Dobbin, *The One-and-a-Half Men: The Story of Jim Brady and Malcolm Norris, Métis Patriots of the Twentieth Century* (Vancouver, BC: New Star, 1981).
54 Ruth Roach Pierson, *"They're Still Women After All": the Second World War and Canadian Womanhood* (Toronto, ON: McClelland and Stewart, 1986), 23.

CHAPTER 6

Paradise Postponed, 1939–50: The Second World War and Its Aftermath

Public opinion polls were a new feature of Canadian public life during the Second World War. The polls told the politicians that an overwhelming majority of Canadians would not countenance a postwar return to Depression conditions. Most favoured the federal government introducing universal social programs, with four in five supporting both a tax-financed compulsory and comprehensive national health insurance scheme, and universal pensions for Canadians over sixty or sixty-five. A majority, impressed with the efficiency with which the wartime economy was regimented and the transition from a surfeit of workers to a labour shortage, also wanted a planned economy for Canada in peacetime.[1]

This chapter discusses the growing demands for welfare state programs from below during the Second World War, and state efforts to fulfil some demands and lower expectations overall. It looks at the politics leading up to the *Report on Social Security* (the Marsh Report) prepared for the federal government in 1943, and Mackenzie King's efforts to stem the growing tide of support for the Co-Operative Commonwealth Federation (CCF) by promising vast social changes. It examines both progressive and regressive features of the legislation of family allowances in 1944 as a vaunted first installment on the welfare state that Canadians were pressuring the government to create; analyzes why the King government largely reneged on its other promises, misleadingly blaming the provinces for its inaction; and explores changing attitudes of elite groups such as business and the medical profession towards social program proposals during the war when radicalism from below was common, and after the war as radicalism subsided.

PLANNING FOR PEACETIME

Early in the Second World War, the Liberal government of Mackenzie King had imposed both wage and price controls, anxious to avoid the cost-of-living increases that had radicalized workers and farmers during the First World War and created postwar unrest. King was also determined to avoid a repeat of the postwar recession that had lingered through most of his first term as prime minister. Having experienced the anguish and militancy of Canadian workers during the Depression, the cautious prime minister reasoned that a postwar return to Depression conditions could precipitate chaos and perhaps revolution. However, as a cautious man, King remained reluctant to commit his government to expensive social programs for which he would then have to impose taxes. Legislating unemployment insurance was a first step, but unemployment insurance alone would hardly keep the postwar economy afloat. King might have left the conundrum of how to balance the need for more social spending with his desire to placate the business interests which funded the Liberal party until after the war, but public skepticism that questioned whether he meant to act at all and a decline in support for the Liberal government forced his hand.

Popular demands for change were fuelled by perceptions that the government's wartime management of the economy was more solicitous of company profits than workers' wages. Labour militancy reached new heights despite government efforts to squelch strikes as impediments to the war effort without addressing the issues of distribution of wealth that they raised. A growing number of Canadians had concluded that a socialist system would work better for Canada than the capitalist system. Polls suggested that two Canadians in five wanted public ownership of the major industries in the country rather than simply state regulation.[2] In September 1943, the respected Gallup poll reported that 29 per cent of Canadians were prepared to vote for the socialist CCF in a federal election versus 28 per cent who would support each of the two established parties. The CCF demonstrated an ability to turn that support into votes in wartime elections. In a federal by-election in Toronto's working-class

York South in February 1942, an unknown CCF candidate, campaigning on a platform of postwar planning and welfare, defeated the former prime minister Arthur Meighen, who campaigned for conscription. Provincially, the CCF almost formed the government of Ontario in 1943 when they carried thirty-four seats in the legislature (they held no seats in the legislature before the vote) and the party won the election in Saskatchewan in 1944, carrying forty-seven of fifty-two seats on election day.[3]

By then, both the Liberals and Conservatives had begun to realize that they needed to embrace the less radical of the CCF's programs, especially social programs and a degree of state economic planning, in order to maintain their popular support and to prevent a peaceful social revolution in Canada in which the economic elites would be humbled. The Conservatives rediscovered the spirit of reform that they had briefly embraced when R.B. Bennett announced his New Deal. J.M. Macdonnell, president of National Trust, took the lead in committing the Conservatives to a measure of welfare liberalism. An unofficial Conservative conference organized by Macdonnell at Port Hope, Ontario, in September 1942 called on a potential Conservative national government to implement national health insurance, a national universal pension plan, a program of social housing, and even to guarantee collective bargaining rights for workers.[4]

The Liberal government had, at that time, failed to make its own plans for social programs known to Canadians, but it had taken several initiatives on the veterans' social policy front. Its first priority was to reassure armed forces personnel that they and their families would be properly cared for by their government when they returned home. There was concern that the common view that Great War veterans had been treated shabbily could potentially harm recruitment and troop morale. A special committee with representatives of several ministries was established in December 1939 and charged with identifying the problems that would arise upon demobilization. This committee's work led to the establishment of the General Advisory Committee on Demobilization and Rehabilitation in October 1940, under the direction of decorated Great War veteran and former Canadian Legion official Robert England.

One year later, influenced by the General Advisory Committee, the government announced pensions and post-discharge payments for veterans that were more generous than what their counterparts received after the Great War. Veterans were guaranteed the right to return to their former jobs or jobs "no less favourable" with the same employer at war's end, the right to free university education or vocational training, preference for civil service jobs, eligibility for unemployment insurance for up to one year, and low-interest loans to go into business. The following year, under the Veterans' Land Act, loans were provided for those wishing to acquire either commercial or hobby farms. The size of benefits kept rising as the war progressed, and the government's promises along with an initial budget of $750 million were combined into a Veterans' Charter in 1944. A Department of Veterans Affairs (DVA) was established to co-ordinate their delivery, and in the end, some $1.2 billion was spent implementing their provisions.[5]

Spending so much money on veterans made sense to the followers of British economist John Maynard Keynes, who gained influence in a variety of government departments, including Finance, during the war. Keynes argued that state intervention, both fiscal and monetary, was necessary to smooth out the booms and busts that characterized the capitalist economic cycle. During the Depression, he collected his thoughts on the subject in his book, *General Theory of Employment, Interest and Money*. Keynes rejected the view that markets were self-correcting and that the severity and length of the Depression were the result of government tampering with private markets. Instead, focusing on aggregate demand, Keynes posited that depressions were caused by imbalances between aggregate output and aggregate demand, and that the price system alone was unable to create a balance between the two. To the shock of orthodox economists, Keynes recommended that governments intervene mightily in the economy when it appeared to be heading into recession, using debt to finance state expenditures and reinvigorate the economy. The debts could be repaid when the private sector revived, at which time the state would retrench its expenditures, while using taxation to create government surpluses and prevent the private sector from overheating.

Many members of the Canadian elite, including Mackenzie King, were skeptical about Keynes's views; they argued that a headlong rush to expand the state's role in the peacetime economy was a prescription for economic disaster, or socialism, or both. King's decisions about how far governments should go down the road of state planning and social insurance policies would be determined by popular pressure rather than economic theory. Even the "Keynesians" within the government tended to reject the proposals of left-wing Keynesians, among whom one could likely count Keynes himself, that called for a permanent state presence in the economy large enough to assure that aggregate demand and output were usually in balance. Canada's right-wing Keynesians reduced the message of the British economist to an exhortation of timed state expenditures that would coincide with economic downturns, with spending to be eased during upswings. Even these moderate Keynesians were at odds with orthodox economists in their insistence that the federal government should prepare to shoulder a relatively large postwar debt in order to prevent the recession that a postwar economic downturn would otherwise bring.[6]

While some conservatives in the government believed that the generous programs for veterans represented sufficient investment in the postwar economy, wartime sentiment in favour of broad social policy initiatives made it impossible for King to follow their advice. His government established an unofficial advisory body on postwar reforms in 1941 and, in September, it became the official Advisory Committee on Reconstruction. Under the chairmanship of McGill University principal Dr. Cyril James, subcommittees were established to make recommendations on economic and social policy, housing, and the status of women.[7] However, House of Commons and Senate committees on reconstruction were also established.

The most publicized subcommittee report was that of the committee examining postwar social security, generally called the Marsh report after its chair, Leonard Marsh. Marsh had headed up an interdisciplinary social science research program at McGill University throughout the Depression years, and had been active in the League for Social Reconstruction (LSR), an organization founded by academics in the 1930s to conduct and publicize research that might lead to progressive social change. Despite a range of views within the LSR, the organization's overall perspectives were similar to the CCF's. Marsh's report endorsed a comprehensive program of social welfare and a government commitment to maintain high levels of employment.[8] His report was made public just two months after a parallel report on social security for Britain, authored by Sir William Beveridge, was released. Beveridge proposed that Britain's underfunded, means-tested social programs be replaced by universal social insurance programs that would provide cradle-to-grave security for the British people after the war.

Meanwhile the housing subcommittee, after amassing evidence of large numbers of Canadians living in overcrowded, or substandard accommodations, had concluded that the private sector could not provide adequate housing for Canada's poor. Its report, prepared by its chair C.A. Curtis, a Queen's University economist, recommended that governments in Canada had to take responsibility for building 30 per cent of new housing.[9]

The subcommittee on the status of women, while failing to challenge gender role stereotypes head-on, recommended that publicly funded half-day nursery schools become generally available to Canadians so that mothers had time away from their children, for paid work if they wished. It hoped to spare most mothers from the necessity of paid work by endorsing family allowances meant to supplement the "family wage" paid to men with monies required for the raising of children. It also supported the full inclusion of domestic workers in social insurance programs such as unemployment insurance and the protection of their rights as workers in federal and provincial labour codes. Perhaps reflecting the middle- and upper-class composition of its entirely female membership, the committee's recommendations regarding state expenditure to train women for the workforce zeroed in on domestic workers who were deemed in short supply. C.B. Macpherson, eventually to become one of Canada's most celebrated political philosophers, was a young Wartime Information Board officer when the subcommittee filed its report. His summary, to the Prime Minister's Office, nicely caught the committee's ambivalence as to whether to promote equity or to strengthen traditional family forms. Noting that the committee supported women's right to enter all occupations and to receive equal pay and possibilities of advancement, he added: "The right to choose their work will not necessarily operate to encourage large numbers of women to leave their homes."[10]

The Marsh Report, as critics have noted, assumed an even more rigid gender-role division. For Marsh, family allowances and social insurance programs that supplemented a worker's wages with a "social wage" were intended to make it possible for a household to be maintained solely by a male "breadwinner." In Marsh's universe, there was no need for publicly supported daycares, for training programs for women, for public services related to work in the home, or for other programs that might allow both members of a couple with children to work. As in the Beveridge Report, the male breadwinner/female housewife model was unquestioned and, indeed, said to be in need of state support.[11]

TOWARDS FAMILY ALLOWANCES

Mackenzie King and many of his ministers regarded Marsh's proposals, taken as a package, as too costly. C.D. Howe, T.A. Crerar, and Angus L. Macdonald objected to the redistribution of wealth that would occur if greater taxes had to be levied on the rich to pay for universal social programs that would benefit mainly those without means.[12] King worried that Canadians, while wanting reforms, would balk at the inevitable price of costly social programs implemented within the context of a capitalist system. In order to prevent a slowdown in corporate investments, the burden of taxation would have to fall on the working people, farmers, and small business owners who would also be the beneficiaries of the new programs. Redistribution of wealth would occur from the well to the ill, from the young to the old, and from the employed to the unemployed, far more than wealth would be redistributed from the rich to the poor. This, as King was aware, created the risk of a tax revolt against a government responsible for both taxing and spending heavily.

Aware, however, that the public temperament demanded a visible sign of the Liberal government's commitment to reform, King decided that the government had to legislate a major social program during the war. This could buy the government time while it pondered the costs and revenue sources for a bolder program of postwar social insurance. A family allowance, supported both by Marsh and the subcommittee on women, had much to recommend it as the first initiative for the government.[13]

In the first place, the government was concerned about keeping the lid on wage settlements and industrial militancy during the war. The unions insisted that the wages paid to a male worker must be high enough to support a relatively large family. Yet many male workers were unmarried, while married workers often had small families or grown families. Government-paid family allowances, as even some corporate executives with no overall love of government social programs argued, would weaken the union argument. A male worker need only receive enough pay to support himself and his wife. The state, rather than the employer, would provide the extra monies required to look after his children. In practice, King had no intention of paying anything close to the full additional costs that each child brought to a household. But even paying part of those additional costs from the federal treasury could help to dampen wage demands.[14]

If the government hoped to restrain the wage demands of male breadwinners, it also hoped to create a monopoly for men over most jobs in the labour force, certainly over the better-paying jobs. Single women would continue to staff low-paying clerical and secretarial jobs ghettoized as women's jobs, and nursing as well as elementary-school teaching positions would continue to be filled by women. Yet the government was determined to send the married women whom it had encouraged to respond to wartime labour shortages back to their homes.[15] In part, this was simply gender prejudice and a commitment to patriarchal hierarchies. It was also a product of the extreme pessimism, in light of the Depression disaster, that the economy could ever produce jobs for all adults who wanted paid work.

Family allowances were part of the equation here. They were meant to compensate women for a portion of the wages they would forego by leaving the labour force. As such, they were the carrot in a set of social policies regarding women that mainly relied on the stick. Federal subsidies as a top-up for provincially subsidized daycare spaces, provided during the war in Ontario and Quebec to make it easier for women to work in war industries, were cancelled. Only one thousand of a grand total of four thousand licensed spaces in Ontario were subsidized in 1944–45 and a fraction of those numbers were licensed in Quebec. Hopes on the part of equality advocates in women's and labour groups that the number of such spaces could be expanded were largely dashed by federal withdrawal of funds for child care. It was part of a concerted strategy to remove married women from the labour force. Wartime guarantees to veterans of a right to return to their old jobs cost most women theirs.

Though employment expanded in the early postwar period, employers were not required to rehire the women they had laid off as new jobs became available. Indeed, government advertising campaigns made it clear that the Canadian state regarded the accepted roles of married women to be restricted to the household. As a disincentive to married women's work, the government reduced the married men's exemption for husbands of income-earning wives. In 1942, at a time when the government wanted married women to participate in the wartime labour force, the Income Tax War Act had been amended to allow men to claim the full married men's exemption until their wives' income was over $750. As of January 1, 1947, that exemption, the value of which had been eroded by inflation, was reduced to $250.[16]

Family allowances had the support of most business groups because of their ideological use in fending off arguments for the need for "family wages" large enough to compensate fathers of big families. Unsurprisingly, then, the trade union movement was suspicious of family allowances. It was partially placated by government promises that such allowances would be linked to a broader program of social spending meant to ensure full employment after the war. King made a point of using Keynesian arguments as family allowances were introduced. Indeed, it was precisely the degree of economic stimulation that the allowances would supply—about $200 million in their first year of operation— that gave them the edge as the first social security program to be legislated.[17]

The Roman Catholic Church supported family allowances because Catholic families, especially in Quebec, were larger on the whole than non-Catholic families. Père Léon Lebel, a Jesuit who had campaigned tirelessly for family allowances since the 1920s, cited the support of the papal encylical, *Rerum Novarum,* for wages for workers that were sufficient to support their families. But he always used pro-natalist arguments as well to ensure the support of the Catholic hierarchy. The size of average French-Canadian families was, in fact, falling steeply throughout the twentieth century despite Church teachings against birth control. Women who were born in the late nineteenth century and married had an average of 6.4 children, while their counterparts born between 1910 and 1920 had an average of 4.4. In the minds of many non-Catholics, however, the presence of families of ten or twelve children in rural Quebec loomed large. Just as the Catholic Church regarded family allowances as an incentive for families to have children, many opponents of allowances rejected such social payments because they potentially discouraged family planning. Support for family planning and anti-Catholicism often seemed to go together in the propaganda of "baby bonus" opponents. Charlotte Whitton's breach with her fellow social workers grew wider when she published *The Dawn of an Ampler Life,* which accepted state intervention to ensure better wages for male "breadwinners" but vociferously opposed family allowances with arguments tainted by paranoid anti-Catholicism.[18]

No political party was disposed to join the hysterical opposition of anti-Catholics to family allowances, though some Conservative MPs shared Whitton's views. The government, not wishing to appear as if it were providing an incentive to couples to have large families, scrapped its plans to make the "baby bonus" a flat payout for each child. Instead, families would receive a smaller payment for all children beyond the fourth. The initial payment set for family allowances in 1945 was between $5 and $8 per child, depending on the child's age.

Family allowances provided a large increase in the standard of living for the poorest families and were a welcome addition to the income of most families. Though some MPs insisted that the allowance should be sent to fathers as the "heads of household," the government acceded to the pressures from women's groups such as the NCWC to send the cheques to mothers. For many housewives, the monthly family allowance cheque was the only family money over which they could exercise any discretion.[19]

Family allowances also played a progressive role in Quebec by encouraging families to keep their children in school longer. Clerical opposition to state intervention in education, along with employer opposition and the opposition of families who needed both the waged and unpaid labour of their children to survive, had delayed efforts to pass compulsory schooling in the province. Only in 1943, during the relatively progressive regime of Liberal Adelard Godbout, did Quebec finally legislate mandatory schooling to age fifteen. But Maurice Duplessis, who was returned to power in 1944, refused to enforce a law that he claimed transferred control over children from parents to the state. By that time, the Roman Catholic Church in Quebec did not share Duplessis's traditionalist views regarding schooling. Anxious that the industrial backwardness of the province had resulted in a continuing large-scale exodus of French-Canadians, the Church moved away from its long-standing idealization of rural life. If the flock were to be kept within the province, it was necessary for the province to industrialize under the leadership of well-educated French-Canadians at all levels. [20]

How, then, to ensure that French-Canadian parents, most of whom had received little education, did not pull their children out of school at a young age? The Church, which controlled the Catholic school boards throughout the province, decided that if the Quebec government would not put pressure on parents to keep their children in school it would turn to the federal government as an alternative partner in enforcing mandatory schooling. Under the family allowances legislation, parents who had not received special permission from the authorities to let their children leave school before turning fifteen did not receive a family allowance payment for those children. However, the family allowances bureaucracy could only determine which families were affected if it received information from the school boards about which children had withdrawn from school. The Catholic school boards surreptitiously provided this information. [21]

The use of family allowances to force children to attend school may be seen as using the state to impose a social right, in this case the right of all children to an education. Yet for some, this compulsion interfered with equally important rights. In the Northwest Territories and the Yukon, administrators decreed that parents who took their children with them as they hunted rather than sending them to school on a regular basis would be deprived of family allowances. This, added to the threat that children who did not attend school would be apprehended, forced many families to break with their traditional lifestyles and live in towns so that their children could attend school regularly. [22]

National surveys suggested that, in the late 1940s, larger working-class and rural families gained between 10 and 20 per cent of their incomes from family allowances; for many families on social assistance, it provided more than a third of household income. Over time, though, the value of the allowances was eroded by inflation, and the federal government simply refused to increase the amount. The government was unmoved by letters and petitions from labour and women's groups calling for indexation. Father Lebel noted, with frustration, that in 1951, with milk retailing at 19 cents a pint, "the monthly allowance of $5.00 given for children of less than six years does not even pay for the pint of milk that doctors recommend as the daily requirement for children and adolescents to ensure the normal development of their body."[23] The government's parsimony in this area reflected a broader postwar retrenchment from wartime promises.

REFORM HITS AN IMPASSE

The three major parties made bold social policy promises during the 1945 federal election. Both of the mainstream pro-capitalist parties attempted to outflank the CCF by promising that cradle-to-grave social security could be made available to Canadians without the need to place industry under state ownership. Along with programs of planned public works intended to ensure full employment, social security programs were meant to guarantee Canadians against fears that old age, illness, or the operations of the business cycle would ever reduce them to destitution again. The CCF won only twenty-eight seats and 15.6 per cent of the vote, just half of the support that national polling had suggested they might win three years earlier. The Liberal and Conservative endorsement of a comprehensive program of social security, or the "welfare state" as it soon came to be identified, allowed these parties to remain Canada's leading political forces.

As the sitting government, Mackenzie King's Liberals had advantages over the Conservatives. Both the party's Veterans' Charter and family allowances programs were in place for the June 1945 election. One month after the election, King's government issued a Green Book entitled *Proposals of the Government of Canada*. These proposals would become the basis for meetings with the provinces to determine the final shape of the emerging Canadian welfare state. The proposals included a universal and nationwide health insurance program, a universal pension program for Canadians sixty-five and older, an extension of federal responsibility for the unemployed to include all employables, and generous federal subsidies for provincial public works. While costs for medical insurance would be shared by the federal and provincial governments, the pension would be funded by the federal government alone.[24]

The federal government was aware of the likely costs of its sweeping reforms. The Department of Finance was primarily concerned with keeping investors happy. If taxation levels on the wealthy and on corporations ran too high, there was a risk of a capital strike. That would leave the federal government with the unpalatable options of either allowing a major recession to occur or of following CCF prescriptions for government operation of the commanding heights of the economy. It was pressure from Finance that tipped the balance in favour of the opponents of social insurance in cabinet in early 1943 when the Department of Pensions and Health proposed a detailed scheme for national health insurance. The following year, Finance Minister J.L. Ilsley encouraged King to ensure investors that demobilization would be accompanied by lower taxes on businesses. He indicated that "a great deal of spending by private industry will shortly be held up if it is not already delayed for lack of any decision as to the tax treatment to be accorded desirable new investment in the period of demobilization."[25]

With Finance concerned to keep taxation within bounds, the Green Book demanded that the federal government become the only significant tax jurisdiction in the country. Specifically, it called for an extension into peacetime of the wartime practice of leaving the national government in full control of income tax on individuals and corporations, along with succession duties. Ottawa would then give the provinces 5 per cent of the money it had collected, to be distributed on a per capita basis. The provinces responded angrily. With citizens clamouring for new schools and highways and better subsidization for hospitals, and municipalities wanting aid with their infrastructural projects, provincial governments needed some flexibility to collect the most lucrative sources of tax: personal income, corporate profits, and death duties.[26]

Provincial opposition was led by Premiers George Drew of Ontario, Maurice Duplessis of Quebec, and Angus L. Macdonald of Nova Scotia. All three were crusty conservative opponents of social insurance and long-time opponents of federal intervention in areas of provincial jurisdiction. This would make it relatively easy later on for the King government to paint a picture in which reactionary premiers destroyed the hopes of a progressive prime minister bent on providing Canadians with cradle-to-grave social security. Historians often accept this portrait of why the federal Liberals' 1945 election promises of social security were all broken.[27] The cynical Liberal mythology notwithstanding, it ignores the larger blame that points to a King government too attuned to the desires of capital to fulfil its election pledges to the people.

The Dominion-Provincial Conference on Reconstruction, organized by King to discuss the Green Book proposals, had its first meetings from 6 August to 10 August 1945. Though the meetings produced a co-ordinating committee consisting of the prime minister and premiers to deal with the issues raised by the Green Book, the premiers were united in their opposition to the centralization of spending and taxing powers in federal hands. Over the next nine months, bureaucrats and cabinet ministers in the federal and provincial governments locked horns on a variety of issues, touching on both social security and taxation.[28]

In his private diaries, Mackenzie King indicated a degree of sympathy with the provincial position that he could never hint at publicly. He regarded the Finance-driven federal position to be unacceptably rigid.[29] There were, as some premiers noted, several ways to break the impasse with the provinces. One was to decouple the social security proposals from the issue of taxation. That would allow the provinces the freedom to raise funds as required to fulfil their duties in the jurisdictions reserved for them by the constitution. The provinces would be placed on the defensive if they tried to prevent social security programs from being legislated for ideological reasons or purely from provincial jealousy of the federal government invading their areas of jurisdiction. But such a decoupling was anathema to Finance and the business community since it raised the prospects of two levels of government taxing and spending with little co-ordination. Another approach might be to follow Angus Macdonald's suggestion to yield the entire field of succession duties to the provinces, to increase the share of corporate and personal income taxes turned over to the premiers, and to foreswear federal rights to a variety of minor taxes, such as fuel and entertainment taxes.

King chose instead to simply fall in line with Finance, insisting that the taxation and social security proposals were linked and non-negotiable, well aware that such an approach would scuttle federal–provincial co-operation regarding the social security proposals in the Green Book. As King's diaries reveal, he had decided that he wanted to shelve the social security program that he had promised the Canadian people. King's conservative economic views influenced his decision. "The argument that our taxes may still be lowered, notwithstanding these increases in contributions to the provinces, is that by this method production can be kept at a high level…[to] permit of increased volume of taxation," he wrote, adding that his own perspective differed: "sooner than later, and perhaps sooner than expected, there could be a complete collapse and depression, as a result of the war financing and the liabilities it has left." Ignoring his wartime and election promises, not to mention the Green Book proposals to which he was supposed to be committed, King confided in his diary: "While I am wholly sympathetic with doing everything to promote health and welfare matters, I do feel that this will have to come very gradually and the people in Canada are in a more fortunate position in dealing with these questions than are the peoples of any other country."[30]

King's new goals were tax reduction and a balanced budget, hardly Keynesian tools for maintaining an economy that was losing war-created employment. Commenting on Minister of National Health and Welfare Brooke Claxton's impassioned defence at the last dominion–provincial plenary of the Green Book social security initiatives, King wrote: "Claxton...has pushed the social legislation to make too many commitments for legislation involving more in the way of taxation by a levy on all classes. I am going to advise Ilsley against doing anything in the budget which means the imposition of further taxes." The wily prime minister told his astounded cabinet in early May that he intended neither to continue the plenary sessions with the provinces regarding the Green Book nor to introduce any new universal social programs during the electoral mandate he had been given just a year before. With the first of the family allowances cheques having been mailed in mid-1945, King felt "that was as far as we should think of going into that class of expenditure until the end of another four or five years." Even health insurance, which he had pledged to Canadians many times, had to be delayed because "we have gotten in far too deeply in the matter of public outlays."[31]

Some cabinet ministers were shocked at King's complete turnaround on social reform, but none left the cabinet over the issue. Instead the federal Liberals successfully pinned the blame for the failure of the Green Book discussions on the premiers.[32] The federal Liberal Party, as a result, suffered no political fallout from its reversal on the issue of comprehensive social security for Canadians.

No doubt, the King government's generous spending on family allowances and the Veterans' Charter programs contributed to the view that the Liberals remained committed to an extension of social reforms. Historian Jeff Keshen suggests: "Not only did World War II result in the defeat of an unquestioned evil, but it helped usher in what most people today consider to be a more humane approach to social and economic affairs. In this development, the Veterans Charter played a major and often pioneering role."[33] The opposite, however, may be the case. As King looked at the financial outlays promised to take care of the veterans, and thought of the taxes required to fund both such outlays and new universal social programs, he balked at the latter. The Charter may indirectly have prompted a huge delay in promised universal programs.

WHY PARADISE WAS POSTPONED

The June 1945 federal election, and the Ontario provincial election that preceded it by six weeks, suggested that the tide of reformism was receding. The

CCF had gone from thirty-four seats and second place in the Ontario legislature to a mere eight seats and third place. As the much-anticipated postwar recession failed to occur, thanks to the government's spending on veterans' programs and family allowances as well as consumer spending of wartime savings, the consensus in favour of reform faded.

The business community, which had been divided in the 1930s on the need for government intervention in the economy, was never completely united, even during the war. However, if only because business leaders feared the CCF and its program of nationalization of industry, most acquiesced publicly to the implementation of social insurance programs, always with the proviso that they must be funded on an actuarial basis so that they did not result in a massive transfer of wealth from the rich to the poor. In this sense, J.M. Macdonnell was no business maverick as he led the Conservative Party effort to nail the masthead of reform to the party platform.

P.S. Fisher, vice-president of Southam Company Ltd., the country's largest newspaper conglomerate, and chair of the Canadian Chamber of Commerce's Postwar Planning Committee, reflected this reformism in an appearance before the House of Commons Special Committee on Reconstruction and Re-establishment in 1943. He commented that "removal of want is not enough. We need, instead, something like a new Bill of Rights for the Canadians of tomorrow." Such a bill of rights would provide for contributory programs to ensure Canadians need not live in fear of illness, old age, or involuntary unemployment. The business community, it appears, wanted to rid itself of the image of greed that was fuelling socialist demands for an end to private ownership. Addressing the Chamber's annual convention in 1943, Fisher presented a conservative vision of social reform in which private enterprise would continue to control the economy, but state bodies would have the responsibility to ensure that employment levels were high and that those unable to work for whatever reason were cared for without private businesses having to assume the costs: "I have suggested that the job of business is in the main to produce, and the job of Government is in the main to regulate. The depression of the 1930s was primarily the result of a breakdown in international and in national regulation. It was essentially a failure of Government. The fact that individual businesses by individual mistakes made the total situation worse did not shift the fundamental responsibility."[34]

Postwar prosperity and the decline in popular socialist fervour emboldened free enterprisers. There were no more speeches before the Chamber by executive members supporting new programs of social spending. Indeed, in 1948, the Chamber indicated explicitly its opposition to any new social spending that required increased business taxes, suggesting that this would reduce capital available for investment in Canada.[35]

One year later, both the medical profession and the life insurance industry withdrew their wartime support for state medical insurance. In 1943, the Canadian Medical Association (CMA) and the Canadian Dental Association (CDA) informed the House of Commons Special Committee on Social Security of their support respectively for compulsory medical insurance and compulsory dental health insurance. Both physicians and dentists had experienced economic hardships in the 1930s when many of their patients were simply unable to pay for treatment. The existing voluntary medical insurance schemes were neither comprehensive nor well subscribed. The CMA noted loftily that patient health was too precious to be compromised by lack of income. Dr. A.E. Archer, president of the CMA when it supported public health insurance, later indicated particular concerns regarding the future of the two thousand or so young doctors who would be demobilized at war's end without ever having operated a private practice, and the likelihood of rural areas and poor regions attracting such doctors. "For these two problems we should consider ourselves fortunate if a health insurance scheme is ready to operate at the time of demobilization."[36]

As the end of the war approached, the prospects of a postwar depression dimmed. The CMA, at its national convention in June 1945, while reiterating support for a national medicare scheme, called for its implementation to be delayed to some unspecified time in the future so that government funding could be directed towards a program of hospital building and improvement. Meanwhile, it suggested that an experimental local program be put in place to determine what the real costs of a compulsory program operating nationwide might be.[37] This cooling down of support gradually led to CMA criticisms of a government-based medical program, and in 1949 it passed a resolution that marked the organization's formal flip-flop on medicare.

There were signs that less elite groups than big business and physicians were also unprepared to pay for the costs of a comprehensive program of social security after the war. For example, the trade union movement, the spearhead of initiatives for social reform during the war, was now at best divided as to how quickly governments should move to implement new programs. The Canadian Congress of Labour (CCL), the upstart organization of industrial unions, was committed to an advanced welfare state, and supported a vast redistribution of wealth via the tax system and the gradual passing of ownership of industry from private hands to the state. But the CCL was too tied to the CCF for

Mackenzie King to much worry about appeasing its demands. He walked out of his annual meeting with the CCL leaders in April 1946 because of their relentless attacks on his government's apparent failure to deliver a program of postwar economic reconstruction. He was more receptive to the leaders of the railway brotherhoods who told him that their members wanted the government to reduce taxes and thereby boost purchasing power.[38]

Perhaps such a tax cut or at least a holding of the line on taxes for railway workers and other Canadians with average or below-average incomes could have been combined with the introduction of a comprehensive social security program if taxes on the wealthy were raised substantially. But King and other ministers were dead set against such tax hikes, arguing that they would cause a shortage of new capital investment. So, boxing themselves in with the options of either introducing both new social insurance programs and tax hikes for working people or delaying such programs, the government convinced itself that "average Canadians" did not want new social programs despite all the public-opinion surveys that contradicted such an assertion. For example in 1946, Louis St. Laurent, King's Quebec lieutenant, lectured the premiers at the faltering Dominion-Provincial Conference: "What the average Canadian wants, and wants now, is lower taxes. Specifically that means lower income taxes. He sees that the war has been over for a year, he feels that if government spending is not away down it ought to be, and he wants a substantial tax cut effective right now."[39]

The general message that the government's information bureau was providing was that the public was apathetic and cynical regarding the negotiations concerning the Green Book.[40] Facing little grass-roots pressure to fulfil his election promises, King could give in to the business point of view that warned against big spending programs, focus on tax reduction, and blame the provinces for his government's failure to introduce social programs. Government revenues were sufficient to allow King, while funding family allowances and veterans' programs, to provide the provinces with assistance for programs to build hospitals and for other health-related endeavours, while also working with them to build infrastructure that would be appreciated by the private sector.[41]

Soon, the government of Louis St. Laurent, who succeeded King as prime minister in late 1948, would have a new justification for slowing down the pace of reform: national security. Canadian defence expenditures remained modest in the early Cold War, which pitted the Soviet-led Communist bloc against the United States and its capitalist allies, but increased dramatically during the Korean War of 1950-53. The conservative St. Laurent had amassed a vast number of corporate directorships before entering politics and feared confrontation with Quebec's conservative nationalist provincial government. Now he had a credible argument for derailing persistent requests for reform. Speaking to the premiers at the 1950 Dominion-Provincial Conference, St. Laurent announced: "The limitations upon what it will be possible to undertake successfully, imposed by the over-riding demands of our national security, are both physical and financial. Until there is convincing evidence of an end to the menace of Communist aggression, a large and growing share of the resources and manpower of our country will have to be devoted to defence purposes." External Affairs Minister Lester B. Pearson, a future Liberal leader and prime minister, in thinking of the socialist threat internationally, conceded that it was insufficient to denounce Communism as promising bread without freedom. "We, on the other hand, cannot hold the loyalty of great masses of people by merely offering them freedom without bread."[42]

Right-Thinking Canadians

The freedom that Canadians enjoyed in these early postwar years was a gendered freedom in which most women would not enjoy economic independence. A virtual industry of psychological experts descended upon Canadians to define the parameters of "normal" behaviour and to ostracize those who did not conform. The psychology profession, perhaps unconsciously, became something of an ideological arm of the state in guiding Canadians towards behaviour patterns that seemed to reinforce both capitalist and patriarchal structures. Its aim was largely focused on mothers, who were given the duty not only to raise their children to adulthood in good physical shape but also to mould their sense of citizenship. Motherhood was to be a full-time job, and women with children who sought a life outside the confines of child-rearing were condemned as being irresponsible to both their families and the nation.[43]

Many of the women who were confined to their homes raising children and did not seek paid employment nonetheless chafed at the limited conceptions of their lives proposed by the psychologists. In the new suburbs, they became community activists who were responsible for initiating and then providing volunteer staffing to community centres and pre-kindergartens, as well as hosting community events from their own homes. In many communities, they took advantage of increasing government funds for recreation programs to build community-controlled democratic structures of decision making in the area of recreation in which women played key roles. Perhaps unsurprisingly, given both the sexist and elitist notions of the era, many of these gave way by the mid-1950s to bureaucratic structures that paid men to be in charge.[44] Whether they remained single, or married and sought work, or married and left the paid labour force, women's choices rarely seemed to follow the prescriptions of the psychologists. But state policies, more often than not, did follow the psychologists' perspective. State layouts on child care, social assistance, and housing could be reduced if the women requiring these services were defined as violating desirable social norms.

Wartime sacrifices strengthened Canadians' convictions that their governments owed them guarantees of decent incomes, free medical care, and old age pensions. The success of government wartime planning in mobilizing the economy and eradicating unemployment suggested the fallacy of leaving the country's economic health to the working of market forces. Political parties competed to convince Canadians that the return of peace meant a partnership of government and business in managing the economy.

But the Liberals and Conservatives, along with the business community, remained committed to a private-enterprise economy in which investors could earn virtually unlimited rewards. Squaring this conservative aim with promises of greater social equality was not easy. An extensive program of social security funded by progressive taxes, along with a state-managed economy in which private investment was important but competed with state investments, could result in a significant redistribution of wealth.

Whatever Canadians were told by Mackenzie King in the 1945 election, "the real Liberal plan, whether by accident or by design, was [C.D.] Howe's. It was based on optimism about the economy, and skepticism about the potentialities of planning. It would not be the economic abstractions of doctrinaire planners in Ottawa that would shape postwar Canada. That would be left to business self-interest, guided, prodded, and shaped by incentives that businessmen would understand. Postwar Canada would be a free enterprise society."[45]

Howe's view, expressed in the Cabinet Committee on Dominion-Provincial Relations in June 1945, was that "the government did not need social security measures" if "the full employment policies were successful." As political economist Harold Chorney observes, Howe subscribed to the "sanitized and vulgar variant of Keynesian policy [that] held sway in Ottawa and at the Bank of Canada." As reconstruction minister, Howe established the parameters of this right-wing Keynesianism in his White Paper on postwar reconstruction presented to Parliament in April 1945. The White Paper, though sometimes said to have committed the government to full employment, in fact was explicit that the government could not successfully deal with seasonal unemployment or unemployment resulting from a decline in trade. It could only increase expenditures and/or reduce taxation when the private sector seemed to be stagnating, and then decrease expenditures and increase taxation during better times. The government would not exercise control over ownership, pricing, or other decisions that traditionally belonged to the private sector.[46]

As we explore the struggles for various social programs in the postwar period in the next several chapters, the debate between these two very different variants of Keynesianism should be kept in mind. There were, of course, socialists who rejected both variants of Keynes's thought as simply props for maintaining the capitalist system. There were also diehard conservatives who rejected the postwar Keynesian consensus. But much of the struggle over social programs seemed to pit left-wing Keynesians against those with Howe's vision of the postwar social order.

NOTES

Much of the material that appears in this chapter appeared earlier in a different form in my article, "Paradise Postponed: A Re-examination of the Green Book Proposals of 1945," in *Journal of the Canadian Historical Association*, New Series 4 (1993): 120–142.

1 Malcolm G. Taylor, *Health Insurance and Canadian Public Policy: The Seven Decisions that Created the Canadian Health Insurance System* (Montreal, QC: McGill-Queen's University Press, 1978), 166; Untitled Study Done for Canadian Chamber of Commerce, 1944, reprinted in "Annual Meeting (19th) Addresses, 1948," Canadian Chamber of Commerce Papers, MG 28.3, Box 62, Vol. 1, Library and Archives of Canada (LAC).

2 For example, Canadians were asked by the Gallup organization in November 1943: "Do you think that workers would be better off if all the industries in Canada were owned and run by the Dominion government after the war, or do you think that workers would be better off if these industries were left under private management?" The response: 39 per cent chose government ownership; 47 per cent chose private ownership and operation; while 14 per cent were undecided. Interestingly, by November 1945, when Gallup asked the question again, only 21 per cent wanted a primarily government-run economy; while 64 per cent opted for private enterprise; and 15 per cent were undecided. National Liberal Federation Papers, MG 28 IV-3, Vol. 961, LAC.

3 Norman Penner, *From Protest to Power: Social Democracy in Canada, 1900–Present* (Toronto, ON: James Lorimer, 1992), 78, 80; Desmond Morton, *The New Democrats 1961–1986: The Politics of Change* (Toronto, ON: Copp Clark Pitman, 1986), 14.

4 Jack Granatstein, *The Politics of Survival: The Conservative Party of Canada, 1939–1945* (Toronto, ON: University of Toronto Press, 1967), 125–50, 207–10.

5 Jeff Keshen, "Getting It Right the Second Time Around: The Reintegration of Canadian Veterans of World War II," in *The Veterans Charter and Post–World War II Canada*, ed. Peter Neary and J.L. Granatstein (Montreal, QC: McGill-Queen's University Press, 1998), 62–69.

6 Harold Chorney, "The Economic and Political Consequences of Canadian Monetarism" (paper presented at the British Association of Canadian Studies Annual Meeting, University of Nottingham, 12 April 1991); Robert Campbell, *Grand Illusions: The Politics of the Keynesian Experience in Canada, 1945-1975* (Peterborough, ON: Broadview Press, 1987).

7 Doug Owram, *The Government Generation: Canadian Intellectuals and the State 1900-1945* (Toronto, ON: University of Toronto Press, 1986).

8 Leonard Marsh, *Report on Social Security for Canada* (1943; reprint, Toronto, ON: University of Toronto Press, 1975).

9 Canada, Advisory Committee on Reconstruction, *Final Report 4: Housing and Community Planning*, Final Report of the Subcommittee, C.A. Curtis, chairman (Ottawa, ON: King's Printer, 1944).

10 C.B. Macpherson, Wartime Information Board, to J.W. Pickersgill, 18 December 1943, William Lyon Mackenzie King Papers, MG 26, J1, Vol. 365, (LAC) p. 317806; Gail Cuthbert Brandt, "'Pigeon-Holed and Forgotten': The Work of the Sub-Committee on the Postwar Problems of Women, 1943," *Histoire sociale/Social History* 15, 29 (1982): 239-59.

11 Nancy Christie, *Engendering the State: Family, Work and Welfare in Canada* (Toronto, ON: University of Toronto Press, 2000), 278-81. A feminist critique of Beveridge is found in Jane Lewis, "Dealing with Dependency: State Practices and Social Realities, 1870-1945," in *Women's Welfare, Women's Rights*, ed. Jane Lewis (London, UK: Croom Helm, 1983), 17-37.

12 Angus L. Macdonald to King, 22 January 1944, King Papers, Vol. 364, p. 315890; T. J. Crerar to King, 8 January 1944, King Papers, Vol. 348, pp. 309918-21. Howe's opposition is mentioned in *Mackenzie King Diaries*, MG 26, J 13, 12 January 1943, LAC.

13 Christie, *Engendering the State*, 11, 290. Christie claims that King "implemented family allowances in 1944 as a means of obviating the further growth of the welfare state, in the belief that such a relatively limited government expenditure would create full employment and thus allow returned soldiers to once again take up their responsibilities as husbands and breadwinners" (11). This may be reading history backwards. During and immediately after the federal election in the spring of 1945, King did commit his government to a variety of social security measures that would have meant "the further growth of the welfare state." There is little evidence that, at the time he introduced family allowances, King had yet decided to pull away from implementing other new social programs.

14 Dominique Marshall, *Aux origines sociales de l'État-providence : familles québécoises, obligation scolaire et allocations familiales 1940-1955* (Montreal, QC : Les Presses de l'Université de Montréal, 1998), 45-53 ; Brigitte Kitchen, "The Introduction of Family Allowances in Canada," in *The Benevolent State: The Growth of Welfare in Canada*, ed. Allan Moscovitch and Jim Albert (Toronto, ON: Garamond, 1987), 234-36. Raymond Blake provides evidence that senior government officials linked family allowances with efforts to control wages, but is skeptical of the role this argument played in King's decision to proceed with the program. Raymond Blake, "The Genesis of Family Allowances in Canada," in *Social Welfare Policy in Canada: Historical Readings*, ed. Raymond B. Blake and Jeff Keshen (Toronto, ON: Copp Clark, 1995), 244-54.

15 Dominique Jean, "Family Allowances and Family Autonomy: Quebec Families Encounter the Welfare State, 1945-1955," in *Canadian Family History: Selected Readings*, ed. Bettina Bradbury (Toronto, ON: Copp Clark Pitman, 1992), 405.

16 Ruth K. Abbott and R.A. Young, "'Cynical and Deliberate Manipulation?' Child Care and the Reserve Army of Female Labour in Canada," *Journal of Canadian Studies* 24, 2 (1989): 28; Ruth Roach Pierson, *"They're Still Women After All": The Second World War and Canadian Womanhood* (Toronto, ON: McClelland and Stewart, 1986), 48-57.

17 Kitchen, "The Introduction of Family Allowances," 230, 233–34; Marshall, *Aux origines sociales de l'État-providence*, 46–48; Christie, *Engendering the State*, 47, 296; Blake, "Mackenzie King," 253.

18 Kitchen, "The Introduction of Family Allowances," 224–25; Christie, *Engendering the State*, 185, 286–90; Paul-André Linteau, René Durocher, and Jean-Claude Robert, *Quebec: A History 1867–1929* (Toronto, ON : James Lorimer, 1983), 22.

19 Marshall, *Aux origines sociales de l'État-providence*, 56, 301.

20 Ibid., 26–39, 53.

21 Ibid., 112–14.

22 Thomas Berger, *Northern Frontier, Northern Homeland: The Report of the Mackenzie Valley Pipeline Inquiry*, vol. 1 (Ottawa, ON: Minister of Supply and Services, 1977); Kativik School Board, *About the KSB: History of Education in Nunavik*, Retrieved from www.kativik.qc.ca.

23 Jean, "Family Allowances," 412–13, 419, quotation on 430.

24 Canada, Dominion-Provincial Conference on Reconstruction, *Proposals of the Government of Canada* (Ottawa, ON: King's Printer, 1945).

25 J.L. Isley to King, 4 January 1944, King Papers, Vol. 362, p. 313209.

26 Canada, Dominion-Provincial Conference (1945); *Dominion and Provincial Submissions and Plenary Conference Discussions* (Ottawa, ON: King's Printer, 1946); Canada, Dominion-Provincial Conference on Reconstruction, *Proceedings*, 6 August 1945, (Ottawa, ON: King's Printer, 1945).

27 Robert Bothwell, Ian Drummond, and John English, *Canada Since 1945: Power, Politics and Provincialism* (Toronto, ON: University of Toronto Press, 1981), 91–98; Marc J. Gotlieb, "George Drew and the Dominion-Provincial Conference on Reconstruction of 1945–6," *Canadian Historical Review* 66, 1 (1985): 27–47; and John English, "Dominion-Provincial Relations and Historical Planning, 1945–46," in *Proceedings of the Canadian Committee for the History of the Second World War* (Ottawa, 1987).

28 Canada, Dominion-Provincial Conference on Reconstruction, *Proceedings*, 6 August 1945, 10, 20, 191; some of the correspondence is detailed in Department of National Health and Welfare Papers, RG 29, Vol. 23, LAC, and continued provincial opposition at the final plenary of the Dominion-Provincial Conference in May 1946 is evident in *Dominion and Provincial Submissions*.

29 *Mackenzie King Diaries*, 31 January 1946; 3 May 1946.

30 Ibid., 23 January 1946; 1 February 1946.

31 Ibid., 3 May 1946; 6 May 1946.

32 So, for example, Finance Minister D.G. Abbott told the Reform Club of Quebec in March 1948: "If Quebec had made a tax agreement it is very likely Ontario would have made an agreement too. If that had happened, the country would have already been on the way toward having better health services, a better system of old age pensions and better insurance against the dangers of another depression than we have at present. In other words, Mr. Duplessis' brand of provincial autonomy has meant higher taxes for Quebec, poorer health services, and less social security, particularly for the aged." D.G. Abbott address to Reform Club of Quebec, 20 March 1948, Department of Finance Papers, RG 19, E2C, Vol. 92, LAC.

33 Keshen, "Getting It Right the Second Time Around," 79.

34 Canada, House of Commons, Special Committee on Reconstruction and Re-Establishment, *Minutes of Proceedings and Evidence*, 28 May 1943, 476–82; "Sixteenth Annual Meeting" *Addresses*, October 1943, Canadian Chamber of Commerce Papers, Vol. 1.

35 "Annual Meeting," *Addresses*, October 1948, Canadian Chamber of Commerce Papers, Vol. 1.

36 The life insurance industry expressed its support for a national health insurance plan as well as "the inauguration and integration of well-prepared and practical social security plans for

the maintenance of a minimum subsistence level of all classes." *Ottawa Citizen*, 8 June 1943. Its repudiation of national medicare in 1949 is noted in Taylor, *Health Insurance*, 108, 196. The medical profession's views in wartime were presented in "A Submission Respecting Health Insurance Presented to the Special Committee on Social Security of the House of Commons by the Canadian Medical Association," 13 April 1943, Special Committee on Social Security Papers, MG 28, I 103, Vol. 345, LAC; Canada, House of Commons Committee on Social Security, *Minutes of Proceedings and Evidence*, 1 May 1943, 8, 22. The dentists' views are in Arthur L. Welsh, president of the Canadian Dental Association, Evidence before Canada, House of Commons Committee on Social Security, *Minutes of Proceedings and Evidence*, 1 May 1943, 241–47. The quotation is from the *Montreal Gazette*, 20 August 1943.

37 *Montreal Gazette*, 13 June 1945.

38 *Mackenzie King Diaries*, 5 April 1946; " Memorandum of Proposed Legislation Submitted by the Dominion Joint Legislative Committee of the Railway Transportation Brotherhoods," submission to Cabinet, King Papers, Vol. 406, pp. 366859–61.

39 Dominion and Provincial Submissions, 2 May 1946, 545.

40 A.B. Dunton, "Confidential Memorandum to Members of the Cabinet," 6 August 1945, King Papers, Vol. 381.

41 Brooke Claxton to J.L. Ilsley, 18 June 1946, King Papers, Vol. 400. p. 362148.

42 Canada, *Proceedings of the Constitutional Conference of Federal and Provincial Governments*, Ottawa, 4–7 December 1950 (Ottawa, ON: King's Printer, 1950), 5–6, 52.

43 Mona Lee Gleason, *Normalizing the Ideal: Psychology, Schooling, and the Family in Postwar Canada* (Toronto, ON: University of Toronto Press, 1999); and Mary Louise Adams, *The Trouble with Normal: Postwar Youth and the Making of Heterosexuality* (Toronto, ON: University of Toronto Press, 1997).

44 Veronica Strong-Boag, "Home Dreams: Women and the Suburban Experiment in Canada, 1945–60," *Canadian Historical Review* 72, 4 (1991): 471–504; Shirley Tillotson, *The Public at Play: Canada and the Politics of Recreation in Postwar Ontario* (Toronto, ON: University of Toronto Press, 2000).

45 Bothwell, Drummond, and English, *Canada Since 1945*, 69.

46 Chorney, "The Economic and Political Consequences of Canadian Monetarism," 16; Canada, Department of Reconstruction, Sessional Paper Number 90, *Employment and Income with Special Reference to the Initial Period of Reconstruction*, 12 April 1945 (Ottawa, ON: King's Printer, 1945)

The Welfare State, 1950–80

Though governments delivered slowly on the promises of cradle-to-grave security made to Canadians in the aftermath of the Second World War, popular
pressures forced them to create social programs after 1950 that caused some
commentators to refer to Canada, in common with other Western nations, as
a "welfare state." In practice, though, governments continued to balance demands from popular movements, trade unions and average workers for programs to redistribute wealth with demands from organized business and other
conservative groups to sanction inequalities in order to promote economic
growth and efficiency.

Part 3 examines the pressures from both above and below in a variety of
arenas in order to evaluate just how comprehensive a welfare state was created
in Canada between 1950 and 1980. These dates correspond to the period in
which the "Keynesian welfare state" held sway. Some historians prefer to use
1945 and 1975 as the beginning and end dates of this period, dates that correspond with the most dynamic economic growth and reformism throughout the
Western countries. But there was a time lag in Canada between the economic
cycle and social legislation. As we saw in chapter 6, no new social programs
were legislated in the 1940s. In the late 1970s, when "stagflation"—the combination of inflation and economic stagnation—slowed the reform impulse,
there were only hints of the drastic cutbacks that would mark the next period
of social policy in Canada.

The chapters in part 3 each deal with social policy in a particular area, out-
lining both popular and elite perspectives on possible reforms. Each chapter
surveys the successes and defeats of popular groups and analyzes the reasons
for both. Chapter 7 deals with the elderly who benefited from new pension
programs, but within limits for which the private insurance industry could take
much of the responsibility. Chapter 8 deals with another limited success of the
"welfare state" period, the creation of the first stage of a national medicare program. Chapters 9 and 10, by contrast, deal with social policy areas in which
activists' successes were far more measured, child care and housing, while
chapter 11 analyzes the complexities of the poverty policy arena in which politicians promised so much but delivered so little.

CHAPTER 7

Social Policy and the Elderly, 1950–80

Writing to the premiers in January 1964, Prime Minister Lester Pearson outlined his design for the proposed Canada Pension Plan. "It should be as universal as is administratively practicable." Yet, he estimated, well over 80 per cent of men would be contributing to the plan at a given time, while only 30 per cent of women would. Still, he believed that most women would have made sufficient contributions by their retirement years to collect a pension. Nobody's earnings-related pension would be especially generous. This was because, while universality was a goal of the federal government, so was maintenance of private pension planning. "It should leave scope for further provision by those who are in a position to make it, and any disturbance to private pension plans should therefore be kept to the practicable minimum." That minimum was in free fall in the government's estimates by January 1964, as Pearson revealed, crediting the provinces for his government's decision to cut a third off the maximum pension proposed to Canadians just months earlier. "Some provincial governments," he noted, feared that the initial benefits proposal "might incline some people to withdraw from private pension plans. To meet this concern, the federal government is prepared to propose that the earnings-related pension be reduced from 30 to 20 per cent of pensionable earnings."[1]

Pearson's proposed compromise demonstrated the limits upon the welfare state as it evolved in postwar Canada. Programs might be devised to benefit a group like the elderly, but they were to do no more than provide bare necessities. They must not interfere with private enterprise and profit making in most sectors of the economy. In the final legislation in 1965, Pearson raised the maximum to 25 per cent, but only on earnings up to $5,000 per year, an average wage at the time. But, for actuarial reasons, the years of contributions required to reach the maximum were also increased, a blow to seasonal workers and most women workers. CCF/NDP Premier Woodrow Lloyd of Saskatchewan questioned the Liberals' priorities: "The economic and social advantages of a satisfactory Canada Pension Plan far outweigh any minor or temporary disturbances to private plans, and we fail completely to see how the millions of Canadians not now covered could possibly withdraw from non-existent private plans."[2]

Some historians of social policy suggest that the policies devised during the Pearson years in office, 1963 to 1968, demonstrated a real willingness on the part of the state to ensure decent incomes for Canadians. Penny Bryden writes: "The achievement of the Canada Pension Plan legislation also demonstrated the successful transformation of the national Liberal Party. By accepting the national responsibility for a fully portable and universal pension scheme, the Pearson Liberals had shifted their administrative emphasis away from the national economy and towards the well-being of the individual citizen."[3]

Certainly, provision for the elderly was an area in which postwar governments proved willing to go beyond the residual welfare state. But how far were they prepared to go? This chapter traces the evolution of state policies for the elderly, observing both their progress and their limitations. In 1980, for example, according to Statistics Canada, 28 per cent of Canadians over sixty-five lived in poverty. The figure dropped to 15 per cent in 1990, by which time the percentage of the elderly living in poverty was slightly lower than the percentage for the overall population.[4] Since the elderly were the major demographic group targeted by non-means-tested programs, even that figure, arguably, demonstrated the parsimony of the national programs in force at the time.

The figures for poverty rates are, in any case, debatable because of differences among policy-makers about what constitutes poverty. Right-wingers are apt to regard poverty as simply a measure of the minimum required to keep a body alive. Left-wingers, by contrast, usually insist that community standards, that is, the nation's overall standard of living, must be considered when calculating the numbers of people whose incomes are relatively too low. Statscan's approach attempts to take both viewpoints into account, though it is closer to the right-wing perspective.

Statscan determines the minimum required by households to pay for subsistence levels of food, shelter, and clothing. Households for which that figure goes over a certain percentage are then deemed to be poor because of a lack of discretionary income. The percentage that Statscan uses has changed over time. In 1961, it used 70 per cent; by the 1980s, it used 58.5 per cent, citing a rising standard of living that meant most Canadians spent a declining portion of income on basic survival.

By contrast, the Canadian Council on Social Development (successor to the Canadian Welfare Congress) and the Senate Committee on Poverty defined poverty as an income far below the average income for households of comparable size. In 1986, according to the Senate's figures, 39.5 per cent of the elderly lived in poverty while Statscan's calculation suggested the correct number was 18.8 per cent. The Social Planning Council of Metro Toronto (SPCMT), using a detailed budget plan for what they considered a standard of living that allowed the elderly to live with dignity though not in luxury, claimed that 52.9 per cent of Canadians over sixty-five were living in poverty.[5] While Statscan considered only a third of that group to be poor, it was clear that most elderly people in Canada had limited means despite a generation of social programs devised to help them.

REMOVING THE MEANS TEST

The national, universal old age pensions program proposed in the 1945 Green Book was scrapped by the government as unaffordable in the wake of its failure to secure a taxation agreement with the provinces. Yet, in 1951, it became the first of those proposals to be lifted off the table and legislated. With the agreement of all provinces, Ottawa was able to propose to Britain that the British North America Act be amended for a second time to allow the federal government to implement a national social insurance program.

Historians and social policy scholars debate the reasons why old age pensions were legislated long before a national medical insurance policy, which was equally popular, and federal financial support for unemployables, which had broad support from the provincial governments. The federal government had tried to fend off a universal program by reforming the means-tested pension. The maximum pension, fixed at $20 from 1928 to 1943, and then raised to $25, was raised again to $30 in 1947 and to $40 in 1949, though some of each increase was simply eaten up by inflation. Eligibility requirements were liberal- ized. Provincial governments, anxious to cater to seniors' votes, often supple- mented the maximum pension. British Columbia and Alberta were the first to provide supplements in 1942, and by the end of the decade, only Ontario, Prince Edward Island, and New Brunswick failed to do the same.[6] Throughout, however, popular pressure for a universal program was growing.

As we saw in chapter 6, the means-tested program had contributed might- ily to the popular view that all elderly citizens should receive a state pension. Historian James Snell argues that, by the 1940s, "a culture of entitlement to state support for the elderly now complemented the continuing familial cul- ture of support."[7] A provincial organization of pensioners had begun with British Columbia in 1932, and province-wide organizations were established in Alberta in 1940, Manitoba and Saskatchewan in 1942, and Nova Scotia in 1947. Even before the Prairie organizations had been formed, Violet McNaughton, the leading Prairie feminist and a columnist for the *Western Producer*, had spearheaded a petition drive across the region in favour of a universal pension at age sixty-five. Aided by the CCF's newspapers across the three provinces, McNaughton collected 40, 553 signatures to forward to Parliament in 1940.[8]

While efforts to hold national meetings of the old age pensioners' organiza- tions foundered on the limited incomes of the old-age activists, the pressures for pensions were felt by politicians across the country as social agencies joined with the pensioners' organizations to press for a universal pension of sufficient size to allow the healthy elderly to live independently. The Montreal Council of Social Agencies, for example, produced a "Charter for the Aged" in 1947 that argued for minimum income guarantees by the state for seniors, state provision for their medical needs, and for institutional care and treatment when they required it, as well as the right to work.

Members of Parliament received angry notes from constituents demand- ing that the Liberals implement an old age pension scheme, with or without provincial co-operation. Ontario MP R.W. Gladstone, for example, forward- ing to the prime minister a frustrated note from a lifelong Liberal activist who was threatening to quit the party if it failed to introduce universal pensions at seventy, observed that "electors in Ontario are not placing the blame on Drew." While many accepted that provinces should contribute 50-50 with the federal government for citizens between ages sixty-five and seventy, the federal govern- ment alone was thought responsible for looking after those who had reached seventy. The Liberal activist, whom Gladstone indicated was a senior of modest means, expressed a common view that the means-tested pension was "a tax on thrift and a gift to the thriftless spenders."[9]

Such views contributed to an increasingly liberal view of eligibility for pensions on the part of most provincial boards in the dying years of the means-tested pension. When the Joint Committee of the Senate and the House of Commons on Old Age Security held hearings in 1950 to consider a universal pension program, it was told by the Canadian Congress of Labour (CCL) that 73.3 per cent of Canadians over seventy had received the maximum pension available under the pension legislation in September 1949. Only the "unduly strict interpretation of the regulations under the Act by the Maritime provinces" kept the figure even that low.[10] The CCL interpreted these figures as evidence of the decline in self-sufficiency in the Canadian population. No doubt, as well, popular support for universal pensions put pressure on boards to grant pensions to people whose eligibility under the rules was questionable.

Labour's support for a universal program of old age pensions was unsurprising, as was the Canadian Association of Social Workers' clarion call for such pensions to be "uniform for all, adequate for a minimum standard of living, and without a means test."[11] The degree of social consensus in favour of universal pensions was evident in the Canadian Chamber of Commerce's urging that "a national basic pension of $30 per month be paid by the Federal Government out of current revenue to all Canadians of age 70 and over." Because the means test was "discriminatory and penalizes the thrifty," the Chamber saw little alternative to replacing the existing pension with a universal one, despite its members' continued concerns that taxation levels in Canada were too high.[12]

How significant a victory was the "citizens' wage?" Certainly, in principle, the universal old age pension was an important achievement for supporters of cradle-to-grave social security. Like family allowances, pensions were "demogrants." If you fit the demographic profile—in the first case, having children under a certain age, in the second case, simply being over a certain age yourself—you received a fixed amount of money from the state. You did not have to prove need and demean yourself in the process. A pension was an absolute right of citizenry.

At $40 a month, however, it was a right consisting of rather thin gruel. While the tax-hating Canadian Chamber of Commerce might have considered $30 a month as a sufficient pension, the CCL qualified $40 a month as "an outrageous pittance."[13] It paid no heed to the social workers' call for pensions that would provide pensioners with an acceptable standard of living. Similarly, the government's decision to leave the pension age at seventy was a disappointment for social agencies and pensioners' groups that had insisted on pensions for men at sixty-five and sixty for women, the age discrepancy explained by the exceptional difficulty women over sixty faced in acquiring or retaining employment in the face of employers' age prejudices.

Nor did the federal Liberal government of Louis St. Laurent prove to be interested in responding to labour, pensioner, and social worker pressures in the years after 1951 for a richer pension. Though the economy boomed, thanks to the Korean War, and inflation reduced the value of pensions along with family allowances, the government's priority was military expenditures while the war dragged on, and tax reduction after the war ended in 1953. Only in the months preceding the 1957 federal election did the government hike the pension, but merely by $6. John Diefenbaker, leader of the resurgent Progressive Conservatives, promised during the 1957 federal election to raise the pension to $55, a promise that he kept. The Conservatives raised the pension once again to $65 a month before the 1962 federal election and, after their victory in 1963, the Liberals kept an election promise by adding an additional $10.[14]

Still, even at $75 a month, a pensioner who was not a homeowner would pay every cent of the pension towards rent for a modest one-bedroom apartment in Canada's cities in the mid-1960s. A study in 1969 demonstrated that half of all unattached individuals over sixty-five and 30 per cent of couples in which one was a senior had incomes that were below Statistics Canada's modest low-income cut-off. Altogether, about 40 per cent of seniors lived below the poverty line, though some argued that this statistic was inflated because the researchers did not determine what percentage of low-income seniors had paid off their homes.[15] By contrast, they did not take into account the larger medical bills that were common for seniors.

It was because the "citizens' wage" that the state was willing to pay was so low that pressures mounted for an earnings-related pension that would allow the existing workforce to escape the poverty in retirement that most of Canada's seniors endured in the 1950s and 1960s. The American Social Security program, legislated in 1935, along with parallel programs in western Europe, became the model for advocates of a better deal for seniors.

POLITICS AND THE CANADA PENSION PLAN

The government committees studying pensions in 1950 considered copying the American Social Security program with its earnings-related contributions and benefits, but the premiers were largely hostile, with Ontario and Quebec objecting to any federal program of this kind. Alberta's Ernest Manning told the 1950 Dominion-Provincial Conference that "the idea that the state should by a system of compulsory contributions require each citizen to lay aside something for his old age is basically inconsistent in a democratic society."[16]

Opposition to a state-operated, contributions-based pension was general throughout the business community. The Canadian Chamber of Commerce and the insurance industry led the charge and held off the political forces favouring such a program for many years. They argued that private pension plans, rather than a state plan, should provide income for seniors. Many companies, though, simply had no plan, and there was no portability of plans from company to company. Workers who lost their jobs with one firm or changed jobs simply lost their pension rights. The Chamber recognized that the small number of private plans and their lack of portability created the overwhelming public support that polls showed for a state-run earnings-related pension regime. All the while decrying increasing state expenditures, the Chamber wanted governments to provide special tax incentives for firms that allowed workers to transfer their pension benefits in and out of the firm.[17]

Business's view of the inadvisability of introducing an earnings-related pension held sway over the Liberal government before its defeat in 1957, and over the Conservative administration that governed from 1957 to 1963. The Liberals had introduced a Registered Retirement Savings Plan in 1957 that allowed Canadians to invest, tax-free, a defined portion of their income each year in private retirement plans. However, this proved mainly a benefit for the well-to-do who could afford to set aside income for this purpose.

In opposition, the floundering Liberals began to reassert their wartime enthusiasm for state-financed social programs. Most ministers from the St. Laurent period, with the exception of Paul Martin Sr., minister of national health and welfare, opposed new social programs, but a set of Young Turks in the Liberal party attempted to move the party leftwards. Led by investment banker Walter Gordon and *Winnipeg Free Press* editor, Tom Kent, the left-leaning Liberals quietly took control of the party machinery, easy enough to do because the Liberal government had largely ignored the party, relying on extensive patronage networks to yield both funds and votes at election time.[18]

Lester B. Pearson, who won the Liberal leadership race over Paul Martin Sr., in 1958, had little experience with domestic policy and seemed to waffle between the positions of the old guard, who cautioned fiscal prudence, and the younger party activists who emphasized social security measures. Force of circumstance seemed to help the activists and to steer the consensus-seeking Pearson in the direction of supporting an expanded set of social security measures. A recession gripped the Canadian economy from late 1957 to the end of 1962, and questions were raised once again about the private marketplace's ability to ensure social security for Canadians. The Canadian Left, decimated in the 1958 election when the CCF dropped from twenty-five to eight seats, created a new party to unite the labour unions with liberal-minded individuals and the democratic socialists of the CCF. This led to the creation of the New Democratic Party (NDP) in 1961, with Saskatchewan's CCF premier, T.C. Douglas, taking the reins of the federal wing of the party. Socially minded Liberals warned that their party risked losing support to the upstart party if it failed to endorse new social programs.[19]

When the Liberals returned to office in 1963, an earnings-related pension, along with a national medicare program, were the two major social security programs on its agenda. But there were a number of obstacles in the way of the proposed pension. In the first place, Quebec, under the leadership of the provincial Liberal Party, was pursuing a nationalist course in the area of social policy. The nationalism of Liberal leader Jean Lesage was very different from that of long-time Union Nationale leader Maurice Duplessis, who died in 1959. Duplessis defended clerical responsibility in the areas of social services and education, appropriating state funds for these sectors but handing them over to the churches and private-sector agencies rather than establishing overarching state policies. By contrast, Lesage, elected in 1960, espoused a statist version of Quebec nationalism in which the provincial government, rather than the Church, would become the defender of the language and unique culture of French-Canadians in the province. The government would seek both to stimulate industrial activity and to provide social services to citizens. The Quebec Pension Plan (QPP), which Lesage's government devised before the federal Liberals had devised a national pension regime, was meant to do both. On the one hand, it would guarantee a livable income for retirees who had participated in the labour force for much of their adult lives. On the other, the monthly payments into the plan, which would be collected via employer contributions, and check-offs from wages of employees, as well as contributions from the self-employed, would provide a huge pool of funds for provincial government investment in industries that agreed to locate in the province.[20]

The Ontario government also considered implementing a provincial plan, but one quite different from Quebec's. Ontario was home to most of the largest insurance companies in the country, and their influence on the Conservative provincial government was immense. The insurance industry was implacably hostile to any government program that might take business away from them. They feared that many Canadians who had invested in private retirement pensions would reduce their private coverage if a generous public program were in place. So, the government of John Robarts set its sights on a provincial pension scheme that would require all employers of fifteen or more employees to provide them with pensions. The province would establish an apparatus to coordinate these pensions and ensure portability, but the private insurers would get the pension business. Unsurprisingly, the Canadian Life Insurance Officers Association and other business groups preferred the proposed Ontario pension over the Quebec scheme. However, they wanted a national plan modelled on Ontario's rather than a patchwork of provincial schemes that produced no portability from province to province.[21]

Thus, instead of opposing a federal plan, Ontario attempted to pressure the federal government to create a national version of its own proposed provincial plan. When the federal government held firm on the public versus private issue, Ontario focused on insuring that the plan would provide only a modest pension, so that better-off Canadians who bought private retirement plans and unions that had negotiated private pension plans for their members would be unlikely to reduce private coverage. With its proposed provincial plan as an ace in the hole, Queen's Park was in a position to significantly limit the federal government's flexibility in shaping the character of the Canada Pension Plan (CPP), and Ottawa compromised on issues other than public control over the new pension.

Other provinces largely favoured a federal earnings-related pension, neither wishing to follow Quebec's lead in establishing a provincial program nor opposing the general principle of state-run earnings-related pensions. Even Premier Manning, who opposed tendencies towards developing a "welfare state" in Canada, begrudgingly supported the proposed CPP on the grounds that lack of portability of private pensions was affecting the mobility of Canadian workers, a grave concern to Alberta whose expanding economy created a constant need for new workers.[22]

Thus, the legislation of a CPP seemed a foregone conclusion after the election of the Pearson Liberals in 1963. Although big-business interests in that party continued to oppose new social welfare legislation, the party's election platform had been designed by reformers. The reformers were aided by the government's minority status. The party was dependent for its survival on the votes of the NDP, which would be more likely to defeat the government if it failed to introduce social legislation. Public polls suggested that more than seven Canadians in ten wanted a national compulsory earnings-related pension.

So the real political debates were less over whether there would be a CPP than what its shape would be, as well as how the CPP would cope with Quebec's separate plan. The latter provoked broad changes in federal-provincial relations. The Pearson government recognized that burgeoning separatist sentiment in Quebec was fed by Ottawa's usurping responsibility for social programs from the province. Pearson, responding to the advice of advisers committed both to a widening of national social programs and the mollification of Quebec's fears of Ottawa's domination, announced that provincial governments could "opt out" of federal programs without financial penalty. In turn, they must establish a provincially administered program that met the objectives of the federal program. In the case of earnings-related pensions, there would be no federal subsidy to the provincial plan, but there would also be no collection of contributions from those employed in the province. Rather, the federal government would simply recognize that the QPP shared the goals of the federal plan and would serve as the provincial equivalent in Quebec.[23] In turn, Quebec agreed to work with the federal government to ensure that the QPP and CPP had similar enough provisions to guarantee portability between them.

Both in Ottawa and Quebec City, the business community's determination to place limits on an earnings-related pension, if they could not block it entirely, played an important role. The organizations of most of the major business sectors had joined in the opposition to the principle of the CPP from the early days of the Pearson administration; although, in the end, business would only delay the CPP legislation.[24] The Canadian Chamber of Commerce led the charge, arguing that the new state pension plans, with their "built-in tax acceleration," would rob the private sector of potential pools of capital.[25] Further, public pressure would likely develop for low payments into and high payouts from the plan, leading to the necessity of subsidizing the plan's fund with general revenues. This, allegedly, was the case with Canada's civil service pension fund and with American social security.[26] Pearson, responding to the vast campaign of the Chamber and its member boards of trade across the country, as well as individual business people,[27] assured business that the plan would not pay out benefits from general revenues. It would operate on sound actuarial principles rather than social welfare notions of what benefits pensioners might require.[28]

The business campaign against the CPP had the support of much of the press in the country, a large portion of which was controlled by a few corporate groups. The *Financial Post* claimed that "Canada already allocates a bigger slice of national income to welfare than its chief trade partners and the imposition of the Canada Pension Plan would make the disparity substantially greater." It then provided false figures meant to demonstrate the case: Canada allegedly spent 12.1 per cent of its gross domestic product on social expenditures in 1960, while Britain spent 8 per cent and the United States 7 per cent. The correct figure for Britain, according to the Organization of Economic Co-operation and Development (OECD), was 13.9, and for the United States 10.9.[29] Yet, on the basis of these false figures, the *Financial Post*, along with other media, claimed that "indeed, we should be thinking of cutting back, not adding, because bigger government deficits are due in good part to rapidly rising welfare costs."[30] In fact, Canadian governments had largely run surpluses on annual accounts in the postwar period, with deficits recorded only at the height of the Korean War due to war expenditures and in the thick of the recession of the late 1950s and early 1960s.

EVALUATING THE PENSION PLANS TO 1990

That the might of the business community failed to prevent the passage of the CPP demonstrates that factors other than the fostering of economic growth held some sway in government thinking in the Pearson years. But how much sway is difficult to assess since the government argued, fairly or not, that it had to introduce a modest program because of the influence of the Ontario government, which, in turn, was in bed with the insurance industry. If business did not get its way completely, other groups had more cause for complaint. The final legislation made provision for widows over sixty-five to receive the CPP payments that would have gone to their husbands. This was little help to never-married and divorced women. Women's organizations had supported a plan design that would recognize the shorter stays and lower incomes of women in the labour force. They urged the restoration of the original plan's provision that would entitle a worker to benefits despite a relatively small number of years of contributions, and condemned the government's plans to closely tie benefits to incomes earned before retirement. As well, business and professional women's clubs had been pointing out for years that pension plans largely ignored the needs of elderly women.[31] Unfortunately, the second-wave women's movement, which would prove strong enough to force the government to establish a Royal Commission on the Status of Women in 1967, was not well enough organized during the CPP debate to have any real influence. Actuarial concerns, along with implicit patriarchal views of how society should be organized, ensured that the plan would benefit men far more than women.

The patriarchal character of the plan was not its only conservative feature. Contrary to business worries that the pension funds collected by the state might be removed from the pool of private capital and used to appease popular demands for various types of government intervention, the Canada Pension Plan Investment Fund was conservatively managed. Initially, Pearson had planned a pay-as-you-go fund that would balance contributions and payouts, with little or no investing of the contributions. Quebec's ambitious investment plans for its fund forced Ottawa to re-examine this model since other provinces hoped to use CPP contributions for their investment needs. In the end, half the funds were given to the provinces for infrastructural investments, but for the most part the fund behaved like any private institutional investor, seeking only to maximize profits. In the late 1970s, the trade union movement began to campaign for a broader mandate for the Fund. In 1977, the Canadian Union of Public Employees proposed that it be used to promote an industrial strategy for Canada and to repatriate key sectors of the economy then under foreign ownership. The Canadian Labour Congress, representing the bulk of Canadian unions, took up the same call the following year. The United Steelworkers of America (Canadian region) proposed in 1979 that the Fund promote a "leading edge" resource development strategy as well as national economic planning.[32]

The model for much of what labour was proposing was the experience of Scandinavian countries, which had been governed for the most part for several generations by social-democratic parties closely aligned with the labour movement. In Sweden, part of the state pension fund surplus was invested in housing, municipal projects, and the promotion of small businesses. An equity fund was targeted to industrial strategy, providing "rich capital for employment-generating areas of the economy and industrial revitalization."[33]

Canada's two major political parties, tied as they were to capitalist fund providers and free-enterprise ideology, rejected the notion of binding social security policies and industrial strategy together. Only in Quebec was there a fairly bold use of pension funds to promote state economic policies, but it was short lived. Initially, the QPP's investment arm, the Caisse de dépôt et de placement, was a passive investor. Beginning in 1980, however, the managers began to accept directorships in companies where the Caisse held large numbers of shares and to use its share ownership to achieve economic objectives of the government, for example, preventing firms from relocating their head offices to other provinces. But the government gave little support or direction to the Caisse, and by 1983 the fund had reverted to more traditional investment policies.

GUARANTEED INCOME SUPPLEMENT

As the government deliberated on the CPP, many older Canadians objected that the government was offering nothing to people already too old to benefit from the scheme. Women's groups protested the poor coverage for many women, and such criticisms were voiced before the Joint Committee on Pensions that reported in February 1965. Though Liberals on the committee stymied Opposition efforts to establish provisions for women and the aged, several pressured the government to respond to such concerns."[34]

The government responded with a third old-age state pension. This was the Guaranteed Income Supplement (GIS), funded from general revenues, and it reintroduced means-testing into Canadian pensions. Only seniors who applied for the GIS and who demonstrated that all their sources of income combined, including OAP and the CPP, were below a floor set by the government, would receive GIS. The lower the income, the higher the GIS, but its ceiling was set at $40 per month. A senior with no other income than the OAP and the GIS would receive a grand total of $115 a month. It was therefore unsurprising that in 1969, 40 per cent of Canadians over sixty-five remained below the poverty line.

Seniors' groups, however, became well organized in the 1970s and lobbied the government continuously for a better deal. The "citizen's wage" argument likely contributed to their success. Seniors were not expected to be in the labour force. While business interests decried state monies going to able-bodied persons of working age as a disincentive for people to accept the work that was on offer at the wages businesses wished to pay, no such argument could be directed against seniors. In 1974, the GIS was pegged to inflation, and in the early 1980s, the Trudeau government raised the GIS sufficiently to contribute to a large reduction in the number of seniors living in poverty as measured by Statscan. By the 1980s, as well, the number of people reaching sixty-five and collecting the full CPP pension had increased because, as the plan aged, the number of Canadians who had made contributions to the plan for a long time increased. Income for seniors from government programs rose by 50 per cent after inflation between 1971 and 1989.

Old Age, Gender, and Social Services

While the focus of seniors' organizations lobbying governments in the 1950s and 1960s was pensions, there were other issues that concerned them. As Canadians began to live longer, and to enjoy somewhat better health, seniors' groups tried to convince governments to follow policies that would encourage seniors' independence. They argued, for example, that rather than placing seniors in senior-care facilities or encouraging their children to care for them, governments should promote policies that allowed seniors to remain in their own homes, taking care of themselves, but with state-financed support visitors helping out as required.

In Manitoba, in 1974, the NDP provincial government established North America's first universal home care program. Seniors who felt that they did not need full-time institutional care would be assessed to determine the level of home care they required in order for them to remain in their own homes.[35] Policy analysts suggested that home care, while it might involve increased state expenditures in its initial implementation phase, would be cheaper over the long term than building senior citizens' lodges. Such lodges were generally privately built and either charged seniors and their families a great deal for their services or charged modest fees but provided grim surroundings, inedible food, and a limited recreational program. As logical as their argument might be, advocates often had difficulty convincing cash-strapped governments of the importance of implementing a broad program of home care.

Women's groups began increasingly in the 1970s to point out the extent to which issues of the elderly required a gender focus. Not only were women outliving men by about seven years on average but they were also more likely than men to experience poverty during their declining years. Married women and widows often had no savings of their own and only the OAP and GIS as income for their retirement years. If they were single and had been in the workforce, they were often in even worse financial shape since they had no claims on a husband's income and had generally earned small salaries and ended up with little or no private pension monies.

The National Council of Women of Canada, in a study published in 1984, found that unattached elderly women received 53.3 per cent of their income from public sources while the corresponding figure for elderly men was 32.3 per cent. These women were only half as likely as the men to be homeowners rather than renters. Economist Mireille Éthier, commenting on the problems inherent in the actuarial approach to pensions from a gender perspective, asked Canadians to consider "the real purpose of public pensions."

"Should Canada favour a redistributive approach, which accepts wealth transfers from men to women and from young to elderly? Or would we prefer a pure savings approach where an individual's pension would strictly depend on his or her past savings? In other words, we must decide whether we want our public system to provide an adequate replacement income or only a safety net for the poorest element of society."[36]

Women over seventy-two, suggested a study by Louise Dulude, experienced a great deal of illness and infirmity. Dulude observed that not only home help but also a network of community recreational activities and health facilities designed with seniors as the audience were needed. But convincing governments that they, rather than charitable organizations should foot the bill for such institutions, proved a difficult struggle.

Government support for seniors had increased substantially from 1950 to 1980, and while a majority of seniors lived modest lives, the destitution that was once the lot of a majority of the elderly was less common. Pressures from popular groups for the CPP convinced the Pearson government to partially stay the course despite the stridency of the corporate campaign against the program. But the modest benefits offered by CPP, restrictions within its coverage, and conservative investment policies indicated the government's unwillingness to remove old-age security from the marketplace altogether.

International comparisons suggest that the elderly in Canada lived less well, in economic terms, than the elderly in most other industrialized countries. In 1980, OECD figures suggested that the real value of public pensions in other wealthy countries was much higher. Furthermore, private pension coverage, thanks to a combination of government legislation and rates of unionization, was also higher in many European countries. While only 44 per cent of paid workers in Canada enjoyed such coverage, 90 per cent of Swedish workers, 80 per cent of the French, 60 per cent of West Germans, and 50 per cent of British workers were covered. Among Canadians earning under $7,500, the figure for coverage fell to 9. 4 per cent while 76.4 per cent of workers earning over $30,000 had pension coverage.[37]

Beyond the question of coverage, there was the issue of democracy. Both with public and private pensions, neither workers nor their unions were provided any say in the direction of investment of the monies that the workers contributed to pension funds. Pension managers were not required to listen to, much less heed, workers' advice as to how these funds might contribute to the betterment of their communities or workplaces. Pension legislation for the elderly in the postwar period represented one of the greatest achievements of the postwar welfare state in Canada, but it also illustrated the limits of the welfare state as it evolved. Redistribution of wealth was to take place within limits that improved the economic position of some of those at the bottom of the heap, but that left the overall inequalities of wealth and power unchallenged.

NOTES

1 Lester B. Pearson to Premiers, 10 January 1964, Lester B. Pearson Papers, MG 26, N-3, Vol. 220, File 632.5, Library and Archives Canada (LAC).

2 Woodrow Lloyd to Pearson, 17 January 1964, Lester B. Pearson Papers, Volume 220, File 632.5.

3 P.E. Bryden, *Planners and Politicians: Liberal Politics and Social Policy 1957–1968* (Montreal, QC: McGill-Queen's University Press, 1997), 122.

4 *The Globe and Mail*, 15 July 1992.

5 Richard Lee Deaton, *The Political Economy of Pensions: Power, Politics and Social Change in Canada, Britain and the United States* (Vancouver, BC: University of British Columbia Press, 1989), 29.

6 James Snell, *The Citizen's Wage: The State and the Elderly in Canada, 1900–1951* (Toronto, ON: University of Toronto Press, 1996), 9–10.

7 Ibid., 97.

8 Ibid., 166.

9 R.W. Gladstone, MP, to King, 24 June 1947, William Lyon Mackenzie King Papers, MG 26, J1, Vol. 424, pp. 385015–6, LAC.

10 "Submission of the Canadian Congress of Labour to the Joint Committee of the Senate and the House of Commons on Old Age Security," 11 May 1950, Canadian Welfare Council Papers, MG 28, I 103, Vol. 195, File 195–13, 1950, LAC.

11 "Brief from the Canadian Association of Social Workers to the Parliamentary Committee on Old Age Security," 1 April 1950, Department of Finance Papers, RG 19, Vol. 440, File 108–8, LAC.

12 "Submission of Executive Council of Canadian Chamber of Commerce to the Parliamentary Committee on Old Age Security," J.H. Brace, chairman, executive council, 25 April 1950, Department of Finance Papers, Vol. 440, File 108–8–1.

13 "Submission of the Canadian Congress of Labour to the Joint Committee ..." Canadian Welfare Council Papers.

14 *Montreal Gazette*, 11 September 1963.

15 Deaton, *The Political Economy of Pensions*, 21.

16 Canada, *Proceedings of the Constitutional Conference of Federal and Provincial Governments*, Ottawa, 4–7 December 1950 (Ottawa, ON: King's Printer, 1950), 55.

17 "Minutes of the Ad Hoc Committee on Old Age Security, 1961–1962," Canadian Chamber of Commerce Papers, MG 28, 111, 62, Vol. 8, LAC.

18 Bryden, *Planners and Politicians*, chap. 2.

19 Bryden, *Planners and Politicians*, chap. 2 and 3, portrays the divisions within the Liberal Party. Bryden downplays the role of the new NDP in aiding the "left" within the Liberal party, 67–69. The view that the NDP's role was crucial is, however, common to academic histories of the party, including Desmond Morton, *The New Democrats, 1961–1986: The Politics of Change* (Toronto, ON: Copp Clark Pitman, 1986).

20 Bryden, *Planners and Politicians*, 115; Kenneth McRoberts, *Quebec Social Change and Political Crisis*, 3rd ed., with Postscript (Toronto, ON: Oxford University Press, 1993), 361, 368.

21 Bryden, *Planners and Politicians*, 88–89.

22 "Proceedings of Third Provincial Premiers' Conference," Victoria, British Columbia, 6 August 1962, 183–85, Ernest C. Manning (Premiers') Papers, Box 40, File 411, Provincial Archives of Alberta (PAA). General support from the premiers for the CPP was expressed at the federal-provincial conference in Quebec City in late March and early April of 1964: "Notes on Federal-Provincial Plenary Conference at Quebec City," 31 March–2 April 1964, Lester B. Pearson Papers, Vol. 64, File 306.2.

23 "Notes on Federal-Provincial Plenary Conference at Quebec City."

24 G.P. Keeping, writing on behalf of the presidents of the Canadian Chamber of Commerce, Canadian Manufacturers Association, Canadian Construction Association, Investment Dealers Association, Canadian Life Insurance Officers Association, and Trust Companies Association of Canada, 30 August 1963, Lester B. Pearson Papers, Vol. 219, File 632.5.

25 "Minutes of the Meeting of the Health and Welfare Committee," 18 March 1964, Canadian Chamber of Commerce Papers, Vol. 9.

26 H.M. Cunningham to Pearson, 24 June 1963. Lester B. Pearson Papers, Vol. 219, File 632.5. Cunningham was the treasurer of a large private pension plan.

27 Lester B. Pearson Papers, Vol. 220, File 632.5, is filled with letters opposing the CPP from local chambers of commerce, company presidents, and actuaries.

28 Pearson to H.M. Cunningham, 9 July 1963, Lester B. Pearson Papers, Vol. 219, File 632.5.

29 Andrew Armitage, *Social Welfare in Canada: Ideas, Realities and Future Paths,* 2nd ed. (Toronto, ON: McClelland and Stewart, 1988), 22.

30 "Why There's Criticism of the Canada Pension Plan," *Financial Post*, 21 September 1963.

31 Business and Professional Women's Clubs of Ontario, to Premier John P. Robarts, n.d. "Legislation Committee Briefs, 1963," Margaret Ashdown, president, Business and Professional Women's Clubs of Ontario Papers, File 5–9–7, Archives of Ontario (AO).

32 Deaton, *The Political Economy of Pensions*, 319.

33 Ibid., 318.

34 Ron Basford, MP, to Pearson, 9 February 1965, Lester B. Pearson Papers, Vol. 220, File 632.5.

35 *Proceedings of the Fourth Manitoba Conference on Aging: Fiction, Fact and the Future,* 21 May to 29 May 1985.

36 Mireille Éthier, "Survey of Pension Issues," in *Income Distribution and Economic Security in Canada*, ed. François Vaillancourt (Toronto, ON: University of Toronto Press, 1985), 220.

37 Armitage, *Social Welfare in Canada*, 22.

CHAPTER 8

The Medicare Debate, 1945–80

"The government sponsors the TB testing of cattle, pays for loss and has blood testing every year free of charge. What about humans? Let's take our hats off to Russia as far as health is concerned."[1] This was the conclusion of a group of farmers in Seaforth, Ontario, meeting in late 1943 to discuss the idea of a national universal medical care program. Sponsored by *Farm Radio Forum*, a CBC radio series, groups of farmers across the country responded to the proposals that were being mooted for state medical insurance. But the proposals being discussed were more radical than Canada's current medicare system. Medical care was to be removed from the private marketplace completely, and the costs of hospital care, doctors' visits, pharmaceutical costs, dental care, and eyecare were to be covered by a state-funded regime.

The farmers' groups revealed that conditions of health care in Canada, particularly in rural areas, were often grim. For example, a farmer in Elderbank, Nova Scotia, stated "Our doctor has 275 miles of highway to travel. Many do not consult him because of cost of services. Immediate federal action is needed." In Leader, Saskatachewan, another reported: "Our school is never visited by either doctor or nurse. This fall one family had a child with contagious disease...finally the school was closed up, as teacher and all pupils were sick. Mothers here, who never have a doctor at the birth of a child, least of all pre-natal care, most of them are wrecks and old long before their time."[2] Polls suggested that a national medicare scheme was the most popular reform discussed during the Second World War and its aftermath. In both 1944 and 1948, 80 per cent of Canadians expressed support, with the Québécois sharing this sentiment despite the claims of their provincial government and the Catholic Church that national medicare posed a threat to Quebec's traditions of individualism and Church control of social services.[3]

The dismal state of health services across the country fuelled the demand for state action. Canadians had reason to believe that they did not enjoy the full benefits of the medical knowledge of their time. While Sweden and New Zealand, both with universal state medical programs, had the world's lowest infant death rates in 1942—29 per 1,000 live births—Canada's rate was 54. In all provinces, the infant mortality rate in rural areas was higher than the urban rate, usually quite significantly, for example 79 to 51 in Nova Scotia, 76 to 43 in Manitoba, and 63 to 30 in British Columbia. Significantly, Saskatchewan, where pressure from women's groups in the interwar period had led to the hiring of municipal doctors and the creation of "union" hospitals (hospitals operated by several municipalities uniting to pay for their construction and operation), had the country's lowest rural death rate for infants. In that province, 52 children per 1,000 died in their first year of life compared with 43 in the province's cities.[4]

Still, the State Hospital and Medical League of Saskatchewan estimated that 34 per cent of all deaths were premature and that half of all provincial residents suffering disabling illnesses could have been free of disease if preventive care had been applied. As Tommy Douglas, soon-to-be premier of that province and generally regarded as the "father of Canadian medicare,"[5] noted in a broadcast in 1943, "If the average person were checked over by a clinic at stated intervals, and treatment were available before the illness had reached a critical stage, not only would we live longer but the cost of health services in the aggregate would be less than it is now."[6] The National Committee for Mental Hygiene reported in 1939 that only 10 per cent of Canadians could comfortably pay for their medical services in a free-market system while 25 per cent were completely dependent on charity; the remaining 65 per cent could pay for normal services but were forced into debt or rejection of treatment if an operation or long-term care was required.[7]

Yet, despite popular support for medicare, it was not implemented in the early postwar period and, over the next two decades, pro- and anti-medicare forces were locked in constant battle. Advocates of medicare seemingly won, but the program that emerged disappointed them both in the limitations of its coverage and the structure of medical care that it embraced. This chapter explores the structures of political decision making, formal and informal, that resulted in the creation of a particular type of medicare in 1968.

From the Green Book to Hospital Insurance

Though the federal government balked at the potential costs of national health insurance in 1945, it recognized that Canadians expected governments at all levels to invest in health care.[8] In 1948, it announced a program of conditional health grants to provinces to build and operate hospitals, train medical personnel, and carry out health research. The wealthier provinces, in turn, also provided funding to expand their network of hospitals and to increase the number of graduates from medical schools. From 1948 to 1953 alone, forty-six thousand hospital beds were added across Canada.[9]

Saskatchewan had elected a CCF government led by T.C. Douglas in 1944, and it had pledged to take steps towards the creation of a universal medicare scheme. Despite the unavailability of matching federal funds after the collapse of the Green Book process, Saskatchewan forged ahead with plans to create universal hospital insurance in the province and end the distinction in hospitals between paying clients and charity cases. It immediately undertook a hospital construction project to ensure that most residents lived close enough to a hospital to receive care close to home. Then it legislated tax-funded hospitalization insurance in 1947, becoming the first jurisdiction in North America to implement such a program. The province's general revenues as well as a prepaid monthly premium levied on families and singles would pay the costs of insuring that need, and not financial means, determined who used Saskatchewan hospitals. Saskatchewan physicians largely supported this measure, while hospital administrators who opposed the legislation kept quiet after the premier threatened that the province could take control of the hospitals if the existing administrators no longer wished to run them.[10]

British Columbia's Coalition government of Liberals and Conservatives faced serious competition from that province's CCF and also decided to implement a universal hospital insurance program, financed by premiums and a 3 per cent sales tax. Claiming that it wanted to blend the concepts of private and public responsibility, it included "co-insurance" (user fees) within its hospital insurance program, despite protests from the CCF and the labour movement.

Alberta presented yet a third model for paying hospital and other medical bills. Decrying both compulsory participation and centralization, the government established a series of health districts in 1946. District boards, which included both physician and consumer representatives, negotiated a health insurance scheme with municipalities, including the services to be covered for a maximum payment of $10 per adult. While most costs were borne by the voluntary subscriber to the insurance scheme, hospital fees were set at $1 per day, with the municipality and the province splitting the remaining operating costs. Manitoba and Newfoundland also had voluntary programs, which had been established before Newfoundland joined Canada, enrolling about half the province's population.[11]

Louis St. Laurent, like Mackenzie King, was less than enthusiastic about the federal government creating a national health insurance scheme. But he was under tremendous pressure from the five provinces that were heavily subsidizing patients' costs to implement a national program and lift at least half the burden of costs from the provinces.[12] Ontario weighed in on the provinces' side in 1955. About 70 per cent of Ontario residents enjoyed some form of hospital insurance coverage, but Premier Leslie Frost faced public pressure for the government to fund hospital insurance. This included pressure from hospital authorities. The community elites that ran the hospitals had been dealt a body blow by the Depression, as the number of paying customers dwindled while charity cases climbed. In the postwar period, they came to believe that their institutions needed the economic stability that public insurance alone could provide.[13]

Frost responded by insisting that federal involvement was required, a viewpoint he stressed at a federal-provincial conference in October 1955. St. Laurent reluctantly agreed to federal-provincial discussions on hospital insurance. These discussions led to the Hospital Insurance and Diagnostic Services Act of April 1957, which established a formula for federal grants to provinces that implemented a provincial hospital insurance scheme. About half of all hospital costs would be borne by the federal government. The provinces chose the method of financing for their plans, but there were penalties for provinces that levied user fees. Passage of the legislation was eased by the lack of opposition from the Canadian Medical Association (CMA), which, since 1949, had supported user-pay hospitals.[14] Their change of heart was dictated by the need to assuage public anger regarding high costs for hospital stays and to avoid more radical medicare programs that included costs of doctors' visits. The private insurance companies were the big losers in the debate, but were determined to fight to maintain the rest of their health insurance business by denouncing further state intervention in medical care.

TOWARDS MEDICARE

The CMA's rejection of public hospital insurance in 1949 was part of a broader rejection of health insurance by Canadian doctors after the war. With average incomes rising quickly, physician groups expanded or launched health insurance plans that proved successful beyond the doctors' expectations. The plans tabulated total annual medical bills for given populations and set insurance rates that would yield the income expected by physicians plus administrative costs needed to run the plan. For physicians, it meant that they collectively set the rates for various types of treatment. Private insurance companies, which covered over 1.5 million Canadians in 1962,[15] were required to accept the physician-dictated rates as the price for having a place in the health insurance industry.

By contrast, if governments were to get involved in medical insurance, it was likely that they would require physicians to accept lower rates for various procedures as a means of reducing overall medical costs. In the United States, the growth of the private health insurance industry, also dominated by physicians, gave the American Medical Association (AMA) an incentive to spend lavishly to lobby politicians and propagandize Americans regarding the evils of a public health insurance program. Their efforts forestalled President Harry Truman's plans in the late 1940s to introduce a national universal medical insurance scheme despite widespread popular support for such a policy. In the context of the Cold War, the AMA painted state medicine as an exemplar of the programs that unfree Communist states imposed upon their hapless citizens, an image that was ironic in light of the introduction of state medicine in Britain and other European democracies. Supported by big business organizations, the AMA developed an impregnable opposition to state medicine in Congress that united northern Republicans with southern Democrats, the latter often wealthy conservatives elected from pro-medicare constituencies but able to avoid the issue by making the preservation of racial segregation the key to their election strategies.[16]

At the federal-provincial conference in 1955, St. Laurent indicated that the federal government would only consider a national health insurance program when a majority of provinces representing a majority of citizens were prepared to institute provincial programs. The three Atlantic premiers responded that they could only consider a program if the federal government promised in advance to provide most of the funding. The premiers of Alberta and Manitoba wanted more unconditional grant money from the federal government in preference to universal medicare, and wanted any universal scheme to incorporate the private insurance schemes already in operation rather than replace them with a public plan. Ontario was only willing to commit to a national study of the possible scope and costs of a federal health scheme while Premier Duplessis of Quebec opposed a federal program.[17]

As with hospital insurance, it was the provinces that stepped up to the plate first to offer universal programs and then put the federal government on the hot seat for failure to make such provision a national responsibility. Once again, it was Saskatchewan's CCF government that led the way. Tommy Douglas, running for re-election in 1960, announced that with the federal government now paying half of Saskatchewan's hospital bills, his government could afford to implement universal medicare. Both the urban and rural poor, including most farmers, were unable to buy medical coverage, and the Saskatchewan government, like other provincial governments, was picking up the tab for medical bills for a growing section of the poor. It argued that this was unfair, first because it stigmatized those required to rely on state aid and discouraged them from seeing doctors, and second because it placed heavy financial burdens on the state that a universal plan would offset with the tax or premium contributions of the better-off, which the private insurers claimed for themselves. But Saskatchewan faced a huge fight in implementing its program.

Saskatchewan had played a pioneering role in the provision of medical services in Canada. Its municipal doctor schemes and union hospitals of the interwar period, the result of the work of the farm women's movement, and particularly Violet McNaughton, challenged the notion of health as a commodity to be purchased by those with the wherewithal to do so. Nonetheless, such programs relied on voluntary participation by doctors rather than state coercion. The CCF's experiments with full-state operation of medical services before the 1960s were limited to a few areas of the province in which the government was able to enlist the support of progressive-minded physicians. However, after the government announced its intentions to have a province-wide medical insurance scheme, a community clinic movement sprang up, a natural outgrowth of the populism that had produced both the major farm movements in Saskatchewan and the CCF itself. Health clinics with a holistic model of health, in which nurses, social workers, nutritionists, and dentists worked alongside

doctors, enrolled about fifty thousand people in thirty-five regional associations in a province of less than 1 million people.[18]

Most physicians had no intention of becoming salaried professionals working in state-run clinics whose policies were determined by elected boards of
non-physicians. In line with the CMA, which aided them in carrying out an
extensive propaganda campaign against the government's plan, Saskatchewan
doctors insisted that individuals and families should pay their medical bills via
private insurance. If the province insisted that all citizens should be insured, it
should direct them to buy insurance from a private plan. Only the poor should
have their bills paid by the state, with the state paying physician-dictated rates
for services that private plans paid. In July 1962, when the government proved
adamant that it would proceed with its plans, the Saskatchewan branch of the
CMA organized a withdrawal of physician services.[19]

Upper- and middle-class supporters of the physicians formed "Keep Our
Doctors" committees that accused the government of imposing an unwork-
able policy for socialist ideological reasons. The corporate-owned daily papers,
always hostile to the CCF government, terrified people by suggesting that the
province might lose most of its doctors. With both the CMA and national business organizations spending extravagantly to reinforce this message through
television and radio advertising, as well as by using the appearances of "expert"
witnesses on news shows, Saskatchewan residents were subjected to non-stop
propaganda against state medicare. This was offset by the support for medicare
from the Saskatchewan Federation of Labour and the major farm organizations, though these groups had limited access to the media.

The doctors' strike ended after twenty-two days as a result of government
negotiations with the Saskatchewan branch of the CMA, in which the doctors
conceded a universal state program and the government conceded many of the
demands of the doctors. There would be no salaries for doctors or payments
by the number of patients that they served. Instead, fee for service, the principle that governed private insurance plans, would remain sacrosanct. Doctors
would continue to operate from their own private offices, and not only would
doctors not be forced to participate in a community clinic, but those who chose
to practise in a clinic would receive direct funding from the state rather than
have to deal with the community clinic board. Finally, doctors would have the
choice of participating directly in the state plan either by requiring patients
to pay bills and then bill the plan or by staying out of the plan altogether and
billing patients with whatever fees they deemed appropriate. This was simply

a face-saving measure since both sides understood that most patients would choose to patronize doctors who were in the prepaid medicare scheme.

THE HALL COMMISSION

Saskatchewan's decision to launch a compulsory, state-run medicare scheme placed pressure on the national political parties to respond to demands from Canadians in all provinces for universal medical insurance. The NDP made implementation of a national medicare scheme a central plank in its platform. Out of office, the Liberals as well recommitted themselves to the national medicare program that they had promised in the 1945 election but had never delivered. Business stalwarts among former ministers, including C.D. Howe, Charles Dunning, and Brooke Claxton, opposed medicare. But the reformers who had taken over the party machinery in the late 1950s convinced delegates at the 1961 national convention to recommit the party to a national medicare program.[20]

While John Diefenbaker faced fewer demands within his party for state medicare, and considerable business pressures against such a measure, he was leery of simply dismissing any solution that might appease public demands for guaranteed access to medical care. He turned in 1961 to Justice Emmett Hall, a fellow Saskatchewan Conservative, to head a commission to study options for improving the health care available to Canadians. Commentators assumed that the commission, largely composed of hand-picked Tory supporters, would opt for a non-compulsory scheme.

While the commission deliberated, the Social Credit governments of Alberta and British Columbia attempted to counter the "socialist" Saskatchewan scheme with state programs that avoided "coercion" of doctors or "conscription" of citizens into a state plan. First, Alberta in 1963, and then British Columbia in 1964, announced voluntary plans that directed most residents into existing doctor-controlled and insurance-company plans, but provided state subsidies for the poor so that they could also receive coverage. The Alberta plan was endorsed by the provincial College of Physicians and Surgeons, which the government consulted as it set the premium and determined what services were covered. Such plans left many families who were just above the low-income cut-offs in the position of having to decide whether they could afford the high costs of private insurance or should risk going without coverage. Even in wealthy Alberta, the province calculated that only 60 per cent of provincial residents were covered by the voluntary medical-care scheme.[21]

The commission heard ample testimony from organized groups as well as individuals who favoured the Alberta and British Columbia approach over the Saskatchewan plan. While 40 per cent of Canadians had no medical insurance and many more had coverage only for catastrophes, elite groups that opposed a universal state program, led by the CMA and the Canadian Chamber of Commerce, insisted that only 15 per cent of Canadians were unable to afford medical coverage.[22] This figure seemed suspicious in light of a Statistics Canada study in 1961 that placed 27 per cent of Canadians below the poverty line and another 14 per cent on or just over that line.[23] However, to admit that private medical insurance was a hardship for almost half of the population would weaken the argument against state medicine.

MEDICARE'S OPPONENTS

Supporters of continued privatization and voluntary participation in medical insurance included the Canadian Medical Association, the Canadian Dental Association, the Canadian Chamber of Commerce, the entire private insurance industry, the pharmaceutical industry, and representatives of most other industries. The premiers of British Columbia, Alberta, Manitoba, and Ontario opposed medicare while Quebec's Premier Lesage was opposed to federal legislation in a sphere of provincial competence. The Atlantic premiers generally supported medicare but wanted the federal government to pay the lion's share of the costs and to give them time to phase in any universal program because they faced shortages of medical personnel. Only Woodrow Lloyd in Saskatchewan was an unequivocal supporter of a fully state-operated scheme.[24]

The advocates of private insurance used a variety of arguments before the commission. For example, the British Columbia Medical Association, following the lead of the CMA,[25] argued that the monies that medicare would absorb could be better spent on "scholarships for medical students, to add rehabilitative and chronic care kids to our hospitals, to extend our mental health programme, and for many other important services." Directing taxes instead towards paying medical insurance was "foolhardy" because it meant "providing a service to those who are already providing it for themselves, as most British Columbians are doing through our system of voluntary health insurance."[26]

The CMA's brief added that the hospital insurance program, which the physicians regarded favourably, had expanded demand for hospital beds. The federal and provincial governments, it suggested, having created this demand by making hospitalization a free good, now had to cough up the money for more beds. Implicit, however, in this argument was that prior to the existence of a public program, the real health needs of the population, in the area of hospitalization, had been underserved despite the availability of private hospitalization insurance.[27] Nor did the physicians try to claim that private health insurance was meeting everyone's needs. They conceded that to achieve universal medical insurance coverage, about 3 million Canadians would have to have their bills paid by taxes collected from the rest of Canadians, who, in turn, would also have to pay for their own private insurance.

The CMA, while avoiding the Cold War rhetoric of its American counterpart in its opposition to state medicine, emphasized that doctors as a group would be hostile to state medical insurance and even more hostile to any efforts by the government to move them away from individual practice into group settings that might also include other types of medical practitioners. "Physicians by nature and by training are strongly individualistic and it is not given to all doctors to function happily and efficiently as a member of a group." It could lead, in any case, to "assembly-line medicine."[28]

The Canadian Dental Association (CDA) also claimed that state moneys could be better directed at other goals than a national insurance program. Admitting that most Canadians had little or no access to dentists, they pointed out that there was a dismal ratio of dentists to population—1 to 3,000, compared with 1 to 1,900 in the United States, with regional gaps that were best demonstrated by Newfoundland and Labrador's ratio of 1 dentist per 11,000 residents. If all Canadians suddenly had access to dental services, there would simply be too few dentists to accommodate them. Steps to increase the number of dentists would have to precede the implementation of any government plan, and, in any case, any such plan had to be placed under the control of dentists. The dentists called for greater state funding for dental programs and lower fees for dental students.

The dentists admitted that "education and income separately and together are strongly associated with going to the dentist." Yet the dentists largely ignored their own insight that money kept many Canadians from properly caring for their teeth, focusing instead on "people's lack of interest in preventative measures" as the way to improve dental health. They recommended that provinces make fluoridation of water supplies mandatory for municipalities, that Canadians consume less sugar, and that more government funds go to dental research. While cool to state involvement in dentistry, outside of dental education and research, the CDA did recognize some need for governments to fund potential consumers of dentists' services. Like the physicians, they supported state funding of necessary services for destitute Canadians. If governments were going to provide state dental service programs, they should restrict their programs to children.[29]

Not one recognized organization of health professionals in Canada placed itself on record as supporting medicare, with the exception of the nurses' association in Saskatchewan where medicare already was an established program.[30] The rest of the nursing profession in Canada, which later would become a militant supporter of public medicine, restricted itself to calling for greater public support for nursing education and better salaries for nurses.[31]

Both pharmacists and the pharmaceutical industry strongly opposed inclusion of prescription drugs in a state medical insurance plan, since it carried the implicit threat of state regulation of drug prices. The Canadian Pharmaceutical Manufacturers' Association (CPMA) reported soothingly that competition was lively at the manufacturing and retail levels of the industry: "The competitive aspect of research and development, combined with behaviour of prices and promotional activities, indicates that a satisfactory level of competition exists in the industry. Furthermore, this competition is directed in a manner which is socially desirable. Growth, product development and the general level of prices have been favourable rather than unfavourable to the consumer."[32] The pharmaceutical manufacturers assured the commissioners that after-tax profits of the industry were modest and the industry's expenditures on promotion were fairly restrained and served the purpose of informing physicians and others about useful pharmaceuticals.

In fact, the industry's profits, measured as a percentage of invested capital, were double the average for Canadian industries as a whole from 1953 to 1958. A study prepared in 1961 for the federal Department of Justice by the director of Investigation and Research, Combines Investigation Act, noted that apart from making large profits, the industry was absolutely profligate in its promotion expenditures, as it worked tirelessly to press physicians to use various new drugs. Patent laws protected drug companies that developed a new pharmaceutical product, and it was the knowledge that they had a monopoly for many years over a particular drug that caused pharmaceutical companies to spend millions trying to convince physicians to prescribe their product.

But, while monopolistic practices affected only "certain drugs" at the manufacturing level, the retail level was a dead loss to market forces despite being wholly private. Wrote the justice investigator: "The practices of retail druggists...have resulted in the virtual elimination of price competition at the retail level."[33] Such monopolistic practices did not lead to calls for either a public takeover of the manufacture and distribution of pharmaceuticals in Canada or for new public regulations over the industry from any segment of the health care industry. Health care providers, such as doctors, dentists, and pharmacy owners, had a common interest in establishing a high price for their services, and happily confounded private provision with competition and efficient pricing.

Ultimately, the two arguments that were heard most frequently to discredit a compulsory public medical system were that it would deprive health practitioners of the freedoms that all business people ought legitimately to have in a democratic society, and that it would be so costly as to provoke crushing levels of taxation that would destroy Canada's industrial competitiveness. The CMA stated starkly: "We consider government intervention into the field of prepaid medical care to the point of becoming a monopolistic purchaser of medical services, to be a measure of civil conscription. We would urge this Royal Commission to support our view that, exclusive of states of emergency, civil conscription of any segment of the Canadian population is contrary to our democratic philosophy."[34] Premier Leslie Frost of Ontario was prominent among anti-medicare politicians to invoke the industrial competitiveness argument. The country, he averred, "has already become a high cost economy. And that is affecting our trading and developmental position."[35]

MEDICARE'S SUPPORTERS

Medicare's supporters suggested that Canadians had collective rights to the best medical treatments that were available regardless of income, and that the right of individuals to receive affordable medical service outweighed the alleged rights of medical practitioners to price their services as they deemed best. Despite the crushing majority support for medicare evident in opinion polls, few Canadians were willing to come forward as individuals and suggest that they had received second-rate medical treatment because they were poor. A careful scouring of the thousands of briefs before the Hall Commission reveals only one case where an individual Canadian denounced her doctors for providing her family mediocre care because of their inability to pay. Her physician's scathing personal attack upon her in response demonstrated why few Canadians had the temerity to reveal personal cases of receiving poor treatment or being driven to bankruptcy to obtain necessary medical attention.[36] Instead, the horror stories that the commissioners heard as well as the main arguments countering the claims of private medicine came from organizations. Trade unions, social worker and welfare organizations, farmers' federations, and the United

Church of Canada convinced the commissioners that they should adopt an ambitious national program.

The Canadian Association of Social Workers placed the case before the Hall Commission that programs that limited free state care to the destitute, which were in operation in many Canadian provinces, did not work. Many were deterred from seeking medical assistance at clinics because several hours might be required for them to fill out forms at the accounting department. Meanwhile, many people of middle means who did not qualify for the state care available to the indigent avoided seeking needed medical care because "it is going to come out of the food budget, or come out of the youngsters' clothing budget or something like this." The social workers observed that the stigma of receiving a charitable service discouraged usage of the service. It also created problems regarding the proper cut-off income for recipients. Better to have medicare available to all Canadians so that no one had to see it as either a special right or a special shame.

The social workers unsurprisingly made a strong pitch for closely co-ordinating health and welfare services so as to improve the physical and mental health of the population. Many of their clients suffered poor health because of poor housing and the stresses that resulted from limited incomes. They also called for the definition of medical services under medicare to include convalescent hospitals, home care and replacement homemakers for convalescing mothers, and the provision of prosthetic appliances.[37]

The Canadian Federation of Agriculture (CFA) and several other major farm groups appeared before the commission and indicated that the majority of farmers could not afford private health insurance.[38] The United Church of Canada, whose General Council had called for a contributory national health plan since 1952, confirmed the CFA's impressions. The United Church brief added that urban immigrants, particularly unskilled workers from southern Italy, were perhaps even more vulnerable. These people were underpaid, illhoused, insecure about their income, and prone as a result to both physical and mental illness. Yet they were too impoverished to be able to set aside the money for private health insurance.[39]

But the trade union movement probably proved the most effective in demolishing the arguments of industry and physicians that Canadians were gradually meeting their medical needs privately. In the postwar period, the trade union movement, which enrolled about a third of Canadian workers thanks to wartime and early postwar organizing successes, had succeeded in winning a variety of "fringe benefits" for their members in addition to wage increases and improvements in working conditions. A medical benefits package had become a common gain for trade unionists, and such prepaid medical insurance swelled the numbers of families whom the private insurance companies could claim as they pooh-poohed the need for a public program.

Unions' characterizations of the limitations of private coverage undermined such insurance industry boasting. National, provincial, and labour federations complained to the Hall Commission that the profit-driven insurance schemes that enrolled their members tended to severely restrict or deny coverage altogether in such areas as preventive health services, rehabilitation, mental health, dental services, and social services. Prescription drugs, nursing aid, appliances, eyeglasses, and hearing aids were rarely covered. Yet most of these plans had "costly deductible and co-insurance charges." As the Canadian Labour Congress (CLC) concluded, "It is too much to expect that a complete range of services can be made available on a universal basis to the Canadian people within the near future through the mere extension of the private pre-payment schemes. It is not physically, financially nor administratively possible."[40]

The CLC led the way in labour's deliberations before the commission, answering point-by-point the claims made to the commission by the CMA. It noted that, even using the CMA's definition of poverty, 4.5 million Canadians would require that their medical bills be paid for by the state. Apart from the layouts for these people, the state would have to spend millions in carrying out the means tests necessary for determining who was eligible, in the process stigmatizing them.[41]

Trade union federations in poorer provinces emphasized the disparities in medical services among Canada's regions that resulted from a market-driven allocation of resources. In Newfoundland, for example, the number of doctors per capita was less than half the Canadian average, while many rural areas had no physicians at all. The imbalance in the availability of nurses with the rest of Canada was similar. There were few dentists outside the two major cities, and St. John's institution for the aged and infirm was "a blot on the decency of the Canadian nation." Not only was a national medicare plan needed, according to the Newfoundland Federation of Labour, but such a plan had to provide for regional hospitals and clinics to be built and staffed in deprived provinces.[42]

The Hall Report and the Implementation of Medicare

Emmett Hall and the majority of his fellow commissioners were won over, in large part, by the values and arguments of the supporters of a universal medicare program. Their 1964 report made some obeisance in the direction of business and physicians by recognizing that no doctor should be forced to join a national medicare program, and that doctors should remain in private practice even if they joined medicare rather than becoming civil servants working in government offices. Even more of a victory for the physicians was the commission's rejection of the National Health Service model of salaried physicians, which the labour movement had endorsed. Instead, the commissioners supported continuation of the fee-for-service model which was a hallmark of private insurance.[43]

However, the overall direction of the report reflected the persuasiveness of the opponents of the argument made by businesses and physicians. Wrote the commissioners: "The achievement of the highest possible health standards for all our people must become a primary objective of national policy and a cohesive factor contributing to national unity, involving individual and community responsibilities and actions. This objective can best be achieved through a comprehensive, universal Health Services Programme for the Canadian people." "Comprehensive," in Hall's view, included "all health services, preventive, diagnostic, curative and rehabilitative, that modern medical and other services can provide."[44] This meant that governments should not only provide universal coverage for physicians' services and for hospitalization but should also cover prescription drug payments for all Canadians, home care and prosthetic services as required, dental services for children, expectant mothers, and public assistance recipients, and eyecare for children and the poor. Most of these programs would exclude user fees, though each prescription would bear a dollar user fee and adults would be expected to pay one-third the cost of eyeglasses, which would however be free for children.[45] Taxation would pay for all Canadians to be covered by the national health program. In short, Hall had rejected the voluntary medical insurance schemes that Ontario, Alberta, and British Columbia had proposed as alternatives to the Saskatchewan plan because only the latter appeared to guarantee the potential of full coverage to all Canadians for all necessary medical services.

Hall recommended that the federal government pay half the costs for any provincial medicare scheme that provided universal coverage. The provinces could determine their priorities in terms of the various components of the medicare scheme and the timing of their introduction. Federal government grants would help to establish the training programs required to produce the additional personnel needed once medical services were universally available, as well as the facilities required to build the medical and dental clinics to house these services. The federal government would, for example, share with the provinces the costs of building mental health wings in regular hospitals so that most inmates of mental health institutions could receive care in their community. It would also aid the provinces in providing funds that allowed parents to raise mildly intellectually disabled children at home.[46]

The Hall Report put pressure on Lester Pearson's Liberal government, which had been elected in 1963, albeit without a parliamentary majority, to live up to its medicare promises. The Liberals had promised a national medicare program that would provide comprehensive services free of charge to children till they left school and to Canadians over sixty-five years of age. Everyone else would have services by general practitioners, specialists, and surgeons, along with diagnostic services, covered, except for the first $25. Even the left-wingers in the government were taken aback by the scope of services that Hall wanted a national program to cover. For a year the government waffled, and even in the throne speech of 1965, the government committed itself to medicare in only the vaguest terms. The NDP, which had endorsed the Hall Report *in toto*, demanded that the government implement its full set of recommendations immediately.[47]

An exhaustive review of the Hall recommendations by the Department of National Health and Welfare demonstrated the substantial bureaucratic support for the tenor of the reforms proposed by the commissioners. Department officials endorsed Hall's views that "deterrent fees," that is user fees, could not be allowed for basic services because they contradicted the principle of universal availability of medical services. Federal funding of medical services along the lines of the existing federal formula for hospitals was "fundamental in making the most effective use of the nation's health resources to achieve the highest possible health standards for residents of Canada." The bureaucrats also endorsed the children's dental program and subsidizing of prescription costs, but with Finance and Privy Council officials serving as observers to the committee's deliberations, they couched such support with indications that both of these sets of services should be phased in over an unspecified period. Potential costs also caused the officials to reluctantly oppose Hall's embrace of government financing of home care.[48]

The eventual compromise reached within the government called for medicare to be introduced in phases. The first phase would add physician and diagnostic services to the existing hospitalization coverage, while other components of the Hall vision would be introduced as fiscal means became available. In practise, though few Canadians could know it at the time, there would be no second phase for medicare, at least during the twentieth century.

The government had a built-in excuse for delay because of the need to convince the provinces to implement medicare programs. There were meetings in April and May of 1965 in which federal officials representing the cabinet and the Departments of National Health and Public Welfare along with the Department of Finance heard the views of ministers of health and their officials from the provinces. Two federal–provincial conferences that year also provided the provinces with a forum for their disparate views, but provided little detail from Pearson regarding the federal government's plans. Pearson did, however, insist that the federal government, following Hall, would insist that federal funds would only go to provincial programs that met four criteria: comprehensive coverage of physicians' services, universality of coverage, public administration, and portability of services so that citizens were covered when they lived outside of their home province.[49]

In Quebec, an exhaustive provincial review of social programs, headed by Claude Castonguay, had recently begun and tentatively looked favourably upon a program of universal medicare. Federal dollars to help fund such a program were desirable, but federal input into the design of the program was unacceptable. Alberta's Premier Manning continued to fulminate against any program that was universal and that did not involve co-insurance. His government was furious that Ottawa had penalized the province financially for its insistence on user fees in the hospitalization plan. Ontario, Manitoba, and British Columbia also insisted that provinces have more scope for the design of medicare than Pearson's four principles might allow. Other provinces accepted the principles of the Hall Report but wanted sufficient federal funding to make it affordable for them to establish a program. Only Newfoundland was anxious for a federal plan to be legislated immediately, though New Brunswick was committed to establishing a plan and Saskatchewan wanted a federal contribution to its program.[50]

The Liberals called a federal election in late 1965 but narrowly failed again to form a majority government. Their commitment to a modified version of the Hall recommendations during the election left them little alternative afterwards but to legislate a medicare bill. In 1966, the government introduced legislation to provide an average of 50 per cent of the costs of provincial schemes that met the four medicare principles (a formula was used that would provide a larger portion of federal funds per capita in poorer provinces),[51] but the legislation lacked a date for implementation. Initially, Pearson aimed for 1 July 1967, the one hundredth birthday of the country. However, continued provincial reluctance to accept the federal principles argued against such speed, as did the change in the balance of forces in the Liberal cabinet after the election.

Walter Gordon, the progressive finance minister, took responsibility for having advised Pearson to hold an early election, and resigned from cabinet. His replacement, Mitchell Sharp, held views similar to those of organized business and appeared in no hurry to implement medicare, which he claimed could have an undue impact on the federal treasury. Robert Stanfield, the new leader of the Conservative party, denounced "a vast new spending program."[52] But Sharp and his supporters were only able to delay medicare's implementation by one year.[53] On 1 July 1968, funds would be available to provinces with a medicare scheme that met the four principles of medicare. Still, the division within the Pearson cabinet encouraged provinces that opposed universality and public administration to move slowly. Only Saskatchewan and British Columbia presented plans in the month after the medicare deadline and began to receive federal funding in July.

By then, the dithering Pearson had been replaced as head of the government by the more decisive Pierre Elliott Trudeau. Trudeau scotched any further attempts from within the cabinet or the provinces to allow for either delays or modification of the medicare legislation. Within a year all provinces but Quebec had announced plans that met the criteria of the Medical Services Act of 1968. Quebec entered the plan in 1972.[54]

MEDICARE, HEALTH, AND HIERARCHY

The Hall Report was less about health overall than about how to ensure that access to physicians was generally available and that physicians were adequately paid.

Hall did not challenge the medical profession's monopoly over medical care. The commissioners heard a variety of briefs from non-allopathic healers, but they largely accepted the equation of physicians with healing. Even the officials of the Department of National Health and Welfare who reviewed the report's recommendations observed the narrowness of Hall's focus: "Attention in the Recommendations was actually focused on personal health services provided mainly by physicians and others in private practice to the exclusion of public health services."[55]

In addition, the commissioners paid little attention to environmental pollution, which a few trade union briefs suggested was a factor in the health of individuals.[56] They had little to say about the roles of fitness, stress, nutrition, and poverty, outside of its impact on ability to pay medical bills. Industrial accidents were not addressed. The commissioners gave no consideration to the community-care model, which had already been piloted in Saskatchewan, accepting unquestioningly a hierarchical model of medical care in which physicians dictated the roles of other medical practitioners and patients had no input into either the character or payment structures of services.[57]

NATIVE PEOPLES AND MEDICAL CARE

Nothing illustrated better the argument that physician care alone could not guarantee a healthy population than the continued oppression and suffering of indigenous Canadians. In 1977, when the average age of death for Canadians was 66, the comparative figure for Natives was 42.4 years. They were four times as likely to die violent deaths in their twenties or thirties as other Canadians. Babies on reserves died in large numbers of gastroenteritis and pneumonia, diseases of poverty. Waters upon which Natives depended for their fish were often poisoned with waste mercury from chemical plants. On poor, isolated reserves with shabby housing and few facilities, Native children sniffed gas while their parents abused alcohol. Though the residential schooling system, which snatched children from their parents and placed them in environments where physical and sexual abuse were often rife, was being phased out, its scars on the Native psyche were reflected in substance abuse and poor parenting skills.

These woes were compounded by a lack of health workers, including doctors and nurses, on many reserves. There were only ten physicians and 221 nurses of Native descent in Canada in the mid-1970s and there was no national program to change this situation.[58] The federal government had over time taken a degree of responsibility for Native health care, always claiming, however, that constitutionally it was not compelled to do so. Until 1945, Indian Affairs had authority over Native health. After 1945, the Department of National Health and Welfare (DNHW) was given charge of this responsibility, and in 1962, a branch of DNHW called Medical Services was formed with a variety of programs under its control, including the former Indian Health Services.[59]

Community control initiatives at the grassroots attempted to compensate for government indifference and to pressure the federal government to provide Native communities with the wherewithal to deal with both their social and health needs. Reserves began to organize their own community medical schemes to hire doctors and nurses, to make up for the lethargy of Medical Services and to establish the right of Native communities to govern themselves in all areas, including health services. Native nurses formed an organization to promote nursing as an occupation for Native girls. Shamanistic healing practices, long suppressed by the colonial authorities on reserves, but never completely eradicated, made a comeback. The colonialism experienced by Native peoples and the health of the Aboriginal population seemed inextricably linked, and campaigns for community control over health services formed part of the struggle to shed the legacy of paternalistic, remote control by Ottawa over Native lives.[60]

The creation of a national network of provincial medicare programs, all subscribing to the principles of comprehensiveness, universality, portability, and public administration, represented a major victory for progressive forces in Canada, backed by overwhelming public opinion. The combination of public campaigning by important social movements, including labour, farmers, and social workers, with support from key elements of the Liberal Party and the civil service, resulted in a Tory-appointed royal commission failing to suggest some sort of public-private mix that largely subordinated health service provision to profit-seeking health insurance companies and physicians. In turn, this led the Liberal government, divided for two decades on whether to implement its promises originally made in 1919 for a national public program, to finally deliver.

The success of reformist forces in Canada in the area of medicare was a contrast with the United States where the politics of race, the lack of a social-democratic party, the bias of public expenditures towards military spending, and the immense power of organized medicine continued to prevent the introduction of a universal medicare program. As Canada legislated universal medicare, American President Lyndon Johnson, spending billions of dollars on an unpopular war in Indochina, felt only able to support medicare for the elderly and a Medicaid program for the destitute that held down costs for medical services for the poor by sending them to special medical clinics, which were generally understaffed and involved long waits for service.[61]

By contrast, Canada's "first phase" of medicare provided far less comprehensive coverage for illness prevention and treatment than the National Health Service in Britain and similar programs in Scandinavia and Holland. The Soviet Union and its Cold War satellites in eastern Europe all provided sweeping free comprehensive medical care programs. The Hall Commission had looked to western European models rather than the United States in framing its recommendations, and the government rhetorically accepted the commission's conclusions. In practice, the desire to keep costs down resulted in a watering down of Hall's proposals that saw medicare's "first phase" limited to coverage of visits to hospitals and physicians, and diagnostic services. Further phases were not legislated. The late 1960s represented the high point of social reform rather than a first installment on social reforms that would fundamentally redistribute wealth in Canada. The next three chapters examine areas in which the postwar welfare state largely failed to meet the needs of Canadians—daycare, housing, and poverty.

Notes

1 Health Study Bureau, *Review of Canada's Health Needs and Insurance Proposals* (Toronto, ON: Health Study Bureau, 1946), 41.

2 Ibid., 40–3.

3 Malcolm G. Taylor, *Health Insurance and Canadian Public Policy: The Seven Decisions that Created the Canadian Health Insurance System* (Montreal, QC: McGill-Queen's University Press, 1978), 166.

4 Health Study Bureau, *Review of Canada's Health Needs*, 3–4.

5 Historian Georgina Taylor nuances the notion of medicare having been single-parented by a male, recalling that farm women, led by Violet McNaughton, had created the prototypes of medicare at a municipal level in the province. See Georgina M. Taylor, "'Ground for Common Action': Violet McNaughton's Agrarian Feminism and the Origins of the Farm Women's Movement in Canada" (PhD thesis, Carleton University, 1997). See also Georgina M. Taylor, "'Let Us Co-operate': Violet McNaughton and the Co-operative Ideal," In *Co-operatives in the Year 2000: Memory, Mutual Aid, and the Millennium*, ed. Brett Fairbairn and Ian Macpherson (Saskatoon, SK: Centre for the Study of Co-operatives, University of Saskatchewan, 2000), 57–78.

6 "CCF Broadcast by T.C. Douglas, MP," William Lyon Mackenzie King Papers, MG 26, J1, Vol. 346, p. 297811, *Library and Archives of Canada*, (LAC).

7 Ibid., p. 297809.

8 Many organizations expressed disappointment that the promised national health insurance program did not materialize. For example, the National Council of Women of Canada voted at their 1947 convention to "commend the Dominion Government on the Health Insurance Plan already prepared and urge its implementation as soon as possible." " Resolutions, Annual Meeting, held in Regina June 6–11, 1947," National Council of Women of Canada (NCWC) Papers, MG 28 I 25, Vol. 90, File 1, LAC.

9 Malcolm G. Taylor, "The Canadian Health-Care System: After Medicare," in *Health and Canadian Society: Sociological Perspectives*, 2nd ed., ed. David Coburn, Carl D'Arcy, George M. Torrance, and Peter New (Toronto, ON: Fitzhenry and Whiteside, 1987), 74.

10 Duane Mombourquette, "'An Inalienable Right': The CCF and Rapid Health Care Reform, 1944–1948," in *Social Welfare Policy in Canada: Historical Readings*, ed. Raymond B. Blake and Jeff Keshen (Toronto, ON: Copp Clark, 1995), 298–302.

11 Taylor, "The Canadian Health-Care System," 74, 84; Margaret A. Ormsby, *British Columbia: A History* (Vancouver, BC: Macmillan, 1958), 487; Alvin Finkel, *The Social Credit Phenomenon in Alberta* (Toronto, ON: University of Toronto Press, 1989), 123.

12 Eugene Vayda and Raisa B. Deber, "The Canadian Health-Care System: A Developmental Overview," in *Social Welfare Policy*, ed. Blake and Keshen, 315.

13 David Gagan and Rosemary Gagan, *For Patients of Moderate Means: A Social History of the Voluntary Public General Hospital in Canada, 1890–1950* (Montreal, QC: McGill-Queen's University Press, 2002).

14 Brief of Canadian Medical Association, April 1962, Canada, Royal Commission on Health Services, RG 33, Series 78, Vol. 19, File 278, LAC.

15 "Brief from Great West Life and Metropolitan Life Insurance Company," n.d., Royal Commission on Health Services, Vol. 15, Exhibit 200.

16 Monte M. Poen, *Harry S. Truman Versus the Medical Lobby: The Genesis of Medicare* (Columbia, MS: University of Missouri Press, 1979); Lawrence R. Jacobs, *The Health of Nations: Public Opinion and the Making of American and British Health Policy* (Ithaca, NY: Cornell University Press, 1993).

17 "Reports of 1955 Federal-Provincial Conference," Department of National Health and Welfare Papers, RG 29, Vol. 918, LAC.

18 Joan Feather, "From Concept to Reality: Formation of the Swift Current Health Region," *Prairie Forum* 16, 1 (Spring 1991): 59–80; Joan Feather, "Impact of the Swift Current Health Region: Experiment or Model," *Prairie Forum* 16, 2 (Fall 1991): 225–48; Stan Rands, "Recollections: The CCF in Saskatchewan," in *Western Canadian Politics: The Radical Tradition*, ed. Donald C. Kerr (Edmonton, AB: NeWest, 1981), 58–64.

19 On the doctors' strike, see Robin F. Badgley and Samuel Wolfe, *Doctors' Strike: Medical Care and Conflict in Saskatchewan* (Toronto, ON: Macmillan, 1967).

20 P.E. Bryden, *Planners and Politicians: Liberal Politics and Social Policy, 1957–1968* (Montreal, QC: McGill-Queen's University Press, 1997), chap. 2 and 3.

21 Finkel, *The Social Credit Phenomenon*, 144; "Discussions with Provinces on Health Services Matters," Meeting with Alberta Officials, 22 April 1965, Department of National Health and Welfare Papers, RG 33, Vol. 45.

22 Evidence of Canadian Medical Association, April 1962, Canada, Royal Commission on Health Services, Vol. 19, File 278; Evidence of Canadian Chamber of Commerce, March 1962, Vol. 14, File 188.

23 Canada, Economic Council of Canada, *The Challenge of Growth and Change*, Fifth Annual Review (Ottawa, ON: Queen's Printer, 1968), 104–105.

24 "Discussions with Provinces on Health Services Matters," Department of National Health and Welfare Papers, Vol. 45.

25 Evidence of Canadian Medical Association, April 1962, Royal Commission on Health Services.

26 Evidence of British Columbia Medical Association, February 1962, Royal Commission on Health Services, Vol. 12, File 150.

27 Evidence of Canadian Medical Association, April 1962, Royal Commission on Health Services.

28 Ibid.

29 Evidence of Canadian Dental Association, March 1962, Royal Commission on Health, Vol. 14, Exhibit 192, 1962.

30 Evidence of Saskatchewan Registered Nurses Association, January 1962, Royal Commission on Health Services, Vol. 9, File 84.

31 See, for example, Evidence of New Brunswick Association of Registered Nurses, 9 November 1961, Vol. 8, File 44; Evidence of Manitoba Association of Registered Nurses, January 1962, Vol. 9, File 65; and Evidence of Association des Infirmières de la Province de Québec, April 1962, Vol. 15, File 219, Royal Commission on Health Services.

32 Evidence of Canadian Pharmaceutical Manufacturers Association, May 1962, Royal Commission on Health Services, Vol. 20, File 291.

33 Canada, Director of Investigation and Research, Combines Investigation Act, "*Material Collected for Submission to the Restrictive Trade Practices Commission in the Course of an Inquiry under Section 42 of the Combines Investigation Act Relating to the Manufacture, Distribution and Sale of Drugs*" (Ottawa, ON: Department of Justice, 1961), 258.

34 Evidence of Canadian Medical Association, 16 October 1962, Royal Commission on Health Services, Vol. 6, File 67.

35 Canadian Press Report of Leslie Frost Interview, 29 March 1961, Royal Commission on Health Services, Vol. 8.

36 Evidence of Mrs. Marguerite Miles, Toronto, n.d, File 355; Evidence of Dr. C. Collins-William, Toronto, n.d., File 375, Vol. 22, Royal Commission on Health Services.

37 Evidence of Canadian Association of Social Workers, 28 May 1962, Royal Commission on Health Services, Vol. 6, File 61.

38 Evidence of Canadian Federation of Agriculture, 27 March, 1962, Royal Commission on Health Services, Vol. 14, File 190.

39 Evidence of United Church of Canada, April 1962, Royal Commission on Health Services, Vol. 22, File 352.

40 Evidence of Canadian Labour Congress, 17 October, 1962, Royal Commission on Health Services, Vol. 6, File 68.

41 Ibid.

42 Evidence of Newfoundland Federation of Labour, October 1961, Royal Commission on Health Services, Vol. 7, File 25.

43 Royal Commission on Health Services, *Report*, vol. 1 (Ottawa, ON: Queen's Printer, 1964), 29.

44 Ibid., 11.

45 Ibid., 19.

46 Ibid., 19, 24–25, 36, 41.

47 "Election 1963 Pamphlets," National Liberal Federation Papers, MG 28, IV–3, Vol. 1024, LAC; Bryden, *Planners and Politicians*, 136.

48 "Departmental Review of the Report of the Royal Commission on Health Services: Departmental Appraisal and Proposals and Recommendations," March 1965, 23, 25, 28, 59, 62, 77, 87–92. Quote is from 28. Department of National Health and Welfare Papers, Vol. 45.

49 Ibid., 142.

50 Bryden, *Planners and Politicians*, 159; "Discussions with Provinces on Health Services Matters," Meeting with Quebec Delegation, 12 and 13 April 1965, Department of National Health and Welfare Papers, Vol. 45; Finkel, *The Social Credit Phenomenon in Alberta*, 150–51.

51 Eugene Vayda and Raisa B. Deber, "The Canadian Health Care System: A Developmental Overview," in *Social Welfare Policy*, ed. Blake and Keshen, 316. In 1973–74, the federal grant to Newfoundland covered 81.5 per cent of the province's medical bills and 57.6 per cent of its hospital costs while the grant to Ontario paid 44.8 per cent of medical care and 49.4 per cent of hospital costs. "For medical insurance, each province received 50 per cent of the average national per capita medical care expenditure multiplied by its population."

52 The continued opposition of the premiers was clear in File 618.4, "Correspondence with Premiers," Lester B. Pearson Papers, MG 26, N-4, Vol. 199, LAC. Other than Saskatchewan and British Columbia, no provinces were clearly prepared to join the medicare program in February 1968. Nova Scotia and Newfoundland were believed by the federal government to be only prepared to join if Ontario did. But Ontario, New Brunswick, and Alberta were unprepared to join the program. Manitoba planned to defer participation for at least a year beyond July 1 in the hopes of convincing the federal government to concede support for a plan more in tune with Manitoba's free-enterprise views.

53 Ibid., 152–63.
54 Ibid., 164–67.
55 Department of National Health and Welfare, "Departmental Review," 2.
56 Evidence of United Electrical, Radio and Machine Workers of America, May 1962, Royal Commission on Health Services, Vol. 21.
57 Donald Swartz, "The Politics of Reform: Conflict and Accommodation in Canadian Health Policy," in *The Canadian State: Political Economy and Political Power*, ed. Leo Panitch (Toronto, ON: University of Toronto Press, 1977), 311–43; and Vivienne Walters, "State, Capital and Labour: The Introduction of Federal-Provincial Insurance for Physician Care in Canada," *Canadian Journal of Sociology and Anthropology* 19, 2 (1982): 157–72.
58 Paul Grescoe, "A Nation's Disgrace," in *Health and Canadian Society*, ed. Coburn, D'Arcy, Torrance, and New, 127–40.
59 James S. Frideres and René R. Gadacz, *Aboriginal Peoples in Canada: Contemporary Conflicts*, 6th ed. (Toronto, ON: Prentice Hall, 2001), 68–69.
60 Maureen K. Lux, *Medicine that Walks: Disease, Medicine, and Canadian Plains Native People, 1880–1940* (Toronto, ON: University of Toronto Press, 2001); T. Kue Young, *Health Care and Cultural Change: The Indian Experience in the Central Subarctic* (Toronto, ON: University of Toronto Press, 1988).
61 Poen, *Harry S. Truman Versus the Medical Lobby*; Paul Starr, *The Social Transformation of American Medicine* (New York, NY: Basic Books, 1982).

CHAPTER 9

The Child Care Debate, 1945–80

In 1972, J. Eric Harrington, president of Canada Vickers Ltd., wrote pointedly to Grace MacInnis, New Democrat MP for Vancouver Kingsway and veteran campaigner for women's rights: "Could you please tell me what on earth 'day centres' of which you claim we need 130,000 and 'family planning centres' of which you claim we need 700, have to do with 'equal rights for women?' Surely family planning and daycare centres for children are purely a family responsibility and a personal matter and don't have a damn thing to do with equal rights."[1] MacInnis replied equally sharply: "The fact that you can believe that family planning and day care centres for children are purely a family responsibility and a personal matter, indicates very clearly that you enjoy an income standard where you and those who surround you are well able to handle such matters from your own resources. Such, I regret to have to tell you, is not the case for a very large percentage of the Canadian people."[2]

This chapter examines some of the limits of the postwar Canadian welfare state. The focus is on the child care arrangements made by mothers with paying jobs and how both state action and public discourse about the desirability of mothers working shaped the choices available to them. This discourse gradually shifted from overwhelming social condemnation to begrudging acceptance. What did not change was the assumption that the nuclear household must remain the major institution for reproduction of social labour, a place where unpaid mothers socialized children, and provided the prepared food, clean house, and happy, wholesome home that guaranteed employers a productive workforce.[3] In the late 1940s, most people assumed that mothers would not be part of that workforce. As paid work outside the home became common for mothers in the 1950s and 1960s, the "double work day" of domestic responsibilities and outside employment became equally common. Feminists denounced women's subordination in both the home and workplace, and called for communal kitchens and other arrangements that challenged the two-parent nuclear household as the locus for social reproduction.[4] But more conventional views of gender roles followed mothers into the workforce, allowing governments to assume that it was a working mother's responsibility alone to arrange for the care of her children while she earned an income. State and capitalist desires to limit public spending meshed with generalized patriarchal social attitudes to hamper efforts to create a state-operated program of free universal daycare.

After the Second World War, state and employer policies, abetted by media propaganda claiming that full-time motherhood was the destiny of married women, produced a large-scale exit of married women from the labour force. The propaganda in favour of a traditional, two-parent nuclear household in which father worked for wages and mother kept the home fires burning was so all-pervasive as to virtually make invisible the many women who both raised children and worked outside the home.[5] Working women and their children were often in desperate straits because of the unwillingness of either the state or employers to see child care as other than a private matter of concern to the nuclear family. Only in the late 1960s did the child care crisis become a publicly addressed issue, and a combination of long-standing patriarchal ideology and neo-conservative ideology that developed as a response to sluggish economic growth after 1970 prevented more than a token response in public policy to the crisis. Daycare advocates argued that the labour market required married women's labour and publicly supported child care was necessary to ensure its availability. But opponents of state-supported child care believed that a sufficient supply of female labour was available in a gender-segregated workforce to meet employers' needs, and therefore argued that it was a woman's business or a family's business to worry about child care arrangements and not the concern of the state or employers.

The Postwar Situation

The behaviour of governments in the daycare area was not uniform. The contrast between Quebec and Ontario in the aftermath of the war is striking. The Quebec government, reflecting the prevalent hostility to working mothers, quickly closed state-subsidized daycares once the war ended, ignoring petitions from the mothers suggesting that because of their poverty, they could not hope to provide their children with equivalent nutrition, health care, and training to what the day nursery provided.[6] The largely anglophone Local Council of Women of Montreal protested the closing of the day nurseries but decided that a prolonged campaign would yield no results. They opted instead for a joint study of the daycare problem with the Montreal Council of Social Agencies, the umbrella group for anglophone charitable organizations. That study would focus equally on half-day nursery programs for preschoolers which were meant to prepare them for collective environments before they reached the school years. In this way the two councils could avoid the ire of opponents of paid work for mothers. Indeed, the resulting study found widespread disapproval of mothers of young children working outside the home. The Community Chest provided some funding for day nurseries in the 1950s but could fund only a limited program because government money was unavailable and a system of licensing for daycares did not exist.[7]

In Ontario, by contrast, a concerted campaign by mothers using the daycares, women's and welfare organizations, as well as the Communist Party and the CCF, persuaded the government to continue provincial support for daycares.[8] Though the province was unwilling to make up the loss of funds from the federal government, it agreed to pay 50 per cent of the costs of daycares for which the municipalities agreed to pay the remaining 50 per cent. Toronto city council and a few others agreed to keep their daycares open on this basis, but balked at establishing new centres since municipalities would be solely responsible for their capital costs. Provincial grants were available only for preschoolers, forcing municipalities to decide whether to bear the full costs of before-and-after-school programs or leave responsibility for care of school-aged children solely with their families.

Toronto, responding to the well-organized campaign for daycare within the city, agreed to maintain existing centres for school children.[9] Daycares for Ontario preschoolers receiving subsidies required a provincial licence, which was issued only to daycares that met fairly strict requirements set out in the Day Nurseries Act of 1946. The Act stipulated the physical and program qualities a daycare had to meet to be licensed so that each served as "a centre of child training" and had "value to the health of children who use their service." The program had to follow the guidelines established by the Institute of Child Study of the University of Toronto, meals were to be nourishing, and supervisors were to have specialized training in care of preschoolers. Petitions from the mothers who used the nurseries subsidized under the wartime legislation had remarked favourably on the attitudes of staff, the physical equipment, and the programming of their daycares, and so the Ontario legislation represented a real victory for them in putting forth the principle that working mothers' children needed quality care rather than just supervision. Their attitude was shared by the Welfare Council of Toronto, which regarded nurseries as a benefit to all children and believed that they should be incorporated into the school system.[10]

Ontario's commitment to daycare soon proved to be limited. Between 1948 and 1951, daycare fees in Toronto had risen sixfold and, though only applications from the most needy applicants received consideration, few needy people could afford licensed daycare at the new rates. Because of the important role of Communists in the daycare struggles of the period, opponents of publicly subsidized daycare Red-baited daycare advocates rather than responding to their arguments. Still, Ontario's initial response to the women's campaign demonstrates the danger of limiting a discussion of the state's response to child care concerns to the question of the "reserve army of labour." The determination of governments to have women dismissed from their jobs when "the boys came home" varied, depending both on the degree to which women protested this supposed solution to male unemployment and the intensity of the campaign of male-dominated organizations (such as the Roman Catholic Church in Quebec) against working mothers.[11] As Linda Gordon warns, the tendency of functionalist arguments that focus on social control is to ignore that "most welfare policies represent the jerry-built compromises which are the artifacts of political and social conflict—a dynamic that functionalism cannot encompass."[12]

It was militancy, not employer needs, that caused the Ontario government to relent on its plan to close day nurseries and daycare centres the very day that a mass meeting in Toronto had been called to protest any closures. Also, if "reserve army" logic had been applied to daycare, the provision of daycare should have increased in periods of increased employer demand for married women's labour. In practice, however, both during the war and the period between 1960 and 1975 when such demand was high, the increase in public child care provision was token and more a response to public criticism of government inaction than a considered attempt to remove child care as an obstacle to women working. Scholars wedded to the "reserve army" argument also tend to ignore that it was working mothers and their supporters in popular organizations who argued that daycare provision would increase the efficiency and workforce longevity of mothers; capitalists rarely asked the state to take an interest in the child care concerns of their employees. Daycare advocates throughout Canada, hoping to influence public opinion, adopted a conservative discourse in which daycare was a preventative measure against juvenile crime.[13] Yet a real daycare program survived only in Toronto where militancy, rather than the persuasiveness of the movement's discourse, allowed at least minimal provision of state-subsidized child care.

The daycare campaign in Toronto made it clear that many women had no choice but to work. Whether they were sole-income providers or had working husbands, these women were poor and victims of the housing crisis that plagued most cities at war's end. Construction began again when peace returned, but the private market was left to be arbiter of the pace and pricing of new housing developments, leaving many families out in the cold. Irene V. Walker, spokeswoman for the Committee of Parents for the Day Care and Day Nursery Association of Toronto, informed Ontario premier George Drew of the desperate position of the women using Toronto daycares. Seventy per cent, she claimed, were sole providers, sometimes because they had no husbands and sometimes because their husbands were mentally or physically unable to work. "In some cases, the family's home consists of one room, where they have to eat, sleep and live. The meals are prepared on a one or two burner gas plate. In some cases there are as many as 21 people in one house where they have to share one bathroom and sometimes the kitchen." In such homes there was "no place for the children to play" and parents worried that their children, forced to play on the streets, would be killed in traffic accidents. The result was that some couples had bought modest homes at outrageous prices, homes they would lose if the working mother could not participate in the labour force.[14]

Some scholars suggest that the apparent contradiction between the "family ethic" and the need of poor women to work was not merely happenstance. Notes American social worker–welfare historian Mimi Abramovitz: "The family ethic, which locked women into a subordinate family role also rationalized women's exploitation on the job. By devaluing women's position in each sphere, the ideology of women's work and family roles satisfied capital's need for a supply of readily available, cheap, female labor. By creating the conditions for continued male control of women at home and on the job, the economic devaluation and marginalization of women also muted the challenge that increased employment by women posed to patriarchal norms."[15]

Public attitudes were clearly against the working mother. A Gallup poll in 1960 asked: "Do you think that married women should take a job outside the home if they want to or should they concentrate on looking after the home when they have young children?" Ninety-three per cent of respondents answered that married women should concentrate on the home against a mere 5 per cent (4 per cent of men and 6 per cent of women) who supported their right to work. Those numbers changed only modestly during the 1960s though afterwards support for the concept of mothers working outside the home began to grow dramatically. Indeed, the dilemma of working mothers was embedded in the widespread patriarchal perspective that men were family providers and should have first claim on jobs. Only 19 per cent of Canadians in 1950 agreed that women "should be given equal opportunity with men to compete for jobs." While that percentage rose to 32 per cent in August 1956, it tumbled to 16 per cent in June 1961 as a prolonged recession made finding a job more difficult generally.[16]

Yet the participation rate of married women in the workforce grew steadily in the postwar period. From the 4.1 per cent of married women engaged in waged or salaried work in 1941, the percentage of married women working for pay jumped to over one in ten in 1951 and to 22.9 per cent in 1963. A similar percentage of divorced, widowed, or separated women worked in 1963 and the married and once-married group together composed half the female labour force. The Women's Bureau of the federal Department of Labour estimated that half of these women had children under sixteen and two-fifths had preschoolers.[17] Most were forced to make child care arrangements without state assistance.

A survey by the Department of Labour in 1958 of married women in the labour force in eight cities found that a tiny minority had recourse to organized daycare facilities. Grandmothers and other relatives, older children, and neighbours looked after young children while mothers worked. The authors of the study suggested "there was a natural tendency for mothers to be protective in replying to questions about the care of their children" and that this might explain "why there was little demand for organized child-care facilities." They added, however, that the mothers surveyed "would have welcomed some place where school-aged children could go after school and spend the time until their mothers returned from work."[18]

By the late 1950s women's and welfare groups were becoming quite concerned that the child care arrangements of many working mothers were haphazard. In Edmonton, for example, two studies suggested unsatisfactory arrangements for daycare. A study done by the Edmonton Council of Community Services in 1956 found children as young as one month "being left at 6 a.m. and being picked up at 7 p.m. in places which cared for 25 or 30 children with one adult in charge." Two years later the University Women's Club investigated fifty-four places that had advertised facilities for care of preschoolers. Again, concerns were raised about the condition of facilities (usually private homes), the competence of supervisors, the lack of programming, and the supervisor-child ratio. Although the Edmonton Council of Community Services called upon city council to set standards for child daycare and the University Women's Club presented their concerns to the provincial government, nothing was done.[19]

In other cities, the situation was similar. The Women Electors Association of Toronto warned the Welfare Department in the early 1950s that, with the cost of spaces in licensed daycares rising rapidly and the number of spaces remaining flat, children were being placed in "precarious private home care and in some cases in black market day care centres." The secretary of the Family and Child Welfare Division of the Community Chest and Council of Greater Vancouver described child care provision for working mothers in his city as "at a very embryonic stage." In British Columbia in 1952, there were only twenty-seven licensed daycare "foster homes," providing services for 277 children. The federal Deputy Minister of National Health and Welfare indicated in 1954 that only Ontario and BC either licensed or subsidized daycares. Three years later, licensing had begun in Manitoba and Saskatchewan and the number of licensed day nurseries in British Columbia had increased to 208 centres caring for 9,636 children. Yet, in the opinion of Eric Smit, secretary of the Family and Child Welfare Division of the Canadian Welfare Council, only Ontario had a "fully developed system of licensing" with close inspection of centres taking place on a continuing basis.[20]

The popular press trivialized the issue of women's paid work by typecasting the working mother as a middle-class wife augmenting her husband's respectable salary so that the household could pile up material possessions and engage in status contests with neighbours. This created a discourse in which the working woman had made a conscious choice to have a "double work day" for fanciful reasons. Charlotte Whitton, then a member of the Board of Control in Ottawa, demonstrated the reaction women might expect when they asked for publicly subsidized daycare: a personal attack. In 1951, the Carling and Merivale Road Mothers' Committees had presented a brief to Board of Control calling for more day nurseries in the city. The controllers rejected their request and Whitton denounced "the woman who much prefers to work outside her own home, though with little or no economic need....What is of more value to a state, a spinster may sententiously enquire, than fully and faithfully to discharge the vocation you chose?"[21]

Even organizations and individuals that defended women's rights to a career and opposed job and pay discrimination on the basis of gender rarely tackled the issue of the right, or indeed the need, of mothers to seek paid employment. In the discourse of the trade union movement, the view that mothers should stay home with children was implicit. While a local trades council, prompted by women activists, might affirm the view that discrimination on the basis of marital status was unjust,[22] the notion of actively encouraging paid work for mothers had little purchase within an overwhelmingly male-dominated labour movement. The Congress of Canadian Labour (CCL), the second largest and the most progressive federation, did call in 1945 for "day nurseries for working mothers, either within individual establishments or on a community basis, whichever seems more effective." For twenty years afterwards, however, both federal and provincial labour organizations gave little consideration to the child care issue, much less to the larger question of the gender division of labour within the home.[23]

Women's organizations confronted the issue of married women's work with more seriousness than the trade union movement, but with great difficulty. The National Council of Women of Canada (NCWC), for example, the major voice of "club women" in the country, could not reconcile its view that discrimination against working mothers should end with its perspective that full-time mothers were the bulwarks of a free society. Largely avoiding the daycare issue, the organization implicitly endorsed the notion that only single women and a handful of professional women, able to afford full-time help in the home, should seek work. There was no need for public programs that actively encouraged mothers to seek paid work.[24] The NCWC had opposed efforts to encourage the employment of married women during the war and was unsurprisingly silent when the federal government withdrew all support from child care at war's end. Long-time national president Laura Hardy argued during the war that while day nurseries and community kitchens might be necessary during the period of demobilization, "the nurseries and kitchens should not be continued longer than is necessary for two reasons, because of the cost to the Government in maintaining them and the need to keep intact the home and the life of the family." This within a speech that reiterated the NCWC's support for equal pay for equal work and denounced the military for not abiding by this principle.[25]

When the war was over, Hardy still defended women's right to equal opportunities with men in the labour force and continued to imply that "women" should be read as "women without children," though her organization officially deplored discrimination against married women. She joined critics of working mothers who blamed them for the perceived increase in juvenile delinquency[26] and told them to stay home and prevent their children from becoming criminals or Communists, or both. "Why not a crusade to maintain to women who are mothers that their greatest contribution to their country is the training of their children for loyal Canadian citizenship and Christian living....May it ever be said of us that we are building for a strong and virile nation; that we are standing shoulder to shoulder with the men as they face momentous problems; that we are fighting all insidious inroads in our national life."[27] Another argument used by Hardy and other traditionalists against proponents of state-organized daycare was that it took power away from individual women and handed it to the state. She told the Canadian Chamber of Commerce in October 1946: "As women, we want to live in a Canada in which we can raise our children in our own homes and in the schools of our choice, not in public institutions under the guidance of the State."[28]

Unwilling to challenge notions of the nuclear family household that made the mother responsible for the care of the children and the upkeep of the home, the NCWC was bound to contradict itself in dealing with issues of women's paid employment. At the same time as the organization turned away from dealing with child care, it campaigned continuously and effectively to end discrimination by the Unemployment Insurance Commission against mothers and expectant mothers who left the workforce. Though the Commission argued that these women did not intend to return to the workforce, the NCWC responded that the case of each person who became unemployed should be considered on its merits and not dismissed on the basis of social prejudices.[29] It was a classic argument of "equal rights feminism" which called for gender-free public policy but failed to deal with the obstacles women faced in attempting to return to the labour force after becoming mothers.

An "equal rights" emphasis perhaps also explains why the Canadian Federation of Business and Professional Women's Clubs and its provincial affiliates did not make child care an issue in the 1950s.[30] Leaders of this organization rarely made use of maternalist rhetoric and focused strongly on equal pay for equal work and the breaking down of barriers to women's participation in decision making at all levels of business and government. They had campaigned strongly for a Women's Bureau in the Department of Labour and for an end to discrimination against married women in the regulations of the Unemployment Insurance Act.[31] Yet their underlying view that differential treatment of the sexes in law and society slowed women's advance perhaps accounted for a reluctance to support legislation meant to give special aid to mothers.

As noted in chapter 6, similar contradictions to those found on the child care issue in the NCWC marked the report on the postwar problems of women prepared by a subcommittee to the federal government's Advisory Committee on Reconstruction. The subcommittee consisted of ten prominent women, though "no representative basis of any kind was used for the choice of members." Overall, the report had a progressive tone and, in addition to supporting a full-employment policy for Canada and a comprehensive program of social security, it stated that a woman's right to choose her occupation "must be conceded as a right to which every citizen is entitled." Women "must also have the right to equality of remuneration, working conditions, and opportunity for advancement." Overcrowded and substandard housing rather than inadequate mothers were blamed for juvenile delinquency, and women's right to play a key role in the planning of housing programs was asserted. Yet, while stating that married women who wished to remain in the labour force should not be pushed out, the subcommittee also supported children's allowances because it could persuade mothers to stay at home: "The addition to the family income from children's allowances paid to the mother and by her spent for the welfare of her children may well be an alleviating factor in the mental attitude which may result from the surrender of the double income."

The subcommittee's stance on daycare was curious given its supposed commitment to equal opportunities for women in the workforce. Omitting all mention of full-workday care, the subcommittee limited its discussion of child care outside the home to nursery schools operating from 9 a.m. to noon. These schools, claimed the subcommittee, promoted the development of children's social skills while giving mothers time for household and community activities difficult to undertake with a child underfoot. Their numbers should be increased and they should be included within the educational system. The schools "would also care for the children of married women who need or wish to work outside their homes, for a part of the day." But obviously they were not to work outside those homes for more than three hours. The exception would be business and professional women who could afford full-time housekeepers. A program to train home aides was recommended as a solution to the perennial shortage of "good help" long decried by club women, a problem exacerbated by wartime prosperity which gave women more job options than ever before. On the whole, the subcommittee favoured social security measures that would make it possible for most households to function without mothers having to seek paid employment. To that extent they confirmed the traditional perspective that society worked best when married men and women performed gender-typed roles. Yet the progressive measures this subcommittee and the Advisory Committee on Reconstruction endorsed to make it possible for women to remain at home with children without being reduced to penury were not implemented.[32]

Some prominent women refused to accept the contradictory arguments that women must have equality with men in the labour force and yet married women should regard "homemaking" as their only real vocation. Dorise Nielsen, a feminist and socialist who was elected MP for North Battleford as a "Unity" candidate in 1940 (she later joined the Communist Party), became a spokesperson in Parliament for "the emancipation of women as wage earners."[33] In a booklet entitled *New Worlds for Women* (1944), she argued that an extensive program of publicly funded and regulated child care was essential if married women were to have real opportunities to work outside the home. Similar arguments were made by the first two CCF women elected to the British Columbia legislature: Dorothy Steeves (member from 1934 to 1945) and Laura Jamieson (member from 1939 to 1945 and 1952 to 1953). Jamieson, author of a feminist book, *Women, Dry Those Tears* (c. 1945), was a legislative voice for the retention of married women in civil service jobs and for better wages and working conditions for women domestics, retail clerks, and factory employees.[34]

There was also somewhat less enthusiastic support for the rights of women to work from the female-dominated social work profession. While feminists such as Nielsen and Jamieson believed that publicly supported child care ought to be the fundamental right of all women, social workers stressed that most working mothers came from low-income households that might be destitute without the fruits of their paid labour. The all-woman Day Nurseries Committee of the Welfare Council of Toronto and District commissioned a social workers' study in 1941 to look at the child care arrangements of 106 of the 500 women whose applications to place their children in the West End Crèche in Toronto were unsuccessful the year before. The results demonstrated "first of all, that these mothers are pretty desperate to take employment, and secondly, that the plans are, on the whole, inadequate." While lack of child care had caused some mothers to abandon the search for work, poverty forced many others to work anyway, and to provide child care as best they could:

Nine had placed them with relatives (three of these with grandmothers and one with a grandfather where the plans were inadequate), one child was with a relative who does not want the child, but is caring for it until further plans are made. In two instances, the children have been sent out of town. In one case, the parents have four children and are running a laundry in their own home, where the children may be in actual danger…One four-year old child was left without any responsible attendant (in the course of the study the child met with a severe accident): in three instances children were left with landladies who will assume responsibility for only a short time.[35]

The Day Nurseries Committee told the Canadian National Conference on Social Work in 1942 that the detailed information they collected on the financial circumstances of the households of the working mothers indicated that "it is not easy to say in such instances that the place of the mother is with her family." They noted approvingly that the vast majority of the working women whom they had interviewed, while poor, had never approached a social agency for support. They predicted correctly: "If women remain in employment to the degree that they were there in the pre-war period without additional services, the outlook can be considered serious; if the trend on their employment continues as it has in previous decades, it will be acute, and there is every reason to believe that the trend will be maintained."[36]

The social workers who supported the extension of daycare facilities received no support from the wartime executive director of the Canadian Welfare Council (cwc), the organization that spoke most authoritatively on behalf of social agencies in Canada. Dr. George Davidson discouraged the entry of more mothers into jobs outside the home. Davidson urged employers to recruit single women first and then married women without children before hiring married women with children under fourteen. If the latter were to be employed, they should only be considered for day shifts and half-day shifts.[37] Significantly, by war's end, Davidson had become federal Deputy Minister of Health and Social Welfare and was then in a position to encourage that his maternalist views form the basis of federal child care policy.

In the postwar period the cwc remained cautious in its questioning of maternalist assumptions. Despite the proddings of Marion Royce, the cwc undertook no national study of the child care crisis. The secretary of its Child Welfare Division from the late 1940s to the mid-1950s, K. Phyllis Burns, also the first permanent secretary of the Canadian Conference on Social Work, regarded the provision of adequate care for children of working mothers as a priority for Canadian social workers. Though she focused on economic need as the main reason why mothers sought work outside the home, she added, unusual for the time, "that some women make better parents when they have an outside interest. And often, if they are not with children too much, they can give them more love and understanding." She was, however, unable to convince the CWC to join her in making child care a major focus of the organization's work in the 1950s. Even Burns, like most social workers before the 1960s, was influenced by the studies that suggested negative effects of daycare on children. She also recognized that "day nursery care was not entirely satisfactory if it still left the mother with all her household duties to be done after she returned from work." She preferred "more adequate provision of public assistance, pensions and other forms of social allowances" so that "mothers who have small children can stay at home."[38]

Social workers' general reluctance in the early postwar period to regard mothers' paid labour as a partial solution to problems of poverty is evident in the pages of *The Social Worker* and *Canadian Welfare* in the 1950s and most of the 1960s. These were the journals of the Canadian Association of Social Workers and the Canadian Welfare Council, respectively. *Canadian Welfare* made only passing, non-committal comments on working mothers and their child care arrangements before 1967. Until an article in November 1968 broke *The Social Worker*'s silence, this journal contained no articles on the daycare issue.

THE 1960S

As the 1960s dawned, however, a shift in the social discourse on child care became evident. The numbers of working mothers had reached a critical mass that caused some reappraisal of the mother-at-home/father-at-work ideal. By the end of the decade many voices challenged the view that it was best for children if their mothers were home. Initially, child care advocates limited themselves to educating the public to accept that increasing numbers of women were entering the paid labour force and that industry clearly could not do without them. In such circumstances, went the argument, the focus ought to be on insuring the best child care for the children of working mothers rather than attempting to devise means of keeping the mothers home. As a 1960 Toronto Social Planning Council document argued, "The real issue, then, is not whether mothers should work but rather the need to ensure that children are cared for adequately while mothers are at work."[39]

The emphasis on educating the public about the reality of working mothers was widely shared by welfare councils. The Welfare Council of Greater Winnipeg, for example, undertaking a study of child care needs for working mothers in

1959 that involved a random sample of fifteen hundred Winnipeg families, had decided in advance that the main value of the study would be educational. As Joyce Rogers, division secretary of the Community Welfare Planning Council of Greater Winnipeg, explained to a Canadian Welfare Council official: "We want to point out that, whether we like it or not, x% of mothers are working and 'Y' children are affected by this phenomenon. These children are not to be forced to suffer from inadequate care because mothers are working."[40]

The eventual study suggested that at least one in five children of working mothers needed improved care. Similar studies were undertaken by social welfare and women's organizations across the country, and by the federal and Ontario Women's Bureaus of the Department of Labour throughout the 1960s, all of which revealed a desperate need for rapid expansion of licensed daycares with subsidies for low-income households. A report on daycare needs prepared by the Community Chest and Council of the Greater Vancouver area in June 1965 studied 32,000 children with working mothers and concluded that 11,500 of these children needed improved care, with 6,000 of them receiving no care at all, care from older siblings kept home from school, or from infirm or alcoholic sitters.[41] What that meant for one family was revealed by Vancouver School Board trustee Carmella Allevato, when she spoke to a House of Commons Special Committee on Child Care in 1985 and recounted her family's experience of twenty years earlier: "I came to Canada when I was 12 and I was the oldest of four children. We came in November and my mother went to work immediately. I remember that my mother was working nights and at one point they changed her shift from midnight to noon, for whatever reason, and my three-year-old sister had to be left at home alone in the mornings. My mother worked about a block away. That is 20 years ago and I am sure that kind of situation is continuing today."[42]

For another Vancouver family unable to afford a sitter for their two preschoolers and one school-aged boy, the choice was to leave two small children to play unattended in the yard of their house for a brief period when both parents were at work or to give up their house and have no yard at all. The president of the Kingcrest Business and Professional Women's Club, who had watched the two and learned that they were locked out of their house each day, spoke to their mother afterwards:

> I was told that the two children were locked out only for a very short time; that the husband left for work at 3:00 p.m. and that the oldest boy came home shortly afterward to unlock the house. The mother said: I consider the two children being safer locked outside than they would be locked in. I come home shortly after 5:00 p.m.

I have to work until the second mortgage is paid off as it was the borrowed money that paid the initial down payment on the house. My husband is making the first mortgage payments. She went on to say that this arrangement was a family project, that even the little children cooperated to make it work. They never had a house before–not a yard to play in or a tree to climb–said the mother.[43]

In many cases, older children became sitters for their younger siblings. Italo Costa, a social worker on the staff of the Italian consulate in Toronto, told *Chatelaine* that she was often asked by school attendance officers to determine why certain school-aged Italian girls were truant. "The fact is they're at home looking after their younger brothers and sisters and missing out on their education."[44]

The Women's Bureau of the federal Department of Labour conducted a major national study of working mothers in the 1960s. Published in 1970 as *Working Mothers and Their Child-Care Arrangements*[45] the study reported that 1,075,000 children under fourteen had working mothers. While only 17 per cent of mothers of preschoolers were in the workforce, 28 per cent of mothers with all kids in school held a job. "There are no regular care arrangements for one in ten children of working mothers," reported the study, noting that this was true for one child in twenty under the age of three. The study indicated that another 73 per cent of the children were in care arrangements "for which the mother presumably does not pay." While 37 per cent of women earning over $10,000 paid for child care, only 16 per cent of women earning under $3,000 were paying for their child care. Advocates of a network of daycare centres, including centres for before-and-after-school care, saw in cases of this kind an argument for their perspective.

However, daycares without close government regulation were proving an inadequate solution for many parents, according to a study by the Canadian Council on Social Development, successor (in 1970) to the Canadian Welfare Council. Examining 1,412 daycare centres across the country with combined enrolments of 54,100, the CCSD concluded that, particularly outside Ontario, many centres made poor provision for the health, education, and social development of their charges, providing a sterile environment with little equipment. The CCSD called for national standards for daycare centres to correct these problems.[46]

Amidst such calls for action, however, were the male defenders of an imagined family ideal who continued to trivialize the problems of working mothers and of women generally. In Vancouver, where the daycare crisis was acute, as noted above, the two daily newspapers greeted the formation of the Royal Commission on the Status of Women in February 1967 with undisguised contempt. The *Vancouver Province*, decrying a "petticoat tyranny" that began with the suffragettes, asked:

"Is a nation's cause really served by an army of servile husbands and fathers wasting their talents on washing dishes, mowing lawns and cleaning the family car?" Columnist James K. Nesbitt in the *Vancouver Sun* thought women were better off making sandwiches for ladies' auxiliaries: "They are but taking their rightful places in society and if they stayed there instead of roaming about all over the place they'd be far happier—and so would their husbands and children."[47]

There was, nonetheless, a greater tendency on the part of newspapers to report the problems working mothers faced in finding adequate child care by the mid-1960s than at any earlier period, though such coverage was rarely either front-page or in-depth news. Reports that stay-at-home motherhood had been "over-sold," as one headline noted, were backed up by research studies and the public addresses of feminist social workers and child care advocates. These views, however, were often at variance with the more traditional ideas expressed by mothers who worked solely because of economic need. Veteran social worker Barbara Chisholm, executive director of Toronto's Victoria Day Nursery, commented: "Sentencing a mother to 24-hour duty, seven days a week, every day of the year can do the children the very harm we wished to prevent." But working mothers of the 1960s, who were more likely than their 1950s counterparts to defend publicly their right to employment, rarely accepted such logic. Those who worked for economic reasons suggested that they would be happy to leave their jobs and return to the home full time if finances permitted. A typical working mom who wrote to *The Globe and Mail* in 1966 said that she worked out of "dire necessity": "It goes without saying that there are instances of women who could and should be at home with their children, yet who persist in leaving the house five days a week from before 9 to after 5 o'clock—women who are bent on 'fulfilling themselves' at the expense of the physical and emotional well-being of their children; women intent on earning extra money for unnecessary luxuries—but I challenge the experts to show that this group is anything but an insignificant minority."[48]

Interestingly, the letter writer was protesting against comments made by Metropolitan Toronto politicians at a Welfare and Housing Committee discussion of day nurseries. The theme of several speakers in the majority group who opposed new expenditures on daycare at that time was that a comprehensive program of daycare, as proposed by Toronto's Alderman Charles Caccia, had communist overtones. For Reeve John MacBeth of Etobicoke, it meant that women were to be held in common, as he imagined they were under Chinese Communism. Reeve True Davidson, who claimed not to oppose day nurseries as such, nonetheless opposed "the holus bolus assumption they had to be provided for everybody...it reminds me of Russia...we pay lip service to family life, yet at the same time we want to remove children from the family."[49]

Davidson's remarks differed mainly in degree from those of the letter writer. The campaigns of welfare organizations to dramatize the large numbers and the plight of working mothers had had some effect. The dominant discourse on women's work and daycare still rejected gender equality in either the home or the workplace; but it was now recognized that some "needy" women must work and that they had a right to claim state aid for child care during hours when there was no parent in the home. There were great differences among those who shared this perspective about what constituted need in Canada in the 1960s. Nonetheless, it was a perspective that, unlike the harder-line maternalist perspective dominant before 1960, did not shame most working mothers into remaining silent. It also offered social workers and women's organizations an opportunity to argue for an expansion of public child care without appearing to attack the "traditional" family structure with its well-defined gender roles.

If daycare had once been attacked as the culprit in juvenile delinquency, it now came to be seen as a preventative measure for those most likely to become social outlaws. The Department of Social Welfare in British Columbia, which began a modest daycare program in 1966, sharing costs with the federal government under the Canada Assistance Plan, reported confidently: "As day care is extended, particularly to children whose homes have limited opportunities, it is foreseen that fewer children will encounter major problems in adjustment to school and in their homes and communities."[50] Social agencies began to see potential in day-cares for identification and correction of children's problems, sometimes using a discourse that smacked of social engineering. The Ontario Welfare Council, calling in 1973 for universal availability of daycare with geared-to-income fees, suggested that daycare settings provided "excellent opportunities for early identification of and assistance in relation to special needs and problems in the areas of health, family relations, and learning skills." The Council wanted health, education, and psychological testing to become part of a daycare program with follow-up services available when problems were uncovered. While such intrusive notions of daycare were rarely proposed by working mothers, mothers' desire for organized daycare in the 1960s was clear.

For example forty-six of fifty-six mothers with preschoolers, women who worked at GWG, a clothing manufacturer in Edmonton, and who had responded to a questionnaire about their child care arrangements, indicated that if a daycare centre were to open near the plant and establish a low fee, they would place their preschoolers in the centre. Among the fifty-six women, care for their children while they were at work was provided as follows: 24 by husbands, 13 by babysitters, 11 by relatives, 2 by older siblings, and six through arrangements not indicated. Studies by the Women's Bureau of the Ontario Department of Labour also suggested that working mothers would generally welcome affordable institutional daycare.[51] The defensiveness noted by Marion Royce regarding child care arrangements had given way, at least in part, to a willingness to assert that society had to help working women with their child care needs.

For supporters of an enlarged state role in daycare, the hearings and eventual report of the Royal Commission on the Status of Women provided their best opportunity in the 1960s to publicize their cause. Traditionalists regarding gender roles certainly made their views known to the commission and their numbers included large and influential groups such as the 165,000-member Catholic Women's League of Canada and the 45,000-member Cèrcles de fèrmieres du Québec. The former group, whose national conventions studiously ignored the issues of working wives and their needs for child care, did however suggest that municipalities and industries should be "encouraged" to provide daycare with a sliding scale of fees and flexible hours.[52]

A host of groups encouraged the commission to recommend, as it eventually did, that each province establish a network of approved daycare centres and day-homes with the federal government contributing most of the capital costs and a large share of the operating costs. The commission, like most of its pro-daycare participants, favoured a sliding scale of fees for daycare based on family incomes as opposed to a free service. Women's groups that twenty years earlier had encouraged mothers to stay home with their children now recognized that the formal equality of women with men that they professed required that mothers have as much right to earn incomes as anyone else. The NCWC, the United and Anglican Churches, trade union and social worker organizations called for daycare services for all children of working parents who desired the service, regardless of income.[53] So did most Quebec organizations that appeared before the commission. While some Catholic organizations restated traditional arguments against working mothers, they were countered by groups such as the 30,000-member L'Association feminine d'éducation et d'action sociale, which defended stay-at-home mothers, but supported meaningful choice for women through a state presence in daycare provision. The most militant position put forward from Quebec came from the Fédération des femmes du Québec, formed in 1966, which not only defended a woman's right to work but called for a reorganization of community services to reduce the workload of women in individual households.[54]

A common element in the briefs presented by organizations proposing more public child care services was support for a change in the definition of women's gender roles so that women would be valued for their mothering and for their contributions to the community via paid work. Good daycare was presented as a means of enhancing the efficiency of women workers at home and in the workplace. As the Ontario Association of Social Workers, Western Branch, put it:

> Greatly expanded day care service is an urgent need. They should be organized and operated as a utility service—available to the total community with service readily available. Working women cannot be expected to operate at their most effective level when the day care facility is inadequate or non-existent. Emotional conflict for the woman can and does enter, resulting in a reduced level of proficiency in both her homemaking and work in the community. Well organized, licensed and economical day care centres could ensure the mother that her children are being well cared for and she will then be able to fill more adequately her various roles.[55]

But if women now had "various roles" for which state aid was required, what was happening regarding men's roles? Briefs to the commission and social discourse more generally tended to ignore this issue. While there was an implication that men did not need to be the only "breadwinners" in a household, it was still generally assumed that women did need to remain principally responsible for raising the children and maintaining the household.[56] There was reason for cynicism about just how "liberating" mothers' participation in the labour force would be, even given an excellent system of publicly funded child care, if working mothers continued to have all the responsibility for child care and housework.

Perhaps, like the suffragists a half century earlier, women who advocated publicly supported daycare feared harming their cause with men by suggesting that legislative means be considered to encourage men to take equal responsibilities for housework and child care. In the incrementalist perspective of this period, it was a step forward for society to place a positive value on women's paid work outside the home and to ease the guilt of these women along with the difficulties for their children that resulted from the necessity for individualist solutions to child care problems.

Certainly, such a strategy was a success in countries such as Sweden where a political consensus favouring full-employment policies existed. It proved less successful in Canada where, even as the Royal Commission on the Status of Women deliberated, the Trudeau government indicated that inflation, not unemployment, would be its main preoccupation. As unemployment began a slow but steady rise in the 1970s and the labour shortages of the 1950s and 1960s faded into memory, governments and corporations demonstrated little interest in the argument that increased public expenditures on child care were in their interest. While there might occasionally be shortages of women workers in such "women's occupations" as nursing and social work, "gluts" of teachers, saleswomen, and clerical personnel discouraged the view that improved child care was essential for improved economic performance. Indeed, as the economy stagnated, the consensus supporting the welfare state began to crack. For the corporate elite, "reforms" remained unacceptable if they had the effect of redistributing income. Rather, reforms must be funded through the extra income generated in an expanding economy; they would be the means by which the state ensured that the poor received their share of the expanding economic pie and everyone ended up relatively the same.

In the 1970s, as the expansion of the economy slowed down, it became clear that new social programs could probably not be financed without wealth redistribution. Cost became the major public argument of elites against a national daycare program, though the notion of child care as entirely a private family matter remained an important subtext. The economically conservative report of the Royal Commission on the Economic Union and Development Prospects for Canada (Macdonald Commission) suggested in 1985 that "day care could constitute a very costly social service area in which government is not now heavily involved. The cost of an even greater degree of government involvement would be higher still, and we Canadians must consider carefully whether or not we wish our governments to spend more public funds on providing daycare services."[57]

The limited impact on state policy of the report of the Royal Commission on the Status of Women is indicated in the Macdonald Commission's frank admission that, in 1985, daycare remained a "social service area in which government is not now heavily involved." There had been some changes: in 1972, child care costs up to a specified amount became tax deductible for single parents and for the lower-income earner in a married couple, a benefit of little value to low-wage women who earned too little to be assessed for taxes. For the needy, the federal government had reintroduced federal spending on daycare on a limited basis in 1966, by including daycare among costs that could be cost-shared with the provinces under the Canada Assistance Plan; gradually, they became slightly more liberal in their definition of need.[58] More low-income-earning women qualified for subsidized daycare. Daycare subsidies to employers became an alternative to welfare payments and, in some provinces, such as Nova

Scotia, daycare monies were available almost exclusively to women who would otherwise be social assistance recipients.[59]

The Royal Commission on the Status of Women tried to disassociate state subsidization of daycare from welfare. But little changed. A study in 1984 indicated that only 8.8 per cent of children thirteen and younger requiring care were in licensed daycare centres or homes. That year, the Social Planning Council of Winnipeg estimated that 200 preschool children had been left on their own the preceding year; so were 200 children between the ages of five and eight and 2,700 children between the ages of nine and twelve. Five years earlier, there were estimated to be 1 million "latch-key" children in Canada, or about one child in five.[60]

Newspaper articles recounted horror stories about daycare in Canada, some of which were compiled in Laura Johnson's book, *The Kin Trade*, a call for a comprehensive child care policy. Children were warehoused in quarters so cramped that closets became their sleep area, in places that were filthy and infested with parasites, places without toys or play areas. In the first four months of 1979, ten babysitters appeared in court in Calgary on ten unrelated charges of sexual attacks on young children. Even children from middle-class families often found themselves shunted from relatives to sitters to a variety of daycares. The six-year-old daughter of St. John's social worker Lynette Pike had been in seventeen different child care situations between her birth in April 1979 and March 1986. Sitters quit for better-paying jobs or were fired for providing poor care, relatives proved willing to provide care only on a short-term basis, and daycare centres closed or proved to be too far away from Pike's work. Both mother and daughter were frazzled from arrangements that often lasted just a few weeks; the longest arrangement had been one and a half years with a woman whose husband was an alcoholic.[61]

The problems regarding child care were stark enough that all three national party leaders pledged themselves to a national daycare program to improve the situation on a televised leaders' debate during the 1984 federal election. The eventual winner, Brian Mulroney, whose government was more concerned about reducing the national debt than in preserving or extending social programs, reneged on his promise. The Conservatives and conservatives within society generally, even when they did not openly criticize the right of married women to work, stressed that this was a decision made by individuals and therefore gave them no claim on the state. Implicit was the view that it was natural and right that nuclear households, and primarily the mothers within these households, continue to raise the next generation of workers and taxpayers, without pay or financial aid. The quotation that opens this chapter demonstrates how a member of the corporate elite could dismiss the issue of public daycare by using this discourse. Daycare was simply a commodity and would have to be purchased by individuals requiring it. It was not to be seen as a social necessity.

The debate over child care from 1945 to the 1980s had many twists and turns, but the assumption that women should have primary responsibility for care of children was a constant. While women's roles as income-earners came to be more accepted over the period, there was division over the implications of the changes in women's social roles for public policy and for the gender roles of men.[62] Several competing discourses vied in public policy debates: the most successful suggested that it was a mother's personal choice to enter the labour force and she must handle the consequences, including the finding of suitable child care; women's equality with men would be achieved by the economic efforts of individual women. But an alternative discourse branded such a view of equality as hollow because it ignored the gendered construction of both home life and the labour market. From this viewpoint, increasingly espoused by the women's movement, social welfare organizations, and trade unions, among others, an attack on the poverty of women and children and a movement towards real equality of the sexes required public policies that addressed the systemic subordination of women both in the home and in the workplace.

NOTES

1 J. Eric Harrington, president, Canada Vickers Ltd., Montreal, to MacInnis, 9 May 1972, Grace MacInnis Papers, MG 32 C 12, Vol. 19, File-"Women, Status of, 1972," Library Archives of Canada (LAC).

2 MacInnis to Harrington, 18 May 1972. Ibid.

3 Useful works on state efforts to shape the family as a locus of social reproduction include Jane Ursel, "The State and the Maintenance of Patriarchy: A Case Study of Family, Labour and Welfare Legislation in Canada," in *Family, Economy and State: The Social Reproduction Process Under Capitalism*, ed. James Dickinson and Bob Russell, (Toronto, ON: Garamond, 1986), 150–92; and Linda Gordon, "The Welfare State: Towards a Socialist-Feminist Perspective," in *Socialist Register 1990*, ed. Ralph Miliband and Leo Panitch (London, UK: Merlin, 1990), 171–200.

4 Feminists in the CCF convinced the party's national convention in 1946 to adopt a "Status of Women" resolution that called for sexual equality "in the economic and cultural life of Canada" and proposed policies for the "emancipation of the housewife." These included "public or co-operative restaurants, laundries, housecleaning services, home nursing services, nursery schools, supervised recreation areas, community centres." It was, implicit, however

that the movement of these women's jobs from the nuclear household into the community would not alter the gendered character of the labour to be performed. "Report of Ninth National Convention Co-operative Commonwealth Federation," 7,8,9 August 1946, Regina, Canadian Labour Congress (CLC) Papers, MG 28, I 103, Vol. 314, File 4–1, LAC.

5 Veronica Strong-Boag, "Canada's Wage-Earning Wives and the Construction of the Middle Class, 1945–60," *Journal of Canadian Studies* 29, 3 (1994): 5–25, and "Home Dreams: Women and the Suburban Experiment in Canada, 1945–60," *Canadian Historical Review* 72, 4 (1991): 471–504.

6 Ruth Roach Pierson, *"They're Still Women After All": The Second World War and Canadian Womanhood* (Toronto, ON: McClelland and Stewart, 1986), 55.

7 Nursery schools had become popular among upper-income parents in Canada in the 1920s. "The result was that only the very poor who were subsidized, or the children of parents who could afford the fees had the advantage of preschool programs, a situation that effectively continues to this day." Status of Women Canada, *Report of the Task Force on Child Care* (Ottawa, ON: Minister of Supply and Services, 1986), 230; "Minutes of the Sub-Executive Committee of the Local Council of Women of Montreal," 9 January 1946, Montreal Council of Women Papers, MG 28 I 64, Volume 2, LAC; Miss Ghislaine Guindon, Assistant Secretary, Family and Child Welfare Division, Canadian Welfare Council, to Mrs. Winifred Moore, Day Care Consultant, United Community Defense Services, Child Welfare League of America, New York, n.d., Canadian Welfare Council /Canadian Council on Social Development (CWC/CCSD) Papers, MG 28, Vol. 50, File 448, LAC.

8 Susan Prentice, "Workers, Mothers, Reds: Toronto's Postwar Daycare Fight," *Studies in Political Economy* 30 (1989): 115–41, The Minister of Public Welfare made clear that he had been impressed by the number of campaigners for daycare who had written him, signed petitions, or appeared before him in delegations, and by their arguments. W.A. Goodfellow, Minister of Public Welfare, to George Drew, 25 February 1946, George Drew Papers, RG 3, Box 455, File 228-G, "Public Welfare, Department of, Day Nurseries," Archives of Ontario (AO).

9 *The Globe and Mail*, 16 October 1947; Margaret J. Newton, Assistant Executive Secretary, Welfare Council of Toronto and District, to Phyllis Burns, secretary, Child Welfare Division, Canadian Welfare Council, 23 March 1953, CWC/CCSD Papers, Vol. 50, File 448D, "Nursery Day Care 1950–6."

10 Though the number of licensed centres grew rapidly, growth in licensed spaces and particularly subsidized spaces was far less spectacular. There were 4,335 licensed spaces in 1945–46 of which 1135 were subsidized, and 11,581 spaces in 1963–64 with 1,291 receiving subsidies. Ruth K. Abbott and R.A. Young, "Cynical and Deliberate Manipulation? Child Care and the Reserve Army of Female Labour in Canada," *Journal of Canadian Studies* 24, 2 (1989): 28; Goodfellow to Drew, 25 February 1946, George Drew Papers, File 228-G; Ontario, Department of Public Welfare, "Regulations Made Pursuant to Section 3 of Day Nurseries Act 1946" (passed by Order-in-Council 6 March 1947), AO; Submission of Nursery School Committee and Day Nursery Committee, Welfare Council, Toronto, Royal Commission on Education in Ontario, RG 18, Series B, B-115, *Briefs*, Box 16, AO.

11 Toronto Public Welfare Department, "Nursery and Day Care Centers," April 1953, enclosed with Margaret J. Newton, assistant executive secretary, Welfare Council of Toronto and District, to Phyllis Burns, secretary, Child Welfare Division, CWC, 23 March 1953, CWC/CCSD Papers, Vol. 50, File 448D, 53; Prentice, "Workers, Mothers, Reds," 130. On the "reserve army of labour" debate, see Pierson, *"They're Still Women After All"*; Abbott and Young, "Cynical and Deliberate Manipulation;" Patricia Connelly, *Last Hired, First Fired: Women and the Canadian Workforce* (Toronto, ON: Canadian Women's Educational Press, 1978); Ronnie

Leah, "Women's Labour Force Participation and Day Care Cutbacks in Ontario," *Atlantis* 7, 1 (1981): 36–44; and Meg Luxton, "Taking on the Double Day: Housewives as a Reserve Army of Labour," *Atlantis* 7, 1 (1981): 12–32.

12 Gordon, "The Welfare State," 186.

13 *Red Feather* 1, 2 (1946), CWC/CCSD Papers, Vol. 77, File 564. Pressure for the establishment of a public presence in the daycare field during the war came from welfare groups such as the Welfare Council of Toronto, whose executive secretary, Bessie Touzel, had presented an ambitious plan for daycare provision to the federal and provincial governments in early 1942. *The Globe and Mail*, 11 April 1942. See also Ruth Roach Pierson, "*They're Still Women After All*," 50. Employers played a negligible role in reinforcing such pressures and were equally inactive in promoting state involvement in child care in the 1960s; see Prentice, "Workers, Mothers, Reds," 120.

14 Irene V. Walker to Drew, 29 July 1946, Drew Papers, Box 455.

15 Mimi Abramovitz, *Regulating the Lives of Women: Social Welfare Policy from Colonial Times to the Present* (Boston, MA: South End, 1989), 39. While Abramovitz's functionalist conclusion perhaps confounds intentions and consequences, it serves as a powerful description of the way in which the "family ethic" restricted all women but particularly oppressed women who had no option but to work. From this perspective, the daycare dilemmas faced by such women were part of something far greater than state unconcern.

16 Monica Boyd, *Canadian Attitudes toward Women: Thirty Years of Change*, prepared for Canada, Women's Bureau, Labour Canada (Ottawa, ON: Labour Canada, 1983), 46, 47, 49; "Gallup Poll Canada-General-1956," in Vol. 1024, and "Gallup Poll 1960–68," in Vol. 960, National Liberal Federation Papers, MG 28 1V-3, LAC.

17 Canada, Department of Labour, Women's Bureau, *Bulletin*, January 1964, Number XI, "Day Care Services for Children of Working Mothers," Library and Archives of Canada.

18 Canada, Department of Labour, *Married Women Working for Pay in Eight Canadian Cities* (Ottawa, ON: Department of Labour, 1958).

19 "Material Given to Mr. Smit by Miss M.V. Royce," June 1957; *Minutes*, Study Group on Family Welfare Services, 24 November 1960, CWC/CCSD Papers, Vol. 50, File 448, "Nursery-Daycare 1957–68."

20 Patricia Vandebelt Schulz, "Day Care in Canada: 1850–1962," in *Good Day Care: Fighting for It, Getting It, Keeping* It, ed. Kathleen Gallagher Ross (Toronto, ON: Women's Press, 1978), 155; Deputy Minister of National Health and Welfare to Canadian Welfare Council, 24 February 1954, Vol. 50, File 448D, "Nursery Day Care 1950–6"; "Telephone Conversation with Mr. Watson [E.F. Watson, Secretary, Family and Child Welfare Division, Community Chest and Council of Greater Vancouver]" included in "Material Given to Mr. Smit by Miss M.V. Royce," June 1957: "Some notes re discussions of day care for children of working mothers in Edmonton, Calgary and Vancouver-June 1957," Vol. 50, File 448; Deputy Minister of National Health and Welfare to Canadian Welfare Council, 24 February 1954, Vol. 50, File 448, "Family Day Care"; Eric Smit to G.A. de Coq, executive assistant, Edmonton Council of Community Services, 6 May 1957, Vol. 50, File 448, "Nursery-Day Care 1957–68," all from CWC/CCSD Papers.

21 P.T. Rooke and R.L. Schnell, *No Bleeding Heart: Charlotte Whitton, A Feminist on the Right* (Vancouver, BC: University of British Columbia Press, 1987), 146.

22 Such a resolution, for example, was passed by the Vancouver Labour Council, Congress of Canadian Labour, in April 1950, but faced criticism from supporters of the "family wage" argument. Vancouver Labour Council Minutes, 25 April 1950, Canadian Labour Congress (CLC) Papers, I 103, Vol. 78, File 178-1.

23 Congress of Canadian Labour, *Political Action by Canadian Labour* [29-point program] (Ottawa, ON: Mutual Press, 1945), CLC Papers, Vol. 345. The indifference federally is clear in the reports

of the Canadian Congress of Labour's annual meetings with the federal cabinet from 1945 to 1955 and the meetings of the Canadian Labour Congress with the government in the five years following, as well as convention reports from this period for the two organizations in the papers of the CLC, Vols. 103, 114, 314. Even progressive documents such as the "Official Program for Social Security of the UAW-CIO in Canada," also called the "UAW-CIO Win the Peace Plan" ignored daycare and other problems associated with the gender division of labour in the household and in the workplace. George F. Addes, international secretary-treasurer, UAW-CIO to Mackenzie King, 26 April 1946, 35919-20, Mackenzie King Papers, MG 26, J1, Vol. 398, LAC.

As for the provinces, daycare was not dealt with at any convention of the Manitoba Federation of Labour (MFL) before 1974. See "Report of Proceedings" for Annual Conventions, 1955-79, P 404 and P 405, MFL Papers, Provincial Archives of Manitoba (PAM). The Alberta Federation of Labour (AFL) similarly did not discuss the issue of child care at conventions from 1945 to 1970: AFL "Proceedings," for Conventions 1945 to 1970, Provincial Archives of Alberta (PAA). On the attitudes of Quebec unions to women in this period, see Mona-Josée Gagnon, "Les Centrales Syndicales et la Condition Feminine," *Maintenant* 140 (1974): 25-27.

24 Women's organizations in Britain after the Second World War, and not just bourgeois ones, assumed a similar stance. See Denise Riley, "'The Free Mothers': Pronatalism and Working Women in Industry at the End of the Last War in Britain," *History Workshop* 11 (1981): 107. The same had been true after the First World War, according to Jane Lewis, *The Politics of Motherhood: Child and Maternal Welfare in England, 1900-1939* (Montreal, QC: McGill-Queen's University Press, 1980), 80.

25 "Minutes of the 50th Annual Meeting and War Conference of the National Council of Women of Canada," 16-19 June, 1943, Toronto, NCWC Papers, MG 28, I 25, Vol. 82, File 1, LAC. The conference passed a resolution to "commend the National Selective Service in stating that married women with young children will not be asked to take employment unless in the utmost urgency." The Hardy speech is in Vol. 82, File 15, "Women and the World We Want," n.d., "President's Speeches: Correspondence, Speeches 1942-1943."

26 The propaganda suggesting that working mothers were responsible for alleged growth in the incidence of juvenile delinquency had some currency among the mothers themselves. Notes Linda Ambrose, on the basis of interviews conducted by the Canadian Youth Commission's Family Committee: "Mothers internalized the problems, accepting the notion that their own work was at least partly responsible, and fearing that they would be held personally responsible for their children's behaviour." Linda M. Ambrose, "'Youth, Marriage and the Family': The Report of the Canadian Youth Commission's Family Committee, 1943-1948" paper presented at the Canadian Historical Association Annual Meeting, Kingston, ON, June 1991.

27 "We Talk of Peace," "National President: Correspondence, Addresses, 1945-6," NCWC Papers, Vol. 87, File 9.

28 "Address by Mrs. Edgar D. Hardy, C.B.E., vice-president, International Council of Women to Luncheon, Canadian Chamber of Commerce, Royal Alexandra Hotel, Winnipeg," 9 October 1946, Canadian Chamber of Commerce Papers, MG 28, 3, 62, Vol. 1, "Annual Meeting" (17th) Addresses, 1946, 6, LAC.

29 "Brief Submitted by the National Council of Women of Canada to the Committee of Inquiry into the Unemployment Insurance Act," 16 October 1961, NCWC Papers, Vol. 132, File 17. See also Ann Porter, *Gendered States: Women, Unemployment Insurance, and the Political Economy of the Welfare State in Canada, 1945-1997* (Toronto, ON: University of Toronto Press, 2003).

30 "The Canadian Federation of Business and Professional Women's Clubs, Reports," 1952-4, 1954-6, 1956-8, 1958-60, 1960-2, Elsie Gregory MacGill Papers, MG 31 K7, Volume 1, LAC, contain not one mention of child care as an issue. The employment conditions committee and the legislation committee of the Ontario provincial organization, while undertaking a variety

of campaigns to improve the position of women in the work force, did not discuss the issue of child care in the 1950s and early 1960s except indirectly on one occasion in 1963, when they asked Premier John Robarts to "set up a training course for certified household assistants" to deal with the shortage of domestics in the province. "Resolution of Business and Professional Women's Clubs of Ontario to John Robarts," Business and Professional Women's Clubs of Ontario Papers, F 207, File 5-5-3, AO.

31 Report of National President (Mrs. Margaret Campbell) to 1954 Convention; "Minutes of Fourteenth Biennial Convention," 26-30 July 1954, Toronto, "The Canadian Federation of Business and Professional Women's Clubs, Reports, 1952-1954," Elsie Gregory MacGill Papers, Vol. 1.

32 Canada, Advisory Committee on Reconstruction, *Final Report 6: Postwar Problems of Women*, 30 November 1943 (Ottawa, ON: King's Printer, 1944), 7, 13-14; Gail Cuthbert Brandt, "'Pigeon-Holed and Forgotten': The Work of the Sub-committee on the Postwar Problems of Women, 1943," *Social History* 25, 29 (1982): 239-59. Brandt observes that committee members "were overwhelmingly well-educated, of British origin, Protestant, and middle-aged," 245. On the home aide issue, see Ruth Roach Pierson, "'Home Aide': A Solution to Women's Unemployment After World War II," *Atlantis* 2, 2 (Spring 1977): 85-97. On the fate of the recommendations of the subcommittee and of the Advisory Committee on Reconstruction, useful readings include: Brandt, "'Pigeon-Holed and Forgotten;'" Brigitte Kitchen, "The Marsh Report Revisited," *Journal of Canadian Studies* 21, 2 (Summer 1986): 38-48; and Robert A. Young, "Reining in James: The Limits of the Task Force," *Canadian Public Administration*, 24, 4 (1981): 596-611.

33 Julie Landau and Margaret Conrad, "Dorise Nielsen: A Tribute," *Atlantis* 6, 2 (1981): 138-39; quote is from *Montreal Gazette*, 30 June 1943.

34 Connie Carter and Eileen Daoust, "From Home to House: Women in the B.C. Legislature," in *Not Just Pin Money*, ed. Barbara K. Latham and Roberta J. Pazdro (Victoria, BC: Camosun College, 1984), 389-405. Joan Sangster, in *Dreams of Equality: Women on the Canadian Left, 1920-1950* (Toronto, ON: McClelland and Stewart, 1989), notes that feminists in left-wing parties received a hostile reception when they attempted to provoke discussion of patriarchy rather than limiting themselves to narrowly defined economic and class-based issues.

35 "Report of Committee on Day Care of Children," Day Nurseries Committee of the Welfare Council of Toronto and District, CWC/CCSD Papers, Vol. 50, File 448E.

36 "Some Social Implications of Recruitment to Industry," Presentation to Canadian National Conference on Social Work, Montreal, May 1942 (authors not indicated), CWC/CCSD Papers, Vol. 50, File 448E.

37 *The Globe and Mail*, 12 June 1942.

38 "Nursery Day Care 1950-6," newspaper clipping, n.d. Vol. 50, File 448D; K. Phyllis Burns, secretary, Child Welfare Division, to Barbara Fraser, Halifax, 23 December 1947, CWC/CCSD Papers, Vol. 77, File 564. The work of John Bowlby was particularly influential in promoting the view that children without stay-at-home mothers suffered emotional damage. Margaret O'Brien Steinfels, *Who's Minding the Children? The History and Politics of Day Care in America* (New York, NY: Simon and Schuster, 1973), 75-76.

39 Address of Freda Manson, Ontario Welfare Council, to federal Women's Bureau consultation meeting on daycare, 17 February 1965, Ontario Welfare Council Papers, F 837, Box 48, "Day Care Papers, 1965," AO.

40 Joyce Rogers, Division Secretary, Welfare Council of Greater Winnipeg, to Kate G. Macdonnell, Assistant Executive Secretary, Welfare Council of Ottawa, n.d.. copied to Canadian Welfare Council 22 August 1961, with a notation "probably 1959," CWC/CCSD Papers, Vol. 77, File 564.

41 Manitoba Volunteer Committee on the Status of Women, 29-31 May 1968, Canada, Royal Commission on the Status of Women in Canada, *Briefs*, RG 33/89, Vol. 16, Brief 318, LAC.

The Welfare Council of Ontario Papers, Box 48, includes studies done in Ottawa, Calgary, Edmonton, Guelph, Hamilton, Montreal, Scarborough, Vancouver, Windsor, Winnipeg, Chicoutimi, and Quebec City between 1964 and 1968; Brief of United Community Services of the Greater Vancouver Area, 18 April 1968, Royal Commission on the Status of Women in Canada, *Briefs*, Vol. 12, Brief 105.

42 Canada, House of Commons, Special Committee on Child Care, 9, 26, 25 March 1986.

43 "The Business and Professional Women's Clubs of British Columbia and Yukon: Brief on Need for Starting Grants of Child Day Care Centres," 21 February 1968, Royal Commission on the Status of Women in Canada, *Briefs*, Brief 261.

44 Margaret Kesslering, "Canada's Backward Thinking on Day Nurseries," *Chatelaine*, April 1966, 67–74.

45 Canada, Department of Labour, Women's Bureau, *Working Mothers and Their Child-Care Arrangements* (Ottawa, ON: Queen's Printer, 1970). A summary of the report's recommendations is found in Canada, *Report of the Royal Commission on the Status of Women in Canada* (Ottawa, ON: Information Canada, 1970), 263–64.

46 "News Release of Canadian Council on Social Development," 5 May 1972, June Callwood Papers, MG 31 K24 Vol. 10, File 22, LAC.

47 *Vancouver Province*, 7 February 1967; *Vancouver Sun*, 8 February 1967.

48 Callwood Papers, File 10–23, newspaper clipping, "Motherhood Oversold, Social Workers Find"; "Letters to the Editor," Letter from Mrs. M.C. Perinchief, *The Globe and Mail*, 1 June 1966.

49 *The Globe and Mail*, 20 May 1966.

50 Province of British Columbia, "*Annual Report of the Department of Social Welfare for the Year Ended 31 March 1967*" (Victoria, BC: Queen's Printer, 1968), 17. In British Columbia, 2,600 children received subsidized daycare in September 1972 just as an NDP administration took over from Social Credit; by the end of 1973, there were 9,500 children receiving subsidized care. Province of British Columbia, *Services for People: Annual Report of the Department of Human Resources* (Victoria, BC: Queen's Printer, 1973). Yet, the national picture for low-income people requiring daycare services was bleak, according to the Canadian Advisory Committee on the Status of Women, *New Directions for Public Policy: A Position Paper on the One-Parent Family* (Ottawa, ON: CACSW 1976).

51 "Presentation to the Task Force on Community and Social Services Action Committee on Day Care, Ontario Welfare Council," April 1973, Ontario Welfare Council Papers, Box 50; Family Service Association of Edmonton, "Day Care Study," 1 March 1966; "What do Women Think About Working? A Survey Conducted by the Women's Bureau-Ontario Department of Labour," August 1964, Business and Professional Women's Clubs of Ontario Papers, F 207, File 5-5-9. All documents are located at the AO.

52 Royal Commission on the Status of Women in Canada, *Briefs*, Vol. 11, Brief 56, 4 June 1968; Brief 102, January 1968. The League brief stated that "the rights of individuals must be subordinate to the good of the entire family" and maintained that "that men should be given consideration in the work force consistent with their role as father and breadwinner of the family." Their indifference to the needs of working wives is evident in their national convention minutes from 1945 to 1975 in Catholic Women's League Papers, MG 28 E 345, Vols. 1 and 2, LAC.

A nuanced discussion of the Cèrcles that places their politics in the framework of "social Catholic feminism" is in Gail Cuthbert Brandt and Naomi Black, "'Il en faut un peu: Farm Women and Feminism in Quebec and France Since 1945," *Journal of the Canadian Historical Association*, New Series, 1 (1990) : 73–96.

53 *Report on the Royal Commission on the Status of Women in Canada*, 271–72; "Brief from the National Council of Women of Canada to the Royal Commission on the Status of Women in Canada," NCWC Papers, Vol. 143, File 89; and Royal Commission on the Status of Women in

Canada, *Briefs*, Vol. 12, Brief 131 (NCWC), 1 October 1968; Vol. 15, Brief 304 (United Church of Canada), February 1968; Vol. 11, Brief 52 (Anglican Church of Canada Brief presented by the Commission on Women's Work, an interim body appointed by General Synod and including leaders of the women's organizations of the Church); Vol. 17, Brief 440 (CLC), 1 October 1968; Vol. 17, Brief 347 (Confédération des syndicats nationaux), June 1968; Vol. 17, Brief 393 (Quebec Federation of Labour), June 1968; Vol. 11, Brief 105, United Community Services of the Greater Vancouver Area, "Day Care Services for Working Mothers."

54 Royal Commission on the Status of Women in Canada, *Briefs*, Vol. 15, Brief 303, 14 June 1968; Vol. 13, Brief 155, March 1968.

55 Royal Commission on the Status of Women in Canada, *Briefs*, Vol. 14, Brief 243, 20 March 1968.

56 Jane Lewis and Gertrude Astrom note that this was also the case in Sweden where advocates of public policies favouring women's right to work, including quality subsidized child care, have been generally successful. They suggest that advocates of women's right to work shied away from advocating public policies that could challenge the gender division of labour in the home. Jane Lewis and Gertrude Astrom, "Equality, Difference, and State Welfare: Labor Market and Family Policies in Sweden," *Feminist Studies* 18, 1 (1992): 59–87.

57 Canada, *Report of the Royal Commission on the Economic Union and Development Prospects for Canada*, vol. 2 (Ottawa, ON: Supply and Services Canada, 1985), 813.

58 Michael Krashinsky, *Day Care and Public Policy in Ontario* (Toronto, ON: Ontario Economic Council, 1977), 17, 40.

59 Suzanne Morton, "From Infant Homes to Daycare: Child Care in Halifax," in *Mothers of the Municipality: Women, Work, and Social Policy in Post-1945 Halifax*, ed. Judith Fingard and Janet Guildford (Toronto, ON: University of Toronto Press, 2005), 169–88.

60 Canada, Status of Women Canada, *Report of the Task Force on Child Care* (Ottawa, ON: Ministry of Supply and Services, 1986), 47, 51, 100. The study was conducted by the National Day Care Information Centre of Health and Welfare Canada and entitled *Status of Day Care in Canada*. Need for child care was conservatively defined to include single-parent families where the parent worked outside the home more than twenty hours per week and two-parent households where both parents worked outside the home more than twenty hours per week.

61 Laura C. Johnson and Janice Dineen, *The Kin Trade: The Day Care Crisis in Canada* (Toronto, ON: McGraw-Hill Ryerson, 1981); Canada, House of Commons, Special Committee on Child Care, 4: 98–104, 18 March 1986, St. John's.

62 In a 1983 Goldfarb poll, half of those surveyed agreed that "mothers working outside the home contribute as much to social development as women who stay at home to raise their family." Yet a Decima poll the same year, a year when the official rate of unemployment in Canada averaged over 12 per cent, found that 51 per cent of men and 45 per cent of women thought that during a recession married men should be given priority in employment over married women. Sandra Best, "Women's Issues and the Women's Movement in Canada Since 1970," in *The Politics of Gender, Ethnicity and Language in Canada*, ed. Alan Cairns and Cynthia Williams (Toronto, ON: University of Toronto Press, 1986), 129–31.

CHAPTER 10

Housing and State Policy, 1945–80

The Vancouver Housing Association (VHA), a non-profit association formed in 1937, promoted better living conditions in the Vancouver area, and was a member organization of the Welfare Council of Greater Vancouver. In March 1946, it published a fifty-seven-page report on accommodations that were available in the central districts of the city. Apart from citing grim statistics, it gave "typical" examples of the dire situations in which many families and individuals lived. These included: "Service man, wife and four children living in basement with no flooring, damp earth. Children sick...Mother and nine children living in chicken house in Burnaby, father sleeps in town as he has to get to work early in the morning...Mr. And Mrs. 'A' and two children, residents of Vancouver for thirty-four years (father returned from overseas after 4 ½ years service) living in unheated attic."

The East Asian population of the city, victims of long-standing racism in employment, was especially badly housed. Families living in the Chinese business quarter west of Dewdney Street shared "wretched accommodations," while single Chinese males lived in boarding-homes that were "crowded, ill-lit and ill-ventilated." The Chinese death rate from tuberculosis was five times that of the city's white population. Before they were evacuated in 1941 to concentration camps, the Japanese had lived in boarding homes and cabins that were "badly constructed, ill ventilated and lacking in adequate sanitary convenience." When they returned to Vancouver, they would be returning to homes that should have been condemned.[1]

To the VHA, it was obvious that government programs that helped people buy their own homes were not the solution to the accommodation problems of low-income Vancouverites. Instead, there had to be short-term rent controls on private landlords and long-term government programs to build publicly owned social housing apartment complexes if the poor were to be adequately housed. Most wage earners in Vancouver could not qualify for a National Housing Act loan that would allow them to buy a well-built two-bedroom home in the city, the cost of which would be about $4,000. Even if a wage-earning family was approved for the maximum 90 per cent loan under the act, it could not make its payments and have sufficient funds for food and clothing without an annual income of $2,100. A family could reduce the required income to $1,500 by purchasing a substandard home for about $2,500. But the 1941 census demonstrated that the "heads of families" of only 15 per cent of wage-earning families in Vancouver earned over $2,000 annually, and only 37 per cent earned over $1,500.[2]

The Vancouver Housing Authority's advocacy of social housing represented one approach to the problem of inadequate shelter for many Canadians. It had the support of a major investigation conducted for the federal government during the war by a committee headed by C.A. Curtis, a Queen's University economist. Ultimately, however, the VHA's approach was not adopted by those who held state power. Though the federal and provincial governments recognized that they had some responsibility in the area of housing, they rejected the view that the government should become either a developer or a landlord. They dismissed the claim of social housing advocates that housing was a public utility like heat and water as opposed to a commodity like a car or a radio. This chapter explores the battle between advocates of different roles for the state in housing policy, focusing on the conflict between advocates of social housing, whether state-owned or co-operative-owned, and advocates of a fully privatized housing industry in which the state would simply serve as a guarantor on the mortgage loans of home buyers.

THE CURTIS SUBCOMMITTEE

The Curtis subcommittee was established to investigate housing and community planning and to make recommendations for postwar government activity in these areas. It was officially a subcommittee of the federal government's Advisory Committee on Reconstruction, best known for the Marsh Report on social insurance. The profile of housing in Canada's cities in the 1940s provided by the subcommittee was not encouraging. During the Depression of the 1930s, Canadian landlords had largely failed to maintain their properties, and little new homebuilding occurred. In Canada's twenty-seven cities with populations over 30,000, over half of the 810,000 dwellings required major repairs or improvements. Rural housing was also in a sorry state. Almost 200,000 farm homes needed repair. In Saskatchewan and Alberta, about four in ten farmers lived in homes in poor condition, and only about one in ten lived in homes in good repair.

Even if all homes requiring repairs were fixed up, however, the major cities would still need another 125,000 dwellings. An equal number of new farm homes were also needed—100,000 alone were needed simply to replace farm dwellings that were beyond repair. Otherwise, hundreds of thousands of Canadians would remain either in housing that was unsafe and unhealthy or doubled up in homes meant to accommodate single families. In the metropolitan areas, just short of two-thirds of all households were rented. Yet, despite the fact that many renters lived in substandard accommodations, a majority paid disproportionately high rents. Though this might have been expected in the case of low-income tenants, the committee found that just over half of middle-income tenants were also forced to pay rents that soaked up an unreasonable portion of their income.[3]

In looking for a way out of this situation, Curtis and his associates turned to the record of public housing in Britain. About two-thirds of British interwar housing had been built by some combination of the national government and local authorities, with the private sector providing only a third of new homes. "The British people have evolved their objective, which is a home for every family, and a home which is adequate from the standpoints of size, equipment, sanitary facilities, and cost. To accomplish this end, it has been recognized that a large measure of government assistance is essential."[4]

By contrast, Canada's major pieces of housing legislation during the 1930s, the Dominion Housing Act of 1935 and the National Housing Act (NHA) of 1938, had done little to serve the needs of the poor. Under these acts, the government attempted to kick-start a moribund housing construction sector— from which jittery mortgage lenders had all but disappeared—by providing low-cost second mortgages to relatively well-off Canadians. This reduced the risk faced by mortgage lenders, who would be able to seize homes with mortgage payments in arrears without fear of losing much money on resale, and the government would carry the risky second mortgage, thus becoming the major speculator on the value of homes. While such legislation, it was argued, would spur housing construction and put construction workers to work, its major benefactors were the better off along with the mortgage lenders. The latter could make risk-free loans, transferring risk to the state.

The NHA did contain provisions that would have allowed the federal government to make low-interest loans to privately financed low-rent housing developments, but in practice, these provisions were too restrictive and no projects had been undertaken by the time of the Curtis subcommittee.[5] Even to the limited extent that the legislation might have allowed some social housing projects to get off the ground, the Department of Finance assiduously placed obstacles in the way of proponents. Efforts by citizen groups in Winnipeg and Montreal were strangled by the department, then under the leadership of Deputy Minister of Finance W.C. Clark, a man with a Canadian academic background but who had come to the department from a career in investment banking in the United States. Clark warned Finance Minister Charles Dunning, who had become a pillar of the Montreal financial establishment in the years before his return to government under Mackenzie King,[6] that if even a small program of rental housing were allowed, there would be "irresistible" political pressures to expand it widely to "cover more than the favoured few."[7]

Curtis and his colleagues were clear "that a very large and long-range program of low-rental housing must be contemplated."[8] Because such housing was not profitable for the private sector, it would have to be built by municipalities and by non-profit citizens' organizations, in both cases with senior levels of government, and especially the federal government, footing most of the tab. "A reasonable target" for the first year after the war, argued Curtis, was for 15,000 of 50,000 new homes to be low-rent dwellings.[9] But, in the twenty years following the report, only 11,000 public housing units had been built in the entire country.[10]

THE BATTLE LINES ARE DRAWN

Most Canadians recognized that poor housing and health were closely related. A Royal Bank pamphlet on housing published in November 1944 observed that in Toronto, in 1933, infant mortality was 72.6 per 1,000 in seven areas of poor housing, and as high as 121.2 per cent in the worst area. By contrast, four areas of good housing averaged 58.3 infant deaths per 1,000 that year.[11] A City of Winnipeg study of health statistics for two crowded downtown areas compared with the rest of the city showed similar results.[12] But how to combat slum housing and overcrowding inspired considerable debate. The report from the Curtis subcommittee set in motion a political battle regarding the appropriate role of the state in insuring housing for all. Some groups—including the trade unions, veterans' groups, the National Council of Women of Canada (NCWC), the Canadian Welfare Council (CWC), and the CCF—lined up behind Curtis's recommendations.[13] To a large degree, so did municipal governments in the country's larger cities. But industry groups balked at a program that gave the state a large role in the housing construction sector and that made housing a social right as opposed to a commodity. Real estate boards, construction companies, and mortgage companies denounced Curtis's major recommendations.[14]

The federal Department of Finance swung behind industry's position, successfully forestalling government initiatives for social housing. The president of the Central Mortgage and Housing Corporation (CMHC), the state agency established to handle government mortgage subsidies, summed up the views of those who opposed federal monies for public housing. Writing in 1952, D.B. Mansur claimed that "in the view of a great number of people in Ontario, housing falls much more into the category of automobiles than it does into the category of hospitalization." They believed, as did he, that "the individual should make his or her own effort to meet his or her housing needs."[15]

The construction industry and the mortgage lenders campaigned to strengthen NHA efforts that funnelled home-building funds to the better off. They argued that upper-middle-class people moving into new and larger homes would leave behind older homes that the lower-middle-class and unionized workers might be able to afford. As home ownership expanded, the numbers of renters chasing after existing renting space would decline, forcing landlords to lower rents and improve facilities for the low-income families and individuals unable to consider home ownership. Government money would fuel the process, but by giving it to the better off and letting benefits trickle down to the poor, the government would ensure that a version of the market system was preserved. The development industry would remain in private hands and the market for the mortgage industry would not shrink.

The NHA of 1944 reflected the industry's point of view. The federal government used taxpayers' dollars to produce the lowest mortgage rates in Canada's history for the 20 per cent of Canadians wealthy enough to qualify for mortgage assistance. Well-off homebuyers could approach mortgage lenders with money already in hand. In 1954, in an effort to make it even more attractive for mortgage lenders to loan money to eligible mortgage applicants under the NHA, the government replaced loans to mortgagees with guarantees on mortgage loans through a homebuyer's insurance pension of 2 per cent of the purchase price of a new home. For the mortgage lenders, it meant that their profits were guaranteed, since only the government could lose money if a mortgagor defaulted.[16]

The advocates of social housing denounced such subsidies to wealthy homebuyers and the mortgage industry, but they had little impact, with the partial exception of veterans' groups such as the Canadian Legion. During the war, pressure from soldiers' groups to house their families properly had led to the creation of Wartime Housing Limited, a publicly operated homebuilding firm, which built 45,930 dwellings in nine years, mostly small frame-construction homes without full basements or many amenities. Though the government attempted to wind up this public firm as quickly as possible at war's end and to sell off the homes, veterans' pressure forced the government to build 10,000 veterans' rental units, generally of better quality than the wartime housing units. When veterans resisted evictions from their homes and organized the occupation of the Hotel Vancouver the government was convinced that veterans would not sit idly by while it denied a responsibility to house the poor.[17]

For the most part, however, the federal government did feel that it could ride out the pressures for social housing. W.C. Clark, as supportive of the private housing industry as he had been before the war, won converts to his point of view among some former social housing supporters with "his plans to reshape the Canadian residential construction industry to design entire communities."[18] Clark promoted the monopoly of particular developers in designing new suburban communities, and argued that this model could produce communities with integrated facilities without the need to resort to direct state involvement. Urban planners came to view this model as more acceptable than the "public housing projects of socialist Vienna and New Deal America," which were their earlier models.[19] No doubt the intensity of Cold War propaganda against direct involvement of the state in enterprises that might otherwise make profits for private businesses played a role in reshaping the views of the planners.

The failure of social housing advocates did not result from their lack of persistence or from the lack of a housing crisis. Though the crisis did become less acute in the 1950s as incomes rose and more Canadian families moved into homes of their own—often by having two income earners in the family or by taking in boarders—immediately after the war, renters were in difficult straits. Their plight was exemplified by Helen Burgess, one of many parents whose children were in an orphanage because of the housing shortage. Burgess was a mother of two children, aged 7 and 8, separated from her husband and working in Toronto. In a 1947 letter to the prime minister she wrote: "I make clear a week $26.09. Out of this I have to live, pay rent for one little room, street car fare and personal expenses. I had to send my two little children to an orphanage as I couldn't keep them with me in a room as nobody will give you a room if you have children. Now please would you help me, tell me what I should do in order that I could have my babies with me. My heart is breaking for them as I need them and want them with me. I miss them terribly and they miss me too."[20]

By the 1960's, housing shortages still received little publicity, even though they remained a fact of life for many single mothers, along with Native and immigrant families in the cities. Michael Di Stasi, minister of St. Paul's United Church in Toronto, provided this report on the housing conditions of the largest pool of unskilled labour in the city—immigrants from the depressed area of southern Italy.

> Because they must live as cheaply as they can, the newly arrived immigrants crowd into a house where every room is a bedroom. They don't want it this way. As soon as a man can, he buys or rents a house and sub-lets every spare room, trying to save towards having a real home. In times of low employment men may work for fifty or sixty cents an hour, walking miles to save carfare. Often the wife helps by earning a little at some menial job.
>
> Overcrowding, unemployment, lack of necessities, anxiety and depression have their effect on health so there is sickness in the immigrant families. And people at their income level cannot provide any pre-paid medical service.[21]

As in the postwar period, such accounts failed to change the government's approach to financing public housing. For several years after the war, the government had denied subsidies under NHA to projects without at least 10 per cent of the capital having been raised by a private subscriber.[22] The CMHC was finally authorized in 1949 to make loans to provinces or municipalities, or their housing agencies, to a maximum of 75 per cent of the costs of acquiring and recovering land for social housing projects, and for development costs. The provinces, which had made it clear the federal government should solve the problem of housing shortages, were expected to pay 25 per cent of these costs. It was a begrudging acceptance of social housing, and the legislation emphasized that social housing projects had to be run on a break-even basis, which placed a restriction on the degree of rental subsidy.

While this legislation produced little new social housing in the 1950s,[23] social reformers in Toronto made use of its provisions to encourage the city to develop public housing as part of the redevelopment of Regent Park.[24] This became the country's first large-scale social housing program since Halifax's Hydrostone project after the First World War. St. John's, Halifax, Hamilton, Windsor, and Vancouver also developed projects, and Saskatchewan's CCF government was fairly vigorous in promoting social housing, particularly in comparison to its neighbours, Manitoba and Alberta, whose governments opposed public housing.[25] Between 1950 and 1960 however, only 1 per cent of housing units built in Canada were public housing units. Though four in five of these units carried rent subsidies, more than half of the subsidized units were built for the elderly under section 16 of the NHA. The failure of Canadian governments to provide homes for families is evident by comparing Canada's record with that of Newark, New Jersey. With less than 3 per cent of the population of Canada, Newark managed to build twice as much public housing as all of Canada during the 1950s.[26] It might be noted, however, that American public housing has been criticized for providing shoddily built, densely packed, amenity-free developments that are essentially ghettoes for poor non-whites.

Municipalities' obligations in such areas as schools, sewage trunk lines, and water mains, with all expenditures undertaken almost exclusively from property taxes, limited their willingness to enter the housing business. The Canadian Federation of Mayors and Municipalities, in the early postwar period, had urged the federal government to regard housing as an area of national responsibility. J.O. Asselin, chair of the City of Montreal's executive committee, commented that the Depression had demonstrated that municipal finances were too vulnerable to the real estate market's conditions. While left-wing councillors often took up the banner of public housing, most city councillors expected a provincial contribution that rarely turned out to be available. The development industry, not unexpectedly, lobbied against all proposed housing projects, claiming that they subsidized one group of citizens at the expense of the ratepayers. Municipal bylaws to finance housing projects such as Regent Park were submitted to ratepayers in plebiscites and occasionally succeeded, but they more usually met defeat thanks to well-organized campaigns of opposition by real estate interests. In 1955, a confidential report by R.B. Bryce, secretary to the federal cabinet, noted that "since such projects cut into the very profitable subdividing operations of local real estate operators and builders, they have frequently been met with influential opposition in the locality, while the possibilities and benefits of this type of project have been so little known that there has been little vocal support for them."[27]

In fact, there was vocal support for social housing, but it did not carry the day. Supporters of social housing had never expected that the municipalities, with their limited ability to raise funds, would play a major role in funding as opposed to managing public housing.[28] The campaigns from the 1940s onwards focused on the federal government's responsibility to take the lead and establish a national program of social housing. The Canadian Welfare Council's brief to the federal government in 1947 provided a typical viewpoint from public housing advocates. It was prepared by a special committee of the Surveys and Research Division of the CWC that included board members, housing experts, and experts in social welfare. The committee, headed by Dr. Harry M. Cassidy who was the director of the University of Toronto's School of Social Work, argued that the nation's "health, vigour and stability" depended upon its population being well housed. Since 53 per cent of urban Canadians were tenants, and almost no new rental housing was being built in the country, it stood to reason that the state would have to step in and build public housing for renters. Noting that the powerful Minister for Reconstruction, C.D. Howe, had argued that the private sector would deliver the housing Canadians needed, Cassidy suggested that few renters would become homeowners: "The number of families who can afford to buy new houses is distinctly limited; in normal times they do not represent more than a third of all families; under present high costs, probably not more than a fifth of the families in the country can afford a new house."[29]

Endless numbers of briefs of this kind were presented to the federal government in the fifteen years following the war.[30] Many conferences of social housing advocates produced calls to governments for public housing projects, backed up with abundant evidence of their need. The National Committee on Housing brought together the unions, social welfare organizations, veterans' groups, and other popular organizations in demanding a national program of action.[31] But nothing caused the state to budge in this period. The private housing industry's influence on the government and, in particular, on the Department of Finance, stymied reformers. The department proved a friend not only to developers but also to existing landlords, arguing that it had to lift wartime rent controls to spur the building of new rental units. In late 1949, it allowed landlords to raise rents by 18 per cent for unheated accommodations and 22 per cent for heated ones.[32] When members of the Quebec Federation of Tenants met with Finance Minister Doug Abbott two years later to elaborate on the hardships that decreasing rent controls had caused low-income tenants, the minister responded that the increase in beer sales suggested tenants could afford to pay more rent.[33]

The provinces insisted that housing was a federal responsibility. They had supported the federal government's move in December 1945 to bring control of housing under the Emergency Transitional Powers Act. The lack of housing for Canadians had become one of the causes of the government's slow demobilization of its wartime forces in Europe, and the provinces accepted that the federal government had to design the programs and spend the money necessary to find accommodation for soldiers, particularly those who were bringing back war brides and children.[34]

While many provincial governments avoided indicating what types of housing programs they thought the federal government should follow, the municipalities were fairly united in supporting Curtis's recommendations. At the annual conference of the Canadian Federation of Mayors and Municipalities in 1947, they called on the federal government to "institute without delay a subsidized low-rental and purchasing housing program along the lines incorporated in the report of the Sub-Committee on Housing and Planning of the Advisory Committee on Reconstruction." They did add, however, a request that "the facilities so provided be made available to private builders and entrepreneurs as well as to government sponsored projects."[35]

But the federal government wanted less involvement in housing, not more. Having allowed rents to rise so sharply, the federal government chose to suppress information that other countries had kept a more effective lid on rent than Canada. A report prepared for CMHC in the fall of 1950 indicated that, in Sweden, for example, rent controls had been introduced "as a permanent aspect of a flexible overall housing policy," and rents had only been allowed to rise 6 per cent since that time despite a 53 per cent increase in the cost of living. In the United Kingdom, rents had risen only 9 per cent since 1939 against a cost of living increase of 49 per cent. Even in the United States, where controls had been imposed in 1942 but were slated to lapse in June 1951, rents had only been permitted to rise 13 per cent while the cost of living rose 40 per cent. D.B. Mansur recommended that the government not release this data since it "was likely to be troublesome to the Government between now and April 30th, 1951," the date when controls were initially scheduled to end. Mitchell Sharp, then an official in Finance, agreed.[36]

The federal government argued that it had to end its early postwar control of rents because the controls interfered with the provinces' jurisdiction over civil rights and property. However, the Congress of Canadian Labour successfully sought a Supreme Court ruling that forced the federal government to maintain controls until the rental shortages exacerbated by the war were satisfactorily alleviated.[37] Nonetheless, in 1953, federal rent controls disappeared altogether. They meant little by that time since a change in the rules in 1948 had removed controls from rental units, though tenants who were already living in a rent-controlled unit were to continue to be protected from rent increases. However, landlords evicted their existing rent-control-bearing residents and filled their apartments with new renters for whom controls did not apply.[38] Polls in the early 1950s suggested that more than four Canadians in five with an opinion on the subject favoured state-imposed rent controls on landlords.[39]

That was hardly a surprise. The Welfare Council of Ottawa provided the following picture of housing for the city's 49,000 families in November 1952. Though this was one of the nation's wealthier cities, one family in six had no hot running water, one in ten had no bath tub, more than 2,400 had no flush toilet, and 4 per cent lived without running water altogether. Furthermore, about 4,200 of Ottawa's dwellings required major repairs, and rents were not cheap despite the modest character of much of the city's rental accommodations. While housing experts argued that families should spend no more than 25 per cent of income on rent (at the time an adequately nutritious diet would require 40 per cent of a family's income), most had to spend far more. Though two-thirds of family heads earned less than $200 a month, only one-third of the housing stock was renting at $50 or less per month, and few dwellings renting at that rate were being built.[40]

FEDERAL HOUSING POLICY IN THE 1960S AND 1970S

In the reformist Pearson years, social housing advocates hoped that the bias in favour of the pro-industry "trickle-down" approach to housing policy might yield to arguments favouring direct help for tenants. While pro-market policies had produced an increase in home ownership, they had left many tenants as badly off as ever. Slum clearance programs became popular in Canadian cities in the 1950s, as developers glimpsed potential dollars in the redevelopment of downtown areas that had become neighbourhoods of working people and the poor over time. The developers claimed that they were doing the homeowners and tenants of such areas a favour by removing them from unhealthy and unsafe environments. So, for example, the general manager of the Halifax Board of Trade alleged a remarkable coincidence between the needs of commercial developers and the interests of slum dwellers: "Wretched disease infected slums are being leveled to be replaced with new-low cost housing, to give today's children a chance to grow into useful productive citizens. Relocating many of these families in already opened residential areas is opening up new land for commercial development."[41]

In fact, as the well-documented and sorry story of Africville, a historic black neighbourhood in Halifax, suggests, "slum clearance" often resulted in the destruction of viable communities that needed an injection of funds and not the dispersal of their residents. In Africville's case, a rich community life was destroyed when the bulldozers moved in to make room for commercial developments. Historic racism in the city had resulted in Africville's four hundred citizens being denied basic urban services such as water, sewage facilities, and garbage collection. Though the obvious solution would have been for Halifax to extend these services to this community, city officials argued that Africville's residents would benefit from moving to other areas where such facilities were already provided.[42]

Across Canada, the private housing market sagged during the recession from 1958 to 1963, despite efforts by the Diefenbaker government to make it easier for developers and homebuyers to obtain government loans.[43] In 1964, the Pearson government amended the NHA to allow provincial or municipal non-profit corporations to borrow, at low interest rates, up to 90 per cent of the funds required to acquire the land and to develop public housing projects. Furthermore, the government offered to pay up to 50 per cent of the operating losses of subsidized projects. Though this fell short of the long-term demands of the social housing movement for the federal government to take full responsibility of public housing funding, it proved far more advantageous than the 1949 amendments to the NHA. The minister responsible for housing, J.R. Nicholson, told the Commons that the government would "concentrate its future lending in the important social areas of greatest need, namely, public housing, housing for elderly people, housing for students and urban renewal."[44] But the right wing of the Liberal Party was not about to concede that housing should become mainly an area of public investment and ownership. A task force was named with pro-business cabinet minister Paul Hellyer at its head to examine all the issues related to housing policy and to recommend policy directions for the federal government.

The federal Liberals had always been vague in their promises in the housing area. Even the ephemeral Green Book proposals of 1945, with their promise of an advanced welfare state, failed to commit the government to a program of social housing, hardly a surprise given the role of the Department of Finance in producing the Green Book. At the time, the CWC had made note of the failure of the government to regard housing policy as part of the fabric of a welfare state,[45] but the political climate in Canada in the late 1960s seemed to support the extension of state intervention into housing. The National Council of Women of Canada (NCWC), the government-appointed and usually conservative advisory body on welfare issues, became more critical of government housing policy, and wanted "an explicit statement on the part of government of its responsibility in the housing field, a statement based on perception of housing as a fundamental right of human beings in the same way we view education and health."[46] This put the NCWC at odds with the CMHC and government policy that placed housing on a par with the purchase of an automobile, not the provision of free health care.

The Canadian Conference on Housing, sponsored by the CWC and held in Toronto in October 1968, took a similar view of housing policy. Almost six hundred delegates—representing labour, architecture firms, co-operatives, welfare groups, universities, industry, churches, and tenants' associations—supported a declaration that all Canadians had the right to be adequately housed, regardless of income. Furthermore, all housing should include provisions for related facilities and services to make the urban environment livable; there should be more choices for appropriate housing for low- and middle-income groups; and tenants should be active participants in the planning and operation of housing projects.[47]

In his capacity as task force chair, Paul Hellyer travelled across the country in 1968 and heard the pro-public-housing views of the NCWC and the CWC,[48] although he was more interested in the business community's point of view. His report in January 1969 emphasized ways of encouraging the private housing industry to meet the needs of all Canadians, with a focus on lower-income Canadians: Hellyer proposed easier mortgage financing, with lower or even no down payments for the poor. There would be higher ceilings on NHA loans, longer amortization periods, and lower property taxes and a federal department of housing and urban affairs would be created to implement these reforms.[49] By proposing a smorgasbord of public programs meant to make low-income Canadians homeowners, he shifted public debate on the housing issue dramatically.

Long-time proponents of public housing, like Albert Rose, the social worker who led the movement to create Regent Park, and Humphrey Carver,[50] retired chair of the CMHC Advisory Group, claimed that Hellyer distorted the evidence regarding the successes and failures of public housing. Rose charged that the report focused too exclusively on Toronto's burgeoning Regent Park North and South, and quoted "costs allegedly required to create these projects which are grossly inaccurate." Having done a detailed and largely favourable study of Regent Park at its ten-year mark, Rose, while critical of the way in which governments had allowed the development to expand without establishing the necessary facilities for community living,[51] regarded Hellyer's treatment of its shortcomings as shallow. "The report further slanders the residents of public housing developments and denigrates their conditions to the point of despair." Even the normally right-wing *Financial Post* commented that the report offered nothing for the poor and instead proposed that public money be given to middle-class homeowners in the curious belief that renting as such was a problem.[52]

Yet many social reform groups that had concentrated for a generation on public housing as the solution to the housing problems of the poor embraced Hellyer's approach. Disillusionment with the character of the public-housing projects that were built in the 1960s often led reformers away from their earlier belief that social housing provided the full answer to the problem of decent accommodations for Canadians.

Federal programs in the 1970s, and accompanying provincial programs, attempted to boost private ownership of homes while making some provision for an expansion of social housing, an expansion that seemed inevitable as housing costs continued to rise in Canadian cities. In 1973, amendments to the NHA raised the funds available for non-profit and co-op housing from the federal government to 100 per cent. Another amendment created the Assisted Home Ownership Program (AHOP), which subsidized interest rates for qualified homebuyers, and seemed to be the modest-income family's equivalent to the CMHC loans available to the rich. Money was available for purchase of modest townhouse and apartment units that became alternative options to detached and semi-detached houses. AHOP did assist some middle-income and a small number of low-income households to become property owners. Though much ballyhooed, AHOP assisted the construction of only 22,000 units by 1976, of which 12,000 would have been built without it.[53]

The continuing problem of increases in housing prices that outstripped increases in family incomes turned Hellyer's dream of a nation in which all families owned their own homes into an illusion. Hellyer's more progressive recommendations had been the granting of federal loans to municipalities for land development as a way to push speculators out of the land business, and an end to urban renewal schemes that simply removed the poor from their neighbourhoods. In the end there would be few limits placed on either the land speculators, who were pushing up the price of homes beyond the reach of many Canadians, or the developers, who destroyed existing neighbourhoods. While the federal government created the Neighbourhood Improvement Program and provinces also established programs to preserve inner-city neighbourhoods, the political will to stop developers from destroying established neighbourhoods did not exist.[54]

As for land assembly, the Hall-Dennis Task Force, established by the government, commented: "federal concerns in the land assembly program have worked to the disadvantage of the low income group. Concern regarding program cost and a desire to support the private market have resulted in deliberate attempts to discourage land banking (to control land costs over the long term) and major land assemblies to flood the market with lots…although initially the resistance to adopting the program to the needs of the low-income group came from CMHC, in recent years the major obstacle appears to be the Department of Finance." The Trudeau government seemed to underline the point that it was more interested in serving land speculators than low-income Canadians by eliminating the small amount of funding that had gone to land banking.[55]

PROVINCIAL PROGRAMS

Ontario, which had both a large tax revenue base and a major urban-housing crunch, was the first to avail itself of the federal funds. Though Ontario's modest public-housing programs in the 1950s created more social housing units than any other province, the province's housing policies mainly aided the middle class, by topping up monies available from CMHC with second mortgage loans meant to reduce a family's down payments by half.[56] In 1964, the province created the Ontario Housing Corporation (OHC) and began purchasing existing properties for conversion to public housing. Within a year, the OHC had begun advertising for builders' proposals for various types of rental homes. In December 1966, Ontario's portfolio of social housing expanded with the creation of the Ontario Student Housing Corporation. By 1972, the province managed 50,000 units, a figure that increased to 85,000 in 1979. At that point the province also subsidized rents on about 9,000 private accommodations.[57]

This fell far short of need. As price increases for private housing easily outstripped increases in income in the 1970s, many young single-income families could not contemplate a house purchase. An increase in the number of two-income families helped to alleviate the problem somewhat, but for many, it was clear that a lifetime of renting was inevitable. Studies by housing experts demonstrated that private-sector landlords charged low-income tenants far more than they could afford to pay and violated housing regulations with impunity.[58] In 1970 the Ontario Welfare Council (OWC) called on the Ontario government to ensure that rental housing for low-income groups composed 17 per cent of the province's housing stock by 1978, which would require that 50 per cent of all new housing stock over the period be built for low-income residents. Interestingly, however, the OWC called for the government to make it possible for OHC tenants to buy their own homes by setting low down payments and very low interests on long-term mortgages. [59]

Many public-housing tenants were dispirited by the bureaucracies that controlled housing developments and by their unwillingness to listen to tenants' problems and suggestions. Shoddy construction of housing projects suggested that even when the state felt forced to provide housing for the poor, it attempted to invest as little as possible in the building of such homes. In 1969, the Canadian Welfare Council (CWC) had called on the federal government to end the practice of treating public housing as ghettoes rather than communities. It called for proper amenities in social housing developments and "tenant participation in management,"[60] a demand that was increasingly heard from the tenants' unions that sprang up in the late 1960s and early 1970s. But despair that the bureaucrats would continue to rule as if the tenants did not count led some reformers to believe that the answer lay in the long-term conversion of public housing to private home ownership. In the meantime, the tenants' unions pressured local authorities and provincial governments to deal with a variety of issues, which included too large a population density, inadequate soundproofing within buildings, and a lack of laundry facilities and access to shops. They also argued against bureaucratic rules that forbade guests after certain hours and other such interventions that homeowners never had to face.[61] By 1973, tenants' groups existed in public housing projects across the country and city-wide tenants' organizations had been formed in the major centres. A national founding convention that year established the National Association of Public Housing Tenants to represent the five hundred thousand tenants living in housing projects across Canada.[62]

The OWC position reflected a change in the former consensus among reformers that social housing was the answer to the problems of low-income Canadians, and was echoed by the Canadian Council on Social Development, the recently renamed CWC.[63] It was advice that the Ontario and federal governments proved willing to heed, at least in part. The provincial government established an Advisory Task Force on Housing Policy in 1972, headed by Eli Comay, a York University professor of environmental studies and the former commissioner of planning for Metropolitan Toronto. The following year the government gave housing a separate ministry and began providing free loans to municipalities for servicing land needed for development. To encourage home ownership among middle-income Ontarians, the Ministry of Housing required developers to make 40 per cent of the homes they built available to families with incomes under $20,000.[64] In 1973, however, few families could earn such a total without two full-time incomes. The Assisted Home Ownership Program (AHOP), it was argued, should look after people with lower incomes. In any case, by the end of the decade, the Ontario government had lost its enthusiasm for housing the poor. The OWC complained in 1978 that the Ministry of Housing had "virtually halted provision of subsidized housing, especially for families."[65] Ineligible for home-buying programs, low-income families were becoming increasingly unable to find accommodation in public housing as the number of units being built dropped precipitously.

The NDP governments of the 1960s and 1970s proved particularly eager to take up the federal monies available for housing. In Manitoba, when the NDP was elected in 1969, there were fewer than 500 public housing units in the province, all of them in Winnipeg.[66] Within six years, the new government built 5,000 family units, about 5,700 units for the elderly, and over 900 rural and Native housing units, with over half of all public housing units being built outside Winnipeg.[67] Supply, however, lagged behind demand. The Winnipeg Tenants' Association, in a brief to the City of Winnipeg in 1972, noted that slumlords in the northern end of the city were allowing the homes that they rented to fall into disrepair rather than making repairs, simply writing them off as tax losses when the Department of Health condemned them. The tenants, who might like to purchase and fix up these homes, lacked the necessary money. Aboriginals, represented by the Indian and Metis Tenants Association, were particularly poor and often ended up in the worst housing. Aboriginal people had left their reserves and poured into Winnipeg during the 1960s in search of employment, but faced a wall of prejudice that generally left them without secure work.[68]

Mount Carmel Clinic, a community clinic that catered to the needs of Aboriginals and immigrants in the poorest North End neighbourhoods, outlined the effects that the appalling housing conditions had on the health of the tenants. In homes that were cold, infested with rats and cockroaches, people caught colds that developed into pneumonia or bronchitis; and scabies, impetigo, running ears, and sore throats were endemic problems. The clinic urged the government to buy and renovate older homes in the area that were not occupied by their owners, then rent them at subsidized rates. It also suggested that homeowners on pensions or with low incomes should receive tax reductions, a piece of advice the provincial government did take.[69]

British Columbia's short-lived NDP government from 1972 to 1975 also proved quite interventionist. It established a Department of Housing in 1973 and bought out a private housing construction company. Apart from building homes—the province was involved in financing two-thirds or more of housing starts in 1974—the government also established a system of rent subsidies and a rent-to-income scale in an effort to prevent public housing from becoming ghettoes for the poor.[70]

Atlantic governments also took some advantage of federal housing money. Beginning with Newfoundland in 1965, each province passed special housing legislation that often focused as much on encouraging home improvements as creating new dwellings. Population was rising slowly relative to other areas of Canada, but housing in the region, like income, remained inferior. In 1961, 42 per cent of Atlantic Canadian dwellings did not have a bath installed as compared with 20 per cent in the country as a whole, and one-third were without indoor toilet facilities compared with one-tenth of all Canadian homes.[71]

Single women loomed large in the ranks of those whom government housing policies ignored across all provinces. The East-Enders Society in Vancouver, for example, told the Royal Commission on the Status of Women in 1967 that "single women without dependents or the support of a spouse are restricted from applying for low-cost government housing until sixty years of age, thereby exerting great hardships on these women." Even single women with good incomes found themselves blocked in efforts to become homeowners. Mortgage lenders refused mortgage loans to women without a male guarantor, and governments were unwilling to force them to stop this discriminatory practice. [72]

CO-OP HOUSING

Apart from providing low-interest loans for public housing, the federal government in the Trudeau period also provided similar low-interest loans to housing co-operatives, as recommended by the Hellyer Report. The Co-operative Union of Canada (CUC) had been urging the federal government since the 1940s to make co-ops eligible for NHA loans, but the CMHC had objected. The one exception had involved Nova Scotia. With the involvement of the provincial government, 3,149 co-operative units had been constructed in the province, all of them financed by CMHC. In contrast almost 10,000 units were built by a Quebec co-operative between 1948 and 1968 without any CMHC funding. A building co-op involved people working together to build their own homes, with ownership generally passing to individual members or families in the building co-op once the project was completed. Thus these co-ops were temporary co-ops.

Building co-ops became less feasible by the mid-1960s as construction codes became more stringent, technologies changed, and the percentage of the population who were "handy" declined. Mainly popular in small towns, building co-ops could not solve the housing problems of fast-growing cities. "Continuing co-ops," which involved the purchase of existing facilities or hiring developers to build new facilities, had emerged as an alternative to building co-ops. In a continuing co-op, the co-op became the permanent owner of the facility and co-op members rented units, generally on a geared-to-income basis. The rents paid initially for the mortgage on the building and later for renovations, repairs, and maintenance. The term "continuing co-op" gave way to "non-profit co-op" once building co-ops ceased to exist. University student co-ops in Toronto, beginning with the Campus Co-operative Residence at the University of Toronto in 1936, were an early example of this type of co-op. In 1966, Willow Park in Winnipeg became the first of a new generation of non-profit co-ops in Canada. A collaboration between co-operators and CMHC, it was followed by another seven projects across the country over the next four years.

In 1968, the CUC had linked up with the Canadian Labour Congress (CLC) and the United Church to found the Co-operative Housing Foundation (later Federation). Its intention was to promote co-op housing at the local level, and the organization influenced Hellyer to recommend that NHA loans, formerly available only to limited-dividend companies, be made available to co-ops as well. The NHA was amended to reflect that recommendation in 1969.[73] The rules for financing new co-ops were liberalized several times during the 1970s and early 1980s.

About sixty thousand co-op units were built before a federal withdrawal of funds in 1992 effectively ended the building of new co-ops.[74] The co-ops were largely planned by middle-class people, but the government required that a minimum percentage of units be reserved for low-income residents. Despite complaints from private-housing interests that the co-op program largely benefited the middle class, most residents were lower middle class or working class, and about half were low income. By contrast, CMHC mortgage guarantees mainly assisted the well off. In the early 1980s, when mortgage rates ran wild, a number of provinces subsidized mortgages, once again insuring that the better off rather than the poor were the chief beneficiaries. Within the co-ops, however, while low-income residents qualified for housing subsidies, other co-operators paid rents determined by the funds required to pay back the NHA loan.

Co-op programs could theoretically have been used as an alternative to both public housing and private housing. In Denmark, for example, by the early 1970s, though only 5 per cent of housing was controlled by public authorities, over a third of all housing was non-profit housing, either housing co-operatives in which residents were both shareholders and tenants or housing companies founded by trade unions or co-operative construction firms. The prime minister of Denmark, a former trade union president, lived in an apartment in a non-profit unit.[75] In Sweden, which, like Denmark, had a long history of trade-union-affiliated Social Democratic governments, one-third of the housing stock was owned by municipalities or co-ops in the early 1970s. The Swedish government enunciated a policy in the 1960s that made it a state responsibility to ensure that there was at least one room for every two persons in a household not counting the kitchen and living room and rents for three-room flats did not exceed 20 per cent of the average industrial wage.[76] But the Canadian government remained too wedded to private-sector solutions to follow Scandinavian examples of encouraging non-profit housing ventures as more than a sideshow to private housing. From 1965 to 1980, the period of greatest expansion in public-housing development in Canadian history, about 5 per cent of all new dwellings were in the social-housing sector.[77]

Tenants, among whom low-income Canadians loomed large, did benefit in 1975 when the federal government imposed a three-year program of wage and price controls in order to stem double-digit inflation. The provinces agreed, as part of their contribution to the effort, to impose rent controls. Unsurprisingly, landlords and developers campaigned vigorously against them, arguing as they had at the end of the Second World War, that controls would inhibit investment in new apartment projects. Of course, such investment might have come from the state. But the enthusiasm for state housing projects of the late 1960s and early 1970s had petered away by the time the anti-inflation economic controls ended in 1978. The NDP governments in British Columbia and Manitoba had been replaced by conservative administrations hostile to further public-housing projects, and the Ontario Conservative government had shifted away from its relative interventionism of the previous decade. As we shall see in greater detail in chapter 12, neo-liberalism became the dominant ideology of the 1980s. In this climate, rent controls disappeared and new public housing projects gradually evaporated.

Housing for the Elderly

Public housing for the elderly had greater public support than public housing for low-income families. Business groups opposing state spending on housing for families insisted that families should work to raise the income for their accommodation needs. But such jibes were meaningless when directed against seniors whom few Canadians believed should be expected to work. Between 1946 and 1973, 67,527 separate units for the elderly were built with funds provided in part under the provisions of the NHA.[78] As with public housing for families, however, social housing for the elderly tended to be cheaply built. Cramped rooms, often shared by several elderly people, in facilities with little in the way of recreation were common in some of the early seniors' housing developments.[79]

Pressures from seniors' groups, women's organizations, the Canadian Council on Social Development, and the trade unions led to some improvements. Given the emphasis on home ownership in Canada, however, it is perhaps unsurprising that some social policy critics had problems with the notion of building special housing units under public control for individuals who had lived in private family housing for most of their lives. Louise Dulude, writing in 1978, observed that most of the elderly in social housing were women, and that many were there because of the income discrimination by gender that marked Canadian society. Many elderly widows attempted to remain in their family homes, she noted, but found that their limited incomes made it impossible. Property tax, maintenance costs, and the like proved difficult to pay when most women had smaller pensions than men. Single women, meanwhile, rarely earned the income required to become homeowners at any point during their lives. The result was that while 75 per cent of households led by a male over sixty-five years of age (and Statistics Canada still regarded any household with both a male and a female as "male-headed") were owner-occupied, the same situation applied to only 55 per cent of households that were female-headed. Dulude argued that better income supports for elderly women would likely lead to more of them staying in their own homes and fewer requesting entry into social housing. Furthermore, she claimed, the institutions where the elderly were housed were "expensive and dehumanizing."[80]

Writing in 1980, Albert Rose, housing expert and one of the main forces behind Toronto's Regent Park public-housing project in 1949, commented:

> There is a solution to the long-term housing problem but a major change in the attitudes of Canadians towards the provision of housing as a *social* need is required and a great deal more planning than has been evident during the past thirty-five years is necessary. We can no longer aspire to be primarily a nation of home owners, because the very pace of our urban economic development makes it absurd to remain wedded to the assumptions of 1945 or 1955. The assumptions of the past with respect to those in need of assistance must be swept away. Furthermore, the term "public housing" should no longer be used to mean assistance only to the very poor. Social housing policy must mean the intervention of all levels of government to ensure that the distribution of housing shall be in the national interest. Moreover, the terms "assisted rental" and "assisted home ownership" are infinitely preferred to "public housing."[81]

Rose's view that housing must be seen as a "social need" rather than an individual need stands far and away from the view of the CMHC president in the 1950s that a shelter was more akin to a car than to a hospital bed. It was something, in short, that the individual could be safely left, for the most part, to provide for himself or herself. In the period from 1945 to 1964, the federal government left little doubt that it shared Mansur's views. Its policies ensured that housing was left entirely to the private sector. Between 1964 and 1974, this changed ever so slightly when the federal government acknowledged the failure of the postwar policies to meet the housing needs of a large section of the Canadian population. Pressure from a variety of organized groups outside the business community had caused the government to compromise on the hard-line anti-public-housing policies of the Department of Finance. But, even as Albert Rose was recommending a further shift to the left in popular attitudes, governments were drifting back to the policies of the early postwar period that favoured government help for the well off to build homes but shunned involvement in housing the poor.

It may be questioned, however, whether "the attitudes of Canadians towards the provision of housing" were equally conservative. Certainly, in the early postwar period, there was a vast social movement in favour of greater public involvement in the provision of lodgings for Canadians. But it proved unable to compete with the political power of the real estate industry, which had the ear of the all-important Department of Finance. Ultimately the social-housing movement had too few friends within the state.

Furthermore, the failure of state policy to deal with housing issues in the postwar period reflected a larger failure to deal with issues of income distribution in Canadian society, even in the 1945–80 period when, in theory, development of the welfare state was in full flight. In chapter 11, state policy relative to issues of wealth and poverty is more fully explored.

NOTES

1 Vancouver Housing Association, *Housing Vancouver: A Survey of the Housing Position in Vancouver* (March 1946), 2–3, 5, Department of Finance Papers, RG 19, Vol. 716, File 203-C-28, Library and Archives of Canada (LAC).

2 Ibid., 19.

3 Canada, Advisory Committee on Reconstruction, *Final Report 4: Housing and Community Planning – Final Report of the Subcommittee*, 24 March 1944 (Ottawa, ON: King's Printer, 1944), 11–12, 96, 102, 108, 120.

4 Ibid., 43. Curtis's rosy view of the motives of Britain's interwar governments is challenged by Michael Ball. He notes: "Prior to the First World War the structure of provision associated with private landlordism collapsed. After the war, in 1919, the only possible way to expand working-class housing provision, given the lack of alternatives, was the large-scale subsidization of council housing. The interests of capital, the working class and particular state functionaries and politicians 'coalesced' to squeeze out the private landlord. It was hardly surprising that this alliance turned out only to be temporary but it introduced a new dimension into housing provision; central government funded council housing, that has existed ever since." See Michael Ball, *Housing Policy and Economic Power: The Political Economy of Owner Occupation* (New York, NY: Methuen, 1983), 359.

5 Canada, Advisory Committee on Reconstruction, *Final Report 4*, 193; Albert Rose, *Canadian Housing Policies 1935–1980* (Scarborough, ON: Butterworth, 1980), 17–19; John C. Bacher, *Keeping to the Marketplace: The Evolution of Canadian Housing Policy* (Montreal, QC: McGill-Queen's University Press, 1993), chap. 3 to 5; Alvin Finkel, *Business and Social Reform in the Thirties* (Toronto, ON: Lorimer, 1979), chap. 7.

6 Finkel, *Business and Social Reform*, 15.

7 John C. Bacher, "Keeping to the Private Market: The Evolution of Canadian Housing Policy: 1900–1949" (PhD diss., McMaster University, 1985) 240.

8 Canada Advisory Committee on Reconstruction, *Final Report 4*, 193.

9 Ibid., 152.

10 Bacher, *Keeping to the Marketplace*, 183.

11 "The Royal Bank of Canada" [pamphlet on housing but simply titled with the bank's name], November 1944, CWC/CCSD Papers, MG 28 I 10, Vol. 54, File 471, LAC. The report to which the bank made reference had been prepared by Dr. Herbert A. Bruce, lieutenant-governor of Ontario. See Humphrey Carver, *Compassionate Landscape* (Toronto, ON: University of Toronto Press, 1975), 52.

12 "Report of the City of Winnipeg Fact Finding Board On Housing in Winnipeg," 2 June 1947, Department of Finance papers, Vol. 716, File 203-C-15.

13 Pat Conroy to Mackenzie King, 28 July 1945, Canadian Labour Congress (CCL) Papers, MG 28, I 103, Vol. 196, File 196-1; "Report of Ninth National Convention of the Co-operative Commonwealth Federation," 7–9 August, 1946, Regina, CCL Papers, Vol. 314, LAC.

14 Bacher, "Keeping to the Private Market," 393–94.

15 D.B. Mansur, president, CMHC, to R.E.G. Davis, executive director, CWC, 2 June 1952, CWC/CCSD Papers, Vol. 54, File 471, "Housing."

16 Rose, *Canadian Housing Policies*, 19; Allan Moscovitch, "Housing: Who Pays? Who Profits?" in *Inequality: Essays on the Political Economy of Social Welfare*, ed. Allan Moscovitch and Glenn Drover (Toronto, ON: University of Toronto Press, 1981), 327.

17 Rose, *Canadian Housing Policies*, 28; Bacher, "Keeping to the Private Market," 422.

18 Bacher, "Keeping to the Private Market," 552. On the changing character of Canada's development industry, see Michael Doucet and John Weaver, *Housing the North American City* (Montreal, QC: McGill-Queen's University Press, 1991), 25, 57, 115–23, 140–48.

19 Doucet and Weaver, *Housing the North American City*, 553.

20 Mrs. Helen Burgess, Toronto, to Mackenzie King, June 1947, William Lyon Mackenzie King Papers, MG 26, J1, Vol. 421, 382099, LAC.

21 Submission of United Church of Canada, Royal Commission on Health Services, RG 33, Series 78, Vol. 22, File 352, LAC.

22 "Public Housing is Essential for Canada—A Statement by the Citizens Housing and Planning Association," November 1945, George Drew Papers, RG3, Box 438, File 134 G, Archives of Ontario (AO).

23 Nonetheless, John Bacher, in *Keeping to the Marketplace*, suggests that this change marked an important enough victory to create considerable doubts about Marxist theories of the state that explain social policy in terms of state efforts to achieve legitimation among the working class and the poor. "Unlike unemployment insurance or family allowances, the 1949 acceptance of subsidized housing cannot be tied to a surge of unrest, since postwar labour militancy had long since peaked by this time" (32). However, Bacher makes clear that "the 1949 acceptance of subsidized housing" was largely an illusion. He notes: "The federal government in 1949 designed public housing according to a complicated three-government formula that frustrated even the Metropolitan [sic] Toronto authorities who were its principal users in the country. In typical Machiavellian fashion, this program was developed by CMHC president David Mansur to limit the growth of public housing" (31). If this is the case, there really is not much for Marxists to explain about "the 1949 acceptance of subsidized housing."

Bacher's monograph focuses on the influence of the "two Clarks" on the evolution of housing policy, largely rejecting social-structural approaches to social policy. He presents the policy battle as one mainly pitting W.C. Clark against the reform-minded but establishment figure Harold Clark (23). A focus on personalities begs the question as to why governments chose W.C.'s views over Harold's in the battle of the Clarks.

24 Albert Rose, *Regent Park: A Study in Slum Clearance* (Toronto, ON: University of Toronto Press, 1958).

25 Rose, *Canadian Housing Policies*, 32; Bacher, *Keeping to the Marketplace*, 10, 14.

26 Ontario Association of Housing Authorities, "Proposal for a Federal-Provincial Study on Public Housing to be Jointly Sponsored by Central Mortgage and Housing Corporation and the Ontario Department of Commerce and Development," 7 November 1961, CWC/CCSD Papers, Vol. 54, File 471.

27 R.B. Bryce, "Draft Interim Report on Public Investment," 1955, Department of National Health and Welfare Papers, RG 29, Vol. 918, LAC.

28 Humphrey Carver calls the 1949 amendment a "shabby trick" since "the provinces had not shown the slightest interest in social responsibilities for housing." He concludes that the federal government at the time "would do almost anything to avoid getting into a policy of public housing." Carver, *Compassionate Landscape*, 110.

29 "Housing Brief 1947—A National Housing Policy for Canadians: A Brief Presented by the Canadian Welfare Council to the Dominion, Provincial and Municipal Governments of Canada," CWC/CCSD Papers, Vol. 54, File 471A.

30 Indeed, they began pouring in before the war ended. For example, the Welfare Council of Greater Vancouver held a public meeting on 8 December 1944 to win support for its demand that there be a fully federally funded program of social-housing projects to be implemented by local housing authorities. Among organizations that wrote the federal government over the next few months in favour of this proposal were the Vancouver Labour Council, nine union locals, the Vancouver Day Nursery Association, the Registered Nurses' Association of British Columbia, the Women's Auxiliary to the Air Services, and the British Columbia Society for the Prevention of Cruelty to Animals. Department of Finance Papers, Vol. 707, File 203-1-A. Many municipalities favoured a City of Winnipeg motion in 1944 to allow municipalities to establish low-rent housing projects with rents fixed at one-fifth of income and all losses borne by the federal government. Municipalities expressing support for this plan to the federal government included Verdun, Moncton, Lévis, Halifax, Stratford, and Vancouver. Department of Finance Papers, Vol. 707, File 203-1-A.

31 S.H. Price, chairman, and G.T. Bates, secretary, National Committee on Housing, to all members, April 1949, CWC/CCSD Papers, File 471/2, "Housing 1947–49."

32 "Rent 1948–49," CWC/CCSD Papers, File 471.

33 *Ottawa Citizen*, 16 December 1949.

34 Drew to Legislature, 7 March 1946, George Drew Papers, Box 459, File 267-G.

35 "Resolutions Adopted at the Tenth Annual Conference of the Canadian Federation of Mayors and Municipalities," Winnipeg, 8–11 July 1947, George Drew papers, Box 431, File 44-2-G.

36 "Confidential," "Housing Progress Abroad," prepared by Economic Research Department, CMHC, September 1950; D.B. Mansur, president, CMHC, to M.W. Sharp, Department of Finance, 21 September 1950, Department of Finance Papers, RG 19 E2C, File 101-102-1-3. Sharp scribbled on the document, "Told Mansur did not think this should yet receive general circulation, MWS."

37 "Executive Committee of the Congress of Canadian Labour, Reports to CCL Convention," "Report to 1950 convention, Rent Control," CCL papers, Vol. 314, File 4-22.

38 *Calgary Herald*, 30 August 1949, reported that after the federal regulations in November 1948 removed rent controls from suites that had been vacated, five thousand families in Toronto alone received notice to leave. Staggering rent increases were then imposed on their suites.

39 Gallup Poll, 24 March 1951, National Liberal Federation (NFL) Papers, MG 28, 1V-3, Vol. 962. LAC. Canadians were asked what they favoured when federal rent controls expired that spring: 44 per cent indicated they wanted rent controls to be renewed by the national government while 36 per cent wanted them taken over by the province. Only 13 per cent wanted them removed entirely and 7 per cent had no opinion. Among renters, only 5 per cent favoured the complete removal of controls.

40 "Welfare Council of Ottawa," November 1952; "Corporation of the City of Ottawa: Public Meeting on Housing," 16 October 1952, CWC/CCSD Papers, File 471, "Housing 1946–1952."

41 Twenty-ninth Annual Meeting of Canadian Chamber of Commerce, *Addresses*, K.A. Ross, General Manager, Halifax Board of Trade, "The Role of the Community Chamber in Preparing for Tomorrow for Better Planning," 7 October 1958, Canadian Chamber of Commerce (CCC) Papers, MG 28, Vol. 1, 3, 62, LAC.

42 Donald H. Clairmont and Dennis William Magill, *Africville: The Life and Death of a Canadian Black Community*, 3rd ed. (Toronto, ON: Canadian Scholars' Press, 1999).

43 John T. Saywell, *Housing Canadians: Essays on the History of Residential Construction in Canada* (Ottawa, ON: Economic Council of Canada, 1975), 202.

44 Ibid., 207–208.

45 "Brief to the Dominion-Provincial Conference on Social Security 1946," CWC/CCSD Papers, Vol. 78, File 568.

46 NCWC Standing Committee on Housing and Community Planning, Study Outline 1967–68, Circular Letter Number 1, NCWC Papers, Vol. 143, File 4, "Housing and Community Planning: Correspondence 1967–1968."

47 Canadian Conference on Housing, Toronto, 20–23 October 1968, NCWC Papers, Vol. 143, File 5, "Housing and Community Planning Correspondence 1968–1969."

48 "Parliamentary Brief-1969-National Council of Women—Submission to Federal Government January 1969 Housing," NCWC Papers, Vol. 143, File 47.

49 Saywell, *Housing Canadians*, 210.

50 Carver's reaction is in the *Ottawa Journal*, 4 February 1969.

51 A detailed analysis of Regent Park is found in Sean Purdy, "'Ripped Off' by the System: Housing Policy, Poverty, and Territorial Stigmatization in Regent Park Housing Project, 1951–1991," *Labour/Le Travail*, 52 (2003): 45–108.

52 *The Globe and Mail*, 5 February 1969; *Financial Post*, 3 February 1969. Bacher, *Keeping to the Marketplace*, regards Hellyer and his supporters as "reformers." He suggests that other reformers, such as Carver and Rose, who opposed the report's approach, were not really that far apart from Hellyer, except that the latter group defended public housing against the stinging attack on the concept in the report (29). The rival positions are obfuscated by labelling Hellyer, the new arch-opponent of social housing, as a reformer.

53 Over a third of Canadian families did not qualify for even the cheapest home that might be bought with an AHOP-guaranteed mortgage before housing prices had risen. Canadian Council on Social Development, *Housing and People*, Vol. 3, 1 (1972); John R. Miron, *Housing in Postwar Canada: Demographic Change, Household Formation, and Housing Demand* (Montreal, QC: McGill-Queen's University Press, 1988), 246.

54 Graham Barker, Jennifer Penney, and Wally Seccombe, *Highrise and Superprofits* (Kitchener, ON: Dumont Press Graphix, 1973); Rose, *Canadian Housing Policies*, 50–51.

55 Michael Dennis and Susan Fish, *Report of the Task Force on Low-Income Housing* (Ottawa, ON: Queen's Printer, 1972), 647; Bacher, *Keeping to the Marketplace*, 28.

56 "Housing Programme—1948," Honourable Dana Porter before the Metropolitan Home Builders' Association, 26 April 1948, Drew Papers, Box 438, File 134-G.

57 Rose, *Canadian Housing Policies*, 103–104, 135.

58 One housing scholar explained the dilemma of poor tenants in conservative economic terms: "The poor pay more per unit of housing than the non-poor because they compete for a limited supply of acceptable areas or central area units. The explanation for this unit/rent disparity is based on conventional market analysis. A profit squeeze arises from vandalism, careless tenants, increasing cost of insurance, poor property management and high operating costs. Many poor people seem to develop a landlord syndrome, in that they will not complain about the key money they pay to get on a waiting list, increases in rent, or abuse of regulations, for fear of eviction, since, if it does happen, they are in no position to seek redress in the courts." Kamal S. Sayegh, *Housing: A Canadian Perspective* (Ottawa, ON: Academy Books, 1987), 336.

59 "Recommendations to the Board of Directors Approved by Conference Delegates at June 14 Meeting," "Housing and Community Development Committee, Meetings, Minister, 1970, June, July," Ontario Welfare Council (OWC) Papers, F 837, Box 53, AO.

60 "A New Deal for Public Housing Tenants," by Michael Audain, Housing Consultant, CWC, 16 December 1969, OWC Papers, Box 53.

61 "Ontario Welfare Council Housing and Community Development Committee," 3 June 1970, lists community groups of the poor in Ontario, many of which were tenants' associations, and the struggles in which they were engaged, OWC Papers, Box 53.

62 Chris Bradshaw, national secretary-coordinator, Working Committee for a National Association of Public Housing Tenants, to Harry Stagmayer, executive director, CCSD, 10 August 1973, CWC/CCSD Papers, Vol. 188, File 13.

63 The CCSD called for public ownership of urban land but indicated that governments should also consider subsidization of home ownership. "Housing and Opportunity," Remarks by Michael Audain, Housing Consultant, CCSD, to Annual Meeting of the Lakehead Social Planning Council, Thunder Bay, 23 November 1970, OWC Papers, Box 53.

64 Rose, *Canadian Housing Policies*, 150.

65 Earl Miller, Program Coordination, OWC, "Housing Is Not Enough: Toward an Integrated Approach to Housing and Human Services," Background Paper for OWC Housing Committee Workshop, 28 May 1979, OWC Papers, Box 56.

66 NCWC Standing Committee on Housing and Community Planning, Study Outline 1967–68, Circular Letter Number 1, 17 November 1967, NCWC Papers, Vol. 143, File 4. Elizabeth Speers, committee chair, reported that there were 165 public housing units in Winnipeg with 309 under construction.

67 Rose, *Canadian Housing Policies*, 86–87.

68 Winnipeg Tenants' Association Brief to City of Winnipeg, June 1972, Winnipeg Council of Self-Help Incorporated Papers, P 840, Provincial Archives of Manitoba (PAM); "Winnipeg's Welfare Program and the Dependent Indian: A Study," by Ian J. Harvey, 30 November 1967, City of Winnipeg, Magnus Eliason Collection, PAM.

69 Mount Carmel Clinic Housing Committee Brief to Howard Pawley, Minister of Municipal Affairs, 5 October 1970, Winnipeg Council of Self-Help Incorporated papers, PAM.

70 Rose, *Canadian Housing Policies*, 82.

71 Ram P. Seth and Janet J. Dickson, *Evaluation of the Housing Programmes Embodied in the Prince Edward Island Development Plan* (Halifax, NS: Institute of Public Affairs, Dalhousie University, 1974), 25.

72 Brief of The East-Enders Society, 17 April 1968, Royal Commission on the Status of Women in Canada, *Briefs*, Vol. 12, Brief 121, LAC.

73 Dennis and Fish, *Report of the Task Force on Low-Income Housing*, 1–3.

74 Writing in 1981, Allan Moscovitch noted that governments had been "completely unwilling to assist co-operative housing, resisting demands to make NHA available to continuing co-operatives." Moscovitch, "Housing," 341.

75 Dr. A. F. Laidlaw, Senior Advisor on Co-operative Housing, "Notes on Denmark"—following the United Nations Seminar on Co-operative and Non-profit Housing, Holte, Denmark, 2–16 September 1973, Grace MacInnis Papers, MG 32 C Vol. 9, LAC.

76 Assar Lindbeck, *Swedish Economic Policy* (London, UK: Macmillan, 1975), 247; Tofte Frykman, "Housing Conditions," in *Welfare in Transition: A Survey of Living Conditions in Sweden 1968–1981*, ed. Robert Erickson and Rune Åberg (Oxford, UK: Clarendon Press, 1987), 180–92.

77 Miron, *Housing in Postwar Canada*, 248.

78 Louise Dulude, *Women and Aging: A Report on the Rest of Our Lives* (Ottawa, ON: Canadian Advisory Council on the Status of Women, 1978), 69.

79 Memo to various politicians. "Subject Relating to the Proposed Housing of the Needy Aged in Ottawa," 23 November 1960, CWC/CCSD Papers, Vol. 192, Files 7, 23.

80 Dulude, *Women and Aging*, 26–27, 64, 70, 75. Quote is from 96.

81 Rose, *Canadian Housing Policies*, 198.

CHAPTER 11

Anti-Poverty Struggles, 1945–80

In 1973, *Council Orbit,* a monthly newspaper in Winnipeg published by the Council of Self-Help Groups, reprinted a Canadian Press story about how welfare mothers with large families coped. Three welfare mothers, each with five to seven children, confessed that they were forced to prostitute themselves as Christmas approached. One said that in the preceding three years, she had twice had nervous breakdowns as a result of the prostitution, but "at least it allowed my family to have a decent Christmas."[1]

The desperation of these welfare mothers demonstrated the limits of what had been achieved in the establishment of a welfare state in Canada since the Second World War. Most households in which old age pensioners did not reside were dependent on private incomes in order to survive. While minimum-wage laws were established in all provinces by the end of the 1940s and social assistance for the jobless was gradually extended, families dependent upon minimum-wage jobs lived in poverty and families dependent upon social welfare lived in abject poverty. Though the absolute numbers of the poor and the degree of destitution of the poor had ameliorated since the Depression, about one Canadian in five in 1980 had no access to the "good life," which is often portrayed as having been available to all North Americans in the postwar period.

This was the case despite the fact that a variety of government policies in the postwar period targeted poor people directly or indirectly. In the 1960s, in particular, the Pearson government appropriated the rhetoric of the Johnson administration in the United States, declaring a "War on Poverty." While Johnson's own War on Poverty was blunted by the diversion of government funds to prosecute the war in Indochina, how to fight poverty became a key public policy debate in both the United States and Canada. This chapter traces the specific policies established by governments in the postwar period to deal with poverty among Canadians too young to collect Old Age Pension (OAP). It looks at the efforts by popular organizations, particularly of the poor themselves, to establish an adequate income for all Canadians, and the counter-efforts by conservative groups to limit the responsibility of the public purse in ensuring greater equality among Canadians.

DEFINING POVERTY

As was noted in chapter 8, the definition of poverty in Canada has been politically contentious. Disagreements became clear within the Toronto social work community at the end of the Second World War. The Toronto Welfare Council had produced a cost of living study in 1939 that became an important weapon in the arsenal of advocates of both higher minimum wages and welfare rates in Ontario. After the war, pressure from the businesses who controlled the city's Community Chest caused the Council, as they updated and reissued their study, to rename it *Guide to Family Spending in Toronto*. While social justice advocates would still find useful information for their campaigns in the guide, the approach that the Council had adopted in order to placate the Chest accepted "the view that incompetency on the part of the homemaker was the problem to be addressed rather than any income policy of the wider community."[2]

During the Cold War, it became common for the media, industry, and politicians alike to dismiss claims of continued widespread poverty in Canada as Communist propaganda. But there was grudging acceptance of an incomes study conducted by the Dominion Bureau of Statistics (DBS), the predecessor of Statistics Canada, for the Economic Council of Canada (ECC) in 1961. The ECC was a government body with representation from elite groups, and its study calculated the income required to purchase a minimally acceptable standard of housing, adequate food, and clothing, and still have enough to pay medical and school costs, church dues and miscellaneous and unforeseen expenses. Using this formula, the ECC, which avoided the word poverty, suggested that 27 per cent of urban Canadians lived below the "low-income cut-off" lines, with another 14 per cent living barely above them.

These figures probably under estimated the extent of Canadian poverty, because the ECC assumed that families with greater than five people could be treated as having the same financial need as families of five. Nor did the study include farmers, because there was little agreement about how much of their own food farmers could provide and how much they needed to pay for shelter when they owned their own farmhouses. But most analysts agreed that farmers and rural residents generally had lagged behind urban residents in the postwar period. Aboriginal Canadians who lived on reserves, most of whom lived in dire poverty, were (and continue to be) excluded from the government's calculation of overall poverty in the country.[3]

Other studies suggested that the distribution of wealth among Canadians was grossly uneven, and that taxation policies and social transfers had not redistributed wealth at all. To the surprise of the Pearson Liberal government, its Royal Commission on Taxation—headed by Kenneth Carter, a supposedly conventional chartered accountant—confirmed popular suspicions that the complicated Canadian tax system favoured the wealthy over everyone else, and that the poor were the big losers because of all the indirect taxes that Canadians faced. Carter's call for taxation of capital gains and an end to various tax writeoffs for corporations and the rich sparked a long-running public debate about how government programs should be funded. Carter noted that comparisons of various European countries suggested that rates of taxation on industry were not a predictor of levels of investment or of national income.[4] Nonetheless, the corporate forces in the country proved more than able to counter Carter's recommendations in the political arena. The federal government delayed its taxation proposals for three years after Carter tabled his report in December 1966, and then proposed only a truncated version of his recommendations in a White Paper on Tax Reform.[5] Those proposals were then significantly modified again over the next three years as the Liberals under Pierre Trudeau sought to pacify their corporate supporters.

Nonetheless, notions of how to define poverty in Canada were evolving in ways that corporate leaders largely rejected. The Senate appointed a Special Committee on Poverty in the late 1960s that held hearings across the country under the leadership of David Croll, a reform-minded Liberal. Though Croll's committee produced recommendations for combating poverty that caused several members of his research staff to proclaim a sellout and quit in protest (he called for governments to make the minimum income available to Canadians

70 per cent of the poverty-line income),[6] Croll's definition of poverty was generally embraced by social-justice advocates.[7] For Croll, community standards were the means by to should determine deprivation. The committee's report claimed that families and individuals who earned less than half the Canadian average for households of a similar composition had insufficient income, deeming one in four Canadians poor in 1969 despite a quarter century of economic growth and a large increase in the number of two-income households during the 1960s.[8] Even the relatively low rates of unemployment in the period, 1963–1969, it seemed, were insufficient to prevent a large portion of the population at any given time from living in relative want.[9] Regional disparities in poverty rates were glaring, with the Atlantic provinces experiencing a rate three times that of Ontario.[10]

THE RIGHT TO AN INCOME

The collapse of the Green Book negotiations in 1946 dealt a blow to advocates of minimum incomes for all Canadians. The Green Book had offered to extend federal support of the unemployed beyond recipients of unemployment insurance (UI), leaving only those deemed unemployable as solely provincial charges. Instead, the federal government focused on seniors and the disabled, broadening support for disabled Canadians, that was previously restricted to the blind. The Disabled Persons Act of 1954, like the Blind Persons Act of 1937, included a means test and split the costs of supporting unemployable disabled people with the provinces. The original Blind Persons Act had provided aid only to the blind over age forty but the age limit was dropped to twenty-one in 1947 and eighteen in 1955. Eighteen was also the minimum age for recipients of disability pensions.[11]

During economic downturns, like the one that befell the country in 1954 as the Korean War ended, charities were overrun with demands for help from unemployed men and women whose UI benefits ran out before they could find new jobs, and from individuals who had never qualified for benefits. In the spring, Montreal's Council of Social Agencies and, in the summer, the Hamilton Council of Community Services complained that they had run out of funds to help the destitute in their cities. Pressure from charities and municipalities forced the federal government to provide temporary extensions for UI recipients whose benefits had run out, but this measure proved inadequate in preventing destitution. In April 1955, the Neighbourhood Workers Association in Toronto reported the sad tale of a family with seven children whose father had insufficient stamps in his UI book to qualify for payments. They gave up their radio, washing machine, icebox, and many personal possessions, but still could not afford to buy clothing or to buy the books required for the high-school aged children. They stopped buying meat and cut down on fruits and vegetables, relying on soups and tinned food, and dropping milk in favour of a cheap milk substitute.

La Fédération Joliettaine des oeuvres de charité reported to the Canadian Welfare Council in December that 600 people—500 men and 100 women—were jobless in Joliette, a city of about 20,000. Almost three times as many people were unemployed within the diocese, though it was largely rural. Among the unemployed, at least 250 had qualified for an extension to their UI benefits, but the Fédération was skeptical that this short-term measure would prove adequate. Perhaps reflecting conservative clerical views, it called for public works rather than an expanded UI program as the means to deal with recurring problems of unemployment. Socialists, however, also regarded insurance programs as too limited to deal with unemployment, and Premier Douglas of Saskatchewan, for example, called for a public investment program, planned jointly by the two senior levels of government.[12]

Public opinion seemed to support Douglas's views, at least in part. A Gallup poll in October 1954, at a time when unemployment was rising, found that 65 per cent of respondents believed that governments had to step in to provide work for Canadians, while only 21 per cent believed that business could handle the job. Contradictorily, in a poll taken about the same time, only four Canadians in ten favoured the view that "the important job for the government" was to "guarantee every person a decent steady job" as opposed to working to ensure "that there are good opportunities for each person to get ahead on his [or her] own."[13]

In addition, the federal government was under pressure from the poorer provinces for financial aid. The Atlantic premiers, for example, worked together to convince Ottawa to establish special programs that would foster economic development in their region. In 1957, the Atlantic Provinces Adjustment grants and the Atlantic Development Board were established to promote economic growth.[14] These were the forerunners to a variety of expensive federal initiatives in the 1960s meant to promote economic development in regions of high unemployment throughout the country. Such programs were largely failures, spooning out huge dollops of government money to ravenous corporations that found ways of taking the money without creating long-term employment in disadvantaged areas. The various regional economic development programs, which were combined in the mid-1960s into the Department of Regional Economic Expansion (DREE), absorbed a great deal of federal and provincial monies that might have gone more profitably into public and co-operative enterprises, and into social programs.[15]

It was difficult politically, however, for any political party to oppose the programs. There was a widespread belief in the country that federal policies, as opposed to the operations of the capitalist system, were largely responsible for the concentration of capital in the country in the Golden Horseshoe region, which extended from Windsor to Montreal. Economists on both the right and the left who challenged the underpinning in economic theory and practice of such arguments had little purchase within a debate that was as much emotional as it was practical.[16]

Citizens in the poorer provinces lacked the quality of education and health care that Canadians in the wealthier provinces enjoyed. Since a well-educated and healthy population was necessary to lure private investors, the poorer provinces argued that it was a federal responsibility to help them with their dilemma. The St. Laurent government agreed and implemented equalization grants in 1957 that redistributed a portion of the taxes collected nationally to provinces with below-average tax revenues. The federal government calculated the per capita average taxes collected by the three wealthiest provinces—Ontario, Alberta, and British Columbia—and made unconditional grants available to the other provinces to decrease the gap between the taxes they collected per capita from their citizens and those collected by the three wealthier ones. Hostility to equalization taxes in the wealthier provinces, particularly Alberta, limited the extent to which the federal government could effect redistribution among the provinces.[17] Equalization occurred in tandem with legislative changes that made the federal government more responsible for aiding the unemployed.

The Canadian Welfare Council (CWC) had been lobbying the federal government since the spring of 1953 for federal financing of programs for "employables" (those who were unemployed and ineligible for unemployment insurance but who were deemed capable of holding down jobs) to be administered by the provinces. It prepared a formal proposal drafted by a committee with representation from labour, management, municipal and provincial welfare offices, family welfare agencies, community welfare councils, and schools of social work and law. By early 1955, the city councils of many of Ontario's largest cities had written to the federal government that, in the wake of a deteriorating unemployment situation, they could no longer handle the costs of social assistance for the unemployed, and called on the senior levels of government to take up the slack. The federal response came at the 1955 federal-provincial conference with an offer to split the costs of aiding unemployables. The CWC and most provincial governments, particularly Quebec, insisted that such assistance would be administered solely by the provinces.[18]

The resulting Unemployment Assistance Act of 1956 proved beneficial to many destitute Canadians. In New Brunswick and Nova Scotia, the provincial governments gradually closed down the poorhouses that had provided most of the social assistance available in these provinces for over a century.[19] Several provinces used the extra federal monies to end the practice of discriminating among different groups of the poor in the calculation of social assistance. Newfoundland, Manitoba, British Columbia, and Alberta, within the next four years, combined most of their social assistance programs. While Ontario maintained its mothers' allowance program, it removed the restrictions previously placed on Natives and immigrants regarding eligibility for general welfare assistance.[20]

But most provinces, except Newfoundland, left the municipalities in charge of determining eligibility for social assistance. The larger the portion of social assistance costs, the larger the incentive to be punitive in determining eligibility for welfare. New Brunswick was the worst, requiring municipalities to pay the full non-federal share of welfare costs. Prince Edward Island provided only 25 per cent of the non-federal share, while Nova Scotia paid 67 per cent, and Ontario and Alberta 80 per cent. All of these provinces allowed municipalities to restrict social assistance to their long-time residents, a severe restriction on the mobility of poor people who might wish to move in search of new jobs or to escape an abusive family situation. In contrast, British Columbia, which paid 90 per cent of the provincial-municipal bill, Saskatchewan, which paid 93 per cent, and Newfoundland, which paid 100 per cent, forbade residence restrictions.[21]

Philosophical differences had produced a hodgepodge of social assistance policies. New Brunswick had moved only slightly from the poorhouse regime's enforcement of the logic of the capitalist marketplace.[22] Newfoundland's more liberal policies reflected long-standing notions on the island that social assistance should aid the destitute, regardless of the cause of their destitution. Tommy Douglas's socialist government was more generous than wealthier Alberta's free-enterprise administration. The CWC's Public Welfare Division, dominated by top bureaucrats in the provincial and federal welfare departments,[23] noted the low rates of social assistance relative to unemployment insurance rates even in the provinces with more liberal assistance policies, and argued for a reconceptualization of public assistance. It favoured federal subsidization of all provincial social welfare costs, with a differentiated cost-sharing formula used to benefit the poorer provinces. Their idea was to "put the *fact* of need ahead of the *cause* of need," and to be "concerned less with *why* a person is unemployed than the fact that he is out of work and may require assistance."[24]

The social work profession had adopted this philosophy in the postwar period, largely rejecting the market-based approaches of Charlotte Whitton with their emphasis on individual flaws as the cause of poverty and the need for the state to separate the "deserving" from the "undeserving" poor in the awarding of welfare. Lobbying by the CWC, the Canadian Association of Social Workers, and labour and progressive groups in the 1960s emphasized the responsibility of society to individuals and families in the framing of social policies. This would be evident in the implementation of the Canada Assistance Plan in 1966 and in the long, though ultimately, fruitless campaign for an above-poverty-level guaranteed annual income in the country.

An end to discrimination among categories of the poor could have been achieved by creating one income-support program for all people below a certain income, but the labour movement feared that the result might be downward pressures on unemployment-insurance rates more than upward pressures on social-assistance rates. The labour movement and the women's movement campaigned for greater inclusion of the active labour force within the UI program. The initial program excluded seasonal workers and most women workers and after the war, the rules regarding eligibility of women workers were tightened.

In 1950, the government gave the Unemployment Insurance Commission the right to make special rules for married women. As a result, the Commission required married women applicants to demonstrate that they had been employed for at least fifteen weeks after their marriage or, if they found a new job after marrying, that they had held that job for at least fifteen weeks. Women who lost a job during pregnancy or after giving birth were assumed to have dropped out of the labour force for at least two years even if they were actively looking for work. These discriminatory clauses, which likely annually disqualified 12,000 to 14,000 women with enough weeks of work to qualify for insurance, were only abandoned in 1957 after a sustained campaign led by the National Council of Women of Canada (NCWC), the Canadian Federation of Business and Professional Women, and the major labour organizations. These organizations also worked to fend off attempts by business organizations to reimpose restrictions against married women during a government review of the unemployment insurance legislation in 1961.[25]

Trade union pressures as well as support from provincial governments resulted in the relaxation of restrictions against seasonal workers after the war.
Seamen and some groups of forestry workers had become eligible for UI by
1954 and, coupled with the declining numerical importance of excluded groups
such as farm labourers, fishers, and domestic workers, this produced an increase in the proportion of the labour force covered by insurance—from 42
per cent in 1940 to 59 per cent in 1954.[26] Three years later, fishers, previously
treated as small business people rather than workers, also won the right to UI
benefits, their cause having been taken up by Atlantic governments anxious to
have more federal monies reaching provincial residents.[27]

The inclusion of some workers in precarious employment positions within
the UI scheme reflected a shift from the actuarial ideology that had governed
the provisions of the 1935 and 1940 UI bills. It occurred in the face of a concerted business campaign to prevent the liberalization of the rules for eligibility
and the size of the benefits. The growth of the trade union movement during and after the war and the lobbying efforts of the women's movement for
equal rights in the 1950s and 1960s contributed to a change in public policy
regarding UI.[28] So did the need of the two larger parties to stem the growth of
the NDP, which received some financial support from organized labour. The
Conservative government of John Diefenbaker appointed a committee chaired
by chartered accountant Ernest C. Gill to re-examine the program in light of
the increased draw on its funds during the recession from 1957 to 1962. But the
government largely ignored Gill's recommendations that it should return to a
program with a solely actuarial bias.[29]

The trade union pressures for social considerations in the UI program also
influenced the Pearson and Trudeau governments. They were reinforced by
the Royal Commission on the Status of Women's recommendation to expand
the UI program to benefit working mothers, a policy that would be less costly
for the government to implement than the commission's suggested national
daycare program. A review of UI undertaken by Minister of Manpower Bryce
Mackasey in 1970 supported the views of the commission and of labour and
women's groups more generally, and the 1971 amendments to the UI program
followed his recommendations. Eligibility for benefits, previously restricted to
people who had worked a full thirty weeks in the two years prior to becoming unemployed, was extended to anyone who had worked eight weeks in the
year prior to losing work. The maximum benefit increased from $53 to $100
per week, a livable wage, at least for a single person. Sickness and maternity
leave payments lasting up to fifteen weeks were also included. However, mater-

nity leave eligibility was restricted to women who had worked ten weeks in the twenty weeks preceding the delivery of their babies, a restriction that women's organizations deplored since it assumed that pregnant women without work in the immediate weeks leading up to delivery must be voluntarily unemployed.[30]

Though actuarial considerations were not uppermost in the minds of the drafters of the changes to the UI legislation in 1971, optimism about the fund's ability to remain largely self-financing played a role in their willingness to interpret the goals of a UI program in a liberal manner. Premiums paid by employers and employees covered 81 per cent of the costs of the fund in 1971 with the federal government paying the remaining 19 per cent, and it was assumed that these percentages would extend into the future. [31]

CANADA ASSISTANCE PLAN AND GUARANTEED INCOMES

Of course, a more generous UI program mainly helped those with both a long-term relationship to the labour force and good wages that qualified them for reasonable benefits. The poor included not only the involuntarily unemployed but also the working poor, single mothers without affordable child care, and, despite the implementation of the Canada Pension Plan, many seniors. Non-whites, particularly Natives and African Canadians, were victims of long-term systemic employment discrimination that largely limited them to part-time or seasonal work that was often not covered by minimum-wage legislation. So, for example, a study by the National Council of Women of Canada of employment prospects for women in Nova Scotia uncovered that black women were systematically excluded from most occupations available to other women in the province. The doors were barred to them for employment as saleswomen and waitresses, as secretaries outside of government offices, as nurses outside of a few hospitals, and as domestics in Halifax.[32]

Though the phrase "feminization of poverty" was not yet in use, there was a growing recognition that elderly single women, as well as single women with children, represented an increasing proportion of Canadians without adequate incomes. A study by the National Council of Welfare on children living in poverty in 1975 found that 21.2 per cent of Canadian children growing up in two-parent family households were living in poverty. This rose to 33.7 per cent in male single-parent homes and reached 69.1 per cent in female single-parent homes.[33] As for female seniors without mates, including both widows and unmarried women, a Canadian Advisory Council on the Status of Women report in 1978 suggested that two-thirds lived below the poverty line.[34] The struggles for government-funded daycare and equal pensions for men and women discussed in earlier chapters were meant to challenge women's poverty. The trade union movement tended to focus on full-employment policies—via government economic planning—as the solution to poverty, noting that social-democratic governments in Scandinavia had made a far greater dent on poverty than Canadian social welfare policies. But welfare officials continued to focus on improvements in social assistance as the best means for helping the poor.[35]

The Boucher Report, released by the Quebec government in 1963, endorsed an end to the punitive approach of the Duplessis period in which categorization of potential social assistance recipients was primordial. It called instead for all social assistance programs to be blended together, and for the state to emphasize efforts to train and find work for the unemployed. Jean Lesage's Liberal government embraced the views of this report and welcomed more federal money for provincial welfare programs, if not other forms of federal involvement.[36] Federal–provincial discussions from 1963 to 1965 looked for ways of improving federal assistance that would help the provinces discharge their obligations to the destitute.[37] For some provinces, this meant being given federal help for assistance programs they already had in place; for others, particularly the cash-strapped Atlantic provinces, it meant an opportunity to offer programs available in other provinces.[38] The Canada Assistance Plan (CAP) of 1966 was the major result. For the Pearson government, it was part of a concerted program to eliminate poverty that was announced in the speech from the throne in 1965. Other components included beefed-up regional and rural development programs, a more aggressive human resources policy, urban renewal, and the establishment of the Company of Young Canadians, whose members were hired to work as problem solvers for poverty-stricken communities.[39]

CAP superseded the Unemployment Assistance Act of 1956. It ended the distinction between employables and unemployables, and committed Ottawa to providing half the costs incurred by the provinces to provide income support for destitute citizens. The earlier law's upper limit on how much the federal government would provide for any one social assistance recipient was removed. Federal monies would also be available, on a fifty-fifty basis, for provincial programs that retrained individuals to encourage their entry or re-entry into the labour force, or that otherwise contributed to individuals being able to find work and get off social assistance. Mothers' allowances, health services to social assistance recipients, subsidies for the working poor, welfare programs of benefit to Native peoples, and the costs of administering provincial welfare programs would also be cost-shared. Lester Pearson predicted that CAP would add two hundred thousand women and their children to the rolls of those receiving a federal contribution either to income subsidies or to efforts in finding work.[40]

Both the Unemployment Assistance Act and CAP produced a large-scale shift in social welfare spending from provincial governments to the federal government. While the provinces increased their welfare spending by 167 per cent from 1959 to 1968, the federal increase was elevenfold.[41] Among other programs, the federal government paid half of the costs provinces doled out in rehabilitation services, counselling, daycare, homemaker services, and community development for CAP recipients. But the federal government, from the start, insisted that only the "needy" would be covered by CAP, and they refused to pay for programs that included the working poor, a limitation that caused friction with several provinces, particularly Quebec.[42]

A province was eligible to receive its federal dollars provided that it used a means test to establish eligibility for programs for which it wanted federal matching dollars but discounted length of residency in the province or a particular locality as a criterion for eligibility. Those denied assistance had to have recourse to an appeal procedure, but this procedure would remain under provincial jurisdiction.[43] Quebec chose to "opt out" of this federal program along with many other federal programs in the 1960s. The opt-out solution, worked out at meetings of federal and provincial representatives and given legislative form in the federal Established Programs (Interim Arrangements) Act of 1965, allowed Quebec to receive federal monies while being nominally outside the purview of a program. In turn, the federal government, by insisting that a province that opted out of a program had to follow the general rules for that program in order to receive its share of program funds, ensured that opting out represented a mainly symbolic victory for Quebec politicians dealing with a growing sovereignty movement in their province.[44]

As payments to the provinces rose rapidly in the first few years of CAP, the federal government produced a fairly conservative definition of "need" and insisted that the provinces not ask for federal reimbursement of any share of costs that fell outside this definition. For example, it reduced the claims of provinces that exempted more than a small share of assets when determining eligibility for social assistance or that provided assistance for more than food, clothing, and shelter for welfare recipients. It argued that it was not preventing provinces from providing more assistance than the federal minimum, but refusing to pay a share of these costs.[45] Three governments chose to provide provincial social assistance to the working poor in the Trudeau years: the NDP administration in

Saskatchewan in 1974, the PQ administration in Quebec in 1979, and the NDP administration in Manitoba in 1981.[46]

However, the social welfare establishment, the trade unions, the women's movement, and the growing grassroots poverty movement continued to emphasize the responsibility of the federal government for ending poverty in the country. During the Second World War and in the early postwar years, the Left in Canada had envisaged the end of poverty occurring via federal ownership and/or regulation of most of the economy, with a commitment to full employment and to high minimum wages. During the Cold War, the country's left-leaning organizations appeared to move away from sweeping economic policies to a de facto acceptance of the capitalist system. Reformist forces became less interested in restructuring the economy than in continuing to expand the welfare state. Anti-poverty activists, therefore, began to focus on state guarantees of annual incomes rather than on changing economic structures as the means to reduce and eventually eliminate glaring social inequalities in Canada.

The guaranteed annual income (GAI) was a policy direction that was much discussed in both Canada and the United States in the late 1960s and early 1970s. Its eventual demise in both countries marked a transition from the welfare state consensus of the postwar period to the gradual triumph of neo-liberalism after 1975. But it is important to note that even had such a program triumphed, it might not have warded off the neo-liberal onslaught. Some of the firmest advocates of a GAI were right-wingers. Milton Friedman, the dean of American supply-side economists, was an early advocate. He called for the GAI to replace all existing social insurance programs. By guaranteeing all citizens a minimum income, he argued, governments removed the necessity of having to implement a variety of social insurance programs, each maintained by an expensive bureaucracy and each inspiring a lobby meant to convince legislators to expand the program. Friedman wanted the GAI set at a bare subsistence level so as to ensure that it did not deter employables from taking work that was on offer from employers. The minimum GAI would be tied to tax reporting, with families and individuals below certain incomes receiving a "negative income tax" in the form of a cheque from the government.

GAI advocates among the popular groups rejected the corporate agenda for a GAI. They wanted the negative income tax to guarantee an above-poverty income for all Canadians regardless of their relationship to the labour force. The three major political parties tried to carve out ground between the two polarized views, but significantly, in the early 1970s, a broad agreement was reached among political elites, at least at the federal level, that a GAI was desirable. The disappearance of the idea from the political radar by 1979 represented a considerable shift to the right in the Canadian consensus on social policy.

THE GUARANTEED ANNUAL INCOME DEBATE

Discussions about guaranteed incomes in Canada from the late 1960s to the mid-1970s were instigated by a growing grassroots movement of anti-poverty activists, mainly organized by poor people but aided and sometimes led by radical middle-class people from the social work profession, the student movement, and the Company of Young Canadians. The latter was an attempt by the Pearson government to co-opt radical youth by hiring them to go into communities and help them deal with their problems; as it became clear that the organizers rejected the pull-up-your-bootstraps proselytizing that the government favoured and called for campaigns against governments and corporations that they labelled as oppressors of the poor, the government pulled the plug on this organization.[47] While the importance of the radicals can easily be exaggerated, anti-poverty organizing owed much to the radical environment of the late 1960s. The civil rights and anti-war movements in the United States and the student revolts in the universities in both Canada and the United States created a general atmosphere of contestation. Many poor people who had formerly felt intimidated by the political system, bureaucrats, and landlords, recognized that they could empower themselves by working collectively with others in similar circumstances.

Conversely, governments, responding to the demands of the poor and their supporters, watched their welfare budgets rise and wondered how they might keep these costs within limits and yet pacify the poor. A Quebec government review of social assistance costs in 1969 lamented a steep rise in social assistance payouts. After average increases in payments from 1961 to 1966 of 6.5 per cent, Quebec experienced a 21 per cent increase in 1966–67 and 43.8 in 1967–68 despite little change in the province's unemployment rate. The province had liberalized eligibility for welfare and had increased social assistance payments, and the report made no bones about why : "The rise in average benefits in Montreal was the consquence of the formation of social protest movements during this period whose activities influenced a greater utilization by the government authorities of grants of special assistance to supplement regular rates of assistance."[48] A fixed provincial GAI struck the authors as a possible way to limit the ability of local citizens' groups to wrest better treatment from local authorities.

For the new organizations of the poor, however, a GAI should be a means to recognize a living income as a right of citizenship. About eight hundred organizations representing low-income people emerged across the country, most of which were involved in helping social-assistance recipients demand adequate income from local or provincial authorities.[49] They also fought policy intrusions by social welfare bureaucrats into social recipients' lives, particularly the notorious "man-in-the-house" rule that required celibacy on the part of single mothers receiving welfare. If a welfare worker determined that a man was sleeping with a woman who was receiving social assistance, the man was assumed to be contributing to the finances of the household and the woman's assistance was cut off. As had once been the case with UI, the onus was placed on the woman to prove that she had not made a false claim for state assistance; the state did not have to demonstrate that a sexual partner was providing a welfare claimant with financial support.

The establishment of the Special Senate Committee on Poverty in November 1968 provided organizations of the poor, along with the traditional organizations supporting enriched state benefits and programs for the poor, with a forum to express their vision for social policy in Canada. Most focused on a GAI as the solution.[50] So, it was unsurprising that the committee's report in 1971 recommended a GAI, though it balanced the needs of the poor with governments' concerns that efforts to alleviate poverty not result in major increases in taxes for the better off. The GAI would be set at 70 per cent of the poverty line for each household size. Also, to raise the monies required for the GAI, family allowances, Old Age Security, and CAP would disappear as separate programs. Only contributory programs such as unemployment insurance and the Canada Pension Plan, along with veterans' allowances, would survive the consolidation of minimum-income programs.[51] The report observed that, despite CAP, social assistance rates throughout the country were too low to provide families with any dignity.[52]

The GAI became an important subject of public debate after David Croll and his fellow senators submitted their report. But the committee's report, in fact, suggested a broad-ranging program to attack poverty, including minimum wages set at 60 per cent of the average wage rates for a province, community-controlled clinics offering comprehensive health and social services, a national daycare program, expansion of public housing programs, and the participation of area residents in urban renewal projects.[53] In short, Croll proposed a variety of social democratic measures that various popular groups of the time were pressing for, but even by the end of the twentieth century, few of the committee's recommendations had been acted upon.

Anti-poverty activists used the momentum created by Croll's committee hearings to publicize their demands. In January 1971, Toronto-area poor people's organizations hosted a national conference, at which it was decided to form a national organization of the poor. The National Anti-Poverty Organization (NAPO) was formally launched the following year in Winnipeg. At the Winnipeg meeting, there were two representatives of each province and one from each territory.[54] By 1980, NAPO was a coalition of about eighteen hundred advocacy groups and co-operatives.[55] But NAPO, from the beginning, was heavily dependent on federal funds, unsurprising since its members were too poor to pay subscriptions to an organization working on their behalf. To the extent that the piper calls the tune, therefore, NAPO was somewhat compromised in its ability to engage in militant actions.[56]

The GAI became the major demand of NAPO and its provincial affiliates, and they were determined that it should provide a livable income to families. NAPO called for a wealth tax that would place an annual levy on individuals that reflected the value of all their assets. They also wanted a steeply progressive corporate tax that was higher for non-resident corporations than domestically controlled ones, and a substantial resources tax on natural resources that left the country. Corporations that eliminated jobs would have to pay a special penalty to the state for each lost job. In turn, while there would be no coercion to work, there would be tax incentives for those who found employment and, in industries that faced labour shortages, state subsidies for workers' wages to prevent the industry from moving to another country. It was an elaborate plan that went beyond middle-class solutions to poverty that required people to work at whatever jobs could be found for them.

Though NAPO rarely matched its radical goals with militancy, local anti-poverty groups sometimes did. The social work establishment in Toronto was shaken in 1970 when about seven hundred people, led by the Just Society Movement, a local anti-poverty group, showed up at the annual meeting of the Social Planning Council (SPC), demanding more control by the poor themselves over the creation of strategies for dealing with poverty. Social workers and social agency managers had long accepted the need to placate the economically powerful, whose influence was paramount in the Community Chests and United Ways that raised much of the money required by organizations whose clients were disadvantaged citizens. But the tide was shifting, and the staff of the spc largely sympathized with the militants. The spc board, dominated by corporate representatives, had held back the grassroots revolt of 1970, but within a few years, they conceded their inability to control staffing of the organization in the face of organized labour's threats to leave the spc if social workers were fired. That would leave the spc exposed as a business-dominated organization. Instead, the corporate leaders offered a compromise in which the staff could not lobby directly for radical groups. They would have to be content with offering advice and funds to community organizations, and the hope was that this intermediary role, governed by a board, would discourage militancy.[57]

Labour's role within social planning councils and charitable organizations such as the Community Chests and United Ways reflected various conflicts within the labour movement and contradictions in labour thinking. During the Cold War, the major trade union federations insisted that individual unions purge Communists from leadership positions and expelled unions that defied such edicts. Worried nonetheless by right-wing smear campaigns that bracketed trade unionism and Communism, union leaders sought to associate their organizations with respectable community organizations, particularly charitable organizations.[58] Yet, in theory, many unions, especially the industrial unions, favoured state policies that would eradicate poverty and make the charities unnecessary. While labour seemed content before the 1970s to go along with business's façade that charities and social planning councils were community organizations without a class bias, it often gave its rhetorical support to radical social workers and poverty groups when such organizations were formed. Before the 1980s, however, the labour movement was rarely involved in coalition work with anti-poverty activists.

Provincial and local governments attempted to co-opt leading militants by providing conditional grants to their organizations and salaries to their leaders. Militants who had been engaged in collective organizing often ended up as information officers to individual poor people, helping them to access whatever monies were available to them within current programs. Advocacy replaced protest.[59] Still, the growth in anti-poverty activism in the early 1970s was remarkable, with the National Council of Welfare producing a directory in 1973 that included five thousand low-income groups across the country. Just five years earlier, the Economic Council of Canada had described Canada's poor as "collectively inarticulate...having few spokesmen and groups to represent them to give voice to their needs."[60]

The demand for a GAI united the organizations of the poor, as well as the Canadian Association of Social Workers (CASW), the government-appointed National Council of Welfare (NCW), and the Canadian Council on Social Development (CCSD).[61] Certainly, some members of the federal government responded positively to the grassroots pressure for a basic income guarantee for Canadians. But their margin for negotiating was reduced first by the Pearson and then the Trudeau government's conservatism regarding taxation issues. Money would be available for only a modest GAI.

Little came of early meetings between federal and provincial officials on the issue. The federal government offered a mini-loaf to Canada's poor in 1971 in the form of a proposed Federal Income Support Plan (FISP). This plan would be financed by using monies saved from denying family allowances to the wealthiest 30 per cent of families to double allowances for families with incomes under $4,500 per year. A graduated family allowance, with $16 per child going to low-income families, would supplement other subsidies for the working poor, including health costs that provincial governments covered for social assistance recipients, aided by CAP payments.[62]

FISP, however, seemed almost designed to create polarization between supporters of universal entitlements and supporters of programs targeted to the poor. Feminist groups balked at the implicit assumption of FISP that women married to wealthy men automatically shared in their incomes. Organizations of the poor, such as NAPO, also strongly preferred to have incomes guaranteed to Canadians either through grants across the board to all citizens or through a negative income tax. John Munro, the minister of national health and welfare, observed that 800 of 900 letters that he received regarding FISP were negative. Nonetheless, he managed to obtain an all-party agreement to change the family allowance system shortly before the House prorogued in 1972. One Conservative member refused, however, to vote with the rest of the House to give the bill the necessary unanimity required to prevent it dying on the Order Paper.[63] An election was held shortly afterwards, and in its wake the Trudeau administration did not reintroduce the measure.

THE BUBBLE BURSTS

Marc Lalonde, the new minister of health and national welfare, produced an Orange Book in 1973 that proposed a modest GAI within a program that attempted to link the government's employment and social insurance policies.[64] In an effort to get the provincial governments on side, it also afforded the provinces greater control over social programs. Family allowance rates would become the responsibility of provinces, which could adjust them as they saw fit for family size, ages of children, and the like. A clear distinction would be made between "employables" and "unemployables," with single mothers placed in the latter camp, a clear signal that the Trudeau government was uninterested in implementing the national daycare program called for by the Royal Commission on the Status of Women. Alleged employables would receive less from the federal government than alleged unemployables.[65] While the Social Security Review begun by Lalonde was supported by Prime Minister Trudeau at the time, there was active opposition from the Department of Finance, which reliably represented the business point of view. John Turner as minister but even more so, his deputy minister, Simon Reisman, argued that markets were the solution to restoring a Canadian economy that had become sluggish in the early 1970s. The GAI, from the viewpoint of finance officials, would reduce incentives to work. As the economy continued to stall, this perspective would win over the Trudeau government.[66]

The sluggishness of the economy in the 1970s deepened cracks in the postwar social welfare consensus. While Canadians as a whole claimed to support income guarantees for the poor, they also protested that they were overtaxed. The economic and political establishment took advantage of these contradictory viewpoints to increasingly scapegoat the rising number of unemployed people as the cause of their own problems. In the early 1970s, the Association of Ontario Mayors and Reeves endorsed "workfare," the notion that employable social assistance recipients should be required to do work for the municipality to earn their welfare cheques. Civic unions feared that workfare would become a means for depriving city workers of their jobs in favour of the cheap labour that welfare recipients would be required to provide. Western Canadian municipal officials went their eastern counterparts one better in mean-spiritedness by calling for a stripping of voting rights from welfare recipients, though this was not implemented.[67]

In this context, Canada's welfare ministers, meeting in 1974, demonstrated little enthusiasm for a GAI program. The three NDP governments—Manitoba, Saskatchewan, and British Columbia—remained supportive of the concept. The Atlantic provinces claimed that they lacked the means to finance their half of the payments required in the Orange Book, while Quebec opposed further federal involvement in income-security programs. The provincial Liberal government had its own approach to income security, which resulted from the report of the Castonguay-Nepveu Commission of Inquiry on Health and Social Welfare that had reported its designs for social security in 1971. The commission proposed three tiers for income security, with the negative income tax as the first tier, social insurance as the second, and means-tested family allowances as the third.

Focusing on providing incentives for the unemployed to join the workforce, Quebec wanted the older notions of the "deserving" and "undeserving" poor to be maintained in a GAI. It was willing to have those it deemed unemployable receive a poverty threshold income, but it wanted potential workers to receive no more than 60 per cent of a poverty income. They could make up much of the rest via family allowances if they had children since the Castonguay-Nepveu Report, as part of a pronatalist strategy, envisioned a family allowance payment amounting to 40 per cent of the income required to raise a child. This distinction between employables and unemployables was unacceptable to the three NDP governments, as well as the social welfare and poverty organizations.[68]

Meetings behind closed doors of federal and provincial officials throughout 1974, 1975, and 1976 failed to produce a GAI, ultimately because the federal government of the time, much like the federal government that had presented the Green Book thirty years earlier, got cold feet about its proposal. In 1975, the provincial welfare ministers agreed to a two-tier system for a GAI along the lines of Lalonde's proposal. There would be income support for unemployables and those unable to find work and income supplementation for the working poor. But the federal government, facing a deficit in 1975 for the first time in many years, balked at the $2 billion price tag for the program the provinces had agreed upon. It countered with a $240 million program that would cover families with children and recipients between the ages of fifty-five and sixty-five. When Ontario objected, the federal government temporarily shelved the project of a guaranteed annual income.[69]

Several provinces had, however, decided to supplement their social programs to produce a modest GAI. In Saskatchewan, the Family Income Plan, implemented in October 1974, gave $1,800 to a family of four with an annual income below $6,647, allowing them to keep half of all income they earned above that figure to a maximum of $10, 247. Ontario and British Columbia implemented even more modest programs. None of the provincial programs came close to the $7,000 payment across the board to all families of four recommended by NAPO.[70]

In 1978, the federal government made one last attempt to revive discussions about a national GAI by proposing to replace the fifty-fifty payment called for in the Orange Book with block funding. The provinces expressed interest, but social workers and poverty organizations decried the lack of guarantees in the program for minimum services in all provinces. The federal government quietly dropped the proposal altogether, unwilling to impose conditions on the provinces with a referendum on Quebec sovereignty known to be in the offing. Instead it legislated a modest Refundable Child Tax Credit in 1978. This provided benefits to two of every three Canadian families, but the monies involved were too limited to have the kind of impact that a GAI might have. Trudeau appears to have acceded to National Health and Welfare Minister Monique Bégin's proposal for the tax credit as a politically judicious offset to cuts the government implemented that year in family allowances.[71]

The federal government ran deficits each year after 1975, and though Keynesian economists emphasized that the deficits were puny and necessary to kick-start the economy, a well-organized business campaign that decried deficits as the road to national bankruptcy was not without effect. Trudeau looked for economies in the federal budget rather than new places to spend money. Accepting business's view that corporations and high-income individuals should receive tax cuts, he was only willing to find money for anti-poverty programs by removing universality in existing programs. Opposition from labour and from recipients of universal benefits prevented him from taking action at all.[72]

Many provincial governments by the late 1970s replaced their war on poverty with a war on the poor. The Social Credit government of Bill Bennett, which defeated Dave Barrett's NDP administration in B.C. in 1975, charged that the outgoing government was soft on welfare cheaters. The next year, Bennett's minister of human resources, Bill Vander Zalm, set up the Ministry Inspectors program, or the "fraud squad" as it was generally labelled, to sniff out welfare cheaters. Ontario, Quebec, and the Atlantic provinces tightened up as well. In 1978, Alberta required that mothers of one child older than four months must seek employment or training for employment.[73] The GAI idea persisted among advocates of the poor, but it disappeared from the politicians' agenda, and from media discussions.

In his detailed examination of policymaking in the area of "poverty reform" between 1958 and 1978, Rodney S. Haddow concludes that state actors, particularly bureaucrats, played the leading role in the debates that resulted in the success or failure of various policy proposals. The political leaders simply adjudicated the debates among the bureaucrats, in the case of CAP, largely deciding in favour of welfare officials and, in the case of the GAI, in finance's favour. In Haddow's view, the Left was too wedded to universal programs and full-employment policies to participate meaningfully in a debate about guaranteed incomes framed mainly in terms of aiding social assistance recipients and the working poor. As for the poor themselves, they were hampered by "their modest material and intellectual resources, their limited capacity to mobilize their respective constituencies, and their financial dependence on the federal government."[74]

Haddow is unkind in suggesting that the "intellectual resources" of the poor were limited. Organizations such as NAPO may have been cowed by their dependence for funds on governments, but they often had detailed ideas about how to restructure Canada's economy to benefit the poorest Canadians. Their ideas, however, were unlikely to convince the corporate community or the Department of Finance, which Haddow notes faithfully represented the views of corporate Canada.

RATES OF POVERTY

In 1975, using the low-income cut-offs established by Statistics Canada, 15.4 per cent of Canadians lived in poverty.[75] This was a substantial decline from the 27 per cent figure established by the federal agency for 1961. In part, this decline might be attributed to government policies, such as increased rates for unemployment insurance and better public support for pensioners. Also important was the 60 per cent increase in constant dollars of the gross national product per capita during this period.[76] Though the income gap among Canadians exclusive of social transfers became increasingly wide, the net effect of social transfers was to leave the distribution of income in the 1970s much the same as it was in the 1950s.[77]

While the increase in GNP per capita helped to reduce the absolute poverty rate, an equally significant contribution was made by the massive increase in the percentage of married women performing paid work. In 1951, only 11.2 per cent of married women worked for pay, accounting for a mere 6.6 per cent of the labour force. By 1979, fully 47.9 per cent of married women were in paid labour, representing 25 per cent of the labour force. That year, the National Council of Welfare estimated that if all married women left the labour force, the rate of poverty for spousal families in Canada would jump by 50 per cent. A majority of the growing number of single mothers in Canada earned very low wages, and so their families lived in poverty; but the very low wages married women earned often lifted a two-income household out of poverty.[78]

NATIVE PEOPLES AND WELFARE

As the Canadian state increasingly accepted its responsibility for insuring a minimum level of social welfare for all citizens, Native peoples' deplorable state of existence became a greater concern. Indigenous peoples lived more like citizens of Third World countries than of Canada. In 1963, they died at an average age of half that of non-Native Canadians, were heavily dependent on federal government welfare payments, and lived in shacks on reserves that were often unheated and without electricity.[79]

In the postwar period government policy had remained focused on the assimilation of Native peoples into the larger society. A joint Senate and House of Commons task force, which reported in 1948, was oblivious to long-standing policies of colonialism towards Aboriginal peoples. But the task force report did recommend the abandonment of earlier efforts to suppress indigenous traditions such as the potlatch among Pacific peoples and the Sun Dance on the Prairies. This was a recognition of the effectiveness of Native resistance to such bans rather than an acceptance of Native culture per se.

Increasingly, in the 1950s and 1960s, government policy spoke of the "integration" of Native peoples into the mainstream. As anti-colonial movements proved successful in winning sovereignty from European powers during this period, the ideology of integration shifted away from older notions of complete assimilation. The carrot was to be used more so than the stick, which had been the key to past policy. Moving the Indian Affairs Branch from the Department of Mines and Resources to the Department of Citizenship and Immigration reflected the view that "Indian policy was to be pro-active in elevating Indians to full citizenship."[80] At the insistence of the Native leadership, strengthened politically by the participation of many Natives in the armed forces during the war, the federal government conceded a degree of self-government on the reserves, reducing the powers of the Indian agents in favour of elected band councils.[81]

Government policy, however, was fraught with contradictions. On the one hand, Indian agents and the residential schools encouraged Native peoples to receive more education and to be involved in the industrial economy. On the other hand, the federal government did nothing to stop provincial governments from building huge dams for hydroelectricity projects that flooded Native communities and ruined their fisheries and tourist lodges. In the name of technological progress, and in the interests of white investors, these communities were relocated from lands where they could both provide for themselves and earn incomes to barren lands that provided no employment.[82] Many Natives migrated off reserves to urban areas in the hope of finding employment; but racism, along with poor education, doomed most of them to extreme poverty in the cities and towns.

In the far North, Natives benefited little from industrial development. Mr. Justice Thomas Berger, commissioned by the Trudeau government to examine the social effects of building pipelines to transport northern energy to the south, concluded that Native peoples had been excluded from the industrial economy and "have paid a high price in terms of social impact whenever the industrial economy has penetrated into the North."[83] The federal government had been expanding its social programs in the region since the 1950s, but Justice Berger noted that programs supposedly meant to create greater social equality had reinforced existing inequities. For example, when Inuvik became the centre for federal operations, replacing Aklavik, comfortable southern-style housing was built for the almost exclusively white employees of the government economic and social development programs. By contrast, shabby housing was built for the Native residents.[84]

Across Canada, the federal government stalled in providing social services to Natives by insisting that the provinces should be providing them. The provinces maintained that as long as the federal government retained jurisdiction over reserves, it must also take all responsibility for the well-being of reserve residents. Nor were Aboriginal peoples keen on having their relationship with the federal government compromised through an off-loading of social services to provincial authorities.[85] The Pearson government, as part of its War on Poverty, sought new ways of dealing with Native poverty and unemployment. In 1964, the cabinet approved a community development program (CDP), involving the hiring of community development officers (CDOs) for reserves whose role would be to initiate projects that would result in reduced federal welfare payments to Natives. While the planning for the CDP was fuzzy, the government believed that these social facilitators could contribute to the creation of employment for reserve residents and win the agreement of the provinces to administer social services on provincial reserves.

However, Natives were not consulted about either the form or the implementation of the program, and none of the twenty-five CDOs or seven supervisors hired in 1965 was Native. But many of the community development assistants, including George Manuel, a future chief of the Assembly of First Nations, were Aboriginal, and they influenced the CDOs in many instances to focus not only on adult education and job training but also on how communities could organize for political purposes. Unfortunately, the Indian agents, whose job was to protect the status quo, clashed with the CDOs and assistants, and Ottawa cancelled the program in 1968. By then, it had become clear that the provinces would not agree to provide social services as long as the federal government retained constitutional control over Natives and their lands. A federal White Paper on Indian Policy in 1969, released while Jean Chrétien was minister of Indian Affairs, focused on provincial demands and promised a repeal of the Indian Act within five years along with a transfer of federal responsibility for Native peoples to the provinces.[86]

But Aboriginal peoples had been emboldened by their earlier postwar struggle for changes in the Indian Act, by the success of decolonization in Africa and Asia, and by the unintended impact of the CDP. They organized to bury the White Paper. The National Indian Brotherhood, formed in 1968, along with its provincial counterparts, led protests that forced the government to abandon its goal of gradually removing Indian status.[87] While the Trudeau government had proclaimed that its objective was equality for all Canadians, the First Nations claimed that this was a mask for genocide against Native peoples who would lose their millennia-old cultures. While the White Paper argued that "a plain reading" of the treaties demonstrated that Ottawa had conceded little to First Nations in the treaties, Native peoples used their oral history to argue that the treaties had promised far more than the federal government had delivered.[88]

The focus of Native efforts after 1969 was on restoring as large an element of Native sovereignty as possible, through land-claims negotiations with governments and in the courts, on the one hand, and through taking over responsibility for social services themselves, on the other. The Champagne/Aishihik band, for example, demanded in 1973 that "control and responsibility over social programs for Yukon Indians must be placed in the hands of the Yukon Indian people."[89] With continued urbanization, however, a large group of Canadian Natives trapped in urban ghettoes became the clients of provincial social service agencies. Federal-provincial negotiations about who was to pay for the services rendered to urban Natives would gradually lead to more agreements about provincial administration of federally paid services on reserves.

In the area of education, considerable progress was evident by 1980. In the mid-1960s, an exhaustive study of the education levels of Prairie Natives indicated that by age sixteen, fewer than 10 per cent of registered Native children were still in school. By 1981, the figure for school attendance for fifteen-to-nineteen-year-old Natives was over 40 per cent, though the figure for non-Natives was 60 per cent. As well, a small number of young Natives had begun to attend colleges and universities.[90] But projects linked to economic development, which might have allowed more Natives who remained on reserves to find work, were not materializing. As late as the early 1990s, only about 4 per cent of Department of Indian Affairs expenditures on reserves were destined for economic development. Wrote economist Helen Buckley in 1992: "The real money—about eighty per cent—goes for schools, housing, various facilities (roads, sewage systems, etc.) and welfare. All of these are needed but they do nothing to turn the situation around. The schools get too few children educated, while welfare and cheap housing lead nowhere. The Hawthorne Report took the Department to task more than twenty years ago for its neglect of economic development (and for the high costs of accounts and record keeping) but nothing has changed."[91]

The period from 1945 to 1980, in retrospect, represented the heyday of Canadian commitment to creating greater economic equality among citizens. As the federal government became more involved in distributing wealth among Canadians, both through equalization and through subsidies to provinces for their social-assistance costs, the provinces also became more liberal in their social-welfare policies. Discrimination in social policy against first employable males and later single mothers decreased. The guaranteed-income debate suggested that policy-makers recognized that the government's goal was not simply to attempt to create equality of opportunity but also to provide a minimum income for citizens as a right of citizenship.

Like so much in the postwar period, however, government commitments to greater social justice were predicated on an expanding economy and an ability to distribute monies to the poor without attacking the privileges of either the rich or the growing middle class. The capitalist system, far more than government programs, was supposed to provide the solution for the problem of want amidst plenty. However, that system seemed unable to deliver much to already disadvantaged regions or to Native communities. Programs that subsidized corporations that relocated to impoverished areas were subverted by their recipients. A guaranteed annual income might have had some impact depending upon how it was designed, but by the end of the 1970s, it was clear that the earlier enthusiasm for such a program had given way to indifference. The progressive redesign of unemployment insurance in 1971, along with CAP, did make a difference in individual lives in all regions. Rising GNP per capita every year between 1961 and 1975, along with two-income households and improved social programs had together reduced the percentage of low-income Canadians.

Unfortunately, the gains of the postwar period came increasingly under attack as the prosperity that caused governments to accede to popular pressures for greater equality for Canadians subsided. Part 4 explores the reasons why the Canadian consensus favouring greater equality began to crack after 1980, and what effects this had on social policy both federally and provincially.

NOTES

1 *Council Orbit,* December 1973, Manitoba Council of Self-Help Groups Papers, Provincial Archives of Manitoba (PAM).

2 Gale Wills, *A Marriage of Convenience: Business and Social Work in Toronto 1918–1957* (Toronto, ON: University of Toronto Press, 1995), 105.

3 Economic Council of Canada, *Fifth Annual Review: The Challenge of Growth and Change* (Ottawa, ON: Queen's Printer, 1968), 108–109; Ian Adams, *The Poverty Wall* (Toronto, ON: McClelland and Stewart, 1970), 16; Canada, *Poverty in Canada: Report of the Special Senate Committee on Poverty* (Ottawa, ON: Information Canada, 1971), 7.

4 Canada, *Report of the Royal Commission on Taxation,* vol. 1, *Introduction, Acknowledgments and Minority Reports* (Ottawa, ON: Queen's Printer, 1966), 44, 201, Low-income families "pay a surprisingly high proportion of their income in taxes to all levels of government," concluded the commissioners (42). Or, as economist Allan Maslove noted in a 1972 study for the Economic Council of Canada, the tax system featured "extreme regressivity…at the lower end of the income scale and the lack of any significant progressivity over the remainder of the income range." Allan M. Maslove, *The Pattern of Taxation in Canada* (Ottawa, ON: Information Canada, 1972), 64.

5 "Proposals for Tax Reform," E.J. Benson, Minister of Finance, 1969, Canada, House of Commons, Standing Committee on Finance, Trade and Economic Affairs, Section 91, Appendix B-49, 137–230.

6 The staff members who resigned outlined their views in Ian Adams, William Cameron, Brian Hill, and Peter Penz, *The Real Poverty Report* (Edmonton, AB: M.G. Hurtig, 1971).

7 In 1973, the CCSD adopted a definition of poverty that also used 50 per cent of the nation's average family income adjusted for family size as the benchmark to measure levels of poverty. Canadian Council on Social Development, *Not Enough: The Meaning and Measurement of Poverty in Canada: Report of the CCSD National Task Force on the Definition and Measurement of Poverty in Canada* (Ottawa, ON: CCSD, 1984).

8 Canada, *Poverty in Canada,* 7–8, 11.

9 Canada's rate of unemployment in the second half of the 1960s hovered between 5 and 6 per cent, the highest rate of unemployment among advanced capitalist industrialized countries of that period. Ibid., 43.

10 Adams, Cameron, Hill, and Penz, *The Real Poverty Report,* 63.

11 Derek P.J. Hum, *Federalism and the Poor: A Review of the Canada Assistance Plan* (Toronto, ON: Ontario Economic Council, 1983), 15.

12 Montreal Council of Social Agencies to CWC, 28 May 1954; Hamilton Council of Community Services to CWC, 21 July 1954; Neighbourhood Workers Association, Toronto, to CWC, 28 April 1955; Maurice Boyer, Secrétaire, La Fédération Joliettaine des oeuvres de charité, to Marie Hamel, Secrétaire, Commission française, Conseil Canadien du bien-être social, 22 December 1954; T.C. Douglas to R.E.G. Davis, executive director, CWC, 4 May 1955; CWC/ CCSD Papers, MG 28 I 10, Vol. 71, File 532, Library and Archives of Canada (LAC).

13 "Gallup Poll Political Issues, 1953, 1954," Polls reported 30 October 1954, and 6 November 1954, National Liberal Federation Papers, MG 28, IV-3, Vol. 962, LAC.

14 Margaret Conrad, "The Atlantic Revolution of the 1950s," in *Beyond Anger and Longing: Community and Development in Atlantic Canada*, ed. Berkeley Fleming (Fredericton, NB: Acadiensis Press/Mount Allison University, Centre for Canadian Studies, 1988), 55–96.

15 Philip Mathias, *Forced Growth: Five Studies of Government Involvement in the Development of Canada* (Toronto, ON: J. Lewis and Samuel, 1978); Annalee Lepp, David Millar, and Barbara Roberts, "Women in the Winnipeg Garment Industry, 1950s–1970s," in *First Days, Fighting Days: Women in Manitoba History*, ed. Mary Kinnear (Regina, SK: Canadian Plains Research Centre, 1987), 149–72.

16 See Kenneth Norrie and Douglas Owram, *A History of the Canadian Economy* (Toronto, ON: Harcourt Brace Jovanovich, 1991), 327, 402; and Kenneth H. Norrie, "Some Comments on Prairie Economic Alienation," *Canadian Public Policy* 2, 2 (Spring 1976): 222. While Norrie, a conservative economist, believes that public policies meant to correct market actions are wasteful, left-wing scholars have argued that state direction of the economy and ownership of major industries would allow governments to work against the logic of the marketplace that concentrates industry in one small region of the country. See Janine Brodie, *The Political Economy of Canadian Regionalism* (Toronto, ON: Harcourt Brace Jovanovich, 1990) and R.J. Brym, ed., *Regionalism in Canada* (Toronto, ON: Irwin, 1986).

17 Alvin Finkel, "Alberta Social Credit and the Second National Policy," in *Toward Defining the Prairies: Region, Culture, and History*, ed. Robert Wardhaugh (Winnipeg, MB: University of Manitoba Press, 2001), 29–49.

18 "Unemployment Insurance in Canada—Some Recommendations," R.E.G. Davis to Premier T.C. Douglas, 17 May 1955, CWC/CCSD Papers, Vol. 71, File 532; *Ottawa Journal*, 24 January 1955.

19 Janet Guildford, "The End of the Poor Law: Public Welfare Reform in Nova Scotia Before the Canada Assistance Plan," in *Mothers of the Municipality: Women, Work, and Social Policy in Post-1945 Halifax*, ed. Judith Fingard and Janet Guildford (Toronto, ON: University of Toronto Press, 2005), 49–75.

20 "Draft—Assistance Programs to the Unemployed," 2 June 1959, CWC/CCSD Papers, Vol. 71, File 532.

21 Ibid.

22 On the different philosophies of provincial governments in Canada regarding social assistance from Confederation to the 1990s, see Gerard William Boychuk, *Patchworks of Purpose: The Development of Provincial Social Assistance Regimes in Canada* (Montreal, QC: McGill-Queen's University Press, 1998).

23 Rodney S. Haddow, *Poverty Reform in Canada, 1958–1978: State and Class Influences on Policy-Making* (Montreal, QC: McGill-Queen's University Press, 1993), 24, 27.

24 "Draft—Assistance Programs to the Unemployed," 2 June 1959.

25 Ann Porter, "Women and Income Security in the Postwar Period: The Case of Unemployment Insurance, 1945–1962," *Labour/Le Travail* 31 (1993): 111–44; Georges Campeau, *De l'assurance-chômage à l'assurance-emploi: l'histoire du régime canadien et de son détournement* (Montreal, QC: Boréal, 2001), 139–41.

26 Ibid., 136–39.

27 L. Richard Lund, "'Fishing for Stamps': The Origins and Development of Unemployment Insurance for Canada's Commercial Fisheries, 1941–71," *Journal of the Canadian Historical Association*, New Series 6 (1995): 179–208.

28 Porter, in "Women and Income Security," documents the male chauvinism in the trade unions' gradual and begrudging turnabout on issues of discrimination against women in the program.

In turn, the NCWC, while strongly opposing discrimination against women, equally favoured opposition to inclusion of seasonal workers in the program. They stood four-square behind the business argument that the program had to be maintained on an actuarial basis. "Brief submitted by the National Council of Women of Canada (NCWC) to the Committee of Inquiry into the Unemployment Insurance Act," 16 October 1961, National Council of Women of Canada Papers, MG 28, I 25, Vol. 132, File 17, LAC.

29 Campeau, De l'assurance-chômage à l'assurance-emploi, 141–47 ; L. Richard Lund, " Income Maintenance, Insurance Principles and the 'Liberal 1960s': Canada's Unemployment Program, 1941–1971," in Canada at the Crossroads? The Critical 1960s, ed. Gustav Schmidt and Jack L. Granatstein (Bochum, Germany: Universitatsverlag Dr. N. Brockmeyer, 1994), 7.

30 Campeau, De l'assurance-chômage à l'assurance-emploi, 153–57.

31 Ibid., 158.

32 Gwendolyn Shand, National Committee on Laws, to Mrs. F.F. Worthington, corresponding secretary, NCWC, 12 August 1955, "The Social Status of Women in Nova Scotia," NCWC Papers, Vol. 101. See also, Wanda Thomas Bernard and Judith Fingard, "Black Women at Work: Race, Family, and Community in Greater Halifax," in Mothers of the Municipality, ed. Fingard and Guildford, 189–225.

33 S. June Menzies, New Directions for Public Policy: A Position Paper on the One-Parent Family (Ottawa, ON: Canadian Advisory Committee on the Status of Women, 1976), 1.

34 Louise Dulude, Women and Aging: A Report on the Rest of Our Lives (Ottawa, ON: Canadian Advisory Committee on the Status of Women, 1978), 95.

35 Haddow, Poverty Reform in Canada 1959–1978, 65, 72.

36 Ibid., 39.

37 Joseph W. Willard, Deputy Minister of National Health and Welfare, to John Munro, Minister of National Health and Welfare, "Annual Report–Canada Assistance Plan Year Ended March 31, 1969," Department of National Health and Welfare Papers, RG 29, Box 1524, File 201-16-1, Pt 6, LAC, traces the steps taken from the federal-provincial conference in September 1963 to the legislation of the CAP. Also useful are "Notes on Federal-Provincial Plenary Conference at Quebec City, March 31–April 2, 1964," Lester B. Pearson Papers, MG 26 N-3, Volume 64, File 306.2, LAC, which indicates the views of the different provinces on the issue of contracting out. Pearson's announcement of the provisions of CAP to the premiers is found in Canada, Federal-Provincial Conference, Ottawa, 19–22 July 1965 (Ottawa, ON: Queen's Printer, 1968), 13–15.

38 Leslie Bella, "The Provincial Role in the Canadian Welfare State: The Influence of Provincial Social Policy Initiatives on the Design of the Canada Assistance Plan," Canadian Public Administration 22, 3 (1979): 439–52.

39 Hum, Federalism and the Poor, 14.

40 Haddow, Poverty Reform in Canada 1958–1978, 40; Canada, Federal-Provincial Conference 19–22 July 1965, 13.

41 Christopher Leaman, The Collapse of Welfare Reform: Political Institutions, Policy and the Poor in Canada and the United States (Cambridge, MA: MIT Press, 1980), 2–3.

42 Hum, Federalism and the Poor, 4–5.

43 Leaman, The Collapse of Welfare Reform, 2–3.

44 Ibid., 334.

45 Joseph W. Willard to provincial deputy ministers, 2 May 1969; John Munro to Willard, 10 April 1969, Department of National Health and Welfare Papers, Box 1524, File 201-16-1, Pt. 5.

46 Hum, Federalism and the Poor, 64.

47 Ian Hamilton, The Children's Crusade: The Story of the Company of Young Canadians (Toronto, ON: P. Martin, 1973); Douglas Owram, Born at the Right Time: A History of the Baby Boom Generation (Toronto, ON: University of Toronto Press, 1996), chap. 9.

48 Gouvernement du Québec, Ministère de la Famille et du Bien-Être Social, *Étude sur l'évolution des coûts de l'assistance sociale*, 15 January 1969, Department of National Health and Welfare Papers, Box 1524, File 202-16-1 Pt 6. Translated by the author.

49 Marjorie Hartling, Burnaby, British Columbia Co-ordinator, National Anti-Poverty Organization (NAPO), to Patricia Godfrey, CCSD, 23 March 23 1972, CWC/CCSD Papers, Vol. 188, File 11.

50 The Senate of Canada, *Proceedings of the Special Senate Committee on Poverty*, Hon. David A. Croll, chairman, 1968-9, 1969-70, 1970-1 (Ottawa, ON: Queen's Printer, 1968-1971).

51 Canada, *Poverty in Canada*, xi.

52 Ibid., 83.

53 Ibid., xvii, xix, xx.

54 *Council Orbit*, 4 August 1972.

55 Leaman, *The Collapse of Welfare Reform*, 51.

56 Haddow, *Poverty Reform in Canada*, 179.

57 Kevin Brushett, "Reaching Out and Biting Back: Grassroots Activism and Toronto's Social Service Community, 1960-75," paper Presented to the Canadian Historical Association Conference, Halifax, NS, May 2003.

58 Shirley Tillotson, "Class and Community in Canadian Welfare Work, 1933-1960," *Journal of Canadian Studies* 32, 1 (1997): 63-92; and "'When Our Membership Awakes': Welfare Work and Canadian Union Autonomy, 1950-1965," *Labour/Le Travail* 40 (1997): 137-169.

59 Darlene Germscheid, first paid co-ordinator of Winnipeg's Council of Self-Help Groups, resigned her position after two years because it restricted her ability to organize demonstrations of the poor and other collective actions, *Council Orbit*, 1 1971.

60 Cited in *Council Orbit*, 6 March 1973.

61 Leaman, *The Collapse of Welfare Reform*, 59.

62 "Notes for An Address by the Honourable John C. Munro to the House of Commons on the Third Reading of Bill C-170 (Family Income Security Plan)," 29 June 1972, Department of National Health and Welfare Papers, Vol. 3351, File 201-11-5, Pt.2.

63 A.W. Johnson, "Social Policy in Canada: The Past As It Conditions the Present," in *The Future of Social Welfare Systems in Canada and the United Kingdom*, ed. Shirley B. Seward (Halifax: Institute for Research on Public Policy, 1987), 57.

64 Johnson, "Social Policy in Canada," 57.

65 Leaman, *The Collapse of Welfare Reform*, 112-22.

66 Haddow, *Poverty Reform in Canada*, 109, 146

67 Leaman, *The Collapse of Welfare Reform*, 59.

68 Ibid., 117. Canadian Council on Social Development, *Guaranteed Annual Income: An Integrated Approach* (Ottawa, ON: CCSD, 1973), 277; Michael Mendelson, "Can We Reform Canada's Income System?" in *The Future of Social Welfare Systems*, ed. Seward, 122-23.

69 Hum, *Federalism and the Poor*, 22.

70 Ibid., 119.

71 Hum, *Federalism and the Poor*, 130, 169-71; Haddow, *Poverty Reform*, 151.

72 Haddow, *Poverty Reform in Canada*, 101.

73 Ibid., 209, 215.

74 Ibid., 165.

75 National Council of Welfare, *Poverty Profile 1999* (Ottawa, ON: NCN, 1999).

76 F.H. Leacy, ed., *Historical Statistics of Canada*, 2nd ed. (Ottawa, ON: Statistics Canada 1983), tables F13, F15.

77 Statistics Canada, *Income Distribution by Size* in Statistics Canada, *Selected Years: Distribution of Family Incomes in Canada* (Ottawa, ON, 1972); Maslove, *The Pattern of Taxation*, 64.

78 Carole Swan, "Women in the Canadian Labour Force: The Present Reality," in *Women and the Canadian Labour Force: Proceedings from a Workshop Held at the University of British Columbia in January 1981*, ed. Naomi Herson and Dorothy E. Smith (Ottawa, ON: Social Sciences and Humanities Research Council of Canada, 1982), 35, 54, 84.

79 Hugh Shewell, "'Bitterness behind Every Smiling Face': Community Development and Canada's First Nations, 1954–1968," *Canadian Historical Review* 83, no.1 (2002): 66.

80 Ibid., 60.

81 Olive Dickason, *Canada's First Nations: A History of Founding Peoples From Earliest Times*, 2nd ed. (Toronto, ON: Oxford University Press, 1997), 304–305.

82 James Waldram, *As Long as the Rivers Run: Hydroelectric Development and Native Communities in Western Canada* (Winnipeg, MB: University of Manitoba Press, 1988); and Sean McCutcheon, *Electric Rivers: The Story of the James Bay Project* (Montreal, QC: Black Rose Books, 1991).

83 Justice Thomas R. Berger, *Northern Frontier, Northern Homeland: The Report of the Mackenzie Valley Pipeline Inquiry*, vol. 1 (Ottawa, ON: Minister of Supply and Services, 1977), 148.

84 Ibid., 158.

85 Shewell, "'Bitterness behind Every Smiling Face,'" 61–66.

86 Ibid., 71–81; Helen Buckley, *From Wooden Ploughs to Welfare: Why Indian Policy Failed in the Prairie Provinces* (Montreal, QC: McGill-Queen's University Press, 1992), 123–24.

87 Arthur J. Ray, *I Haved Lived Here since the World Began: An Illustrated History of Canada's Native People* (Toronto, ON: Lester/Key Porter, 1996), 334–36.

88 Helen Buckley, *From Wooden Ploughs to Welfare*, 124.

89 Brian Wharf, *Community and Social Policy in Canada* (Toronto, ON: McClelland and Stewart, 1992), 111.

90 Buckley, *From Wooden Ploughs to Welfare*, 133.

91 Ibid., 135–36.

PART 4

Neo-Liberalism

As we have seen, the period from 1945 to the mid-1970s was a period of advances in social provision for Canadians. It was also a period of contestation between popular groups and elites, and, in most areas of social policy, legislation represented a compromise between the demands of the former for social justice and demands of the latter for low taxes and preservation of the status quo. A buoyant economy allowed governments to pacify popular demands without producing a net redistribution of wealth among social classes. As well, there was widespread support for the Keynesian perspective that regarded government spending as contributing to aggregate demand and smoothing out the historic booms and busts of the business cycle.

As the economic boom of the postwar decades ran out of steam in the 1970s, however, the business attack on Keynesianism became more sophisticated and more effective. Conservatives attributed the latest crisis in capitalism to alleged years of government overspending on social programs. The solution, they argued, was a return to "liberal," that is marketplace, economics that required a dramatic reduction in government regulation of the economy and provision for the unfortunate. While few called for a full return to the Poor Law, the underlying argument of neo-liberalism was that Canadians had become too reliant on state handouts for their well-being and required the discipline of market forces to smarten them up. Social activists were placed on the defensive as the well-funded business rhetorical onslaught influenced government policies in all areas. Chapter 12 assesses victories and defeats in the era of neo-liberalism, while chapter 13 evaluates the prospects for more progressive developments in social policy once the neo-liberal paradigm, which has lost much of its popular allure, has run its course.

The Welfare State since 1980

X.Y. was an Edmonton mother who was in great economic difficulty in the summer of 2003. A single working mom of three school-aged children, she had benefited a few years earlier from a non-profit agency program that bought and repaired older homes and then sold them, without financial markup, to lower income families. Though she earned barely more than the minimum wage at her clerical job, she could just afford the mortgage payments on the house. But, in the winter of 2003, the combination of colder than usual weather and government deregulation of utility rates doubled and then tripled her heating and electricity bills. Though she made use of food banks and worked extra hours, she could not pay these bills in addition to her mortgage, school fees, and the usual costs associated with raising children and running a household.

X.Y. invited social workers with the provincial Department of Social Services to help her with her financial dilemmas. While they were initially sympathetic, their focus shifted when the utility companies cut off her heat and electricity. They felt it was their duty to question whether her children could remain with her in conditions that were unsafe. Other children had been seized from parents who had become homeless or lived in unheated homes, even though there was no question of their parenting skills or devotion to their children. X.Y. was unwilling to part with her children. She could sell her old home at a loss. But she would then have to rent a substandard home in a crack-infested "welfare" district where she could never feel comfortable about her children's safety. Instead, she decided to face the uncertainty of life in another province where some regulation of utility costs remained and social assistance provisions were slightly better.

Few Canadians would have believed in 1970 that three decades later their fellow citizens might face X.Y.'s choices. Freshly minted reports from government commissions and task forces recommended guaranteed annual incomes, a fairer tax system, guaranteed spots for children in a national daycare network, and an extension of social housing. By the early 2000s, these reports were yellowed with age, their recommendations having been ignored by successive governments. Almost one Canadian in ten relied on social assistance for all or part of household income in 1999 (only tightened eligibility rules kept many more from collecting), 2 million in a population of 30 million relied on food banks for at least some of their food that year, and 200,000 Canadians were homeless.

Was the political will to enhance social equality in Canada ever really there? The 1965 annual convention of the Canadian Chamber of Commerce had listened somberly to the results of an extensive survey which concluded that the Chamber's efforts to influence Canadians' attitudes to social programs had backfired. Respondents had discounted the organization's research and public stances as the self-interested propaganda of the greedy rich.[1] Gradually, corporate leaders sought other ways to turn public thinking against social equality, particularly through funding of superficially independent research institutes that could become the main spokespersons for the corporate viewpoint. The Fraser Institute in British Columbia, the C.D. Howe Institute in Ontario, and the Atlantic Institute for Market Studies presented themselves as disinterested organizations of academics. The findings of their well-financed studies were regularly distributed to the corporate-controlled media and reported on as if they were news rather than editorials. Judging by public opinion polls that showed Canadians in the early 1990s to be more right wing than their counterparts in the late 1960s, the steady stream of alleged research results from the institutes influenced Canadian attitudes towards the proper balance between social spending and taxation. Left-wing institutes such as the Canadian Centre for Policy Alternatives were established as a counter-response to the corporate-financed institutes. These institutes were funded by labour, social work, women's, and environmental groups, sponsors which lacked the financial means and media contacts to get their message across as effectively as the corporations did.

To a degree, neo-liberal ideas took hold in all of Canada's major political parties by the 1980s. They became especially entrenched in the national arena though the Reform Party, formed in 1986, and its successor, the Canadian Alliance (CA), formed in 2000, as well as the Progressive Conservative (PC) Party. The reconstructed Conservative Party of Canada, formed in 2004, which merged the CAS and PCS, made neo-liberal economics the cornerstone of its policy. Even the Liberal federal government, first elected in 1993, while rhetorically centrist, had been captured by neo-liberal forces, particularly in the person of Paul Martin Jr., finance minister from 1993 to 2002, and prime minister as of December 2003.

Most provincial regimes elected after 1980 subscribed to some version of neo-liberal ideology: the Progressive Conservatives in Alberta swung sharply to the right in 1993; Ontario's Progressive Conservative government elected in 1995 followed suit, as did the British Columbia Liberals elected in 2002 and the Quebec Liberals elected in 2003; and both old-line parties in the Atlantic provinces toed the neo-liberal line. The New Democratic regimes elected at various times in Ontario, Saskatchewan, Manitoba, and British Columbia, along with the Parti Québécois regimes, represented only partial exceptions to the neo-liberal thrust.[2] In Quebec, the vision of the Castonguay-Nepveu Report of the early 1970s, which promised to make a huge dent on poverty in the province, was quietly abandoned in 1984. The PQ had spent its early years in office raising the minimum wage and increasing social assistance payments, only to allow both to be eaten up by inflation in subsequent years. In its 1984 budget the PQ cut provincial taxes and spending despite the recession.[3]

Family allowances, CAP, and federal financial support for social housing had all disappeared by the 1990s. Two-tiered medical care, in which the better off could purchase services outside the public sector, had made some gains. The percentage of unemployed Canadians eligible to collect unemployment insurance had been eroded to levels unseen since the early 1950s. Yet the movements that had fought for the creation of social programs as citizen entitlements before the 1980s did not stand idly by as governments tried to rewrite the social contract. This chapter traces the evolution of both neo-liberal forces and popular forces in the struggle to control social policies after 1980.

PRELUDE TO NEO-LIBERALISM

The origins of the neo-liberal assault lie in the economic stagnation of the 1970s. As both inflation and unemployment rose in tandem throughout the decade, conservatives questioned the efficacy of the Keynesian approach to economic policy that supposedly had been utilized by governments since the war to keep both inflation and unemployment in check. They argued that government attempts to reduce unemployment were causing inflation without affecting joblessness. The funds required for stimulative expenditures were being financed by government deficits, which, in turn, were financed by loans from financial institutions both at home and abroad. The loans by these institutions to government allegedly "crowded out" loans to the private sector, forcing interest rates up to record levels. In turn, this fuelled inflation. With companies unable to make loans, jobs in the private sector were disappearing at a faster rate than those that could be created in the public sector. Such viewpoints were joined to the more traditional conservative ones that argued the provision of state aid to those without incomes encouraged them to refuse the jobs that were on offer.[4]

A minority of economists disputed the neo-liberal version of economic events as both ahistorical and lacking in rigour. The links between inflation and government deficits that neo-liberals claimed as fact were unsupported by historical evidence and, government surpluses in the early 1950s had not prevented double-digit inflation from occurring in later years. In any case, they argued, federal financial policy in the 1970s did not follow Keynesian prescriptions. While fiscal policy, which focused on unemployment, was mildly expansionary, monetary policy, which focused on inflation, was restrictionist. The two seemed to cancel each other out. Neo-liberal perspectives were firmly entrenched in the Bank of Canada, and after 1975, the Trudeau government, co-operating with the Bank, regarded tight money policies as a key ingredient in its efforts to stem inflation rates that had reached double digits annually. Opponents of this approach pointed out that Canada's unemployment rate, which had doubled from 4 per cent in 1970 to 8 per cent in 1978–79, would remain high until interest rates fell.[5]

Trudeau's embrace of contradictory economic policies was also evident when he campaigned against wage and price controls during the federal election of August 1974, only to turn around in October 1975 and impose controls for a three-year period in order to contain inflation. Trudeau did not embrace the full-blown neo-liberalism espoused by Margaret Thatcher, who was elected British prime minister in 1979, and Ronald Reagan, elected American president in 1980. However, faced with declining revenues, he was unwilling to embrace the Carter Commission's recommendations for radical changes in the taxation system or to follow Keynesian monetary policies. Instead, he cut social spending so as to contain the rapidly growing deficits incurred by his government from 1975 onwards. Though he remained a supporter of social entitlements in theory, he lost interest in the guaranteed annual income that his government had earlier extolled.

Trudeau was also alarmed by the above-inflation increases in publicly financed health spending in the mid-1970s. Provincial health programs had responded in the early years of medicare to growing demands from patients and doctors for services. In 1977, Trudeau ended the guarantee of federal matching funds for provincial expenditures on health care and post-secondary education. Instead, the federal government would provide an annual Established Programs Funding (EPF) grant to provinces, based on past spending that was indexed to inflation. By handing over unconditional tax points to the provinces equal to about half of the monies they were already receiving annually from Ottawa for health care and post-secondary education, Trudeau softened criticisms from some premiers that the federal government was beginning a process that would lead to a federal withdrawal of funds to the provinces in these areas.[6]

The provinces responded to declining revenues from the federal government by trying to reduce the rate of growth in their health care and post-secondary education expenditures. Allowing universities to hike tuition fees by large amounts was the usual solution to the latter problem, along with reduced expenditures on the upkeep of buildings and eventually on programs. In health care, physicians' fees were curbed somewhat, but in some provinces, the doctors were allowed to recoup their losses by extra-billing patients. Federal National Health and Welfare Minister Monique Bégin denounced extra-billing as a violation of medicare's promise of accessibility to medical services, and in 1984, the federal government introduced the Canada Health Act, which imposed penalties on provinces that allowed extra-billing. Their annual EPF grants would be reduced by an amount equal to the number of dollars that physicians had been allowed to extra-bill patients. The premiers, recognizing that their voters were more opposed to extra-billing than to federal intervention in areas of provincial jurisdiction, beat a retreat.[7]

The Trudeau government also raised the Guaranteed Income Supplement in the early 1980s. The increase reduced the poverty rate for seniors, as measured by Statistics Canada, from 27 per cent in 1980 to 19 per cent in 1985, but poverty rates remained much higher for elderly women without partners. The Special Senate Committee on Poverty's community-linked standard determined that a third of the elderly in Canada were poor. The Social Planning Council of Metropolitan Toronto calculated that in that city alone, over half of seniors lived in straitened circumstances.[8]

Trudeau's efforts to balance capitalist and popular demands seemed in doubt with the onset of a worldwide recession in 1982. The tight-money policies of the Reagan and Thatcher governments[9] fuelled a massive contraction in international investment and trade. Between 1979 and 1982 unemployment rates almost tripled in Britain, doubled in the United States, and shot up from 8 per cent to almost 13 per cent in Canada. Trudeau clung to tight-money policies while making relatively minor cuts to public expenditures as compared with his American and British counterparts, having little idea about how to reinvigorate the Canadian economy. He appointed a royal commission to plan the path forward, placing at its head Donald Macdonald, a former finance minister who had become a leading figure on Bay Street. Before the royal commission reported, Trudeau retired from politics. His replacement, John Turner, another former finance minister with close connections to Bay Street, called a summer election in 1984.

Both Turner and his principal opponent, the new Progressive Conservative leader, Brian Mulroney, decided that Canadians were not prepared to accept a forthright neo-liberal agenda. Though both promised to decrease government expenditures, they were vague about which programs would be cut. Mulroney, during his run for the leadership of the PCs the year before, had castigated the Trudeau government as "socialist," but during the campaign insisted that a government led by him would not slash social programs established by the Liberals. Universal social programs, proclaimed the would-be prime minister, were a "sacred trust, not to be tampered with."[10] During a national pre-election debate of the party leaders, hosted by the National Action Committee on the Status of Women, all three promised to initiate a federal daycare program that would guarantee subsidized daycare spaces to all working mothers seeking quality child care while they worked. But Mulroney, the ultimate winner of the election, had other priorities.

Neo-Liberalism in Action

Brian Mulroney was the first Canadian prime minister since Louis St. Laurent who was at once a member of both the corporate and political elite. Sharing the corporate elite's view that well-financed social programs pushed up taxation rates unnecessarily, Mulroney hoped to cut social spending early in his regime so that Canadians would forgive him by the time of the next election. But his first effort in that direction backfired. In 1985 he announced that old age pension payments, which rose annually by the rate of inflation, would only be partially indexed to inflation. Seniors, said the new prime minister cheerfully, recognized that all Canadians needed to make a contribution in the fight against inflation and ballooning government deficits. Seniors proved him wrong. The "grey power" movement of seniors' organizations had grown apace in the 1970s and 1980s as their numbers in the country grew. Demonstrations by old people embarrassed the government, particularly in one instance when Solange Denis, an Ottawa senior, confronted the prime minister and told him, with the network television news crews recording the moment, that if he did not rescind his change to the pension it would be "goodbye Charlie Brown" come the next election.

Mulroney's pension plans, along with earlier indications from Finance Minister Michael Wilson in November 1984 that the government planned to stiffen the UI program, sparked the creation of Solidarité Populaire Québec, which brought together seventy-five organizations, including the three competing trade union federations as well as women's, welfare advocacy, and seniors' groups.[11] Mulroney beat a strategic retreat, and turned his attention to the less politically charged area of EPF grants to the provinces. He announced in 1986 that his government would cut these grants by 2 per cent per year, a decrease that amounted to 6 per cent a year in real dollars when inflation was taken into account. Though his government held hearings regarding a national daycare program, no program was announced.

In part, because of Mulroney's apparent betrayal of the "sacred trust," though also because of scandals in the government and internal bickering within the Liberal Party, the NDP began a rise to the top of the polls. Canadians, who were somewhat ambivalent about neo-liberalism, were attracted to the social-democratic party's pitch for higher taxes on the wealthy and on corporations as the means to maintain and enrich Canada's social programs. But, by the time of the 1988 federal election, Mulroney appeared to have chosen a neo-liberal issue that would win him re-election: free trade. The Macdonald Commission's report, heavily influenced by business groups, suggested that a free-trade deal with the United States was the answer to Canada's economic woes. Canada, the report argued, should end wasteful expenditures meant to protect Canadian jobs with tariffs and to keep Canadian industries in Canadian hands. The free market would bring jobs and prosperity to most Canadians if the heavy hand of government regulation were only lifted.[12]

This view was consistent with the view increasingly being expressed by corporate leaders throughout the Western world that government protection of industry and of individuals was hampering economic development. "Globalization" became a buzzword for neo-liberal ideologues who believed that no country should be barring capital or trade from another country to protect domestic companies or workers because this only reduced international economic growth. "Free markets," not governments, could be counted on to dispense economic justice.[13]

Recognizing, however, that some Canadians would continue to fail to meet their economic needs via the marketplace, Macdonald did support reviving the idea of the Guaranteed Annual Income (GAI), but only if it replaced most other social insurance programs. The Canadian Labour Congress (CLC) responded with a proposed program that would strengthen existing social insurance programs and make their benefits available to far more Canadians, using the GAI as a last-resort program for those who received insufficient income from other sources, including social insurance programs.[14]

In the 1988 federal election, both opposition parties opposed the Free Trade Agreement (FTA), arguing that the agreement's provisions against providing unfair advantage to firms in one's own country would place Canada's social programs on the chopping block. The Conservatives responded that social programs were exempt from the provisions of the FTA for fair competition between the two countries.[15] Opponents of free trade won more votes in the 1988 election than its supporters, but the Mulroney government kept its Commons majority. The election over, Mulroney nuanced his argument about how the FTA would affect social programs. The logic of the agreement, though not the letter, argued for Canada to bring its social programs in line with their less generous American counterparts. If Canadian taxes on corporations and investors exceeded American taxes, Canada would lose industry and investors.

Daycare disappeared from the public agenda after the 1988 election, and universality was removed from old age pensions and family allowances, as the government introduced a clawback of part or all of the payments made to individuals netting more than $50,000 in a year.[16] Then, in 1990, the government announced a speed-up in the annual decreases to federal transfer payments for health care and post-secondary education, with 2004 targeted as the date when such transfers would end. A limit was also placed on CAP payments to the three wealthiest provinces, while unemployment insurance eligibility rules were tightened. By the end of the Mulroney years in 1993, federal social spending accounted for 8.5 per cent of the GDP, a decline from 10.5 per cent in 1984.[17]

Cuts to social programs proved unpopular if only because they occurred at the same time that a nasty recession arrived in 1990, causing double-digit unemployment throughout the first half of the decade. Though an international slowdown played a role, Canada's job losses exceeded those in the United States and Europe and the government's tight-money policies, once hardly commented upon, began to draw a great deal of fire. Keynesian ideas still seemed to resonate with Canadians who expressed anger at the government for failing to respond to a recession with low interest rates that would lead businesses to create jobs.

Mulroney's neo-liberal thinking regarding monetary policy was shaped by the Bank of Canada and its governor, John Crow. Crow argued that keeping inflation under control rather than alleviating unemployment must be the government's first order of business, borrowing a term popular with right-wing economists to justify his monetary policies: NAIRU or non-accelerating inflation rate of unemployment. The new orthodoxy at the Bank and in the business community became that, even when the economy was buoyant, monetary and fiscal policy should ensure that 8 per cent of Canadians were both unemployed and recipients of minimal government funding through either unemployment insurance or social assistance. This would moderate the demands for wage improvements on the part of the employed, and allow business profits to rise to levels that had been reduced over a generation because of a combination of inflation and worker militancy. Reducing inflation to the lowest level possible, perhaps eradicating it altogether, became the goal of the Bank of Canada.[18]

RETURN OF THE LIBERALS

The election of NDP governments in Ontario, Saskatchewan, and British Columbia in 1990 and 1991 demonstrated disillusionment with neo-liberalism. However, the NDP governments, while instituting social reforms, largely accepted the neo-liberal thrust in Canadian policy-making. The Ontario NDP government, for example, having promised before its election to spend mightily to restore Ontario's unemployment-ridden economy, soon got cold feet. In his first year in office, Premier Bob Rae expanded social housing, substantially increased daycare spaces and the pay of daycare workers, and increased health care and education spending. By mid-1991, however, faced with business threats of a capital strike, Rae began to emphasize debt reduction over reducing unemployment.[19] He rescinded his promise to nationalize the province's auto insurance industry, and later alienated the public-sector unions by imposing pay cuts of 5 per cent on all public-sector workers earning over $30,000 per year.

The perceived betrayal of Ontario voters by the Rae government gave the Liberals, both provincially and federally, a chance to reassert their reformist credentials. When the election writ was handed down in 1993, the federal Liberals, led by Jean Chrétien, were ready with a Red Book of vague promises that pledged the Liberals would defend the social legislation they had introduced in earlier years. They would end cuts in EPF grants to the provinces, and there were hints that cuts already made would be restored. A national daycare program would be established. Brian Mulroney's successor, Kim Campbell, took up the cudgels for neo-liberalism, but she faced an even more right-wing opponent in the Western-based Reform Party. The Reformers wanted massive cuts in federal spending, an end to federal supervision of monies granted to the provinces, and the conversion of the CPP into a program in which individuals would manage their own pension accounts.

The Liberals won a huge victory, winning all the seats in vote-rich Ontario, but they largely ignored their Red Book promises. Reduction in government deficits and debt remained paramount in government policy, resulting in further tightening of UI payments; additional cuts to health care, post-secondary education, and social assistance payments; and an end to family allowances. Paul Martin's budget speech in 1995 slashed government spending by $25 billion in three years, including $7 billion in transfers to provinces. That amounted to a 40 per cent cut in federal transfers.[20] A modest daycare program was announced but then withdrawn when the provinces, which would have to match federal funds, responded unfavourably.

Before facing the electorate for re-election in 1997, the Liberals had completely undone both CAP and family allowances, two programs that were part of the Liberal welfare-state heritage in Canada. CAP had disappeared in 1996 as the federal government, seeking to reduce its overall responsibility in areas of provincial jurisdiction, combined its expenditures in health care, post-secondary education, and social assistance into one cheque called the Canada Health and Social Transfer (CHST).[21] There would no longer be any question of the federal government holding back money from provinces whose welfare regime seemed too restrictive, as there had been with CAP in place. Although the Canada Health Act remained on the books, the Chrétien government continued to allow the federal contribution to the provinces for health care to decline annually. It turned a blind eye to provincial actions that eroded universal access, such as a flat $50 fee for an eye exam conducted by an optometrist in Alberta, and rationed access to psychiatric, physiotherapist and other health services in many provinces.

The Liberals' acceptance of provincial supremacy in the social-welfare field was evident in the Social Union Framework Agreement announced on 4 February 1999. Though Quebec's separatist government refused to be part of the agreement, insisting on provincial sovereignty over its social services, all other provinces and territories signed on with Ottawa. The agreement restricted Ottawa's right to intervene in existing or future provincial programs and guaranteed it would never introduce a program before it had won the support of a majority of provinces and territories. The provinces and territories, in turn, promised to work together to homogenize their social policies as much as possible, and to limit discrimination in the delivery of social provision to migrants from other provinces.[22]

The combination of federal cutbacks and federal unwillingness to impose national standards for social programs could not have come at a worse time, from the point of view of social advocates. The neo-liberal orthodoxy, which regarded deficits and debts as immoral even in times of high unemployment and social need, had gripped most provincial governments. Ralph Klein's government in Alberta, which slashed health spending by almost 20 per cent in 1994, while reducing welfare rolls by over half in a single year, became the poster-boy administration for neo-liberals.[23] Provincial governments in the Atlantic provinces had been administering cuts for years by that time, and Ontario fully joined the neo-liberal column in 1995 after the election of a Progressive Conservative government headed by Mike Harris. Harris, a devotee of tax cuts for the well off, matched and then exceeded Ralph Klein's zeal in cutting social programs.

As the Canadian economy began to recover in the late 1990s, organized public opposition to cuts in social programs forced governments to restore some of the funding cuts of the previous decade. But social advocates were largely on the defensive, trying to restore cuts to programs that still existed, rather than calling for the reinstatement of programs such as CAP and family allowances, or demanding new programs, such as a national daycare program, a guaranteed annual income, or an expansion of medicare's coverage. The right wing's call for tax cuts continued to resonate with many citizens who believed themselves to be overtaxed. Even if the result of tax cuts was that a corporate executive saved about $10,000 while the middle-income taxpayer saved $500, the $500 was much appreciated. The Liberals' tax cuts in the 2001 election, which heavily favoured the rich, seemed to win popular support. They were coupled with promises to increase the annual payout of federal funds to the provinces for health care, though the increases that Jean Chrétien announced did not even restore federal funding to 1993 levels.[24] The next section looks in detail at the role neo-liberalism played in the fate of social programs after 1975.

(Un)employment Insurance

As a result of the 1971 reforms to UI, 96 per cent of unemployed Canadians were eligible to receive insurance when they lost their jobs. Additional changes to the rules in the 1970s and 1980s reduced the eligible group to 85 per cent of the unemployed by 1989. But it was in the 1990s that the rules became especially restrictive and, by 1997, only 41 per cent of the unemployed were eligible for the renamed employment insurance (EI), a figure one percentage point below estimates of the eligible group in 1940 when UI was first introduced.[25] Both actuarial concerns and the government's desire to control wage demands by at once elevating unemployment levels and making the prospect of unemployment look as grim as possible destroyed the view of (un)employment insurance as social justice for Canadians unable to find work. By 2000, the program looked rather like it did in 1940: primarily a tax grab meant to deal with government deficits in other programs, and very secondarily, a program to help a subset of the unemployed.

When the program was liberalized in 1971, it was estimated that the rate of unemployment would remain at a 5 per cent level, which had been the average in the 1960s. But relative economic stagnation in the 1970s pushed unemployment rates to 8 per cent by the end of the decade. To keep the unemployment insurance fund solvent, the federal government had to increase its share of payments from 19 per cent in 1971 to 51 per cent in 1975. Conservatives argued that UI's availability made it more attractive for workers to leave jobs, but statistics demonstrated that only 10 per cent of people who left jobs voluntarily applied for insurance. Moreover, in 1978, Statistics Canada reported that there were twenty times as many unemployed people in Canada as there were job openings.[26]

Beginning in 1975, the government began to tinker with the 1971 reforms, reducing benefits and increasing the weeks of employment required before an unemployed person could qualify for benefits.[27] But it was Brian Mulroney, in his second term of office, who was responsible for shredding the philosophy underlining the 1971 changes. During his first term of office, Mulroney had appointed a commission, headed by former Quebec Liberal cabinet minister Claude Forget, to review and make recommendations regarding the UI system. The corporate and trade union representatives on the commission had opposing views, and the commission issued two reports. The majority report, written by Forget and supported by the business representatives, wanted UI returned to its original actuarial principles which excluded insurance for high-risk people. The unions, by contrast, denounced the logic that seasonal, short-term, and part-time workers should be ineligible for insurance because they had such a high likelihood of losing their jobs.[28]

In 1990 the Mulroney government, heeding Forget's advice, increased the number of weeks that a worker had to have worked within the previous year before becoming eligible for UI. So, for example, in Montreal, a high unemployment city where 10 weeks of work in the previous 52 had previously been enough to earn a right to a maximum of 32 weeks of insurance, it was now necessary to have worked a minimum of 16 weeks to collect any insurance, and that could last no more than 27 weeks. The minimum waiting time for eligibility for workers who had left a job or been fired, as opposed to laid off, was increased from 6 to 12 weeks after the employment ended.

Adding salt to the wounds of the unemployed who could not collect insurance, the government announced that it would expand its practice of dipping into the fund to find money for training programs and other "active" programs for the unemployed. Already using 2 per cent of the fund for such purposes, the government envisioned raising that amount to 15 per cent of the payouts from the fund. The trade union movement claimed that this was a raid on monies intended for income support to the unemployed, and that it constituted a subsidy to employers. While the government blamed the unemployed for their own fate—they allegedly lacked the necessary training to be flexible within an economy that required highly skilled labour—and bemoaned "dependency" on UI, social activists noted that the unemployed were the victims of capitalist restructuring. Ironically, they argued, the very people who were tossing workers out of their jobs would benefit from not having to pay to retrain those workers for new jobs in the economy.[29] Study after study would suggest in the years that followed that available training programs provided few skills that workers needed for the jobs that were opening up in Canada.[30] The women's movement argued that most of the jobs that women were being trained for reinforced, rather than reversed, their unequal position in the labour market.[31]

The final Tory reform of UI in 1993 excluded workers who voluntarily left jobs, regardless of the reason for their departure, as well as workers who were fired for misconduct, as judged by the employer. Rates of insurance payouts for those still eligible for insurance were also reduced so that no one could earn more than 57 per cent of their previous income, continuing a decline from the 75 per cent that was possible in 1971.[32] The Liberals cut even further. In Paul Martin's first budget in 1994, the 57 per cent maximum of former earnings was reduced to 55 per cent for 85 per cent of recipients, weeks of work required for eligibility were increased, and only minor adjustments were made to the Tory restrictions on fired workers and voluntary job leavers.

The new Liberal government also continued the former government's policy of at once reducing the government's contribution to the fund and at the same time taking monies away from insurance payments and putting them into "active" programs designed for reintegrating the unemployed into the workforce. Then, in 1995, the government, following the Forget Commission majority's suggestion, began using hours of work rather than weeks of work to determine eligibility for insurance. This removed many part-time workers, mainly women, from the eligibility many had gained for the first time in 1971 for the right to state aid as unemployed workers rather than as social assistance recipients.[33] The result of such policies, which were not accompanied by any lowering of the rates that workers and employers were required to pay into the fund, was that the fund began to accumulate a surplus as the percentage of unemployed able to qualify for EI continued to fall. By the early 2000s, the federal government was using the EI fund much as Mackenzie King used it during the Second World War—as a cash cow to finance other government programs.

There were sporadic workers' protests against growing restrictions on UI benefits. In the late 1970s, a group known as Action-Chômage, organized by left-wing groups in Quebec, counselled workers who had been denied UI and attempted to create a solidarity network among unemployed workers. Quebec's rate of unemployment at the time was consistently about 50 per cent higher than the Canadian average, placing unemployment in the province at about 12 per cent in 1978. It was several points higher in the Atlantic provinces, with Newfoundland consistently posting the country's highest rates of joblessness. But it took the recession of 1982, which pushed national joblessness to 12.8 per cent, to provoke the various provincial federations of labour to establish separate organizations for the unemployed. These organizations made UI a key focus, and their lack of success in influencing government policy testified to labour's growing political weakness. Demonstrations in the Atlantic provinces in the late 1990s and the election of opposition members in formerly Liberal ridings in the region in 1997 caused some relaxation of the strict rules governing EI. But, on the whole, changes in UI/EI policy over the post-1975 period represented a victory for neo-liberals.

HOUSING POLICY

Housing policy in the early 2000s also looked a bit more like housing policy in 1945 than in the 1970s. As with UI, the state's move away from public responsibility represented a victory of bourgeois interests over those of the working class and especially the poor. During the 1990s, the tap on social housing was turned off almost as tightly as it had been in the 1940s and 1950s.

The period of liberalism in housing policy lasted throughout the 1970s and for much of the 1980s, but within clear limits. The federal government continued to provide a substantial portion of the funds required for provincial agencies that built and maintained social housing. During these two decades, about 400,000 social housing units were developed, with 91,000 units added by non-profit co-ops and the rest by municipal and private non-profit organizations. This included housing for families and for seniors, though much of the family housing was cheaply constructed and segregated from neighbourhoods of family owned housing. Organizations of the poor sometimes called for rental subsidies as an alternative while others continued to support social housing, but demanded that it be better built, dispersed throughout communities, and run by its tenants. Efforts to turn boarding houses into non-profit permanent homes went awry as developers bought the properties on which they developed condominiums and office towers.[34]

Federal cuts to housing programs began during the late Trudeau period, escalated under Brian Mulroney, and reached their apogee under Jean Chrétien. Sister Monique Picard, assistant to the executive director of Les Oeuvres de la Maison du Père, described the extent of the abandonment in federal help for Quebec at a housing conference in 1990: "In 1979, the federal government was involved in the production of 10,000 public, co-operative or non-profit housing units in the province of Quebec. By 1986, that figure had dropped to 3,000. Yet, more than 35,000 people in Quebec alone are still on public-housing waiting lists."[35]

Cuts in social housing budgets and the relaxation of rent controls hit women hardest. According to Femmes et Logement, a Montreal lobby group for women's rights in housing, half of the province's households headed by women paid between 43 and 46 per cent of their income for housing compared with only 5.5 per cent of families headed by men. Quebec's reduced payments for subsidized housing forced women to live in poorly maintained buildings, and often resulted in frequent moves that left families rootless in their neigh- bourhoods. Middle-class men became the chief beneficiaries of Quebec's hous- ing programs since "eighty-four per cent of the housing subsidies granted by government go to landlords in the form of tax shelters and assistance to home- ownership or renovation programs."[36] Women in the Atlantic provinces fared even worse than their counterparts in Quebec. Families in New Brunswick on social assistance typically paid 65 per cent of their income on rent, usually for an inadequate shelter.[37]

Poor single men in Canada were also victims of public policies that favoured the interests of the wealthy over the poor in the area of housing. In Vancouver, the Downtown Eastside Residents' Association (DERA) was formed in 1973 to defend the interests of area residents. Most of the community's ten thousand residents were elderly males, half of whom were disabled, and virtually all of whom had monthly incomes of about $425 that permitted them to live only in closet-sized hotel rooms without cooking facilities. Their lives were made even more desperate by constant evictions. DERA had campaigned in the 1980s to prevent EXPO 86, which Vancouver hosted, from precipitating the relocation of poor downtown residents from their homes. Perhaps one thousand residents were evicted during EXPO and, in the next few years, another two thousand lost their homes as developers erected luxury condominiums and high-rise office towers along with parking lots. People in wheelchairs ended up in rooms above the ground floor in hotels or walk-ups that lacked elevators. DERA was able to develop some housing co-ops for area residents, but the developers' policies caused the number of homeless to rise each year.[38]

Aboriginals, both female and male, who lived in urban centres, were espe- cially grimly housed. In Winnipeg, in 2000, a study suggested that the city's fifty thousand Aboriginal residents, while less than 10 per cent of the popu- lation, provided half of the city's homeless. Three-quarters lived in substan- dard housing, and most paid half their income towards rents for their bleak accommodations.[39]

As difficult as the 1980s were for advocates of social housing, the 1990s were worse. In 1993, the federal government cut off all funds for social housing to the provinces, and most provinces simply stopped building social housing al- together. Even the NDP governments elected in Ontario in 1990 and British

Columbia in 1991, though carrying out ambitious housing projects before 1993, largely stopped building new housing once the federal government pulled the plug.[40] Only in Quebec, under the PQ government in the late 1990s, did a modest program of developing new social housing survive.

By 1996, Canada had at least two hundred thousand homeless people, and a significant proportion of tenant households—44 per cent in wealthy Ontario alone—paid more towards rent than the 30 per cent of income that Statistics Canada believed was the upper limit of what households could afford to pay.[41] In 2002, the federal government announced that it would re-enter, in a modest way, the business of sharing social housing costs with the provincial governments, promising to spend $320 million over five years. Social housing advocates hoped that this pittance would encourage the government to resume its social responsibility for sheltering all Canadians.

CHILD CARE

A task force headed by Katie Cooke, established by the Trudeau government in its dying days, demonstrated that provincially approved and licensed daycare spaces remained at a premium in Canada. Only an estimated 8.8 per cent of households where there was no stay-at-home parent had access to such spaces. In Toronto, a survey indicated that 49 per cent of parents regarded a child care centre as the ideal arrangement they would prefer for their children; but only 10 per cent had their kids in daycare. After 1976, mothers' participation rates in the labour force dramatically increased, and by 1986 a majority of mothers with children under twelve years of age, including mothers with preschoolers, were in the labour force.[42]

A national movement for daycare had emerged by the 1984 federal election in the form of the Canadian Day Care Advocacy Association, founded in Winnipeg in 1982. Most daycare advocates campaigned for a national program of publicly operated child care centres, though there were also calls for state support for parent-created, co-operatively run daycares. Daycare advocates were generally united in their support for strict government standards for child care operations and for the banning of private, for-profit centres that, in their view, treated children as commodities. Even Quebec's daycare advocates wanted federal money provided for the support of *garderies*.[43]

Brian Mulroney's commitment to lower government spending trumped his commitment to a national daycare program. The Macdonald Commission set the pace for the business community's denunciations of plans for an expanded government role in daycare by arguing that such a program would require vastly expanded taxes and thereby restrict Canada's competitiveness in world markets.[44] The Mulroney government established a special committee in November 1985 to consider the extent of the child care crisis in Canada and to make recommendations. Though the committee heard many stories from parents who were unable to find affordable, stable, safe child care while they worked,[45] the Tory majority on the committee endorsed the views of business lobbyists who called for the child care expense allowance to be increased as an alternative to funding daycare directly.[46]

The Liberals, running for election in 1993, promised in the party's Red Book that a Liberal administration would increase the number of daycare spaces in the country by fifty thousand each year that the economy grew by more than 3 per cent.[47] But, although the economy grew by that amount seven times in the following nine years, this commitment was not fulfilled. Human Resources Minister Lloyd Axworthy offered the provinces $700 million in matching grants for adding new daycare spaces, but as it became clear that the monies offered would simply be redistributed from existing shared federal-provincial programs, this initiative was abandoned.

By 2005, there was nothing to show for either the Tory or Liberal promises of a national daycare program, although some progress had been made by a few provinces. Quebec initiated a program in 1997 whose goal was to publicly subsidize and operate daycare for all mothers of children under age twelve. The cost of daycare would be fixed at $5 dollars a day per child. There were several reasons for this bold step. The PQ were aware that women were more cautious about its sovereignty option than men, and so it made an effort to support demands from the women's movement that would establish the party as women-friendly. The women's movement, in turn, made special efforts to convince PQ governments, which were somewhat more progressive than Liberal administrations, to support its agenda. In 1995, a massive March for Bread and Roses, organized by the Fédération des femmes du Québec, emphasized the social power of the women's movement in the province and strengthened feminist forces in the PQ government.

The daycare policy formed part of a family policy that would increase state support for low-income families while providing a large subsidy to daycare centres so that they need charge parents only $5 a day to use their facility. Poor households would receive a subsidy that reduced that rate even further. The government proceeded to build a large number of new child care centres, though this expansion never matched demand, creating some backlash against the PQ from parents whose children were not accommodated. The PQ government also negotiated a contract with unionized child care workers in 1999 that increased pay rates by 38 per cent. That still left this college-educated group with modest salaries, but it gave them higher salaries than daycare workers in the wealthier provinces of Alberta and Ontario.[48] Though $5-a-day daycare soon became a program that no political party dared to attack openly, the provincial Liberals, upon their re-election in 2003, decided that the program would have to be re-examined and later raised the fees.[49] But thanks to a well-organized campaign of feminists and trade unions, the eventual increases proved relatively small despite the neo-liberal inclinations of Jean Charest's administration.

Other provincial governments were largely unfriendly to child care advocates. Alberta had cut its child care subsidies by 20 per cent in 1995, and Ontario and British Columbia also became home to regimes favouring tax cutting and privatization, and with little interest in copying Quebec's approach to child care. In 1998, about 10 per cent of all children in the country under twelve years of age with working mothers were in daycare spaces that had been licensed by their province or territory as meeting government-established standards regarding staff qualifications, staff-to-children ratio, facilities and programs. In Newfoundland that figure fell to 5 per cent, and in Saskatchewan, 3.9 per cent. Interestingly, Prince Edward Island, with spaces available for 15.4 per cent of children in the province, beat the other two Maritime provinces by more than two to one.[50] But only in Quebec was there much of an improvement over the next several years, as the province increased its spending on early childhood care and education from less than $300 million in 1997–98 to over $1 billion in 2001–02.[51] In 2005, the federal government began another round of consultations with the provinces regarding a national daycare program.

In summary, outside Quebec, public support for child care in 2005 was restricted to the poorest families. Governments rejected the view that the state had an obligation to ensure that all families had access to quality child care and that child care workers had a right to a decent wage. Tougher rules for collecting social assistance made labour-force attachments compulsory for most single mothers, but child care subsidies often failed to provide the working poor with licensed daycare spaces. Women in small towns and the countryside, in particular, found that the market did not provide them with good potential daycare arrangements, and they made do as best they could.[52]

Pensions and the Lives of Seniors

Seniors' groups, women's groups, and labour all campaigned for richer pensions for Canadians. Only 36.8 per cent of employees in Canada were covered by occupational pension plans in 1984, a figure unchanged since 1976. Public pensions provided a large part of the incomes of seniors, particularly women. Unattached elderly women received 53.3 per cent of their incomes from state programs, versus 32.3 per cent for unattached elderly men. This led advocates of greater equity for women to demand that pensions be revisited and payments to the elderly poor be increased.[53]

While popular groups were pressuring the government to enrich public-pension programs, the private-pension industry promoted a focus on employer-based schemes. When the federal government announced its reforms for pension programs in 1987, it was obvious that the interest of business groups had prevailed. Public programs were slightly enriched by bringing in early retirement benefits, at a reduced rate for sixty-year-olds, and improving survivor benefits. But shortly afterwards, the Mulroney government restored the means test to the OAP that had been lifted in 1951, with retirees having an income over $50,000 simply excluded from receiving pensions. Private pensions were reformed to a degree. There would be some coverage for part-time workers, and some provisions for vesting pensions after two years of membership in a plan. Survivor benefits became mandatory and pension benefits were to be split in the case of a marriage or common-law relationship breakdown.[54]

Trade union researcher Rick Deaton sums up the results of the Mulroney pension reforms as follows: "The public policy review of retirement income arrangements in Canada and the remedial reform 'package,' however, failed to expand either the private or the public pension system. As a result of conflicting views and pressures concerning the extent and nature of pension reform based on the opposing class interests of the major actors, the critical issues of coverage, inflation-proofing and an adequate income replacement rate were left unresolved."[55] Nor are the monies collected from working people to fund public pensions used to promote social objectives, either job creation or investment in social infrastructure. Sweden, by contrast, uses pension funds both to promote an industrial strategy meant to ensure low unemployment and to enrich social programs. Canada's private pension schemes are marked by unilateral control by employers, "a reflection of the imbalance in the distribution of power between labour and management under conditions of collective bargaining in capitalist countries."[56]

The government's failure to increase pensions often meant that seniors, who were living longer than ever past retirement, were often without means to purchase home care services as they became less able to care for themselves. Provincial governments established or expanded home care programs that covered both seniors and disabled persons, but often these involved minimal state funding and contracting out of service provision to private firms.[57] As with daycare, the degree of privatization and the question of universal coverage depended upon the ideology of provincial governments, with Manitoba's NDP government deciding in 1974 to operate a universal and completely public program.[58] Most other provinces linked services to income, and gave regional health authorities the right to contract out services, leading the Canadian Association on Gerontology to note in 1999 that "Canada does not have a universally accessible, comprehensive home care policy or program."[59] Families and volunteers, they suggested, provided about 70 or 80 per cent of the care required by seniors, though governments in Canada were spending about $2 billion annually on home care.

Most of the staff hired for paid home care were women, and their wages, like those of child care staff, were at poverty levels. This was particularly the case for women working for subcontractors to regional health authorities, who, unlike Manitoba's government-employed workers, were non-unionized. Competition among potential subcontractors was often based on little more than who could pay the lowest wages and benefits to their casually employed workers. In turn, with most of the unpaid caregiving being provided by women, there was a ripple effect on women's mental health and opportunities for social advancement. Burned out by long hours of care for children and parents, many qualified women were unable to take senior jobs in industry, government, and the professions.[60]

Governments were touchy on the issue of the gendered nature of cutbacks and privatization. It was women who lost state caregiving jobs, women whose jobs were privatized, and women in the home who had to take on the work that state-employed caregivers would no longer provide. When researchers at the University of Alberta concluded that the Klein cuts of 1994 affected women disproportionately, a Conservative MLA demanded that these professors be fired.[61]

POVERTY AND INCOME SUPPORTS

The combination of an increase in GNP per capita, a vast increase in the number of two-income households, and improved social programs reduced poverty levels in Canada from 27 per cent in 1961 to 15.4 per cent in 1975. However, recessions and cutbacks reversed that progress. The Statscan measure of low-income Canadians climbed to almost 20 per cent during the steep recessions of 1982–84, and 1990–93, though the return of an economic boom allowed the rate to drop to 16.2 per cent in 1999.[62] The National Council of Welfare commented in July 2002, "Our patchwork system of social programs is clearly not doing what it takes to seriously address the causes and consequences of poverty. And there is no forum for Canadians outside government, especially for low-income Canadians and hungry children, to come to the table with governments to talk about their own realities, aspirations, priorities and solutions."[63]

As governments began putting the squeeze on social assistance and unemployment insurance, citizens' groups made efforts to deal with the growing problems of poverty and hunger in Canada. Food banks first appeared in Alberta in June 1981. When the economy collapsed in 1982, they spread across the country. Unemployed Action Centres, connected with the trade union movement, operated close to one-third of the food banks in 1986.[64] Many church leaders were also involved in operating food banks, and their disgust that charity was required to prevent Canadians from starving led to the Roman Catholic bishops' condemnation in 1983 of public policies that put corporate profits ahead of the needs of workers and the poor.[65] Half of those being fed. were children.

Poverty in Canada was both racialized and gendered. *Nellie's Newsletter* in Toronto reported that, while just over one-fifth of Canadian children lived in poverty according to the 1996 census, that figure increased to 52.1 per cent for Aboriginal children, 42.7 per cent for visible minorities, and 37 per cent for children with disabilities.[66] Women accounted for three-fifths of the adult poor, with single mothers and elderly women without partners experiencing especially high rates of poverty.[67] But it was child poverty that social advocates focused on. In part, this was because efforts to press for policies that recognized the increasing "feminization of poverty" faced a conservative backlash. While social justice advocates demanded equal wages for work of equal value and more income subsidies, their successes were limited. Conservatives, looking at the increasing number of single and divorced mothers, balked at public policies that would contribute to women's independence rather than a return to the "traditional" family. They had the support of industrialists and state employers who benefited from using women as cheap labour. Social advocates decided that they might win more public support if they focused on poor children rather than on their mothers.

This approach seemed to bear some fruit when the House of Commons voted unanimously in 1989 to eliminate child poverty by the end of the century. That year, a year of prosperity, the national child poverty rate was 14.4 per cent, but by 1996, the census reported that the rate had increased to 21.1 per cent. In 2001, there was an encouraging fall to 15.6 per cent,[68] but the decline was the result of a booming economy and there was little to prevent its rising again when the economy stagnated once more. The politicians proved unable to achieve the 1989 goal mainly because social policies that increased poverty among adults inevitably increased poverty for their children. The restrictions on UI pushed many households into poverty; so did provincial efforts to attract employers by raising minimum wages by less than inflation. In 2003, a one in-come, minimum-wage family of two adults and one child received on average only 40 per cent of a poverty-line income.[69]

The provinces also made it more difficult to collect social assistance and slashed assistance rates, even though they were already quite low. In Ontario, for example, in 1995, the Conservative government of Mike Harris reduced rates by 22 per cent. Welfare recipients who had been unemployed for longer than four months were forced into "workfare" schemes, part-time make-work job schemes meant to subsidize private or public employers while supposedly providing work experience for the unemployed.[70] Ignoring the state of mental health, family responsibilities, and availability of transportation of many aid recipients, provincial governments required them to attend job-training courses, summarily cutting off those who failed to do so. In the country as a whole, income was being redistributed in favour of the wealthy. The net wealth of the top 20 per cent of families with children rose 43 per cent between 1984 and 1999 in Canada, but it only rose by 3 per cent for the middle-income group. For the bottom 20 per cent of Canadians, there was a 51 per cent decline.[71]

The federal contribution to ending child poverty proved feeble, a reflection of its priority of debt and tax reduction over social spending. In 1993, the Liberals followed through on a Conservative plan to end family allowances. They created the New Integrated Child Tax Benefit (NICTB), an income-related benefit meant to assist low-income mothers. However, the small amount of extra income that this benefit directed to mothers living in poverty was largely undone by provincial cuts in social assistance rates. In turn, the federal reduction in transfers to the provinces for all purposes encouraged the provinces to cut welfare spending, the least politically sensitive of all social expenditures. With CAP tossed into the dustbin in 1996, the provinces no longer had to demonstrate that a set portion of their federal funds was being spent to aid the destitute.

In 1997, the federal government replaced the NICTB with the Canada Child Tax Benefit. This benefit to children living in poverty was supposed to free up money for the provinces to spend on such programs as early childhood education for children at risk, child care, pharmacare, and dental health. In practice, the provinces, with federal support, used the monies they received for work incentive payments, often as subsidies to employers. A program whose title implied that it was meant to benefit the children of the poor discriminated against children whose mothers stayed home with them, while leaving mothers well below the poverty line if they chose to accept the provincial work incentives.[72]

Though there continued to be a large community of policy advocates who supported the rights of low-income Canadians, its political power during the 1990s and early 2000s seemed marginal. Although the cutbacks in education and health raised a sufficient ruckus so that most of the funds cut in the 1990s were restored in the early 2000s, there was no parallel enrichment of social assistance budgets, minimum wages, unemployment insurance, or social housing. The poorest Canadians, it seemed, were bearing the brunt of the neo-liberal agenda. Little wonder that there was a revival of militancy among the poor. Organizations of the poor in the major cities sponsored workshops and a variety of political campaigns meant to apply public pressure against recalcitrant politicians. The Ontario Coalition Against Poverty (OCAP), organized in 1995 as the Harris cuts began, proved the most willing to use physical confrontations to challenge government efforts to dispossess the poor. Responding to rising homelessness among those cut off social assistance, OCAP evicted Conservative Finance Minister Ernie Eves from his office in June 2000, with a number of the demonstrators, including OCAP's lead organizer, John Clarke, being arrested as a result.[73]

A summary of OCAP's activities before that time by an activist evokes the state's all-round attack on the most oppressed members of the Canadian working class in the 1990s and the willingness to fight back on the part of some of the victims:

OCAP mounts large collective actions, often with our union allies or the Mohawk warrior society of the Tyendanaga First Nation Reserve, around a specific economic issue such as the withdrawal of provincial and federal governments from public housing, or Toronto's policy, mimicking New York's, for the "social cleansing" of panhandlers and homeless from the downtown tourist areas. We have picketed and enforced semi-embargos on businesses investing in a redevelopment scheme which, by closing a hostel, threw homeless men back on the street. To enforce specific demands, we have instituted a campaign of continuing "economic disruption"—snake marches, demonstrations, mass panhandling—of bourgeois activities, fairs, festivals, and film shoots. And we have mobilized the larger actions...challenging police power: in Ottawa, a march on Parliament Hill "to persuade the prime minister of the seriousness of the homelessness crisis," interrupted by arrests by the RCMP, whose line we broke; the occupation of a Toronto city park, designating it "safe" from police harassment for the homeless, and holding it for three days until we were violently removed, with arrests, by the police; and most recently, the second, more powerful march on Parliament in November 1999. Each of these was a small, but in our present situation, real victory.[74]

HEALTH CARE

Though the poor had always suffered greater problems of health and access to treatment for illnesses than other Canadians, and therefore suffered the most when public health care was undermined, the saving grace of Canadian medicare in neo-liberal times was that all Canadians had access to the public health care system. This meant that middle-class and some upper-class Canadians had considerable affinity for the public health care program that had begun with hospital insurance in 1957 and was enriched with medicare in 1968. Free access to certain medical services became, in most Canadians' minds, a right of citizenship. There was considerable chafing when provincial governments allowed physicians to bill patients directly for services for which the doctors felt governments underpaid them. In Saskatchewan, Premier Ross Thatcher's "deterrent fee" of $2 per visit to a physician helped to defeat his Liberal government in 1971. The Canada Health Act of 1984, which threatened federal financial penalties for provincial violations of the principles of medicare, was immensely popular.[75]

Campaigns to further enlarge medical protection by placing dentists' bills, non-hospital pharmaceutical costs, and eyeglasses within medicare received limited support from the middle class and the unionized working class because many of them already enjoyed these protections from employers. But there was a strong desire to preserve and extend the availability of both physicians' services and hospital care that underlay the prepaid medicare schemes that the provinces had constructed in the spirit of the 1968 legislation.

This did not prevent deep cuts in health care spending in the early 1990s. Health care was rivalling education as the top item in provincial budgets, and deficit-cutting, tax-cutting premiers had no option within a neo-liberal paradigm but to cut health care budgets. While these cuts were proportionately far smaller than the cuts in the programs that targeted the poor, they were significant. In Alberta, the Klein cuts of 1993–96 shaved 17 per cent off the annual health-spending budget over a three-year period.[76] In the Atlantic provinces, where cuts started earlier, annual cuts of 5 to 6 per cent over several years added up to even greater cutbacks than the much-publicized Alberta cuts.

Often, politicians who planned to make drastic cuts in medicare promised voters just the opposite. The federal Liberal Red Book in 1993 promised to halt the bleeding of federal money to the provinces for medicare. But, when EPF was lumped together with CAP in 1995 to form the CHST, the total package was reduced by $7 billion over a three-year period. Conservative Mike Harris, promising to slash "welfare" spending as he ran for election in Ontario in 1995, also assured voters that health care would dodge the bullet. So did the conservative Liberal, Gordon Campbell, running for election in British Columbia in 2001. Once elected, both made deep cuts to the health care system.

Because all polls indicated that over 90 per cent of Canadians wanted to hold on to medicare, and indeed that they regarded Canada's publicly operated health care schemes as superior to American's private medicine, no major politician openly called for an end to the public system. There were, however, calls by Klein and Harris for the private sector to play a major role in the delivery of medical services. Much of the privatization that occurred was at the expense of the lowest-paid hospital workers and of low-income consumers of health services. Food services and maintenance work in hospitals were often contracted out, transforming modest-paying unionized jobs into minimum-wage non-union work. Certain once-free medical services were "delisted," that is removed from a provincial health department's list of services paid for as part of medicare, or were provided in more limited circumstances. Such changes saved provincial medical systems only token amounts, and sometimes resulted in increased costs, for example when provinces contracted out medical services for workers' compensation recipients to for-profit providers.

The decentralization of provincial programs to local health boards, charged with finding slack in the system and cutting it away, also resulted in limited savings. Most of the money in the health care system went to paying fees for physicians' services and salaries for nurses. The political clout of the Canadian

Medical Association and its provincial branches, and the carefully cultivated mystique of the medical profession made an assault on physician control of the medical system too dangerous for any provincial government to seriously consider. While efforts were made to cap payments to doctors, talk of replacing fee-for-service payments with salaries played a minor role in policy discussions regarding the future of medicare. Physicians also successfully resisted most efforts to increase the role of other, less highly paid health professionals within the medical system. Their efforts also resulted in a limited inclusion of non-allopathic practitioners within both state and privately funded health-insurance schemes.[77]

Inevitably, then, much of the initial assault on the costs of the medical system fell upon nursing staff in hospitals. Hospitals sent patients home quickly, and pressured patients' families to carry out tasks in the hospital once carried out by nurses. They attempted to reduce drastically both the numbers of nurses and the wages of the nurses who remained. By 2000, there had been an 8 per cent drop in the number of registered nurses in Canada relative to the population, and a 21 per cent decline in licensed practical nurses. Patients chafed as waiting times for "elective" surgeries increased, and even life-and-death operations seemed to require a waiting period. Families of patients who had been dismissed too early complained bitterly when the result was a death or the need to bring the patient back to hospital within a short time, sometimes in worse shape than when she or he had been sent home.[78] Hospital closings resulted in huge protests.

By the end of the twentieth century, cutbacks in health care were clearly unpopular with voters, and governments began to reinvest in the health system. Medical spending had been cut by 5 per cent per capita in constant dollars in Canada between 1991 and 1996. But, according to the Canadian Institute for Health Information, government health spending in Canada increased by about $20 billion, or 35 per cent, from 1997 to 2003, while inflation during that period was only about 15 per cent.[79] The federal government had gradually increased the size of the CHST. In 2000, after meetings with the provinces, it announced a 35 per cent increase in the CHST over the next five years.[80] That would restore federal funding to about the numbers, with inflation and population increases factored in, in force when the Liberals had taken power.

The federal government's partial turnaround did not create a new consensus regarding medicare. Several provinces, particularly those with NDP governments as well as the PQ government in Quebec, were committed to expanding the services that they provided their citizens in the public system, particularly in such areas as home care and pharmaceuticals. They wanted the CHST to reflect these new obligations. Other provinces, led by Alberta and, before the defeat of its Conservative government in 2003, Ontario, also wanted more funds but wanted Ottawa to permit an expansion of privately run but publicly funded services. The opening of a private hospital in Calgary in 2001, to denunciations from Friends of Medicare, the trade union movement, and the two major opposition parties, seemed to many the thin edge of the wedge of privatization. The Ontario Conservatives had also laid the groundwork for privatization of several hospitals.

In part, the neo-liberal drive towards both cost cutting and privatization within medicare was frustrated by consumer resistance. But, in turn, the role of physicians and nurses in publicizing the dangerous consequences of the changes that were occurring contributed to popular opposition to government cutbacks. Both groups also proved quite militant in defending their economic positions. Nurses had once constituted one of Canada's poorest paid professional groups. Beginning in the 1970s, however, nurses increasingly joined unions, and struck for better wages and working conditions.

A feminist consciousness had emerged in a number of so-called women's professions, including nursing, in the wake of the women's liberation movement of the late 1960s and onwards. "We are not Florence Nightingales," United Nurses of Alberta president Margaret Ethier insisted during the 1980 strike of nurses in that province, the first of three such strikes. These strikes were illegal under Alberta's Essential Services Act and the union paid heavy fines for counselling its members to strike. But the hospitals, in each case, were forced to award handsome settlements to the nurses in order to end the strikes. During the late 1990s, as well, nurses and their unions limited, and sometimes altogether foiled, efforts by provincial governments to erode their wages and working conditions. To the chagrin of many governments, nurses appeared to be able to mobilize significant sections of Canadian society on their behalf.

Because of concerns about the long-term sustainability of medicare, and the perception that various provincial initiatives threatened the guarantee to Canadians of prepaid medical services, the federal government established a one-man commission on medical services in 2001. Prime Minister Chrétien named Roy Romanow, the former NDP premier of Saskatchewan, as commissioner. In hearings across the country, it became clear that, apart from business groups and conservative governments, there was little popular support for tinkering with medicare. Privatization appealed to chambers of commerce and to potential investors but repelled most Canadians, and particularly the trade unions, members of the health professions (with some ambivalence on the part of physicians), social workers, and the churches. Even in Alberta, the commissioners heard mainly from opponents of two-tier medicine that allowed the wealthy to purchase medical services that were unavailable to the rest of the population.[81]

THE ROMANOW REPORT AND BEYOND

The Romanow Report, while not a radical document, destroyed the arguments of the neo-liberal think tanks and the governments of Alberta and Ontario that medical costs were strangling the national economy and that increased privatization was the solution both to reducing costs and improving national medical standards. Romanow concluded that Canada's health spending was comparable to other countries in the OECD and considerably less than American spending. While the rise in spending was not dramatic, it had increased from 7 per cent of the gross domestic product in 1970 to 9.1 per cent in 2000, a modest amount in light of the aging of the population, the costs of new medical technologies, and the growth of public perceptions of various medical services as a right of citizenship rather than commodities for people with means. Public spending on health care had only increased from 5 per cent to 6.5 per cent of GDP during that period, reflecting a decline in the portion of medical costs covered by public sources, from about 77 per cent in 1970 to 67.6 per cent in 2001–02. That was significantly less than coverage in the Scandinavian countries and the United Kingdom, but somewhat more than the American figure of 60 per cent.

The U.S. figure included expenditures for the minority of Americans who benefited from state programs—Medicare for the aged, and Medicaid for the destitute—and tax deductions for private insurance purchasers. The real losers in the American system were people too poor to carry full insurance (an estimated 44 million Americans had no health insurance at all in 2003, while many others were underinsured) but not poor enough or old enough to qualify for state medical coverage. Provincial spending on health care had increased from 28 per cent of provincial budgets in 1974 to 35 per cent in 1999–2000, most of the increase attributable to the decline in federal grants per capita over that period. Canada's health system, noted the report, was largely a success. In 1999, life expectancy at birth for Canadians was 75.4 years for men and 81.2 years for women, which made Canadians the fifth longest-living people in the world.[82]

Romanow noted that evidence that privatization, delisting, and public–private partnerships improved the efficiency of the medical system "has not been forthcoming." The evidence from the U.S. was that a private system of medicine was far more expensive to administer than a public one. In the U.S., the combination of private insurance systems with systems required to track eligibility for and amounts of tax subsidies accounted for far greater administrative costs per person than in Canada: $1,151 to $325. The Americans also had to pay for the profits of their private-care providers.[83]

But Romanow was critical of gaps in the public health system in Canada. The whole, he wrote, seemed less than the sum of its parts: "We must transform our health care 'system' from one in which a multitude of participants, working in silos, focus primarily on managing illness, to one in which they work collaboratively to deliver a seamless, integrated array of services to Canadians, from prevention and promotion to primary care; to hospital, community, mental health, home and end-of-life care."[84] He proposed that the federal government boost health care spending to the provinces in a targeted manner, with special payments for diagnostic care, services to rural and remote areas, primary health care, home care, and pharmaceutical programs, particularly catastrophic drugs. Altogether, he suggested, that within three years, the CHST should be increased by $6.5 billion to reflect the total number of new dollars needed.[85]

Romanow also noted disparities in services across the country. These were partly the result of philosophical differences and partly the result of poorer provinces and territories being unable to match expenditures on health per capita in wealthier provinces. He proposed a Health Council of Canada that would establish indicators and benchmarks that could be monitored to assess how well governments were doing over time to meet the health needs of Canadians.[86] While the Romanow Report dealt with gender issues only cursorily, it did recommend that home caregivers should receive special benefits under the EI program.[87] He ignored proposals from feminists that family caregivers dealing with individuals who might otherwise require institutional care or paid home care receive a salary for their work.

One area where Romanow believed that special efforts were required was mental health. Deinstitutionalization of mental health patients, which had begun in earnest in the 1960s, potentially constituted a progressive course of action. It was more just to allow psychiatric patients to remain part of their families and the community than to lock them away from society. But, often deinstitutionalization had been motivated more by cost-saving concerns than by considerations of social justice. Expensive-to-maintain mental institutions were closed or scaled down while their inmates were thrown onto the streets with few services to take the place of the programs that the asylums offered. Romanow agreed with the Canadian Mental Health Association that governments had to offer programs to reduce "barriers to access to community life in areas such as employment, education and housing."[88]

Public reaction to the Romanow Report was overwhelmingly positive, according to opinion polls. Government reaction was more mixed. Poorer provinces welcomed the promise of more federal funds, and Jean Chrétien endorsed the tenor of the report. But the governments of Ontario and Alberta, which were promoting privatization, quickly proclaimed that they would resist any incursion of the federal government in an area of provincial jurisdiction. They wanted more money from the "feds" for health care but with no strings attached as to how it should be spent. Alberta had established an advisory panel on medical care as a rival to the Romanow Commission. It was chaired by former Conservative cabinet minister Donald Mazankowski. Since Mazankowski was a director of several insurance companies and had been Mulroney's minister of privatization, his committee, as expected, supported greater privatization of the delivery of medical services. Romanow bowed at least a little in the direction of the right wingers by suggesting that food and cleaning services for hospitals could continue to be privatized—a suggestion that the unions denounced—and demurring from federal financial penalties for provinces that privatized or created public–private partnerships in the health sector.[89]

A federal-provincial meeting in February 2003 produced the joint responses of the federal and provincial governments to the Romanow Report. The First Ministers' Health Accord promised $17.3 billion in increased health funding over three years and a total of $34.8 billion in five years. The money was meant to fund increases in provincial and territorial spending in the areas mentioned by Romanow. A Health Council "to monitor and make annual reports on the implementation of the Accord, particularly its accountability and transparency provisions" also formed part of the Accord.[90] However, some of the monies promised by the federal government appeared to simply double count funds promised to the provinces in 2000. Nor, in line with the Social Union

Framework of 2000, did the provinces have to account for how they would spend the extra funds they received. Instead, the federal government would rely on the publicity of Health Council reporting to keep premiers and territorial leaders on track with national priorities.

Before year's end, however, Alberta's premier Ralph Klein refused to even have his province participate in the Health Council, which he regarded as an intrusive measure that would meddle into provincial policies. The Accord made no mention of privatization or of public–private partnerships, thus leaving the field open to premiers to continue to contract out various parts of the health system.[91] In 2004, the federal election focused heavily on medicare financing, and Paul Martin, as leader of a minority Liberal government after the June vote, provided another increase in federal funding to provinces for medicare several months afterwards, though again with few strings attached. The funds committed demonstrated the power of the pro-medicare lobbies in Canada, while the successful resistance of several provincial governments to stipulations against privatization and public–private partnerships demonstrated the continued political strength of health entrepreneurs.

First Nations and the Welfare State

The Romanow Report, following the spirit of the Royal Commission on Aboriginal Peoples (RCAP), noted that the health of Native peoples required a special approach. Native peoples' demands for self-determination, along with federal jurisdiction over registered Indians and Inuit, excluded the possibility of delegating Aboriginal health to the provinces. Yet what Romanow had heard from Native leaders paralleled what the commissioner recommended with respect to Canadians' health generally: a holistic approach to health, one which did not create airtight silos that separated social needs and health. For First Nations, it meant that health was inseparable from the empowerment of its citizens and the strengthening of cultural identity. By 2000, the health of Native peoples had dramatically improved compared with forty years earlier. In 1963, life expectancy for a registered Native person was only half that of other Canadians. By 2000, Native men lived, on average, 7.4 years less than other Canadian men and Native women, 5.2 years less than other Canadian women.[92]

As well, First Nations were increasingly managing their own social affairs. As the residential schools began to close in the 1960s and 1970s, band councils campaigned to have on-reserve schools controlled by First Nations rather than to be forced to send children to off-reserve schools run by non-Natives. By the 1990s, the on-reserve school controlled by a Native school authority had become the norm. First Nations also turned their attention to gaining control over health services on the reserves. An early precedent was the Kateri Mohawk Hospital Centre, which opened in 1955, the result of a Mohawk women's initiative that secured funding from both the Quebec government and the Mohawk Council of Kahnawake. The James Bay and Northern Quebec Agreement of 1975 created autonomous Aboriginal health and social service boards, though the communities in question struggled to keep the provincial and federal governments from interfering with their new-found authority. Then, in 1979, the Inuit created the Labrador Independent Health Commission in Labrador.[93]

By 2001, an estimated 46 per cent of eligible Native communities had signed agreements with the federal government to manage health services themselves and most other reserves were in the process of negotiating similar arrangements. In addition, Native leaders and various federal government departments had worked together to create programs that would address epidemic problems on the reserves, including the Aboriginal Diabetes Initiative and the National Native Alcohol and Drug Abuse Program. The federal government provided funding to individuals on reserves for prescription drugs, dental treatment, vision care, and transportation to health facilities off reserve as required.[94]

But such services, noted Romanow, did not reflect a clear federal government commitment to providing comprehensive medical services to Natives. Earlier efforts to off-load responsibility for Natives' health onto the provinces continued apace, and the notion remained that the federal government was the "payer of last resort." There had been no repudiation of a 1974 ministerial statement that summarized the federal government's role in the health arena as "giving financial assistance to indigent Indians to pay for necessary services when the assistance [was] not otherwise provided."[95]

Romanow called for an end to the dispersal of responsibility for Native health among federal and provincial government departments. What was required, instead, was to "consolidate Aboriginal health funding from all sources and use the funds to support the creation of Aboriginal Health Partnerships to manage and organize health services for Aboriginal peoples and promote Aboriginal health." The Partnerships would identify specific health needs of Native communities and make use of community resources to guide health programs. Wherever possible, Native health care providers would be hired, and when non-Natives were hired, Natives would sensitize them to the norms and needs of their communities. In 2002, the percentage of trained Native nurses and physicians in Canada, while much improved compared with a few decades earlier, remained well below the percentage of Natives within the population as a whole—1 per cent versus 3 per cent.[96]

The federal government attempted, in particular, to limit its responsibility for off-reserve Natives, including former reserve residents who had moved to urban locations because of the lack of employment opportunities on reserves. By 2000, about half of all Native peoples lived in cities and towns, and the federal government balked at providing them the autonomous institutions that their reserve counterparts increasingly enjoyed. Organizations of urban Natives placed pressure on governments to recognize that Native peoples who moved to cities should have the right to self-determination. In 2003, there were murmurings about "urban reserves" but no framework for their operation was announced that year, seven years after RCAP had called upon governments to ensure that the needs of all Native peoples, regardless of place of residence, were respected. Federal monies to registered Indians for health purposes covered only reserve residents.[97]

RCAP, which reported in 1996, had provided the comprehensive social policy framework that became the keystone of Native demands. Headed by former Assembly of First Nations (AFN) grand chief Georges Erasmus, RCAP called on governments to make a definitive break with past colonialist and cost-cutting objectives in their dealings with First Nation peoples. The report noted that the goal should be "to pave the way for Aboriginal self-government by enhancing the capacity of Aboriginal citizens to engage in nation building."[98]

This meant ending the control of outsiders over Aboriginal family life. In the postwar period, there had been a drastic increase in intervention by provincial social welfare agencies in the area of Native child welfare. While the social workers sought to protect children from unsafe environments, they operated within a limited framework. Children were seized from Native homes judged by European middle-class standards to be inappropriate and placed in institutional care or adopted out to European families deemed to meet such standards. Often that meant placing the children in families in different provinces from their birth parents and even in the United States. No efforts were made either to involve the Native communities in determining the fate of their children or in working with these communities to create conditions that would make so much intervention into individual households unnecessary. In British Columbia, 34.2 per cent of all children in care in 1964 were Native. By 1981–82, Native children represented 63 per cent of those in care in Saskatchewan and 41 per cent in Alberta. Nationally, 4.6 per cent of Native children were in agency care compared with 1 per cent of non-Native children.[99]

First Nations organizations documented the disastrous impact on many of the children who had been apprehended and on their families and communities. The children grew up in a nether world, discriminated against because of their Native heritage but with no connection to that heritage. Native adults were made to feel that they were inferior parents whose children had to be taken from them, and Native communities were deprived of their young people. In 1981, responding to pressure from the AFN and other Native organizations, the Department of Indian Affairs and Northern Development (DIAND) signed its first agreement with a First Nations agency to deliver child welfare services. Ten years later, there were thirty-six agencies receiving DIAND funding to provide child and family services to 212 bands. By the mid-1990s, several Native child and family agencies in urban centres had signed agreements with the federal government, and Métis agencies began to emerge with the signing of a provincial agreement in Alberta. All three Prairie provincial governments promised to move quickly to implement Native control of the delivery of welfare services to non-reserve Native families.[100]

Though the assimilationist philosophy that once governed relations between the state and First Nations was crumbling, it was unclear that it was giving way to the holistic philosophies espoused by the RCAP and the Romanow Report. Government willingness to fund the programs required to provide Natives with the resources to establish both autonomy for their communities and a standard of living comparable to other Canadians foundered on the neo-liberal rock of government funding. So, for example, as Natives assumed control over medical programs formerly administered by Ottawa, the funds provided were inadequate to integrate medical and social services. Glen Ross of the Cree Nation Tribal Health Centre at The Pas, Manitoba, told the RCAP commissioners: "[Even after transfer], there remain a number of issues which are barriers to providing comprehensive health care services for the Tribal Council membership. Some of these are that we have inadequate community-based mental health programs; we lack adult care; we lack services for the disabled, we have poor, inadequate medical transportation services. Transportation is a non-insured benefit, and we protest that those benefits are not on the table for transfer of control."[101]

Federal resistance to spending new money was particularly evident in the area of housing. While 9.8 per cent of dwellings in Canada needed major structural repairs, the figure for Native accommodations was 19.6 per cent. That figure rose to 26 per cent on reserves and to 33 per cent in Inuit communities. Native families were almost alone among Canadians in still having a substantial group whose homes lacked piped water or bathroom facilities. Valerie Montague, a social service administrator in Christian Island, Ontario, noted: "We have families that are doubled and tripled up. We have up to 18 and 20 people sometimes living in a single unit built for one family."[102]

Many of the homes built with government assistance on reserves in the postwar years had been shoddily constructed. Lack of fire-protection services on reserves led to an average of two hundred reserve dwellings in Canada (out of seventy-four thousand) burning to the ground each year. Solid-waste dumps in the North and inadequate sewage treatment created environmental hazards for the food consumed by Natives in that region. Housing programs implemented in the 1970s and 1980s had alleviated the worst housing conditions of the immediate postwar period. The Rural Housing Program for Aboriginal People added about twenty-five thousand units of Native housing from 1974 to 1994 before the construction of new units was suspended. Native housing co-operatives built another ten thousand units with government financial assistance. Tenant interviews suggested that residents in these co-ops enjoyed a stable environment and a strong cultural identity, but monies for more co-ops disappeared in 1994. RCAP determined that the cost of replacing unrepairable shacks, repairing the homes with structural damage, and building enough new dwellings to ensure adequate housing for all Natives within ten years would be $228 million the first year with costs rising to $774 million by the tenth year. But the payoff would be healthier, more productive communities.[103]

As it was, a large percentage of the monies that governments were spending on Natives in Canada was on funds for their incarceration. Though they made up only 3 per cent of the population, Natives accounted for 17 per cent of the prison population. Before the 1970s, the justice system denied that systemic racism resulted in higher incarceration rates for Native men and women. Pressures from Aboriginal communities after that time resulted in the gradual introduction of Native community policing, Native courts that focused on healing as much as retribution, and rehabilitation programs operated entirely by First Nations or in conjunction with corrections officials. Successful rehabilitation programs "have focused on linking the prisoner with his/her community, e.g., school, family, social service organization, neighbourhood organization."[104]

Corporate Canada, using front groups such as the pseudo-academic "institutes" and aided by a compliant media dominated by a few corporate syndicates, made significant inroads in popular thinking regarding the desirable role of the state in the last quarter of the twentieth century. Focusing on government deficits and debts, the right wing was able to convince many Canadians that the state interventionism of the previous thirty years was strangling the country's economic potential. This softened up the population for the cutbacks in government programs and spending that marked much of this period. But Canadians' attachment to their social programs, and increasing organization and militancy on the part of opponents of cutbacks, caused politicians to promote "reinvestment" in social infrastructure as the twenty-first century began. This did not mean that the influence of neo-liberal ideology disappeared, particularly with reference to programs affecting the poor. Though a subset of the poorest Canadians remained militant, governments took advantage of the passivity of the majority, a passivity often resulting from fear of state retribution if they participated in political life. The War on Poverty had largely given way to a War on the Poor.

NOTES

1 Address by J.M. Keith, *Addresses*, 29 September 1965, 36th Annual Meeting, Canadian Chamber of Commerce Papers, MG 28, 3, 62, Vol. 4, Library and Archives of Canada (LAC).

2 A trenchant analysis of the move towards neo-liberal thinking on the part of Saskatchewan's NDP is found in Phillip Hansen, *Taxing Illusions: Taxation, Democracy and Embedded Political Theory* (Halifax, NS: Fernwood, 2003).

3 Michael Mendelson, "Can We Reform Canada's Income Security System?" in *The Future of Social Welfare Systems in Canada and the United Kingdom* ed. Shirley B. Seward (Halifax, NS: Institute for Research on Public Policy, 1987), 123.

4 The attack on Keynesianism in Canada is documented in Arthur W. Donner and Douglas D. Peters, *The Monetarist Counter-Revolution: A Critique of Monetary Policy 1975–1979* (Toronto, ON: James Lorimer, 1979); Harold Chorney and Phillip Hansen, "The Falling Rate of Legitimation: The Problem of the Contemporary Capitalist State in Canada," *Studies in Political Economy* 4 (1978): 65–98; and Harold Chorney, *The Deficit: Hysteria and the Current Economic Crisis* (Ottawa, ON: Canadian Centre for Policy Alternatives, 1989).

5 Robert Campbell, *Grand Illusions: The Politics of the Keynesian Experience in Canada, 1945–1975* (Peterborough, ON: Broadview Press, 1987); Thomas J. Courchene, *The Strategy of Gradualism: An Analysis of Bank of Canada Policy from Mid-1975 to Mid-1977* (Montreal, QC: C.D. Howe Institute, 1977); Harold Chorney, "The Economic and Political Consequences of Canadian Monetarism" (paper presented to the British Association of Canadian Studies, University of Nottingham, Nottingham, UK, 12 April 1991), 31.

6 Malcolm Taylor, "The Canadian Health care System: After Medicare," in *Health and Canadian Society: Sociological Perspectives*, 2nd ed., ed. David Coburn, Carl D'Arcy, George M. Torrance, and Peter New (Toronto, ON: Fitzhenry and Whiteside, 1987), 84–86.

7 Mike Burke and Susan Silver, "Universal Health Care: Current Challenges to Normative Legacies," in *Canadian Social Policy: Issues and Perspectives*, 3rd ed., ed. Anne Westhues (Waterloo, ON: Wilfrid Laurier University Press, 2003), 171; Taylor, "The Canadian Health care System," 93–100.

8 Richard Lee Deaton, *The Political Economy of Pensions: Power, Politics and Social Change in Canada, Britain and the United States* (Vancouver, BC: University of British Columbia Press, 1989), 37.

9 Two key works on the New Right of this period in the United States and Britain are Frances Fox Piven and Richard Cloward, *The New Class War: Reagan's Attack on the Welfare State and Its Consequences* (New York, NY: Pantheon, 1982); and Ramesh Mishra, *The Welfare State in Crisis: Social Thought and Social Change* (Brighton, UK: Wheatsheaf, 1984).

10 Sylvia Bashevkin, *Welfare Hot Buttons: Women, Work, and Social Policy Reform* (Toronto, ON: University of Toronto Press, 2002), 28.

11 Monique Simard, "Coalition Politics: The Quebec Labour Movement," *Socialist Studies* 4 (1988): 77.

12 Canada, *Report of the Royal Commission on the Economic Union and Development Prospects for Canada*, vols. 1 and 2 (Ottawa, ON: Supply and Services Canada, 1985).

13 The philosophy of globalization and its impact on social programs are dissected in Gary Teeple, *Globalization and the Decline of Social Reform: Into the Twenty-First Century* (Toronto, ON: Garamond, 2000).

14 Mario Iacobacci and Mario Seccareccia, "Full Employment versus Income Maintenance: Some Reflections on the Macroeconomic and Structural Implications of a Guaranteed Income Program for Canada," *Studies in Political Economy* 28 (Spring 1989): 142; Rodney Haddow, "Canadian Organized Labour and the Guaranteed Annual Income," in *Continuities and Discontinuities: The Political Economy of Social Welfare and Labour Market Policy in Canada*, ed. Andrew F. Johnson, Steven McBride, and P.J. Smith (Toronto, ON: University of Toronto Press, 1994), 350–66.

15 On the contemporary debate regarding the impact of free trade on social policy, see Glenn Drover, ed., *Free Trade and Social Policy* (Ottawa, ON: Canadian Council on Social Development, 1988).

16 John English and William R. Young, "The Federal Government and Social Policy in the 1990s: Reflections on Change and Continuity," in *Canadian Social Policy*, ed. Westhues, 245.

17 Bashevkin, *Welfare Hot Buttons*, 34.

18 Chorney, "The Economic and Political Consequences," 35–39.

19 Support for the pre-election plan of the NDP to focus on unemployment is found in Harold Chorney, "Deficits-Fact or Fiction? Ontario's Public Finances and the Challenge of Full Employment," in *Getting on Track, Social Democratic Struggles for Ontario*, ed. Daniel Drache (Montreal, QC: McGill-Queen's University Press, 1992), 186–201.

20 John Loxley, *Alternative Budgets: Budgeting as If People Mattered* (Halifax, NS: Fernwood, 2003), 9; Bashevkin, *Welfare Hot Buttons*, 82.

21 Anne Westhues, "An Overview of Social Policy," in *Canadian Social Policy*, ed. Westhues, 11.

22 Burke and Silver, "Universal Health Care," 172.

23 On the Klein cuts, see Trevor Harrison and Gordon Laxer, eds., *The Trojan Horse: Alberta and the Future of Canada* (Montreal, QC: Black Rose, 1995); Kevin Taft, *Shredding the Public Interest: Ralph Klein and Twenty-five Years of One-Party Government* (Edmonton, AB: University of Alberta Press, 1997); and Christopher J. Bruce, Ronald D. Kneebone, and Kenneth J. McKenzie, eds., *A Government Reinvented: A Study of Alberta's Deficit Elimination Program* (Toronto, ON: Oxford University Press, 1997).

24 Candace Johnson Redden, *Health Care, Entitlement, and Citizenship* (Toronto, ON: University of Toronto Press, 2002), 71.

25 Georges Campeau, *De l'assurance-chômage à l'assurance-emploi* (Montreal, ON: Boréal, 2001), 117, 153, 281.

26 Ibid., 155, 164.

27 Ibid., 166, 167, 170.

28 Ibid., 179–82,

29 Ibid., 219–21, 231–32.

30 Thomas Dunk, Stephen McBride, and Randle W. Nelson, eds., *The Training Trap: Ideology, Training and the Labour Market* (Halifax, NS: Fernwood, 1996); Marjorie Griffin Cohen, ed., *Training the Excluded for Work: Access and Equity for Women, Immigrants, First Nations, Youth and People with Low Incomes* (Vancouver, BC: University of British Columbia Press, 2004).

31 Submission by the Canada Advisory Council on the Status of Women, September 1989, Canada, House of Commons, Legislative Committee Hearings on Bill C-21, An Act to Amend the Unemployment Insurance Act.

32 Campeau, *De l'assurance-chômage à l'assurance-emploi* 241–45.

33 Ibid., 263–5, 271.

34 Canadian Housing and Renewal Association, *Access to Housing: Proceedings of the Twenty-first Annual Symposium of the Canadian Housing and Renewal Association* (Ottawa, ON: CHRA, 1990), 8.

35 Ibid.

36 Ibid., 23.

37 Ibid., 111.

38 Ibid., 6–8; Tim Falconer, *Watchdogs and Gadflies: Activism from Marginal to Mainstream* (Toronto, ON: Penguin, 2003), 192–96.

39 Lea Caragata, "Housing and Homelessness," in *Canadian Social Policy*, ed. Westhues, 75.

40 Ibid., 79.

41 Ibid., 72, 77.

42 Canada, Status of Women, *Report of the Task Force on Child Care* (Ottawa, ON: Minister of Supply and Services, 1986), 51, 100; Canada, House of Commons, *Report of the Special Committee on Child Care* (March 1987), 8, quoting Statistics Canada, *The Labour Force*, Cat. No. 71-001, May 1982, December 1986.

43 Jane Jenson, "Family Policy, Child Care and Social Solidarity: The Case of Quebec," in *Changing Child Care Advocacy and Policy in Canada*, ed. Susan Prentice (Halifax, NS: Fernwood, 2001), 42; Canada, House of Commons Special Committee on Child Care, 1985–1986, *Hearings and Evidence*, particularly Mrs. Alice Taylor, Director, Holland College Child Study Centre.

44 Canada, *Report of the Royal Commission on the Economic Union and Development Prospects for Canada*, vol. 2, 813.

45 Canada, House of Commons, *Minutes of Proceedings and Evidence of the Special Committee on Child Care*, 1985–1986.

46 So, for example, the Canadian Manufacturers Association, appearing before the committee, claimed that "current government spending on social programs and income support, in total, exceeds what Canada can afford" and recommended an increase in the child care expense deduction as an alternative to government funding of daycares. Canada, House of Commons, *Minutes of Proceedings and Evidence of the Special Committee on Child Care*, May 16, 1986.

47 Liberal Party of Canada, *Creating Opportunity: The Liberal Plan for Canada* (Ottawa, ON: Liberal Party of Canada, 1993). See also Bashevkin, *Welfare Hot Buttons*, 56.

48 The politics of daycare in Quebec is outlined in Jane Jenson, "Family Policy," 39–62.

49 *The Globe and Mail*, 13 October 2003.

50 Child care Resource and Research Unit, *Early Childhood Care and Education in Canada: Provinces and Territories, 1998* (Toronto, ON: Centre for Urban and Community Studies, University of Toronto, 2001), 72, 126,

51 Jocelyne Tougas, "Child Care in Quèbec: Where There's a Will, There's a Way," a paper of the Child Care Advocacy Association of Canada (n.d.). Retrieved from www.child careadvocacy. ca/resources/pdf/QUE_Child care.pdf.

52 Government of Alberta, MLA Committee to Review Low-Income Programs, *Low-Income Programs Review: What We Heard* (Edmonton, AB: Government of Alberta), November 2001.

53 Deaton, *The Political Economy of Pensions*, 81; Mireille Éthier, "Survey of Pension Issues," in *Income Distribution and Economic Security in Canada*, ed. François Vaillancourt (Toronto, ON: University of Toronto Press, 1985), 220.

54 Deaton, *The Political Economy of Pensions*, 108–14.

55 Ibid., 114.

56 Ibid., 161.

57 Sheila Neysmith, "Caring and Aging: Exposing the Policy Issues," in *Canadian Social Policy*, ed. Westhues, 189.

58 In 2003, this program provided services to 34,300 Manitobans and employed 5,500 casual staff. Though the Manitoba government regarded its program as "universal" and "comprehensive," there were enough gaps to allow private providers to find a market within the province. *Manitoba Health, Manitoba Home Care Program*. Retrieved from www.gov.mb.ca/health/home care.

59 Canadian Association on Gerontology, "Policy Statement: Home Care in Canada" (n.d.). Retrieved from www.cagacg.ca/publications/552_e.php.

60 See the essays in Sheila Neysmith, ed., *Restructuring Caring Labour: Discourse, State Practice and Everyday Life* (Toronto, ON: Oxford University Press, 2000), as well as Jane Aronson and Sheila Neysmith, "The Retreat of the State and Long-Term Care Provision: Implications for Frail Elderly People, Unpaid Family Carers and Paid Home Care Workers," *Studies in Political Economy* (1997): 37–66.

61 Ecumenical Health Care Network, "Home Care: Fact Sheets on Key Health Care Issues" (May 2005). Retrieved from www.united-church.ca/health care/pdf/home care.pdf.

62 Alvin Finkel, *Our Lives: Canada after 1945* (Toronto, ON: Lorimer, 1997), 299; National Council of Welfare, *Poverty Profile 1999* (Ottawa, ON: NCW, 1999).

63 Allyce Herle, acting chair, quoted in "Youngest Canadians at Highest Risk of Chronic Poverty." Press release, National Council of Welfare, 29 July 2002. Retrieved from www.ncwcnbes. net/htmdocument/principales/povertypro99Press_e.htm.

64 Graham Riches, *Food Banks and the Welfare Crisis* (Ottawa, ON: Canadian Council on Social Development, 1986), 15, 31–32.

65 Canadian Conference of Catholic Bishops, *Ethical Reflections on the Economic Crisis* (Ottawa, ON: Episcopal Commission for Social Affairs, 1983).

66 *Nellie's Newsletter*, August 2002. In possession of the author.

67 In 1993, as in 1982, the ratio of adult women to men who lived in poverty was 1.33 to 1. Andrew Armitage, *Social Welfare in Canada Revisited: Facing Up to the Future* (Toronto, ON: Oxford University Press, 1996), 61.

68 Garson Hunter, "The Problem of Child Poverty in Canada," in *Canadian Social Policy*, ed. Westhues, 32; Social Planning Council of Winnipeg (SPCW), *Children: An Overlooked Investment: Manitoba Child Poverty Report Card 2002* (Winnipeg, MB: Social Planning Council of Winnipeg, 2002); *Toronto Star*, 30 July 2002; *The Globe and Mail*, 25 November 2003.

69 SPCW, *Manitoba Child Poverty Report Card 2002*.

70 Jean Swanson, *Poor-Bashing: The Politics of Exclusion* (Toronto, ON: Between the Lines, 2001), 123.

71 Canadian Council on Social Development, *The Progress of Canada's Children* (Ottawa, ON: CCSD, 2002).

72 Swanson, *Poor-Bashing*, 110–14; Hunter, "The Problem of Child Poverty," 42–44.

73 John Clarke, "Fight to Win," *Labour/Le Travail* 50 (Fall 2002): 383–90.

74 Norman Feltes, "'The New Prince in a New Principality: OCAP and the Toronto Poor," *Labour/Le Travail* 48 (Fall 2001): 146.

75 Redden, *Health Care, Entitlement, and Citizenship*, 46–47; Burke and Silver, "Universal Health Care," 171.

76 Simon Renouf, "Chipping Away at Medicare: 'Rome Wasn't Sacked in a Day,'" in *The Trojan Horse*, ed. Harrison and Laxer, 230.

77 Renouf, "Chipping Away at Medicare," 86–92; Roy J. Romanow, *Final Report: Building on Values: The Future of Health Care in Canada, Commission on the Future of Health Care in Canada* (Ottawa, ON: Government of Canada 2002), 136.

78 Romanow, *Final Report*, 128, 174.

79 *Edmonton Journal*, 7 November 2003, 5.

80 Redden, *Health Care, Entitlement, and Citizenship* 71.

81 Romanow, *Final Report*, 17.

82 Ibid., 40, 46, 62, 67, 76.

83 Ibid., 21, 96.

84 Ibid., 19.

85 Ibid., 104.

86 Ibid., 25.

87 Ibid., 32–33.

88 Ibid., 213.

89 Canadian Union of Public Employees (CUPE), *On the Front Line*, 17 February 2003.

90 Health Canada, Health Care System, "2003 First Ministers' Accord on Health Care Renewal" (2003). Retrieved from www.hc-sc.gc.ca/english/hca2003/accord.html.

91 *The Globe and Mail*, 6 February 2003; CUPE, *On the Front Line*, 17 February 2003; *Friends of Medicare*, 6 February 2003.

92 Romanow, *Final Report*, 253.

93 Canada, Royal Commission on Aboriginal Peoples (RCAP), *Final Report*, vol. 3, *Gathering Strength* (Ottawa, ON: Minister of Supply and Services, 1996), chap. 3, "Health and Healing."

94 Romanow, *Final Report*, 248–49.

95 Ibid., 247.

96 Ibid., 34, 255.

97 RCAP, *Final Report*, vol. 3, chap. 3, "Health and Healing."

98 Ibid., chap. 1, section 1, "Social Policy in Context."

99 Ibid., chap. 2.

100 Ibid.

101 Ibid.

102 Ibid., vol. 3, chap. 4, "Housing."

103 Ibid.

104 James S. Frideres and René R. Gadacz, *Aboriginal Peoples in Canada: Contemporary Conflicts*, 6th ed. (Toronto, ON: Prentice Hall, 2001), 125–42; quotation from 136.

CHAPTER 13

The New Millennium
and Social Policy Directions

In the mid-1990s, the United Nations named the Cree community of Oujé-Bougoumou one of fifty exemplary communities in the world. Just a decade earlier, the Grand Council of the Cree of Quebec had cited the scattered First Nations people of the area as among the most destitute people of the developed world. They had been forced to move seven times in five decades, their community shoved aside by mining developments from which it drew no benefit. By the mid-1970s, they were dispersed among other communities or living in shacks next to logging roads. Eventually, the Cree had had enough. They blockaded the main logging road to Nemeska and forced the provincial government to come to terms. In 1989, a negotiated agreement gave them surface rights to 167 square kilometers of land along with $25 million to build a village for their 525 residents. Three years later, the federal government contributed $50 million to the project.

The Cree hired Alberta First Nations architect Douglas Cardinal to design a village that reflected their spiritual and cultural heritage, their environmental values, and their need for economic development. Among its features were buildings that united teepee shapes with modern forms, with the buildings laid out to reflect traditional patterns of a Cree community; a roofless pavilion that served as a meeting place in summer and a local skating rink in winter; a district heating system that used sawdust waste from the area's lumber mills which prevented the by-product from polluting the local environment; a home ownership program with payments geared to income; and a combined village centre and school. The community tried to foster the participation of all of its residents through implementing frequent workshops to deal with the transition from a dispersed to a united community and offering a summer work program for youth. Chief Abel Bosum, at the opening of the medical clinic, asked residents to think of the entire village as a healing centre. "Now we are no longer the 'forgotten Crees.' We are no longer the passive victims of industrial forces, no longer the pathetic, oppressed people seeking the sympathy of others. Instead, we have become daring innovators and self-confident planners."[1]

The success of Oujé-Bougoumou harkens back to pre-contact Aboriginal cultures in which areas such as the economy, religion, health, and the sharing of goods were all closely linked rather than compartmentalized in government bureaucracies. In recent years, as Aboriginal peoples have gained ground in their struggles for autonomy, there has been a revival of ancient practices, which are often married to European technologies. So, for example, the Blood First Nation's Kainai Continuing Care Centre in southern Alberta has both practitioners of Native medicine and the latest in medical technology. The ceremonial lodgepoles in front of the centre announce an institution in which the Sun Dance, ancient herbal remedies, smudges, and face paint are as important as intravenous machines. Historian Maureen Lux notes that the centre is "not an innovation so much as a return to an approach to health care that recognizes patients' needs as Aboriginal people. It is also a reflection of the people's adamant refusal to forsake their own medicine, spirituality, and culture despite the considerable might of the federal government."[2]

Summary of Social Policy History

As we have seen, the European societies that were established in today's Canada from the 1600s onwards lacked the holistic practices of the Aboriginal peoples. Class-divided and elite-controlled, these societies featured wealthy business people, professionals, government officials, artisans, farmers, labourers, and paupers. Each of these societies needed a means to deliver various social services to the poor and the unlucky while the wealthy purchased medical care, schooling, and child care as commodities. In New France, the Church, and particularly the nuns, provided charitable services to the poor, as much to save the souls of their charges as to keep them alive. In British North America, non-denominational Protestant charitable organizations, largely run by middle- and upper-class women, provided similar services to non-Catholics.

These organizations made a distinction between the "deserving poor," who merited relief in the home, and the "undeserving poor," whom the state had to take care of in the Houses of Industry that were established in the nineteenth century. In the Atlantic colonies, in particular, the Houses of Industry quickly became the dumping grounds for the poor. The workhouses and poorhouses were emblematic of the new industrial order: capitalists wanted cheap labour and the purpose of social policy was to ensure that they had a plentiful supply. Since the lives of working families were often grim, the lives of families without a wage earner must be made even grimmer so as to scare workers from either resisting employer control or quitting their jobs. The Poor Law philosophy would stalk Canadian workers and their families for generations to come, and arguably, in a modified way, continues to do so.

As industrialization and urbanization continued apace, the charitable systems established during periods when most colonists were self-sufficient farmers proved inadequate to deal with a growing number of social problems. Polluted, unsafe cities required state intervention to ensure adequate water supplies and sewage disposal, to reduce the risk of fire, and to deal with epidemics. From penniless old people to the mentally disturbed to wayward youth, the state increasingly stamped its mark on society in an effort to create an efficient industrial society.

Gradually, the working-class and farmers, as well as the growing middle classes, began to question the individualistic ethic that had been prevalent within the country even before Confederation. The Great Depression of the 1930s, which many regarded as an indictment of the entire capitalist system, became the catalyst for proposals for comprehensive social policies meant to promote greater equality in Canada. Such plans foundered on the rock of "sound finance" and were stymed by the elites' attempts to ensure that social reforms did not attack their wealth. In any case, most campaigns for reforms that would benefit workers provoked a section of the business community to respond with a "reform" program of its own, one that would cost the rich little and indeed benefit the well off more so than the working class. So, for example, the campaign for non-contributory unemployment insurance was drowned out by an employer campaign for an actuarially based, contributory UI. Calls for social housing lost out to programs that rewarded construction companies and banks for housing the well off.

There were no universal social programs in Canada before the Second World War. Unemployment insurance, introduced in 1940, was not initially universal in character, excluding over half of the workforce. Family allowances, introduced as the war ended, provided the country with its first universal social program. The introduction of the allowances had both a progressive side—all families benefited and the allowances were paid to women—and a reactionary side—they were meant to compensate married women for being thrown out of their wartime jobs. Popular demands that the government legislate programs to prevent another Depression and look after the needy resulted in thirty years of reformist legislation.

Such legislation, however, was always a compromise between the demands of popular groups for change and the pressure from conservative groups, especially business, for low taxes. Thus, pensions were kept below a poverty-line level so that Canadians had an incentive to buy life insurance and otherwise invest in private companies during their working years. Medicare covered hospital stays and visits to physicians, but many medical costs, including dental care, prescription drugs, and visits to non-allopathic practitioners remained as private costs. Social housing was available only to the very poor and the old, and usually cheaply constructed and segregated from middle-class residential areas. Finally, daycare, which raised issues of gender roles, was largely limited as a public good to the poorest of the poor. There were many programs directed at alleviating poverty, with the Unemployment Assistance Plan of 1956 and the Canada Assistance Plan of 1966 regarded as the apogee of federal government efforts to reverse the Poor Law philosophy that had historically guided government policies. In practice, though, even when the last poorhouses were closed down, the poor continued to receive such miserable incomes from the state and were subject to so much surveillance that the Poor Law message of "less eligibility" for those without jobs remained strikingly apparent.

As limited as the gains made in the three decades following the war might have been, they did represent incremental improvements. They were also a tribute to the trade unions, women's organizations, and Native people's organizations and other community groups fighting for social justice. In many cases, however, these gains were nothing more than temporary compromises made by governments responding to pressures in times of prosperity. When the economy began to perform in a somewhat less stellar fashion after the mid-1970s, cutbacks were the order of the day. CAP and family allowances disappeared, federal payments to the provinces for medicare and post-secondary education were slashed, and neo-liberal rhetoric that harkened back to pre-Depression days became common among politicians. Yet the cutbacks always faced organized opposition from popular groups and, by the early 2000s, at least some of the social programs, particularly medicare, were receiving new injections of government cash. Unfortunately, however, in the areas of daycare, housing, and poverty policy, the losses of the 1980s and 1990s were not reversed.

ADDING IT UP

Citizens wanting reforms tended to focus on specific program initiatives such as medicare, pensions, housing, daycare, or income supplements. These programs were implemented in a piecemeal fashion, each with their own bureaucracy at the provincial level, often at the federal level in Ottawa, and sometimes at the municipal level. Occasionally, a task force on an issue presented a more integrated approach: the Marsh Report, the Royal Commission on Medical Care, the Royal Commission on the Status of Women in Canada, Quebec's Castonguay-Nepveu Report, the Royal Commission on Aboriginal Peoples, the Senate Report on Poverty, and the Romanow Report travelled the country and spoke to all levels of society. Civil society groups, including women's groups, poverty groups, mainstream churches and others, for example, put forward a progressive social vision to the Macdonald Commission. However, as with most task forces, the commissioners chose to ignore the recommendations.[3]

During the period when CAP was in operation, social critics observed that an extension of its services to the entire population—services that included counselling, rehabilitation, daycare, homemaker services, and community development—would effect a positive social evolution for Canada.[4] But all of these needed to be supplemented with programs that guaranteed a decent income to all Canadians, whether through work-related earnings or an income directly from the state. In practice, the piecemeal approach to social policy and health care continued to dominate government thinking at the dawn of the new millennium.

Research increasingly demonstrated the links between health, education, employment, and income. Two studies reported in 1996, and involving 76,000 people between them, observed a close link between levels of education and income and good health. A third reported the somber link between unemployment and poor health and between unemployment and suicide rates. That study was conducted by a professor of preventative medicine and biostatistics who was also a community medicine resident and a consultant to the Workers' Compensation Board. He found that Canada had spent between $850 million and $1.2 billion in 1993 alone to pay for the medicare costs that resulted from the mental and physical problems associated with unemployment.[5]

This finding underscores the importance of employment to psychological well-being, especially in a society that values the work ethic.[6] Some scholars, however, regard the work ethic itself as a social problem. Political scientist Phil Resnick observes that in a society well able to produce and distribute necessary goods with a minimum of labour, traditional notions of full employment mean simply perpetuating "a social order that revolves around mindless consumerism and routine, mind-numbing work."[7] Workers in such fields as advertising, private insurance, and the military, arguably do the work that serves the ideological needs of the economic system rather than the social needs. But, setting aside the issue of which jobs are socially necessary, the issue remains: How can the work be spread around equally?

The phenomenon in the early 2000s of an ever-increasing number of Canadians working overtime while the unemployment rate stubbornly hugs the 8 per cent mark underscores this dilemma. As economists Diane Bellemare and Lise Poulin Simon have observed, a full employment policy "is more than a commendable social objective." It is "a key factor in the attainment of such objectives as efficiency, equity and stabilization…The pursuit of full employment ensures that even when a society prizes efficiency, the losers will be compensated. Employment generates an allocation of income which satisfies the important social values embodied in the industrial work ethic. And finally, full employment serves to stabilize employment and prices all at once. In other words, the pursuit of full employment becomes the invisible hand."[8]

The definition of "employment" in such an equation, however, is extremely important. As feminist critiques have emphasized, the caring work in the home, usually performed by women, needs to be valued monetarily even as efforts are made to spread it more evenly between the sexes. Full employment policies also need to include the disabled, who are often counted as "unemployables" in an economic system that is characterized by far fewer paid jobs than potential workers. Of course, as many supporters of guaranteed incomes observe, too great a focus on people working can draw attention away from what citizens need to live with dignity, regardless of whether they work or don't work. Notions of who is eligible and who isn't should be combated rather than embraced in a comprehensive program of social policy.

BLAMING THE VICTIM

But capital, a sometimes almost invisible player in the arena of social policy, has an integrated vision of social programming as well, and it is one in which the "welfare state" must remain residual. The Macdonald Report, which linked free trade with a modest guaranteed annual income that was meant to replace all other social programs in the country, provided a compelling vision from the right of the minimal responsibility of the state towards citizens.

Advocates of the "residual" welfare state denounce universal programs as too costly and argue that state expenditures that provide benefits to better-off citizens can be chopped altogether. This would reduce overall government spending and leave most of the funds at the government's disposal to meet the needs of the destitute. But it is no coincidence that there is a better distribution of both income and social services in countries where universal programs prevail relative to countries where programs are mainly residual. For example, Scandinavia and Holland, which exemplify states with universal entitlements, offer their poorest citizens far better services than does the United States, which exemplifies the "residualist" approach. In Canada, though there are fewer universal programs than in Scandinavia, universal medicare is defended across all social strata, except perhaps by big business. The consequence has been that even though conservatives have tried to tame medicare, the system continues to service most Canadians, including the poor.

In contrast, in the United States, where only the old and the destitute receive free medical services from the public purse, state governments have cut away the medical services available to the poor. Burdened with laws requiring them to balance revenues and expenditures annually, and fearing the consequences of increasing taxes, thirty-four states chose to remove many working-poor residents from the Medicaid program. An estimated 1.6 million Americans, half of them children, lost their entitlement to state medicine in 2002 and 2003, while many of the programs that had earlier been available to them, such as children's health programs, closed down or were scaled back.[9]

The views of the major industrialists and bankers on social policy rarely have a direct impact on the viewpoints of Canadians at large. However, as suggested at various points in this book, both the corporate-controlled think tanks and the media parrot the ideology of the capitalists, and the education system at all levels, sometimes unthinkingly, reproduces it. As for politicians, even those nominally on the Left tend to take for granted the fact that social policy must not threaten the profits and privileges of the wealthy.

The wealthy were certainly tossed a scare by the Great Depression of the 1930s. During that decade, many saw their profits tumble, could only be cautious about new investments, and watched with angst as workers and the unemployed organized and expressed contempt for the existing economic system. Unable to end the economic mess themselves, many captains of industry were willing to have the state exercise greater economic direction and to implement social insurance programs, always with the caveat that this must be done without redistributing income from the rich to the poor. In the postwar period, such programs were implemented and provided a modicum of social security while redistributing income only slightly. But the capitalist class was not amused when workers demanded more and more income and privileges from both employers and the state as the "reserve army of labour" depleted in the wake of historically low unemployment rates.

Meanwhile, under pressure from American multinational corporations and the American state, the world economy was becoming more integrated. National tariffs and quotas were reduced and opportunities for capital to shift from country to country, always important to the capitalist system, expanded. This "globalization" of capital put pressure on national governments to reduce state demands on corporations that potentially crimped profits, everything from employee safety standards to environmental standards. Globalization threatened workers' jobs when their wages outstripped those in other countries where an equally skilled labour force might be available. It was the antithesis of local control and democracy. But, according to its advocates, it was absolutely inevitable and would have the long-term effect of creating the greatest industrial efficiency imaginable. In turn, that would create immense wealth that the marketplace, through its mystical operations, would share with the peoples of the world.

As corporations became more globalized, they threatened to withdraw capital from countries with high taxes and generous social programs. The failure of the authoritarian command economies of the Soviet Union and its allies, and the ultimate collapse of most of the Communist regimes, was used to discredit not only the idea of a socialist economy but also the state operations of services of any kind. State-owned corporations in capitalist countries, most of which offered excellent public services at reasonable costs, were "privatized" in many countries. Canada was no exception.

The notion that state intervention was rarely the answer to a problem—except perhaps in the case of providing police protection to property owners at home and military protection to property owners abroad—was easily extended to the welfare state. The private sector could provide better health and education services than the public sector. Social housing, social assistance, and public daycare created dependency and contributed to crime, immorality, and a breakdown of society. As we have seen, the arguments regarding health and education proved a tough sell since the middle class and the working class, however persuaded about the virtues of profit-oriented operations overall, liked the idea of prepaid services and wanted public money to be used to improve these services rather than to enrich private companies.

In other areas, though, the constant propaganda about welfare state failures seemed to be relatively successful. If one believed the mainstream media, public monies for Aboriginal programs were all being frittered away by corrupt First Nations politicians, social assistance payments kept the unemployed from seeking work, and social housing projects were the new slums, if not breeding grounds for crime and immorality. Conservatives went further, claiming that social assistance and subsidized daycare for single mothers encouraged young women to have children out of wedlock, higher minimum wages discouraged job creation, and unemployment insurance caused individuals to choose unemployment over work.[10] Of course, this assumed that state policy should actively limit people's choices about whether to work and to marry. To a great extent, the work issue seemed to be a red herring, since the rate of unemployment continued to be a function of economic performance, which was largely in the hands of investors and not workers. Though it was more difficult and less profitable to receive either (un)employment insurance or social assistance than it had been in the 1970s and 1980s, unemployment rates in the late 1990s and early 2000s were no lower than in those earlier periods, if the devastating recession of 1982–85 is factored out.

As for the punishment of single women by legislating many of them into poverty, it did little but punish their children. The numbers of single-parent families were growing in most countries. What distinguished various nations was the extent to which they accommodated the phenomenon as opposed to punishing those who ended up, whether by design or choice, as single moms. In France, where close to one-quarter of all mothers were unmarried by the late 1800s, it was the practice to provide crèches for their preschoolers (and for non-working mothers who chose to use them) as part of the school system. By the late 1900s, employment policy gave single moms preference over all others in terms of employment training. Such policies resulted in poverty rates for single mothers that were only slightly above those for the population as a whole. In Sweden, where the poverty rate was very low, similar policies had almost eliminated an association between poverty and single motherhood. By contrast, in Canada, as in the United States, the supposedly "moral" approach to single motherhood accounted for this group and their children comprising a very large portion of the poor.

Just as the experience of other nations demonstrated that state spending could eliminate the notion of single motherhood as a "problem" (if one set aside the moral objections, supposedly based on religious beliefs), it also demonstrated that social housing could be an answer to housing crises rather than being the crisis itself, as neo-liberals argued it had become in Canada. In several Scandinavian countries, as was suggested in chapter 10, state subsidies for co-operative housing projects run by the residents themselves helped to nurture healthy communities. By contrast, Canadian social housing projects seemed to be depressing and difficult places to live. Toronto's Regent Park was one of the largest of the projects and became emblematic of social housing's failure. But, as Sean Purdy, detailing the collapse of the early promise of that community, argues:

> Contrary to the "blame the victim" conjectures of "underclass" theories, the causes of the socio-economic inferiority of Regent Park tenants rests squarely on state housing practices and the inability of a profit-oriented economic system to adequately attend to the employment and shelter needs of low-income families. Regent Park residents became trapped, not by the welfare or public housing system itself, but by the glaring lack of affordable public and private shelter spaces, subdued investment in project facilities and services, moralistic assumptions about proper tenants, low welfare benefits and related social services, and a shrinking labour market.[11]

Ironically, in 1958, on the tenth anniversary of Regent Park, Albert Rose, a social worker who had played a large role in promoting its development in the first place, argued in a book that the project was a huge success.[12] The project, in its early years, provided homes for the working poor, many of whom had previously lived in rundown rental dwellings, unable to afford better accommodation. It developed its own "slum" status from the 1960s onwards as many of its earlier residents bought their own homes and left the project, and the organization of the Canadian economy and society created a hard core of unemployed who became Regent Park's principal residents. Governments tried to deal with the increasing number of people in social housing by spending less and less on them per capita. Then they threw up their hands as social housing conditions deteriorated, blaming the residents for all the problems.

The extent of the corporate attack on the welfare state raises questions about how much redistribution of income and power is possible within the capitalist system. Some argue that the Keynesian welfare state established between 1945 and 1975 demonstrated that some degree of progress is possible within the confines of capitalism. Others, such as Claus Offe, have argued that "the Keynesian welfare state involves the unintended but undesirable consequences of undermining both the incentives to invest and the incentives to work."[13] This pessimistic viewpoint appears, on the surface, to be a left-wing version of the neo-liberal argument, a "revolutionary defeatist" argument that suggests no change is possible if the capitalist system is to function properly. This argument is ahistorical, since, as mentioned earlier, there is adequate research disproving the link between economic performance and levels of social spending. Scandinavia and Holland, despite their lavish social expenditures, are thriving capitalist countries. But, certainly, in an age of global capitalism, Offe is correct, at least in theory, when he argues that "the power position of private investors includes the power to define reality."[14] If corporations wish to boycott a country because it promotes policies that favour workers over investors, there is little that can be done to stop them within the capitalist system.

THE WAY FORWARD

If underfunding was a big problem for welfare-state initiatives, it was symptomatic of larger problems. There were many contradictions within the welfare state, some of which were discussed in the introduction and touched on elsewhere in the book. On the one hand, the welfare state became necessary because face-to-face communities that looked after their unfortunate had largely disappeared. On the other hand, the whole notion of the welfare state was that the "community," as represented by the state, was to take the place of local communities in caring for those who required health or social services. How, however, were members of a community as abstract as that of a nation, province, or large city to relate to a system of caring that most experienced only as taxpayers and consumers? When it came to issues such as housing and daycare, those who could afford to provide these services for themselves were often easily swayed by conservatives who argued that they should not have to pay for these services for others. Since the "others" were no longer necessarily their neighbours (or perhaps they were the neighbours they didn't know in the new urban and suburban agglomerations), it was not always easy to identify with the recipients of social assistance. For social advocates, the problem of arguing for "community spirit" in communities that were communities only in name was never easy.

Nor was it always easy to argue the virtues of the state bureaucracies' employees who delivered the welfare-state services to consumers. Civil servants, teachers, physicians, nurses, social workers, university professors, and the like may have believed that in following the rules set out by governments to deliver a variety of services they were serving the public good. But the recipients often experienced these services differently. Women whose children were seized by social workers, parents whose children ran into difficulties at school, citizens who ran afoul of bylaw officers and correctional officials, patients who experienced indifferent care in hospitals and doctors' offices, were often disillusioned by the impersonal welfare state. Concerns about professionalism on the part of the service deliverers protected their high wages and prestige, yet their sanctimony often offended workers in the private sector who worked in poorer conditions doing more physically demanding jobs for less pay. Of course, public-sector workers, who had unionized in force in the 1960s, were largely following a social script in which each group of workers tried to use its education, experience, skills, and tasks to get better wages and working conditions than other workers. Without this script, their treatment by the state, their employer, would surely have been worse.

What, then, does the history of struggles for social programs suggest as the way forward for progressives who want social policy to reflect social justice concerns rather than the interests of capital? The successful campaign for medicare in the 1960s and the campaign to prevent its erosion in the 1990s point to the importance of progressive groups working together towards a common cause. In most provinces, trade unions, the women's movement, and a variety of community groups worked together to defend medicare, forcing politicians who wanted to be re-elected to provide a minimal degree of support for its egalitarian principles. Both within the community groups and throughout the health services, with the exception of physicians, there is increasing support for the view that medicare will best be protected not by cutbacks but by an extension of the system to embrace all aspects of health care. Clinics and centres in which the various professions work together and in which clients have a degree of control over the overall operations offer a counter model to the bureaucratic and elitist model of silos of care that the Romanow report criticized. Examples of such clinics and centres have been found in Canada since the early postwar period, and their numbers have increased.

Pressure for popular control over other social services, long a concern of the anti-poverty movement, is also important in efforts to defeat neo-liberalism and its Poor Law approach to people's needs. Social movements, particularly the co-op housing movement, have emphasized that if residents of social housing were given adequate resources and the democratic right to make the major decisions about their communities, the problems with past social housing policies would be alleviated. Similarly, daycares run by boards of parents and pension schemes controlled by their contributors would strengthen Canadian democracy. As a greater number of Canadians join movements, based on class, gender, ethnicity, and region, and take up the call for their democratic rights within Canadian life, the Poor Law underpinnings will once again be under attack, just as they were during the Great Depression and the Second World War.

"Social policy" requires constant redefinition. In Canada's recent past, it has become too associated with the state and its mandarins, a vehicle for a small number of ambitious individuals as much as the source of care for many. We seem to be very far from the notion that the British social scientist R.M. Titmuss once identified as the abiding popular ethos behind the postwar welfare state: "The fundamental and dominating historical processes which led to these major changes in social policy were connected with the demand for one society; for non-discriminatory services for all without distinction of class, income or race;...for services that would manifestly encourage social integration."[15]

NOTES

1 Canada, Royal Commission on Aboriginal Peoples (RCAP), *Final Report*, vol. 3, *Gathering Strength* (Ottawa, ON: Minister of Supply and Services, 1996), chap. 4, "Housing," section 7.2, "Political, Social, and Cultural Benefits."

2 Maureen K. Lux, *Medicine That Walks: Disease, Medicine, and Canadian Plains Native People, 1880–1940* (Toronto, ON: University of Toronto Press, 2001), 225.

3 Daniel Drache and Duncan Cameron, eds., *The Other Macdonald Report: The Consensus on Canada's Future that the Macdonald Commission Left Out* (Toronto, ON: James Lorimer, 1985).

4 Derek P.J. Hum, *Federalism and the Poor: A Review of the Canada Assistance Plan* (Toronto, ON: Ontario Economic Council, 1983), 4–5.

5 *University Affairs*, February 1996, 15.

6 Note that the Marsh Report also emphasized employment as the key to improving lives, even as it outlined a myriad of social programs that did not seek to punish the unemployed in the distribution of social goods. Brigitte Kitchen, "The Marsh Report Revisited," *Journal of Canadian Studies* 21, 2 (1986): 38–48.

7 Duncan Cameron and Andrew Sharpe, eds., *Policies for Full Employment* (Ottawa, ON: Canadian Council on Social Development, 1988), 6.

8 Diane Bellemare and Lise Poulin Simon, "Full Employment: A Strategy and an Objective for Economic Policy," in *Policies for Full Employment*, ed. Cameron and Sharpe, 88.

9 *New York Times*, 31 December 2003.

10 The impact of this conservative discourse in Canada, the United States, and Britain, with an emphasis on gender, is discussed in Sylvia Bashevkin, *Welfare Hot Buttons: Women, Work, and Social Policy Reform* (Toronto, ON: University of Toronto Press, 2002).

11 Sean Purdy, "'Ripped Off' by the System: Housing Policy, Poverty, and Territorial Stigmatization in Regent Park Housing Project, 1951–1991," *Labour/Le Travail* 52 (2003): 107.

12 Albert Rose, *Regent Park: A Study in Slum Clearance* (Toronto, ON: University of Toronto Press, 1958).

13 Claus Offe, *Contradictions of the Welfare State* (London, UK: Hutchinson, 1984), 199.

14 Ibid., 151.

15 Richard M. Titmuss, *Commitment to Welfare*, 2nd ed. (London, UK: Allen and Unwin, 1976), 191.

Bibliography

MANUSCRIPT COLLECTIONS

Archives of Ontario (AO)
Business and Professional Women's Clubs of Ontario Papers, F 207
George Drew Papers, RG 3
Ontario Welfare Council (OWC) Papers, F 837
Royal Commission on Education in Ontario, RG 18

Library and Archives of Canada (LAC).
Canadian Chamber of Commerce Papers, MG 28
Canadian Labour Congress (CLC) Papers, MG 28, I 103
Canadian Welfare Council/Canadian Council on Social Development
(CWC/CCSD) Papers, MG 28
Canadian Welfare Council Papers, MG 28, I 103
Catholic Women's League Papers, MG 28 E 345
Department of Finance Papers, RG 19, E2C

Department of National Health and Welfare Papers, RG 29, RG 33
Elsie Gregory MacGill Papers, MG 31 K7
Grace MacInnis Papers, MG 32 C 12
June Callwood Papers, MG 31 K24
Lester B. Pearson Papers, MG 26, N-3, N-4
Mackenzie King Diaries, MG 26, J 13
Mackenzie King Papers, MG 26 J1
Montreal Council of Women Papers, MG 28 I 64
National Council of Women of Canada (NCWC) Papers, MG 28, I 25
National Liberal Federation Papers, MG 28 IV-3
Royal Commission on Health Services, RG 33
Special Committee on Social Security Papers, MG 28, I 103
Royal Commission on the Status of Women in Canada, *Briefs*, RG 33/89,

Provincial Archives of Alberta (PAA)
Ernest C. Manning (Premiers') Papers

Provincial Archives of Manitoba (PAM)
Magnus Eliason Collection
Manitoba Council of Self-Help Groups Papers
Manitoba Federation of Labour (MFL) Papers, P404, P405
Winnipeg Council of Self-Help Incorporated Papers, P 840

GOVERNMENT DOCUMENTS

Canada. Advisory Committee on Reconstruction, *Final Report 4: Housing and Community Planning*. Ottawa, ON: King's Printer, 1944.
———. *Final Report 6: Post-War Problems of Women*. Ottawa: King's Printer, 1944.
Canada. Canadian Advisory Committee on the Status of Women. *New Directions for Public Policy: A Position Paper on the One-Parent Family*. Ottawa, ON: CACSW, 1976.
Canada. Department of Reconstruction, Sessional Paper Number 90, *Employment and Income with Special Reference to the Initial Period of Reconstruction*, 12 April 1945. Ottawa: King's Printer, 1945.
Canada. Director of Investigation and Research, Combines Investigation Act. *"Material Collected for Submission to the Restrictive Trade*

Practices Commission in the Course of an Inquiry under Section 42 of the Combines Investigation Act Relating to the Manufacture, Distribution and Sale of Drugs." Ottawa, ON: Department of Justice, 1961.

Canada. Department of Labour. *Married Women Working for Pay in Eight Canadian Cities.* Ottawa, ON: Department of Labour, 1958.

Canada. Department of Labour, Women's Bureau. *Working Mothers and Their Child-Care Arrangements.* Ottawa, ON: Queen's Printer, 1970.

Canada. Dominion-Provincial Conference (1945), *Dominion and Provincial Submissions and Plenary Conference Discussions.* Ottawa, ON: King's Printer, 1946.

Canada. Dominion-Provincial Conference on Reconstruction, *Proceedings*, 6 August 1945. Ottawa, ON: King's Printer, 1945.

Canada. Economic Council of Canada. *The Challenge of Growth and Change: Fifth Annual Review.* Ottawa, ON: Queen's Printer, 1968.

Canada. *Federal-Provincial Conference, Ottawa, 19-22 July 1965.* Ottawa, ON: Queen's Printer, 1968.

Canada, House of Commons, *Report of the Special Committee on Child Care.* Ottawa, ON: Supply and Services Canada, 1987.

Canada. *Poverty in Canada: Report of the Special Senate Committee on Poverty.* Ottawa, ON: Information Canada, 1971.

Canada. *Proceedings of the Constitutional Conference of Federal and Provincial Governments, Ottawa, 4-7 December 1950.* Ottawa, ON: King's Printer, 1950.

Canada. *Report of the Royal Commission on Taxation.* Vol. 1, *Introduction, Acknowledgments and Minority Reports.* Ottawa, ON: Queen's Printer, 1966.

Canada. *Report of the Royal Commission on the Economic Union and Development Prospects for Canada.* Vols. 1 and 2. Ottawa, ON: Supply and Services Canada, 1985.

Canada. *Report of the Royal Commission on the Status of Women in Canada.* Ottawa, ON: Information Canada, 1970.

Canada. Royal Commission on Aboriginal Peoples, *Final Report.* 5 vols. Ottawa, ON: Minister of Supply and Services, 1996. Available online from www.ainc-inac.gc.ca/ch/ rcap/sg/ sgmm_e.html.

Canada. The Senate of Canada. *Proceedings of the Special Senate Committee on Poverty*, Hon. David A. Croll, Chairman. Ottawa, ON: Senate of Canada, 1968-69, 1969-70, 1970-71.

Canada. Status of Women Canada. *Report of the Task Force on Child Care.* Ottawa, ON: Minister of Supply and Services, 1986.

Canadian Council on Social Development. *Guaranteed Annual Income: An Integrated Approach.* Ottawa, ON: CCSD, 1973.

———. *Not Enough: The Meaning and Measurement of Poverty in Canada: Report of the CCSD National Task Force on the Definition and Measurement of Poverty in Canada.* Ottawa, ON: CCSD, 1984.

———. *The Progress of Canada's Children.* Ottawa, ON: CCSD, 2002.

Dennis, Michael, and Susan Fish. *Report of the Task Force on Low-Income Housing.* Ottawa, ON: Queen's Printer, 1972.

Economic Council of Canada. *Fifth Annual Review: The Challenge of Growth and Change* Ottawa, ON: Queen's Printer, 1968.

Government of Alberta. MLA Committee to Review Low-Income Programs, *Low-Income Programs Review: What We Heard.* Edmonton: Government of Alberta, November 2001.

Health Canada. Health Care System. "2003 First Ministers' Accord on Health Care Renewal." Available online from www.hc-sc.gc.ca/english/hca2003/accord.html.

Health Study Bureau. *Review of Canada's Health Needs and Insurance Proposals.* Toronto, ON: Health Study Bureau, 1946.

Liberal Party of Canada. *Creating Opportunity: The Liberal Plan for Canada.* Ottawa: Liberal Party of Canada, 1993.

National Council of Welfare. *Poverty Profile 1999.* Ottawa, ON: NCW, 1999.

Ontario. Commission on Laws Relating to the Liability of Employers to Make Compensation to Their Employees for Injuries Received in the Course of Their Employment. *Final Report.* Toronto, ON: King's Printer, 1912–13.

Province of British Columbia. *Annual Report of the Department of Social Welfare for the Year Ended 31 March 1967.* Victoria, BC: Queen's Printer, 1968.

———. *Services for People: Annual Report of the Department of Human Resources.* Victoria, BC: Queen's Printer, 1973.

Romanow, Roy J. *Final Report: Building on Values: The Future of Health Care in Canada, Commission on the Future of Health Care in Canada.* Ottawa: Government of Canada 2002.

Social Planning Council of Winnipeg. *Children: An Overlooked Investment: Manitoba Child Poverty Report Card 2002.* Winnipeg: Social Planning Council of Winnipeg, 2002.

Statistics Canada. *Income Distribution by Size in Canada, Selected Years: Distribution of Family Incomes in Canada*. Ottawa, ON: Statistics Canada, 1972.

BOOKS AND JOURNALS

Abbott, Ruth K., and R.A. Young. "'Cynical and Deliberate Manipulation?' Child Care and the Reserve Army of Female Labour in Canada." *Journal of Canadian Studies* 24, 2 (1989): 23–38.

Abel, Kerry. *Drum Songs: Glimpses of Dene History*. Montreal, QC: McGill-Queen's University Press, 1993.

Abramovitz, Mimi. *Regulating the Lives of Women: Social Welfare Policy from Colonial Times to the Present*. Boston, MA: South End, 1989.

Adams, Ian. *The Poverty Wall*. Toronto, ON: McClelland and Stewart, 1970.

Adams, Ian, William Cameron, Brian Hill, and Peter Penz. *The Real Poverty Report*. Edmonton, AB: M.G. Hurtig, 1971.

Adams, Mary Louise. *The Trouble With Normal: Postwar Youth and the Making of Heterosexuality*. Toronto, ON: University of Toronto Press, 1997.

Allen, Richard. *The Social Passion: Religion and Social Reform in Canada, 1914-28*. Toronto, ON: University of Toronto Press, 1971.

Ambrose, Linda M. "'Youth, Marriage and the Family': The Report of the Canadian Youth Commission's Family Committee, 1943–1948." Paper presented at the Canadian Historical Association Annual Meeting, Kingston, ON, June, 1991.

Ames, Herbert Brown. *The City Below the Hill*. 1897. Reprint, Toronto, ON: University of Toronto Press, 1972.

Arblaster, Anthony. *The Rise and Decline of Western Liberalism*. Oxford, UK: Basil Blackwell, 1984.

Armitage, Andrew. *Social Welfare in Canada: Ideas, Realities and Future Paths*. 2nd ed. Toronto, ON: McClelland and Stewart, 1988.

———. *Social Welfare in Canada Revisited: Facing Up to the Future*. Toronto, ON: Oxford University Press, 1996.

Arnott, Teresa L. "Black Women and AFDC: Making Entitlement out of Necessity." In *Women, the State, and Welfare*. Edited by Linda Gordon, 280–98. Madison, WI: University of Wisconsin Press, 1990.

Arnup, Katherine. *Education for Motherhood: Advice for Mothers in Twentieth-Century Canada*. Toronto, ON: University of Toronto Press, 1994.

Aronson, Jane, and Sheila Neysmith. "The Retreat of the State and Long-Term Care Provision: Implications for Frail Elderly People, Unpaid Family Careers and Paid Home Care Workers." *Studies in Political Economy* (1997): 37–66.

Artibise, Alan. *Winnipeg: An Illustrated History.* Toronto, ON: James Lorimer, 1977.

Asher, Robert. "Failure and Fulfillment: Agitation for Employers' Liability Legislation and the Origins of Workmen's Compensation in New York State, 1876–1910." *Labor History* 24 (Spring 1983): 198–222.

Axtell, James. "Through Another Glass Darkly: Early Indian Views of Europeans." In *Out of the Background: Readings on Canadian Native History.* 2nd ed. Edited by Ken Coates and Robin Fisher, 17–29. Toronto, ON: Copp Clark, 1996.

Babcock, Robert H. "Blood on the Factory Floor: The Workers' Compensation Movement in Canada and the United States." In *Social Welfare Policy in Canada: Historical Readings.* Edited by Raymond B. Blake and Jeff Keshen, 107-21. Toronto, ON: Copp Clark, 1995.

Bacher, John C. "Keeping to the Private Market: The Evolution of Canadian Housing Policy: 1900-1949." PhD diss., McMaster University, 1985.

———. *Keeping to the Marketplace: The Evolution of Canadian Housing Policy.* Montreal, QC: McGill-Queen's University Press, 1993.

Badgley, Robin F., and Samuel Wolfe. *Doctors' Strike: Medical Care and Conflict in Saskatchewan.* Toronto, ON: Macmillan, 1967.

Baehre, Rainer. "Paupers and Poor Relief in Upper Canada." *Historical Papers* 60 (1981): 57–80.

Bailey, A.G. *The Conflict of European and Eastern Algonkian Cultures 1504-1700: A Study in Canadian Civilization.* 2nd ed. Toronto, ON: University of Toronto Press, 1969.

Baillargeon, Denyse. "Gouttes de lait et soif de pouvoir : les dessous de la lutte contre la mortalité infantile à Montréal, 1910–1953." *Canadian Bulletin of Medical History* 15 (1998): 27–57.

Baldwin, Doug. "'But Not a Drop to Drink': The Struggle for Pure Water." In *Gaslights, Epidemics, and Vagabond Cows: Charlottetown in the Victorian Era,* edited Doug Baldwin and Thomas Spira, 103–24. Charlottetown, PEI: Ragweed Press, 1988.

Ball, Michael. *Housing Policy and Economic Power: The Political Economy of Owner Occupation.* New York, NY: Methuen, 1983.

Baribeau, Claude. *La Seigneurie de la Petite-Nation 1811–1854 : le rôle économique et social du seigneur.* Hull, QC: Éditions Asticou, 1983.

Barker, Graham, Jennifer Penney, and Wally Seccombe. *Highrise and Superprofits.* Kitchener, ON: Dumont Press Graphix, 1973.

Barkwell, Peter A. "The Medicine Chest Clause in Treaty No. 6." *Canadian Native Law Reporter* 4 (1981): 1–23.

Bashevkin, Sylvia. *Welfare Hot Buttons: Women, Work, and Social Policy Reform.* Toronto, ON: University of Toronto Press, 2002.

Bella, Leslie. "The Provincial Role in the Canadian Welfare State: The Influence of Provincial Social Policy Initiatives on the Design of the Canada Assistance Plan." *Canadian Public Administration* 22, 3 (1979): 439–52.

Bellemare, Diane, and Lise Poulin Simon. "Full Employment: A Strategy and an Objective for Economic Policy." In *Policies for Full Employment.* Edited by Duncan Cameron and Andrew Sharpe, 69–93. Ottawa, ON: Canadian Council on Social Development, 1988.

Berger, Justice Thomas. *Northern Frontier, Northern Homeland: The Report of the Mackenzie Valley Pipeline Inquiry.* Vol. 1. Ottawa, ON: Minister of Supply and Services, 1977.

Bernard, Wanda Thomas, and Judith Fingard. "Black Women at Work: Race, Family, and Community in Greater Halifax." In *Mothers of the Municipality: Women, Work, and Social Policy in Post-1945 Halifax.* Edited by Judith Fingard and Janet Guildford, 189–225.Toronto, ON: University of Toronto Press, 2005.

Best, Sandra. "Women's Issues and the Women's Movement in Canada Since 1970." In *The Politics of Gender, Ethnicity and Language in Canada,* 129–31. Edited by Alan Cairns and Cynthia Williams. Toronto: University of Toronto Press, 1986.

Bilson, Geoffrey. *A Darkened House: Cholera in Nineteenth-Century Canada.* Toronto, ON: University of Toronto Press, 1980.

Blake, Raymond. "The Genesis of Family Allowances in Canada." In *Social Welfare Policy in Canada: Historical Readings.* Edited by Raymond B. Blake and Jeff Keshen, 244–254. Toronto, ON: Copp Clark, 1995.

Bliss, Michael. *A Living Profit: Studies in the Social History of Canadian Business, 1883–1911.* Toronto, ON: McClelland and Stewart, 1974.

———. *Plague: A Story of Smallpox in Montreal.* Toronto, ON: Harper Collins, 1991.

Bock, Gisela. "Challenging Dichotomies: Perspectives in Women's History." In *Writing Women's History: International Perspectives*. Edited by Karen Offen, Ruth Roach Pierson, and Jane Rendall, 1–23. Bloomington, IN: Indiana University Press, 1991.

Boris, Eileen. "The Power of Motherhood: Black and White Women Redefine the Political." In *Mothers of a New World: Maternalist Politics and the Origins of Welfare States*. Edited by Seth Koven and Sonya Michel, 213–45. New York, NY: Routledge, 1993.

Bothwell, Robert, Ian Drummond, and John English. *Canada Since 1945: Power, Politics and Provincialism*. Toronto, ON: University of Toronto Press, 1981.

Boychuk, Gerard William. *Patchworks of Purpose: The Development of Provincial Social Assistance Regimes in Canada*. Montreal, QC: McGill-Queen's University Press, 1998.

Boyd, Monica. *Canadian Attitudes toward Women: Thirty Years of Change*. Prepared for Canada, Women's Bureau, Labour Canada. Ottawa, ON: Labour Canada, 1983.

Bradbury, Bettina. "The Family Economy and Work in an Industrializing City: Montreal in the 1870s." *Historical Papers* 58 (1979): 71-96.

———. "Elderly Inmates and Caregiving Sisters: Catholic Institutions for the Elderly in Nineteenth-Century Canada." In *On the Case: Explorations in Social History*. Edited by Franca Iacovetta and Wendy Mitchinson, 129–55. Toronto, ON: University of Toronto Press, 1998.

———. and Tamara Myers, eds. *Negotiating Identities in Nineteenth and Twentieth Century Montreal*. Vancouver, BC: University of British Columbia Press, 2005.

———. *Working Families: Age, Gender and Daily Survival in Industrializing Montreal*. Toronto, ON: McClelland and Stewart, 1993.

Brennan, Patrick H. "'Thousands of Our Men Are Getting Practically Nothing at All to Do': Public Works Relief Programs in Regina and Saskatoon, 1929–1940." In *Age of Contention: Readings in Canadian Social History, 1900–1945*. Edited by Jeffrey Keshen, 316–30. Toronto, ON: Harcourt Brace, 1997.

Brodie, Janine. *The Political Economy of Canadian Regionalism*. Toronto, ON: Harcourt Brace Jovanovich, 1990.

Brown, Lorne. *When Freedom Was Lost: The Unemployed, the Agitator and the State*. Montreal, QC: Black Rose Books, 1987.

Brown, R. Craig, and G. Ramsay Cook. *Canada, 1896–1921: A Nation Transformed.* Toronto, ON: McClelland and Stewart, 1974.

Brown, Wendy. "Finding the Man in the State." *Feminist Studies* 18 (1992): 7–34.

Bruce, Christopher J., Ronald D. Kneebone, and Kenneth J. McKenzie, eds., *A Government Reinvented: A Study of Alberta's Deficit Elimination Program.* Toronto, ON: Oxford University Press, 1997.

Brundage, Anthony. *English Poor Laws 1700–1930.* Houndmills, Basingstoke, Hampshire, UK: Palgrave, 2002.

Brushett, Kevin. "Reaching Out and Biting Back: Grassroots Activism and Toronto's Social Service Community, 1960–75." Paper presented at the Canadian Historical Association Conference, Halifax, NS, May 2003.

Bryce, R.B. "The Canadian Economy in the Great Depression." In *Interpreting Canada's Past.* Vol. 2, *Post-Confederation.* Edited by J.M. Bumsted, 467–86. Toronto, ON: Oxford University Press, 1993.

Bryden, Ken. *Old age pensions and Policy-Making in Canada.* Montreal, QC: McGill-Queen's University Press, 1974.

Bryden, P.E. *Planners and Politicians: Liberal Politics and Social Policy 1957–1968.* Montreal, QC: Kingston: McGill-Queen's University Press, 1997.

Brym, R.J., ed. *Regionalism in Canada.* Toronto, ON: Irwin, 1986.

Buckley, Helen. *From Wooden Ploughs to Welfare: Why Indian Policy Failed in the Prairie Provinces.* Montreal, QC: McGill-Queen's University Press, 1992.

Bullen, John. "Hidden Workers: Child Labour and the Family Economy in Late-Nineteenth-Century Urban Ontario." *Labour/Le Travail* 18 (1986): 163–87.

——. "Children of the Industrial Age: Children, Work and Welfare in Late Nineteenth-Century Ontario." PhD thesis, University of Ottawa, 1989.

——. "J.J. Kelso and the 'New' Child-Savers: The Genesis of the Children's Aid Movement in Ontario." *Ontario History* 82 (1990): 107–28.

Burke, Mike, and Susan Silver. "Universal Health Care: Current Challenges to Normative Legacies." In *Canadian Social Policy: Issues and Perspectives.* 3rd ed. Edited by Anne Westhues, 164–81. Waterloo, ON: Wilfrid Laurier University Press, 2003.

Burke, Sara Z. *Seeking the Highest Good: Social Service and Gender at the University of Toronto, 1888–1937.* Toronto, ON: University of Toronto Press, 1997.

Cameron, Duncan, and Andrew Sharpe, eds. *Policies for Full Employment.* Ottawa, ON: Canadian Council on Social Development, 1988.

Campbell, Robert. *Grand Illusions: The Politics of the Keynesian Experience in Canada, 1945–1975.* Peterborough, ON: Broadview Press, 1987.

Campeau, Georges. *De l'assurance-chômage à l'assurance-emploi : l'histoire du régime canadien et de son détournement.* Montreal, QC: Les Éditions du Boréal, 2001. A translated version is Georges Campeau. *From UI to EI : Waging War on the Welfare State,* translated by Richard Howard. Vancouver, BC: University of British Columbia Press, 2005.

Canadian Association on Gerontology. "Policy Statement: Home Care in Canada" (n.d.). Available online from www.cagacg.ca/publications/552_e.php.

Canadian Conference of Catholic Bishops. *Ethical Reflections on the Economic Crisis.* Ottawa, ON: Episcopal Commission for Social Affairs, 1983.

Canadian Housing and Renewal Association. *Access to Housing: Proceedings of the Twenty-First Annual Symposium of the Canadian Housing and Renewal Association.* Ottawa, ON: CHRA, 1990.

Caragata, Lea. "Housing and Homelessness." In *Canadian Social Policy: Issues and Perspectives.* 3rd ed. Edited by Anne Westhues, 67–89. Waterloo, ON: Wilfrid Laurier University Press, 2003.

Cardinal, Harold, and Walter Hildebrandt. *Treaty Elders of Saskatchewan: Our Dream Is that Our Peoples Will One Day Be Clearly Recognized as Nations.* Calgary, AB: University of Calgary Press, 2000.

Carter, Connie, and Eileen Daoust. "From Home to House: Women in the B.C. Legislature." In *Not Just Pin Money: Selected Essays on the History of Women's Work in British Columbia.* Edited by Barbara K. Latham and Roberta J. Pazdro, 389–405. Victoria, BC: Camosun College, 1984.

Carver, Humphrey. *Compassionate Landscape.* Toronto, ON: University of Toronto Press, 1975.

Chen, Xiaobei. *Tending the Gardens of Citizenship: Child Saving in Toronto, 1880's–1920's.* Toronto, ON: University of Toronto Press, 2005.

Charles, Aline. *Travail d'ombre et de lumière : le bénévolat féminin à l'Hôpital Ste-Justine, 1907–1960.* Quebec, QC: IQRC, 1990.

Child care Resource and Research Unit. *Early Childhood Care and Education in Canada: Provinces and Territories, 1998.* Toronto, ON: Centre for Urban and Community Studies, University of Toronto, 2001.

Chorney, Harold. *The Deficit: Hysteria and the Current Economic Crisis.* Ottawa, ON: Canadian Centre for Policy Alternatives, 1989.

———. "The Economic and Political Consequences of Canadian Monetarism." Paper Presented to the British Association of Canadian Studies Annual Meeting, University of Nottingham, Nottingham, UK, 12 April 1991.

———. "Deficits-Fact or Fiction? Ontario's Public Finances and the Challenge of Full Employment." In *Getting on Track, Social Democratic Struggles for Ontario.* Edited by Daniel Drache, 186–201. Montreal, QC: McGill-Queen's University Press, 1992.

Chorney Harold, and Phillip Hansen. "The Falling Rate of Legitimation: The Problem of the Contemporary Capitalist State in Canada." *Studies in Political Economy* 4 (1978): 65–98

Christie, Nancy. *Engendering the State: Family, Work, and Welfare in Canada.* Toronto, ON: University of Toronto Press, 2000.

Clairmont, Donald H., and Dennis William Magill. *Africville: The Life and Death of a Canadian Black Community.* 3rd ed. Toronto, ON: Canadian Scholars' Press, 1999.

Clarke, John. "Fight to Win." *Labour/Le Travail* 50 (Fall 2002): 383–90.

Clio Collective. *Quebec Women: A History.* Toronto, ON: Women's Press, 1987.

Cohen, Marjorie Griffin, ed. *Training the Excluded for Work: Access and Equity for Women, Immigrants, First Nations, Youth and People with Low Incomes.* Vancouver, BC: University of British Columbia Press, 2004.

Cohen, Yolande. *Paroles de femmes : une histoire des Cercles de fermières.* Montreal, QC: Le Jour, 1990.

———. *Profession infirmière : Une histoire des soins dans les hôpitaux du Québec.* Montreal, QC: Presses de l'Université de Montréal, 2000.

Cohen, Yolande, and Esther Lamontagne. "Le bénévolat féminin dans le secteur de la santé : distribution de services et développement d'expertises." Paper presented at the Canadian Historical Association Conference, Toronto, ON, June 2002.

Comacchio, Cynthia R. *"Nations Are Built of Babies": Saving Ontario's Mothers and Children, 1900–1940.* Montreal, QC: McGill-Queen's University Press, 1993.

———. *The Infinite Bonds of Family: Domesticity in Canada, 1850–1940.* Toronto, ON: University of Toronto Press, 1999.

Connelly, Patricia. *Last Hired, First Fired: Women and the Canadian Work Force.* Toronto, ON: Women's Educational Press, 1978.

Connor, J.T.H. *Doing Good: The Life of Toronto's General Hospital*. Toronto, ON: University of Toronto Press, 2000.

Conrad, Margaret. "The Atlantic Revolution of the 1950s." In *Beyond Anger and Longing: Community and Development in Atlantic Canada*. Edited by Berkeley Fleming, 55–96. Fredericton, NB: Acadiensis Press/Mount Allison University, Centre for Canadian Studies, 1988.

Cook, Ramsay. *The Regenerators: Social Criticism in Late Victorian English Canada*. Toronto, ON: University of Toronto Press, 1985.

Copway, G. or Kah-Ge-Ga-Gah-Bowh, Chief of the Ojibway Nations. *The Traditional History and Characteristic Sketches of the Ojibway Nation*. 1850. Reprint: Toronto, ON: Coles, 1972.

Corrigan, Philip, and Derek Sayer. *The Great Arch: English State Formation as Cultural Revolution*. Oxford, UK: Basil Blackwell, 1985.

Cortiula, Mark. "Social Class and Health Care in a Community Institution: The Case of Hamilton City Hospital." *Canadian Bulletin of Medical History* 6 (1989): 133–45.

Courchene, Thomas J. *The Strategy of Gradualism: An Analysis of Bank of Canada Policy from Mid–1975 to Mid–1977*. Montreal, QC: C.D. Howe Institute, 1977.

Cowherd, Raymond G. *Political Economists and the English Poor Laws: A Historical Study of the Influence of Classical Economics on the Formation of Social Welfare Policy*. Athens, OH: Ohio University Press, 1977.

Creese, Gillian. "The Politics of Dependence: Women, Work and Unemployment in the Vancouver Labour Movement before World War II." In *British Columbia Reconsidered: Essays on Women*. Edited by Veronica Strong-Boag and Gillian Creese, 364–90. Vancouver, BC: Press Gang, 1992.

Cross, Michael S., ed. *The Workingman in the Nineteenth Century*. Toronto, ON: Oxford University Press, 1974.

Crowe, Keith J. *A History of the Original Peoples of Northern Canada*. Rev. ed. Montreal, QC: McGill-Queen's University Press, 1991.

Cuneo, Carl J. "State, Class and Reserve Labour: The Case of the 1941 Canadian Unemployment Insurance Act." *Canadian Review of Sociology and Anthropology* 16 (May 1979): 147–70.

Curtis, Bruce. "Social Investment in Medical Forms: The 1866 Cholera Scare and Beyond." *Canadian Historical Review* 81, 3 (2000): 347–79.

------. *State Formation, Statistics, and the Census of Canada, 1840–1875.* Toronto, ON: University of Toronto Press, 2001.

------. *Building the Educational State: Canada West, 1836–1871.* London, ON: Althouse Press, 1988.

Cuthbert Brandt, Gail. "'Pigeon-Holed and Forgotten': The Work of the Sub-Committee on the Post-War Problems of Women, 1943." *Histoire sociale/Social History* 15, 29 (1982): 239–59.

Cuthbert Brandt, Gail, and Naomi Black. "'Il en faut un peu': Farm Women and Feminism in Quebec and France Since 1945." *Journal of the Canadian Historical Association*, New Series 1 (1990): 73–96.

Dale, Jennifer and Peggy Foster. *Feminists and State Welfare.* London, UK: Routledge and Kegan Paul, 1986.

Davies, Megan J. "'Services Rendered, Rearing Children for the State': Mothers' Pensions in British Columbia, 1911–1931." In *Not Just Pin Money: Selected Essays on the History of Women's Work in British Columbia.* Edited by Barbara K. Latham and Roberta J. Pazdro, 249–63. Victoria, BC: Camosun College, 1984.

------. *Into the House of Old: A History of Residential Care in British Columbia.* Montreal, QC: McGill-Queen's University Press, 2003.

Deaton, Richard Lee. "The Fiscal Crisis of the State in Canada." In *The Political Economy of the State Québec, Canada, U.S.A.* Edited by Dimitrios Roussopoulos, 18–56. Montreal, QC: Black Rose, 1973.

------. *The Political Economy of Pensions: Power, Politics and Social Change in Canada, Britain and the United States.* Vancouver, BC: University of British Columbia Press, 1989.

Dechêne, Louise. *Habitants and Merchants in Seventeenth-Century Montreal.* Montreal, QC: McGill-Queen's University Press, 1992.

Dickason, Olive Patricia. *Canada's First Nations: A History of Founding Peoples from Earliest Times,* 2nd ed. Toronto, ON: Oxford University Press, 1997.

Dobbin, Murray. *The One-and-a-Half Men: The Story of Jim Brady and Malcolm Norris, Métis Patriots of the Twentieth Century.* Vancouver, BC: New Star, 1981.

Donner, Arthur W., and Douglas D. Peters. *The Monetarist Counter-Revolution: A Critique of Monetary Policy 1975–1979.* Toronto, ON: James Lorimer, 1979.

Donovan, Kenneth. "Tattered Clothes and Powdered Wigs: Case Studies of the Poor and Well-to-Do in Eighteenth-Century Louisbourg." In *Cape Breton at 200: Historical Essays in Honour of the Island's Bicentennial*

1785–1985. Edited by Kenneth Donovan, 1–20. Sydney, NS: University College of Cape Breton Press, 1985.

Doucet, Michael, and John Weaver. *Housing the North American City*. Montreal, QC: McGill-Queen's University Press, 1991.

Drache, Daniel, and Duncan Cameron, eds. *The Other Macdonald Report: The Consensus on Canada's Future that the Macdonald Commission Left Out*. Toronto, ON: James Lorimer, 1985.

Dulude, Louise. *Women and Aging: A Report on the Rest of Our Lives*. Ottawa, ON: Canadian Advisory Council on the Status of Women, 1978.

Dunk, Thomas, Stephen McBride, and Randle W. Nelson, eds. *The Training Trap: Ideology, Training and the Labour Market*. Halifax, NS: Fernwood, 1996.

Drover, Glenn, ed. *Free Trade and Social Policy*. Ottawa, ON: Canadian Council on Social Development, 1988.

Eccles, W.J. *Essays on New France*. Toronto, ON: Oxford University Press, 1987.

Ecumenical Health Care Network. "Home Care: Fact Sheets on Key Health Care Issues" (May 2005). Available online from www.united-church .ca/health care/pdf/home care.pdf.

Einhorn, Barbara. *Cinderella Goes to Market: Citizenship, Gender and Women's Movements in East Central Europe*. London, UK: Verso, 1993.

English, John. "Dominion-Provincial Relations and Historical Planning, 1945-46." Ottawa: Proceedings of the Canadian Committee for the History of the Second World War, 1987.

English, John, and William R. Young. "The Federal Government and Social Policy in the 1990s: Reflections on Change and Continuity." In *Canadian Social Policy: Issues and Perspectives*. 3rd ed. Edited by Anne Westhues, 240–60. Waterloo, ON: Wilfrid Laurier University Press, 2003.

Errington, Elizabeth Jane. *Wives, Mothers, School Mistresses and Scullery Maids: Working Women in Upper Canada*. Montreal, QC: McGill-Queen's University Press, 1995.

Esping-Anderson, Gøsta. *The Three Worlds of Welfare Capitalism*. Cambridge, UK: Polity, 1990.

Éthier, Mireille. "Survey of Pension Issues." In *Income Distribution and Economic Security in Canada*. Edited by François Vaillancourt, 215-49. Toronto, ON: University of Toronto Press, 1985.

Fahmy-Eid, Nadia. "L'éducation des filles chez les Ursulines de Québec sous le Régime français." In *Maîtresses de maison, maîtresses d'école : femmes, famille et éducation dans l'histoire du Québec*. Edited by Nadia Fahmy-Eid and Micheline Dumont, 49–76. Montreal, QC: Boréal Express, 1983.

Falconer, Tim. *Watchdogs and Gadflies: Activism from Marginal to Mainstream.* Toronto, ON: Penguin, 2003.

Feather, Joan. "From Concept to Reality: Formation of the Swift Current Health Region." *Prairie Forum* 16, 1 (Spring 1991): 59–80.

———. "Impact of the Swift Current Health Region: Experiment or Model." *Prairie Forum* 16, 2 (Fall 1991): 225–48.

Feltes, Norman. "The New Prince in a New Principality: OCAP and the Toronto Poor." *Labour/Le Travail* 48 (Fall 2001): 125–55.

Ferguson, Gerry. "Control of the Insane in British Columbia, 1849–78: Care, Cure, or Confinement." In *Regulating Lives: Historical Essays on the State, Society, The Individual and the* Law. Edited by John McLaren, Robert Menzies, Dorothy E. Chunn, 63–96. Vancouver, BC: University of British Columbia Press, 2002.

Fingard, Judith. "The Winter's Tale: The Seasonal Contours of Pre-Industrial Poverty in British North America." *Historical Papers* 53 (1974): 65–94.

———. "The Relief of the Unemployed: The Poor in Saint John, Halifax and St. John's, 1815–1860." In *The Canadian City: Essays in Urban and Social History*. Edited by Alan J. Artibise and Gilbert Stelter, 341–67. Montreal, QC: McGill-Queen's University Press, 1984.

Finguard, Judith, and Janet Guildford, eds., *Mothers of the Municipality: Women, Work, and Social Policy in Post-1945 Halifax*. Toronto, ON: University of Toronto Press, 2005.

Finkel, Alvin. "Welfare for Whom? Class, Gender, and Race in Social Policy." *Labour/Le Travail* 49 (2002): 247–61.

———. "Alberta Social Credit and the Second National Policy." In *Toward Defining the Prairies: Region, Culture, and History*. Edited by Robert Wardhaugh, 29–49. Winnipeg, MB: University of Manitoba Press, 2001.

———. *Our Lives: Canada after 1945.* Toronto, ON: Lorimer, 1997.

———. "Changing the Story: Gender Enters the History of the Welfare State." *Tijdschrift voor Sociale Geschiedenis* 22, 1 (1996): 67–81.

———. *The Social Credit Phenomenon in Alberta.* Toronto, ON: University of Toronto Press, 1989.

———. *Business and Social Reform in the Thirties.* Toronto, ON: James Lorimer, 1979.

Forest, Pierre-Gerlier, Gregory P. Marchildon, and Tom McIntosh, eds. *Changing Health in Canada: Romanow Papers, Volume 2.* Toronto, ON: University of Toronto Press, 2004.

Foucault, Michel. *The Birth of the Clinic: An Archaeology of Medical Perception.* New York: Vintage, 1973.

———. *Discipline and Punish: The Birth of the Prison.* London, UK: Pantheon, 1977.

Fox Piven, Frances, and Richard Cloward. *The New Class War: Reagan's Attack on the Welfare State and its Consequences.* New York, NY: Pantheon, 1982

Fraser, Derek, ed. *The New Poor Law in the Nineteenth Century.* New York, NY: St. Martin's Press, 1976.

Fraser, Derek. *The Evolution of the British Welfare State: A History of Social Policy since the Industrial Revolution.* 2nd ed. Houndmills, Basingstoke, Hampshire, UK: Macmillan, 1984.

Frideres, James S., and René Gadacz. *Aboriginal Peoples in Canada: Contemporary Conflicts.* 6th ed. Toronto, ON: Prentice Hall, 2001.

Frykman, Tofte. "Housing Conditions." In *Welfare in Transition: A Survey of Living Conditions in Sweden 1968–1981.* Edited by Robert Erickson and Rune Åberg, 180–92. Oxford, UK: Clarendon Press, 1987.

Gagan, David. "For Patients of Moderate Means: The Transformation of Ontario's Public General Hospitals, 1880-1950," *Canadian Historical Review,* 70 (1989): 151–79.

———. *"A Necessity among Us": The Owen Sound General and Marine Hospital, 1891–1915.* Toronto, ON: University of Toronto Press, 1990.

Gagan, David, and Rosemary Gagan. *For Patients of Moderate Means: A Social History of the Voluntary Public General Hospital in Canada, 1890–1950.* Montreal, QC: McGill-Queen's University Press, 2002.

Gagnon, Mona-Josée. "Les Centrales Syndicales et la Condition Feminine." *Maintenant* 140 (1974): 25–27.

Gidney, R.D., and W.P.J. Millar. "From Voluntarism to State Schooling: The Creation of the Public School System in Ontario." *Ontario History* 66, 4 (1985): 443–73.

Glassford, Larry A. *Reaction and Reform: The Politics of the Conservative Party under R.B. Bennett, 1927–1938.* Toronto, ON: University of Toronto Press, 1938.

Gleason, Mona Lee. *Normalizing the Ideal: Psychology, Schooling, and the Family in Postwar Canada*. Toronto, ON: University of Toronto Press, 1999.

Godfrey, W.G. "Private and Government Funding: The Case of the Moncton Hospital, 1898–1953." *Acadiensis* 31, 1 (Autumn 2001): 3–34.

Gordon, Linda. *Heroes of Their Own Lives: The Politics and History of Family Violence: Boston, 1880–1960*. New York, NY: Viking, 1988.

———. "The Welfare State: Towards a Socialist-Feminist Perspective." In *Socialist Register, 1990*. Edited by Ralph Miliband and Leo Panitch. London, UK: Merlin, 1990.

———. *Pitied but Not Entitled: Single Mothers and the History of Welfare, 1890–1935*. Boston, MA: Free Press, 1994.

Gotlieb, Marc J. "George Drew and the Dominion-Provincial Conference on Reconstruction of 1945–6." *Canadian Historical Review* 66, 1 (1985): 27–47.

Gough, Ian. *The Political Economy of the Welfare State*. London, UK: Macmillan, 1979.

Guildford, Janet. "The End of the Poor Law: Public Welfare Reform in Nova Scotia before the Canada Assistance Plan." In *Mothers of the Municipality: Women, Work, and Social Policy in Post-1945 Halifax*. Edited by Judith Fingard and Janet Guildford, 49–75. Toronto, ON: University of Toronto Press, 2005.

Granatstein, Jack. *The Politics of Survival: The Conservative Party of Canada, 1939–1945*. Toronto, ON: University of Toronto Press, 1967.

Grant, H.M. "Solving the Labour Problem at Imperial Oil: Welfare Capitalism in the Canadian Petroleum Industry, 1919–1929." *Labour/Le Travail* 41 (1998): 69–96.

Greer, Allan. *The Patriots and the People: The Rebellion of 1837 in Rural Lower Canada*. Toronto, ON: University of Toronto Press, 1993.

———. *The People of New France*. Toronto, ON: University of Toronto Press, 1997.

Grescoe, Paul. "A Nation's Disgrace." In *Health and Canadian Society: Sociological Perspectives*. 2nd ed. Edited by David Coburn, Carl D'Arcy, George M. Torrance, and Peter New, 127–40. Toronto, ON: Fitzhenry and Whiteside, 1987.

Guest, Dennis. *The Emergence of Social Security in Canada*. 3rd ed. Vancouver, BC: University of British Columbia Press, 1997.

Guildford, Janet, and Suzanne Morton, eds. *Separate Spheres: Women's Worlds in the Nineteenth-Century Maritimes*. Fredericton, NB: Acadiensis Press, 1994.

Haddow, Rodney S. *Poverty Reform in Canada, 1958–1978: State and Class Influences on Policy-Making*. Montreal, QC: McGill-Queen's University Press, 1993.

———. "Canadian Organized Labour and the Guaranteed Annual Income." In *Continuities and Discontinuities: The Political Economy of Social Welfare and Labour Market Policy in Canada*. Edited by Andrew F. Johnson, Steven McBride, and P.J. Smith, 350–66. Toronto, ON: University of Toronto Press, 1994.

Hagopian, John. "Debunking the Public Health Myth: Municipal Politics and Class Conflict During the Galt, Ontario Waterworks Campaigns, 1888–1890." *Labour/Le Travail* 39 (1997): 39–68.

Haig-Brown, Celia. *Resistance and Renewal: Surviving the Indian Residential School*. Vancouver, BC: Tillacum Library, Arsenal Press, 1988.

Hamilton, Ian. *The Children's Crusade: The Story of the Company of Young Canadians*. Toronto, ON: P. Martin, 1973.

Hamilton, Roberta. *Feudal Society and Colonization: The Historiography of New France*. Gananoque, QC: Langdale Press, 1988.

Hansen, Phillip. *Taxing Illusions: Taxation, Democracy and Embedded Political Theory*. Toronto, ON: Fernwood, 2003.

Harrison, Trevor, and Gordon Laxer, eds. *The Trojan Horse: Alberta and the Future of Canada*. Montreal, QC: Black Rose, 1995.

Heidenreich, Conrad. *Huronia: A History and Geography of the Huron Indians 1600–1650*. Toronto, ON: McClelland and Stewart, 1971.

Heron, Craig, and Robert Storey. *On the Job: Confronting the Labour Process in Canada*. Montreal, QC: McGill-Queen's University Press, 1986.

Holter, Harriet, ed. *Patriarchy in a Welfare Society*. Oslo, Norway: Universitets-forlaget, 1984.

Hopkins, J. Castell, ed. *Canadian Annual Review of Public Affairs*. Toronto, ON: Annual Review Publishing Company, 1914.

Houston, Susan, and Alison Prentice. *Schooling and Scholars in Nineteenth-Century Ontario*. Toronto, ON: University of Toronto Press, 1988.

Howard, Victor. *"We Were the Salt of the Earth!" The On-to-Ottawa Trek and the Regina Riot*. Regina, SK: Canadian Plains Research Center, 1985.

Howell, Colin D. "Medical Science and Social Criticism: Alexander Peter Reid and the Ideological Origins of the Welfare State in Canada." In

Canadian Health Care and the State. Edited by C. David Naylor, 16–37. Montreal, QC: McGill-Queen's University Press, 1992.

Hum, Derek P.J. *Federalism and the Poor: A Review of the Canada Assistance Plan.* Toronto, ON: Ontario Economic Council, 1983.

Hunter, Garson. "The Problem of Child Poverty in Canada." In *Canadian Social Policy: Issues and Perspectives.* 3rd ed. Edited by Anne Westhues, 29–49. Waterloo, ON: Wilfrid Laurier University Press, 2003.

Iacobacci, Mario, and Mario Seccareccia. "Full Employment Versus Income Maintenance: Some Reflections on the Macroeconomic and Structural Implications of a Guaranteed Income Program for Canada." *Studies in Political Economy* 28 (Spring 1989): 137–73.

Irving, Allan. "The Development of a Provincial Welfare State: British Columbia, 1900–1939." In *The "Benevolent" State: The Growth of Welfare in Canada.* Edited by Allan Moscovitch and Jim Albert, 155–74. Toronto, ON: Garamond, 1987.

———. "'The Master Principle of Administering Relief': Jeremy Bentham, Sir Francis Bond Head and the Principle of Less Eligibility in Upper Canada." *Canadian Review of Social Policy* 23 (1989): 13–18.

Jacobs, Lawrence R. *The Health of Nations: Public Opinion and the Making of American and British Health Policy.* Ithaca, NY: Cornell University Press, 1993.

Jaenen, Cornelius J. "Amerindian Views of French Culture in the Seventeenth Century." In *Out of the Background: Readings on Canadian Native History.* Edited by Robin Fisher and Kenneth Coates, 102–33. Toronto, ON: Copp Clark Pitman, 1988.

Jean, Dominique. "Family Allowances and Family Autonomy: Quebec Families Encounter the Welfare State, 1945–1955." In *Canadian Family History: Selected Readings.* Edited by Bettina Bradbury, 401–37. Toronto, ON: Copp Clark Pitman, 1992.

Jenson, Jane. "Both Friend and Foe: Women and State Welfare." In *Becoming Visible: Women in European History.* 2nd ed. Edited by Renate Bridenthal, Claudia Koonz, and Susan Stuard, 535–56. Boston. MA: Houghton Mifflin, 1987.

———. "Family Policy, Child Care and Social Solidarity: The Case of Quebec." In *Changing Child Care Advocacy and Policy in Canada.* Edited by Susan Prentice, 39–62. Halifax, NS: Fernwood, 2001.

Jenson, Jane, and Ruth Kantrow. "Labor Market and Family Policy in France: An Intersecting Complex for Dealing with Poverty." In *The Feminization of Poverty: Only in America?* Edited by Gertrude Schaffner Goldberg and Eleanor Kremen, 107–28. New York, NY: Greenwood, 1990.

Johnson, A.W. "Social Policy in Canada: The Past as It Conditions the Present." In *The Future of Social Welfare Systems in Canada and the United Kingdom.* Edited by Shirley B. Seward, 1–33. Halifax, NS: Institute for Research on Public Policy, 1987.

Johnson, J.K. "'Claims of Equity and Justice': Petitions and Politicians in Upper Canada 1815–1840." *Histoire sociale/Social History* 28, 55 (1995): 219–40.

Johnson, Laura C., and Janice Dineen. *The Kin Trade: The Day Care Crisis in Canada.* Toronto, ON: McGraw-Hill Ryerson, 1981.

Johnson, Leo. "Land Policy, Population Growth and Social Structure in the Home District, 1793–1851." *Ontario History* 63,1 (March 1971): 41–60.

Jones, Andrew, and Leonard Rutman. *In the Children's Aid: J.J. Kelso and Child Welfare in Ontario.* Toronto, ON: University of Toronto Press, 1989.

Jones, Jacqueline. *Labor of Love, Labor of Sorrow: Black Women, Work, and the Family from Slavery to the Present.* New York, NY: Vintage, 1985.

Kalecki, Michael. *Essays on the Dynamics of the Capitalist Economies.* Cambridge, UK: Cambridge University Press, 1971.

Kelley, Ninette, and Michael Trebilcock. *The Making of the Mosaic: A History of Canadian Immigration Policy.* Toronto, ON: University of Toronto Press, 1998.

Kelm, Mary-Ellen. *Colonizing Bodies: Aboriginal Health and Healing in British Columbia, 1900–1950.* Vancouver, BC: University of British Columbia Press, 1998.

Keshen, Jeff. "Getting It Right the Second Time Around: The Reintegration of Canadian Veterans of World War 2." In *The Veterans Charter and Post-World War II Canada.* Edited by Peter Neary and J.L. Granatstein, 62–84. Montreal, QC: McGill-Queen's University Press, 1998.

Kesslering, Margaret. "Canada's Backward Thinking on Day Nurseries." *Chatelaine,* April 1966, 67–74.

Keynes, John Maynard. *General Theory of Employment, Interest and Money.* 1936. Reprint, London: Macmillan, 1973.

Kitchen, Brigitte. "The Marsh Report Revisited." *Journal of Canadian Studies* 21, 2 (Summer 1986): 38–48.

——. "The Introduction of Family Allowances in Canada." In *The Benevolent State: The Growth of Welfare in Canada.* Edited by Allan Moscovitch and Jim Albert, 221–41. Toronto, ON: Garamond, 1987.

Klaus, Alisa. *Every Child a Lion: The Origins of Maternal and Infant Health Policy in the United States and France, 1890–1920.* Ithaca. NY: Cornell University Press, 1993.

Krashinsky, Michael. *Day Care and Public Policy in Ontario.* Toronto, ON: Ontario Economic Council, 1977.

Lachance, André. *Vivre, aimer et mourir en Nouvelle-France : la vie quotidienne aux xvii è et xviii è siècles.* Montreal, QC: Libre Expression, 2000.

Lake, Marilyn. "A Revolution in the Family: The Challenge and Contradictions of Maternal Citizenship in Australia." In *Mothers of a New World: Maternalist Politics and the Origins of Welfare States.* Edited by Seth Koven and Sonya Michel, 378–95. New York, NY: Routledge, 1993.

——. "The Independence of Women and the Brotherhood of Man: Debates in the Labour Movement Over Equal Pay and Motherhood Endowments in the 1920s." *Labour History* 63 (1992): 1–24.

Land, Hilary. "The Introduction of Family Allowances: An Act of Historic Justice?" In *Change, Choice, and Conflict in Social Policy.* Edited by Phoebe Hall, Hilary Land, Roy Parker, and Adrian Webb, 159–230. London, UK: Heinemann, 1975.

Landau, Julie, and Margaret Conrad. "Dorise Nielsen: A Tribute." *Atlantis* 6, 2 (1981): 138–9.

Leacy, F.H. ed. *Historical Statistics of Canada.* 2nd ed. Ottawa, ON: Statistics Canada, 1983.

Leah, Ronnie. "Women's Labour Force Participation and Day Care Cutbacks in Ontario." *Atlantis* 7, 1 (1981): 36–44.

Leaman, Christopher. *The Collapse of Welfare Reform: Political Institutions, Policy and the Poor in Canada and the United States.* Cambridge, MA: MIT Press, 1980.

Lepp, Annalee, David Millar, and Barbara Roberts. "Women in the Winnipeg Garment Industry, 1950s–1970s." In *First Days, Fighting Days: Women in Manitoba History.* Edited by Mary Kinnear, 149–72. Regina, SK: Canadian Plains Research Centre, 1987.

Lévesque, Andrée. "Deviants Anonymous: Single Mothers at the Hôpital de la Miséricorde in Montreal 1929–1939." In *Rethinking Canada: The Promise of Women's History.* 2nd ed. Edited by Veronica Strong-Boag and Anita Clair Fellman, 322–336. Toronto: Copp Clark Pitman, 1991. First published in *Historical Papers* 63 (1984):168–84.

——. *La norme et les déviantes: des femmes au Québec pendant l'entre-deux-guerres.* Montreal, QC: Éditions du rémue-ménage, 1989.

Lewis, Jane. "Gender and the Development of Welfare Regimes." *Journal of European Social Policy* 2 (1992): 159–73.

———. "Dealing with Dependency: State Practices and Social Realities, 1870–1945." In *Women's Welfare: Women's Rights*. Edited by Jane Lewis, 17–37. London, UK: Croom Helm, 1983.

———. *The Politics of Motherhood: Child and Maternal Welfare in England, 1900–1939*. Montreal, QC: McGill-Queen's University Press, 1980.

Lewis, Jane, and Gertrude Astrom. "Equality, Difference, and State Welfare: Labor Market and Family Policies in Sweden." *Feminist Studies* 18, 1 (1992): 59–87.

Lindbeck, Assar. *Swedish Economic Policy*. London, UK: Macmillan, 1975

Linteau, Paul-André, René Durocher, and Jean-Claude Robert. *Quebec: A History 1867–1929*. Toronto, ON: James Lorimer, 1983.

Little, Margaret Hillyard. *No Car, No Radio, No Liquor Permit: The Moral Regulation of Single Mothers in Ontario, 1920–1997*. Toronto, ON: Oxford University Press, 1998.

———. "The Introduction of Mothers' Pensions in B.C." In *Family Matters: Papers in Post-Confederation Family History*. Edited by Lori Chambers and Edgar-André Montigny, 91–114. Toronto, ON: Canadian Scholars' Press, 1998.

———. "He Said, She Said: The Role of Gossip in Determining Eligibility for Mothers' Allowance." *Journal of Policy History* 11, 4 (1999): 433–54.

Loxley, John. *Alternative Budgets: Budgeting as If People Mattered*. Halifax, NS: Fernwood, 2003.

Lund, L. Richard. "Income Maintenance, Insurance Principles and the 'Liberal 1960s': Canada's Unemployment Program, 1941–1971." In *Canada at the Crossroads? The Critical 1960s*. Edited by Gustav Schmidt and Jack L. Granatstein. Bochum, Germany: Universitatsverlag Dr. N. Brockmeyer, 1994.

———. "'Fishing for Stamps': The Origins and Development of Unemployment Insurance for Canada's Commercial Fisheries, 1941–71." *Journal of the Canadian Historical Association*, New Series 6 (1995): 179–208.

Lux, Maureen K. *Medicine that Walks: Disease, Medicine, and Canadian Plains Native People, 1880-1940*. Toronto, ON: University of Toronto Press, 2001.

Luxton, Meg. "Taking on the Double Day: Housewives as a Reserve Army of Labour." *Atlantis* 7, 1 (1981): 12–32.

MacDowell, Laurel Sefton. "Relief Camp Workers in Ontario During the Great Depression of the 1930s." *Canadian Historical Review* 76, 2 (1995): 205–28.

MacNaughton, Colleen. "Promoting Clean Water in Nineteenth-Century Public Policy: Professors, Preachers, and Polliwogs in Kingston, Ontario." *Social History* 32, 63 (1999): 49–61.

Maioni, Antonia. *Parting at the Crossroads: The Emergence of Health Insurance in the United States and Canada*. Princeton, NJ: Princeton University Press, 1998.

Malcolmson, Patricia. "The Poor in Kingston, 1815–1850." In *To Preserve and Defend: Essays on Kingston in the Nineteenth Century*. Edited by Gerald Tulchinsky, 281–97. Montreal, QC: McGill-Queen's University Press, 1976.

Marchildon, Gregory, Tom McIntosh, and Pierre-Gerlier Forest, eds. *The Fiscal Sustainability of Health Care in Canada: The Romanow Papers*, Volume 1. Toronto, ON: University of Toronto Press, 2004.

Marks, Lynne. "Indigent Committees and Ladies Benevolent Societies: Intersections of Public and Private Poor Relief in Late-Nineteenth-Century Small Town Ontario." *Studies in Political Economy* 47 (Summer 1995): 61–87.

Marsh, Leonard. *Report on Social Security for Canada, 1943*. Toronto, ON: University of Toronto Press, 1975.

Marshall, Dominique. *Aux origines sociales de l'État-providence : familles québécoises, obligation scolaire et allocations familiales 1940-1955*. Montreal, QC: Les Presses de l'Université de Montréal, 1998. An English translation is Dominique Marshall, *The Social Origins of the Welfare State: Quebec Families, Compulsory Education, and Family Allowances, 1940–1955*, translated by Nicola Doone Danby. Waterloo, ON: Wilfrid Laurier University Press, 2006.

Maslove, Allan M. *The Pattern of Taxation in Canada*. Ottawa, ON: Information Canada, 1972.

Mathias, Philip. *Forced Growth: Five Studies of Government Involvement in the Development of Canada*. Toronto, ON: J. Lewis and Samuel, 1978.

McCallum, Margaret E. "Corporate Welfarism in Canada, 1919–39." *Canadian Historical Review* 71 (1990): 46–79.

McCutcheon, Sean. *Electric Rivers: The Story of the James Bay Project*. Montreal, QC: Black Rose Books, 1991.

McIntosh, Tom, Pierre-Gerlier Forest and Gregory P. Marchilton, eds. *The Governance of Health Care in Canada. Romanow Papers, Volume 3.* Toronto, ON: University of Toronto Press, 2004.

McLaren, Angus. *Our Own Master Race: Eugenics in Canada, 1885–1945.* Toronto, ON: McClelland and Stewart, 1990.

McPherson, Kathryn. *Bedside Matters: The Transformation of Canadian Nursing, 1900–1990.* Toronto, ON: Oxford University Press, 1996.

McRoberts, Kenneth. *Quebec Social Change and Political Crisis.* 3rd ed. Toronto, ON: Oxford University Press, 1993.

Mendelson, Michael. "Can We Reform Canada's Income System?" In *The Future of Social Welfare Systems in Canada and the United Kingdom.* Edited by Shirley B. Seward, 117–46. Halifax, NS: Institute for Research on Public Policy, 1987.

Menzies, S. June. *New Directions for Public Policy: A Position Paper on the One-Parent Family.* Ottawa, ON: Canadian Advisory Committee on the Status of Women, 1976.

Michel, Sonya. *Children's Interests/Mothers' Rights: The Shaping of America's Child Care Policy.* New Haven, CT: Yale University Press, 1999.

Midwinter, Eric. *The Development of Social Welfare in Britain.* Buckingham, UK: Open University Press, 1994.

Miller, J.R. *Shingwauk's Vision: A History of Native Residential Schools.* Toronto, ON: University of Toronto Press, 1996.

Miron, John R. *Housing in Postwar Canada: Demographic Change, Household Formation, and Housing Demand.* Montreal, QC: McGill-Queen's University Press, 1988.

Mishra, Ramesh. *The Welfare State in Crisis: Social Thought and Social Change.* Brighton, UK: Wheatsheaf, 1984.

Mitchinson, Wendy. "Early Women's Organizations and Social Reform: Prelude to the Welfare State." In *The Benevolent State: The Growth of Welfare in Canada*, edited Alan Moscovitch and Jim Albert, 77–92. Toronto, ON: Garamond, 1987.

———. *The Nature of Their Bodies: Women and Their Doctors in Victorian Canada.* Toronto, ON: University of Toronto Press, 1991.

Moffatt, Ken. *A Poetics of Social Work: Personal Agency and Social Transformation in Canada, 1920–1939.* Toronto, ON: University of Toronto Press, 2001.

Mombourquette, Duane. "'An Inalienable Right': The CCF and Rapid Health Care Reform, 1944–1948." In *Social Welfare Policy in Canada: Historical Readings.* Edited by Raymond B. Blake and Jeff Keshen, 293–312. Toronto, ON: Copp Clark, 1995.

Montigny, Edgar-André. *Foisted Upon the Government? State Responsibilities, Family Obligations, and the Care of the Dependent Aged in Late-Nineteenth-Century Ontario*. Montreal, QC: McGill-Queen's University Press, 1997.

Moogk, Peter N. "'Les Petits Sauvages': The Children of Eighteenth-Century New France." In *Childhood and Family in Canadian History*. Edited by Joy Parr, 17–43. Toronto, ON: McClelland and Stewart, 1982.

Moran, James E. *Committed to the State Asylum: Insanity and Society in Nineteenth-Century Quebec and Ontario*. Montreal, QC: McGill-Queen's University Press, 2000.

Morgan, Cecilia. *Public Men and Virtuous Women: The Gendered Language of Religion and Politics in Upper Canada, 1791–1850*. Toronto, ON: University of Toronto Press, 1996.

Morrison, Terrence R. "The Child and Urban Social Reform in Late-Nineteenth-Century Ontario." PhD diss., University of Toronto, 1971.

———. "'Their Proper Sphere': Feminism, the Family, and Child-Centred Social Reform in Ontario, 1875–1900." Part 1, *Ontario History* 68, 1 (1976): 45–64.

———. "'Their Proper Sphere': Feminism, the Family, and Child-Centred Social Reform in Ontario, 1875–1900." Part 2, *Ontario History* 68, 2 (1976): 65–74.

Morton, Desmond. *The New Democrats 1961–1986: The Politics of Change*. Toronto, ON: Copp Clark Pitman, 1986.

———. *Fight or Pay: Soldiers' Families in the Great War*. Vancouver, BC: University of British Columbia Press, 2004.

Morton, Desmond, and Glenn Wright. *Winning the Second Battle: Canadian Veterans and the Return to Civilian Life, 1915–1930*. Toronto, ON: University of Toronto Press, 1987.

Morton, Suzanne. *Ideal Surroundings: Domestic Life in a Working-Class Suburb in the 1920s*. Toronto, ON: University of Toronto Press, 1995.

———. "From Infant Homes to Daycare: Child Care in Halifax." In *Mothers of the Municipality: Women, Work, and Social Policy in Post-1945 Halifax*. Edited by Judith Fingard and Janet Guildford, 169–88. Toronto, ON: University of Toronto Press, 2005.

Moscovitch, Allan. "Housing: Who Pays? Who Profits?" In *Inequality: Essays on the Political Economy of Social Welfare*. Edited by Allan Moscovitch and Glenn Drover, 314–47. Toronto, ON: University of Toronto Press, 1981.

Myles, John. *Old Age in the Welfare State: The Political Economy of Public Pensions*. Boston, MA: Little, Brown and Company, 1984.

Neatby, H. Blair. *The Politics of Chaos: Canada in the Thirties*. Toronto, ON: Macmillan, 1972.

Neysmith, Sheila, ed. *Restructuring Caring Labour: Discourse, State Practice and Everyday Life*. Toronto, ON: Oxford University Press, 2000.

———. "Caring and Aging: Exposing the Policy Issues." In *Canadian Social Policy: Issues and Perspectives*. 3rd ed. Edited by Anne Westhues, 182–99. Waterloo, ON: Wilfrid Laurier University Press, 2003.

Noel, Jan. "'Femmes Fortes' and the Montreal Poor in the Early Nineteenth Century." In *Canadian Women: A Reader*. Edited by Wendy Mitchinson et al., 68–85. Toronto, ON: Harcourt Brace, 1996.

Northcott, Herbert C., and Donna M. Wilson. *Dying and Death in Canada* Toronto, ON: Garamond, 2001.

Norrie, Kenneth H. "Some Comments on Prairie Economic Alienation." *Canadian Public Policy* 2, 2 (Spring 1976): 211–24.

Norrie, Kenneth, and Douglas Owram. *A History of the Canadian Economy*. Toronto, ON: Harcourt Brace Jovanovich, 1991.

O'Brien, Martin, and Sue Penna. *Theorising Welfare: Enlightenment and Modern Society*. London, UK: Sage, 1998.

O'Connor, James. *The Fiscal Crisis of the State*. New York: St. Martin's, 1973

Offe, Claus. *Contradictions of the Welfare State*. London, UK: Hutchinson, 1984.

———. *Disorganized Capitalism: Contemporary Transformations of Work and Politics*. Cambridge, MA: MIT Press, 1985.

Oliver, Peter. "'Terror to Evil-Doers': Prisons and Punishment in Nineteenth-Century Ontario*. Toronto, ON: University of Toronto Press, 1998.

Orloff, Ann Shona. "The Political Origins of America's Welfare State." In *The Politics of Social Policy in the United States*. Edited by Ann Shona Orloff and Theda Skocpol, 37–79. Princeton, NJ: Princeton University Press, 1988.

Ormsby, Margaret A. *British Columbia: A History*. Vancouver, BC: Macmillan, 1958.

Ouellet, Fernand. *Lower Canada, 1791–1840: Social Change and Nationalism*. Toronto, ON: McClelland and Stewart, 1980.

Owram, Doug. *The Government Generation: Canadian Intellectuals and the State 1900–1945*. Toronto, ON: University of Toronto Press, 1986.

———. *Born at the Right Time: A History of the Baby Boom Generation*. Toronto, ON: University of Toronto Press, 1996.

Pal, Leslie. *State, Class and Bureaucracy: Canadian Unemployment Insurance and Public Policy*. Montreal, QC: McGill-Queen's University Press, 1988.

Palmer, Bryan D. *Working-Class Experience: Rethinking the History of Canadian Labour, 1800–1991*. Toronto, ON: McClelland and Stewart, 1992.

Parr, Joy. *Labouring Children: British Immigrant Apprentices to Canada, 1869–1924*. Montreal, QC: McGill-Queen's University Press, 1980.

Pascall, Gillian. *Social Policy: A Feminist Analysis*. London, UK: Tavistock, 1986.

Pearce, Diana M. "Toil and Trouble: Women Workers and Unemployment Compensation." *Signs* 10 (1985): 435–59.

Penner, Norman. *From Protest to Power: Social Democracy in Canada, 1900–Present*. Toronto, ON: James Lorimer, 1992.

Pentland, H. Clare. *Labour and Capital in Canada, 1650–1860*. Toronto: James Lorimer, 1981.

Pierson, Ruth Roach. "'Home Aide': A Solution to Women's Unemployment After World War II," *Atlantis* 2, 2 (Spring 1977): 85–97.

———. *"They're Still Women After All": The Second World War and Canadian Womanhood*. Toronto, ON: McClelland and Stewart, 1986.

———. "Gender and the Unemployment Insurance Debates in Canada, 1934–40." *Labour/Le Travail* 25 (1990): 77–103.

Pitsula, James M. "The Treatment of Tramps in Late Nineteenth-Century Toronto." *Historical Papers* 59 (1980): 116–32.

Piva, Michael J. "The Workmen's Compensation Movement in Ontario." *Ontario History* 67 (1975): 39–56.

Piven, Frances Fox, and Richard A. Cloward. "Welfare Doesn't Shore Up Traditional Family Roles: A Reply to Linda Gordon." *Social Research* 55 (1988): 631–47.

Poen, Monte M. *Harry S. Truman Versus the Medical Lobby: The Genesis of Medicare*. Columbia, MO: University of Missouri Press, 1996.

Porter, Ann. "Women and Income Security in the Postwar Period: The Case of Unemployment Insurance, 1945–1962." *Labour/Le Travail* 31 (1993): 111–44.

———. *Gendered States: Women, Unemployment Insurance, and the Political Economy of the Welfare State in Canada, 1945–1997*. Toronto, ON: University of Toronto Press, 2003.

Prentice, Alison. "The Feminization of Teaching." In *The Neglected Majority: Essays in Canadian Women's History*. Edited by Susan Mann Trofimenkoff and Alison Prentice, 49–65. Toronto, ON: McClelland and Stewart, 1977.

Prentice, Alison, et al. *Canadian Women: A History*. Toronto, ON: Harcourt Brace Jovanovich, 1988.

Prentice, Susan, ed. *Changing Child Care: Five Decades of Child Care Advocacy and Policy in Canada*. Halifax, NS: Fernwood, 2001.

———. "Workers, Mothers, Reds: Toronto's Postwar Daycare Fight." *Studies in Political Economy* 30 (1989): 115–41.

Purdy, Sean. "'Ripped Off' by the System: Housing Policy, Poverty, and Territorial Stigmatization in Regent Park Housing Project, 1951–1991." *Labour/ Le Travail*, 52 (2003): 45–108.

Puttee, Alan, ed. *Federalism, Democracy and Disability Policy in Canada*. Montreal, QC: McGill-Queen's University Press, 2002.

Quadagno, Jill. *The Color of Welfare: How Racism Undermined the War on Poverty*. New York, NY: Oxford University Press, 1994.

Quinn, Herbert F. *The Union Nationale: A Study in Quebec Nationalism*. Toronto, ON: University of Toronto Press, 1963.

Rands, Stan. "Recollections: The CCF in Saskatchewan." In *Western Canadian Politics: The Radical Tradition*. Edited by Donald C. Kerr, 58–64. Edmonton, AB: NeWest, 1981.

Ray, Arthur J. "Periodic Shortages, Native Welfare, and the Hudson's Bay Company, 1670-1930." In *The Subarctic Fur Trade: Native Social and Economic Adaptations*. Edited by Shepard Krech III, 1–20. Vancouver, BC: University of British Columbia Press, 1984. Also published in *Out of the Background: Readings on Canadian Native History*. Edited by Ken S. Coates and Robin Fisher, 83–101. Toronto, ON: Copp Clark, 1996.

———. *I Haved Lived Here Since the World Began: An Illustrated History of Canada's Native People*. Toronto, ON: Lester/Key Porter, 1996.

Ray, Arthur, and Donald Freeman. *Give Us Good Measure: An Economic Analysis of Relations between the Indians and the Hudson's Bay Company before 1763*. Toronto, ON: University of Toronto Press, 1978.

Ray, Arthur, Jim Miller, and Frank Tough. *Bounty and Benevolence: A History of Saskatchewan Treaties*. Montreal, QC: McGill-Queen's University Press, 2000.

Redden, Candace Johnson. *Health Care, Entitlement, and Citizenship*. Toronto: University of Toronto Press, 2002.

Renouf, Simon. "Chipping Away at Medicare: 'Rome Wasn't Sacked in a Day.'" In *The Trojan Horse: Alberta and the Future of Canada*. Edited by Trevor Harrison and Gordon Laxer, 223–38. Montreal, QC: Black Rose, 1995.

Riches, Graham. *Food Banks and the Welfare Crisis*. Ottawa: Canadian Council on Social Development, 1986.

Riley, Denise. "'The Free Mothers': Pronatalism and Working Women in Industry at the End of the Last War in Britain." *History Workshop* 11 (1981): 59–118.

Robertson, Brian. *Capital, Labor, and State: The Battle for American Labor Markets from the Civil War to the New Deal.* Lanham, MD: Rowman and Littlefield, 2000.

Robeson, Virginia R., ed. *Upper Canada in the 1830s.* Toronto: Ontario Institute for Studies in Education, 1977.

Roe, Jill. "The End Is Where We Start From: Women and Welfare Since 1901." In *Women, Social Welfare and the State in Australia.* Edited by Bettina Cass and Cora V. Baldock, 1–19. London, UK: Allen and Unwin, 1983.

Rooke, Patricia T., and R.L. Schnell. *Discarding the Asylum: From Child Rescue to the Welfare State in English Canada (1800–1950).* Landham, MD: University Press of America, 1983.

———. *No Bleeding Heart: Charlotte Whitton, A Feminist on the Right.* Vancouver, BC: University of British Columbia Press, 1987.

Rose, Albert. *Regent Park: A Study in Slum Clearance.* Toronto, ON: University of Toronto Press, 1958.

———. *Canadian Housing Policies 1935–1980.* Scarborough, ON: Butterworth, 1980.

Rose, Nancy E. "Gender, Race, and the Welfare State: Government Work Programs from the 1930s to the Present." *Feminist Studies* 19 (1993): 319–42.

Rosenthal, Marguerite G. "Sweden: Promise and Paradox." In *The Feminization of Poverty: Only in America?* Edited by Gertrude Schaffner Goldberg and Eleanor Kremen, 129–55. New York, NY: Greenwood, 1990.

Ruddel, David-Thiery, and Marc La France, "Québec: 1785–1840: problèmes de croissance d'une ville coloniale." *Histoire sociale/Social History* 18, 36 (1985): 315–33.

Rutherford, Paul, ed. *Saving the Canadian City: The First Phase, 1880–1920.* Toronto, ON: University of Toronto Press, 1974.

Ruyle, Eugene. "Slavery, Surplus and Stratification on the Northwest Coast: The Ethnogenetics of an Incipient Stratification System." *Current Anthropology* 14, 5 (1973): 603–17.

Sangster, Joan. *Dreams of Equality: Women on the Canadian Left, 1920–1950.* Toronto, ON: McClelland and Stewart, 1989.

———. *Girl Trouble! Female Delinquency in English Canada.* Toronto, ON: Between the Lines, 2002.

――. *Regulating Girls and Women: Women, Family and the Law in Ontario.* Toronto, ON: Oxford University Press, 2001.

Sagard, Father Gabriel. *The Long Journey to the Country of the Huron.* Edited by George M. Wrong. Toronto, ON: Champlain Society, 1939.

Sassoon, Anne Showstack. "Women's New Social Role: Contradictions of the Welfare State." In *Women and the State: The Shifting Boundaries of Public and Private.* Edited by Anne Showstack Sassoon. London, UK: Hutchinson, 1987.

Sayegh, Kamal S. *Housing: A Canadian Perspective.* Ottawa, ON: Academy Books, 1987.

Saywell, John T. *Housing Canadians: Essays on the History of Residential Construction in Canada.* Ottawa, ON: Economic Council of Canada, 1975.

Schaffner, Gertrude, and Eleanor Goldberg, eds. *The Feminization of Poverty: Only in America?* New York, NY: Greenwood, 1990.

Schulz, Patricia Vandebelt. "Day Care in Canada: 1850–1962." In *Good Day Care: Fighting For It, Getting It, Keeping It.* Edited by Kathleen Gallagher Ross, 137–58. Toronto, ON: Women's Press, 1978.

Scott, Bruce. "A Place in the Sun: The Industrial Council at Massey-Harris, 1919–1929." *Labour/Le Travailleur* 1 (1976): 158–92.

Seth, Ram P., and Janet J. Dickson. *Evaluation of the Housing Programmes Embodied in the Prince Edward Island Development Plan.* Halifax, NS: Institute of Public Affairs, Dalhousie University, 1974.

Sharp, Paul F. *Whoop-Up Country: The Canadian-American West, 1865–1885.* Norman, OK: University of Oklahoma Press, 1973.

Shewell, Hugh. "'Bitterness Behind Every Smiling Face': Community Development and Canada's First Nations, 1954–1968." *Canadian Historical Review* 83, 1 (2002): 58–84.

――. *"Enough to Keep Them Alive": Indian Welfare in Canada, 1873–1965.* Toronto, ON: University of Toronto Press, 2004.

Simard, Monique. "Coalition Politics: The Quebec Labour Movement." *Socialist Studies*, 4 (1988).

Simmons, Christina. "'Helping the Poorer Sisters': The Women of the Jost Mission Halifax, 1905–1945." *Acadiensis* 14 (1984): 3–27.

Smith, Dorothy E. *The Conceptual Practice of Power: A Feminist Sociology of Knowledge.* Toronto, ON: University of Toronto Press, 1990.

Snell, James G. *In the Shadow of the Law: Divorce in Canada, 1900–1939.* Toronto, ON: University of Toronto Press, 1991.

———. "The Newfoundland Old Age Pension Program, 1911–1949. *Acadiensis* 13, 1 (Autumn 1993): 86–109.

———. *The Citizen's Wage: The State and the Elderly in Canada, 1900–1951.* Toronto, ON: University of Toronto Press, 1996.

Splane, R.B. *Social Welfare in Ontario, 1791–1893: A Study of Public Welfare Administration.* Toronto, ON: University of Toronto Press, 1965.

Starr, Paul. *The Social Transformation of American Medicine.* New York, NY: Basic Books, 1982.

Steinfels, Margaret O'Brien. *Who's Minding the Children? The History and Politics of Day Care in America.* New York: Simon and Schuster, 1973.

Stewart, Stormie. "The Elderly Poor in Rural Ontario: Inmates of the Wellington County House of Industry, 1877–1907." *Journal of the Canadian Historical Association,* New Series 3 (1992): 217–33.

Storey, Robert. "Unionization Versus Corporate Welfare: The Dofasco Way." *Labour/Le Travailleur* 12 (1983): 7–42.

Strange, Carolyn, and Tina Loo. *Law and Moral Regulation in Canada, 1867–1939.* Toronto, ON: University of Toronto Press, 1997.

Strikwerda, Eric J. "From Short-Term Emergency to Long-Term Crisis: Public Works Projects in Saskatoon, 1929–1932." *Prairie Forum* 26, 2 (2001): 169–86.

Strong-Boag, Veronica. *The New Day Recalled: Lives of Girls and Women in English Canada, 1919-1939.* Toronto, ON: Copp Clark Pitman, 1988.

———. "Home Dreams: Women and the Suburban Experiment in Canada, 1945–60." *Canadian Historical Review* 72, 4 (1991): 471–504.

———. "Canada's Wage-Earning Wives and the Construction of the Middle Class, 1945–60." *Journal of Canadian Studies* 29, 3 (1994): 5–25.

———. "'Wages for Housework': Mothers' Allowances and the Beginnings of Social Security in Canada." In *Social Welfare Policy in Canada: Historical Readings.* Edited by Raymond B. Blake and Jeff Keshen, 122–36. Toronto, ON: Copp Clark, 1995.

Struthers, James. *No Fault of Their Own: Unemployment and the Canadian Welfare State, 1914-1941.* Toronto, ON: University of Toronto Press, 1983.

———. "A Profession in Crisis: Charlotte Whitton and Canadian Social Work in the 1930s." In *The "Benevolent" State: The Growth of Welfare in Canada.* Edited by Allan Moscovitch and Jim Albert, 111–25. Toronto, ON: Garamond, 1987.

———. *The Limits of Affluence: Welfare in Ontario, 1920–1970*. Toronto, ON: University of Toronto Press, 1994.

Sullivan, Michael. *The Development of the British Welfare State*. London, UK: Prentice Hall/Harvester Wheatsheaf, 1996.

Sutherland, Neil. *Children in English-Canadian Society: Framing the Twentieth-Century Consensus*. Waterloo, ON: Wilfrid Laurier University Press, 2000.

Swan, Carole. "Women in the Canadian Labour Force: The Present Reality." In *Women and the Canadian Labour Force: Proceedings from a Workshop Held at the University of British Columbia in January* 1981. Edited by Naomi Herson and Dorothy E. Smith, 29–103. Ottawa, ON: Social Sciences and Humanities Research Council of Canada, 1982.

Swartz, Donald. "The Politics of Reform: Conflict and Accommodation in Canadian Health Policy." In *The Canadian State: Political Economy and Political Power*. Edited by Leo Panitch, 311–43. Toronto, ON: University of Toronto Press, 1977.

Taft, Kevin. *Shredding the Public Interest: Ralph Klein and Twenty-five Years of One-Party Government*. Edmonton, AB: University of Alberta Press, 1997.

Taylor, Georgina M. "'Ground for Common Action': Violet McNaughton's Agrarian Feminism and the Origins of the Farm Women's Movement in Canada." PhD diss., Carleton University, 1997.

———. "'Let Us Co-operate': Violet McNaughton and the Cooperative Ideal." In *Canadian Co-operatives in the Year 2000: Memory, Mutual Aid, and the Millennium*. Edited by Brett Fairbairn and Ian Macpherson, 57–78. Saskatoon, SK: Centre for the Study of Co-operatives, University of Saskatchewan, 2000.

Taylor, Malcolm G. *Health Insurance and Canadian Public Policy: The Seven Decisions That Created the Canadian Health Insurance System*. Montreal, QC: McGill-Queen's University Press, 1978.

———. "The Canadian Health-Care System: After Medicare." In *Health and Canadian Society: Sociological Perspectives*. 2nd ed. Edited by David Coburn, Carl D'Arcy, George M. Torrance, and Peter New, 73–101. Toronto, ON: Fitzhenry and Whiteside, 1987.

Teeple, Gary. *Globalization and the Decline of Social Reform: Into the Twenty-First Century*. Toronto, ON: Garamond, 2000.

Therborn, Goran. "Classes and States: Welfare State Developments 1881-1984." *Studies in Political Economy* 13 (1984): 7–41.

Thompson, David. *Explorations in Western America, 1784–1812.* Edited by J.B. Tyrell. Toronto, ON: Champlain Society, 1916.

Tillotson, Shirley. "Class and Community in Canadian Welfare Work, 1933–1960." *Journal of Canadian Studies* 32, 1 (Spring 1997): 63–92.

———. "'When Our Membership Awakes': Welfare Work and Canadian Union Autonomy, 1950–1965." *Labour/Le Travail* 40 (1997): 137–69.

———. *The Public at Play: Canada and the Politics of Recreation in Post–War Ontario.* Toronto, ON: University of Toronto Press, 2000.

Titmuss, Richard M. *Commitment to Welfare.* 2nd ed. London, UK: Allen and Unwin, 1976.

Tougas, Jocelyne. "Child Care in Québec: Where There's a Will, There's a Way." A paper of the Child Care Advocacy Association of Canada (n.d.). Available online from www.child careadvocacy.ca/resources/pd-fQUE_Child care.pdf.

Trattner, Walter I. *From Poor Law to Welfare State: A History of Social Welfare in America.* 3rd ed. New York: Free Press, 1984.

Treaty 7 Elders and Tribal Council, with Walter Hildebrandt, Sarah Carter, and Dorothy First Rider. *The True Spirit and Original Intent of Treaty 7.* Montreal, QC: McGill-Queen's University Press, 1996.

Trigger, Bruce. *The Huron: Farmers of the North.* Rev. ed. New York, NY: Holt, Rinehart and Winston, 1990.

Tucker, Eric. *Administering Danger in the Workplace: The Law and Politics of Occupational Health and Safety Regulation in Ontario, 1850–1914.* Toronto, ON: University of Toronto Press, 1990.

Ursel, Jane. "The State and the Maintenance of Patriarchy: A Case Study of Family, Labour and Welfare Legislation in Canada." In *Family, Economy and State: The Social Reproduction Process Under Capitalism.* Edited by James Dickinson and Bob Russell, 150–92. Toronto, ON: Garamond, 1986.

———. *Private Lives, Public Policy: 100 Years of State Intervention in the Family.* Toronto, ON: Women's Press, 1992.

Vachon, André. *Taking Root: Canada from 1700 to 1760: Records of Our History.* Ottawa, ON: Public Archives of Canada, 1985.

———. *Dreams of Empire: Canada before 1700.* Ottawa, ON: Public Archives of Canada, 1982.

Valverde, Mariana. "The Mixed Social Economy as a Canadian Tradition." *Studies in Political Economy* 47 (Summer 1995): 36–60.

Vanast, Walter J. "'Hastening the Day of Extinction': Canada, Quebec, and the Medical Care of Ungava's Inuit, 1867–1967." In *Social Welfare Policy in Canada: Historical Readings*. Edited by Raymond B. Blake and Jeff Keshen, 44–65. Toronto, ON: Copp Clark, 1995

Vayda, Eugene, and Raisa B. Deber. "The Canadian Health Care System: A Developmental Overview." In *Social Welfare Policy in Canada: Historical Readings*. Edited by Raymond B. Blake and Jeff Keshen, 313–25. Toronto, ON: Copp Clark, 1995.

Vickers, Jill. "The Intellectual Origins of the Women's Movement in Canada." In *Challenging Times: The Women's Movement in Canada and the United States*. Edited by Constance Backhouse and David H. Flaherty, 39–60. Montreal: McGill-Queen's University Press, 1992.

Wade, Jill. *Houses for All: The Struggle for Social Housing in Vancouver, 1919–1950*. Vancouver, BC: University of British Columbia Press, 1994.

Waldram, James. *As Long as the Rivers Run: Hydroelectric Development and Native Communities in Western Canada*. Winnipeg, MB: University of Manitoba Press, 1988.

Wallace, Elisabeth. "The Origin of the Social Welfare State in Canada, 1867–1900." *Canadian Journal of Economics and Political Science* 16, 3 (1950): 383–93.

Walters, Vivienne. "State, Capital and Labour: The Introduction of Federal-Provincial Insurance for Physician Care in Canada." *Canadian Journal of Sociology and Anthropology* 19, 2 (1982): 157–72.

Ward, W. Peter. "Unwed Motherhood in Nineteenth Century English Canada." *Historical Papers* 60 (1981): 34–56.

Warsh, Cheryl Krasnick. *Moments of Unreason: The Practice of Canadian Psychiatry and the Homewood Retreat, 1883–1923*. Montreal, QC: McGill-Queen's University Press, 1989.

Watkins, Ernest. *R.B. Bennett: A Biography*. London, UK: Secker and Warburg, 1963.

Wharf, Brian. *Community and Social Policy in Canada*. Toronto, ON: McClelland and Stewart, 1992.

Webber, Jeremy. "Labour and the Law." In *Labouring Lives: Work and Workers in Nineteenth-Century Ontario*. Edited by Paul Craven, 105–203. Toronto, ON: University of Toronto Press, 1995.

Wetherell, Donald. "To Discipline and Train: Adult Rehabilitation Programmes in Ontario Prisons, 1874–1900. " *Social History* 12, 23 (1979): 145–65.

Wilbur, R.H. *The Bennett Administration*. Ottawa: Canadian Historical Association, 1969.

Wills, Gale. *A Marriage of Convenience: Business and Social Work in Toronto 1918–1957*. Toronto, ON: University of Toronto Press, 1995.

Wilson, Elizabeth. *Women and the Welfare State*. London, UK: Tavistock, 1977.

Wishart, James M. "Class Differences and the Reformation of Ontario Public Hospitals, 1900–1935: 'Make Every Effort to Satisfy the Tastes of the Well-to-Do.'" *Labour/Le Travail* 48 (2001): 27–61.

Witt, John Fabian. *The Accidental Republic: Crippled Workingmen, Destitute Widows, and the Remaking of American Law*. Cambridge, MA: Harvard University Press, 2004.

Woodsworth, J.S. *Strangers within Our Gates*. 1909. Reprint, Toronto, ON: University of Toronto Press, 1973.

Wylie, William T.N. "Poverty, Distress and Disease: Labour and the Construction of the Rideau Canal, 1826–32." *Labour/Le Travailleur* 11 (1983): 7-29.

Young, Robert A. "Reining in James: The Limits of the Task Force." *Canadian Public Administration* 24, 4 (1981): 596–611.

Young, T. Kue. *Health Care and Cultural Change: The Indian Experience in the Central Subarctic*. Toronto, ON: University of Toronto Press, 1988.

Index

as recommended by Curtis subcommittee, 224; and restrictions on single women, 238; "slum clearance," as industry alternative to, 231–32; in U.S., 228; women, as victims of cuts to, 297–98

Howe, C.D., 130, 143–44, 176, 229

Hudson's Bay Company, 56–57, 119

Hydrostone housing project (Halifax), 99, 228

immigrants, 41–42, 49, 52–54, 85, 181, 206, 207, 221–22, 227

income tax, 73, 97, 136–38, 141

Indian Affairs and Northern Development, Department of, 274, 317

infants, 72–73; mortality rates of, 72, 74, 170, 187, 224

infectious diseases, 32, 44, 51, 52–54, 71, 76–80, 88

inflation: control of, as neo-liberal strategy, 286–87, 291; during First World War, 96, 97, 126; and family allowances, 134–35, 156; of 1970s, 286–88; and old age pensions, 154, 156, 289

insurance industry, 158–59, 161, 172–73

Inuit, 19–20, 120

Kelso, J.J., 70–71, 81–82, 100

Keynes, John Maynard, 128; and theory of welfare state, 128–29, 132, 143–44, 149

King, William Lyon Mackenzie, 101, 125–26, 140–41, 172, 224; and committees on postwar reform, 129; and deals with Labour Party, 105–106; and family allowances, 130–35; and Green Book of social policy reforms, 135–38, 141; and industrial councils, 108; and refusal of social assistance, during Depression, 110; as skeptical of Keynesian theory, 128–29; social programs of, as politically expedient, 105–106, 125, 131; and UI, 115–17, 296

Klein, Ralph, 293, 303, 308, 314

Korean War, 141, 156, 161, 252

labour. See trade unions; workers

Labour, Department of, 198, 202, 206, 207

Labour Party, Canadian, 105–106, 113

Lalonde, Marc, 266–67, 268

Lebel, Léon, 132, 134–35

Lesage, Jean, 158, 177, 259

"less eligibility," principle of, 50, 58, 68, 328

Liberal Party/governments, 105–106, 125, 126–27, 135, 138, 143, 292–94, 300, 305; and CPP, 151–52, 156–61, 162; and dependence on NDP, 159–60; left wing of, as influencing social policy, 157–58, 159, 176, 188; and medicare, 184–86, 188; neo-liberalism of, 285; and social housing, 231, 232–35

Macdonald, Donald, and royal commission on economy, 212, 288, 289–90, 299–300, 329, 331

Manitoba, 100, 164, 172, 228, 237–38, 240, 303

Manning, Ernest, 157, 159, 185

Maritime provinces, 45, 52, 53, 66, 68, 99, 101; housing programs in, 238; and medicare, 173–74, 177; and old age pensions, 155; poorhouses/workhouses in, 49, 58, 68, 101, 107, 120, 255

Marsh, Leonard, and social security subcommittee of, 129

Marsh Report, 8, 125, 129, 130–31, 223, 329

Martin, Paul, Jr., 285, 292, 296, 314

Martin, Paul, Sr., 157

Mazankowski, Donald, and Alberta medical care committee, 313

McNaughton, Violet, 154, 174

means testing: for early old age pensions, 96, 104, 105, 106, 154–55; for GIS, 163

media, as supporting economic elites, 160–61, 175, 207–208, 284, 285, 333

medicare: arguments against, 177–80; arguments for, 180–82; CMA opposition to, 140, 172, 173, 177–78, 180, 182; delays in implementing, 184–86; dentists' opposition to, 178–79; and extra-billing by physicians, 287, 307; federal legislation on, 185–86, 188; federal-provincial negotiations on, 172, 173–74, 185; forerunners of, 171–72; Hall Commission on, 176–77, 188; Hall Report on, 182–87, 188–89; as implemented internationally, 170, 173, 188; as needed in poorer provinces, 173–74, 177, 182; as proposed in Green Book, 135, 138, 171; public support for, 169–70, 180, 307, 309, 310–11, 314; as right of citizenship, 307, 311; in Saskatchewan, 171, 174–76, 176–77, 183; success of, 311–14; U.S. plans for, as unsuccessful, 173, 178, 188